Handbook of Multivariate Process Capability Indices

Handbook of Multivariate Process Capability Indices

Ashis Kumar Chakraborty
Moutushi Chatterjee

CRC Press is an imprint of the
Taylor & Francis Group, an **informa** business

A CHAPMAN & HALL BOOK

First edition published 2021
by CRC Press
6000 Broken Sound Parkway NW, Suite 300, Boca Raton, FL 33487-2742

and by CRC Press
2 Park Square, Milton Park, Abingdon, Oxon, OX14 4RN

© 2021 Taylor & Francis Group, LLC

CRC Press is an imprint of Taylor & Francis Group, LLC

Reasonable efforts have been made to publish reliable data and information, but the author and publisher cannot assume responsibility for the validity of all materials or the consequences of their use. The authors and publishers have attempted to trace the copyright holders of all material reproduced in this publication and apologize to copyright holders if permission to publish in this form has not been obtained. If any copyright material has not been acknowledged please write and let us know so we may rectify in any future reprint.

Except as permitted under U.S. Copyright Law, no part of this book may be reprinted, reproduced, transmitted, or utilized in any form by any electronic, mechanical, or other means, now known or hereafter invented, including photocopying, microfilming, and recording, or in any information storage or retrieval system, without written permission from the publishers.

For permission to photocopy or use material electronically from this work, access www.copyright. com or contact the Copyright Clearance Center, Inc. (CCC), 222 Rosewood Drive, Danvers, MA 01923, 978-750-8400. For works that are not available on CCC please contact mpkbookspermissions@tandf.co.uk

Trademark notice: Product or corporate names may be trademarks or registered trademarks and are used only for identification and explanation without intent to infringe.

Library of Congress Cataloging-in-Publication Data
Library of Congress Control Number: 2020946029

ISBN: 978-0-367-02997-5 (hbk)
ISBN: 978-0-429-29834-9 (ebk)

Dedicated to
wife, Purnima Chakraborty, and daughter, Paulami Chakraborty,
of the first author
&
parents, Subhash Chatterjee and Reba Chatterjee, of the second
author

Contents

Preface	xiii
Acknowledgements	xv
Biography of First Author	xvii
Biography of Second Author	xviii

1 Introduction — 1

1.1 Concept of Process Capability Index 2
1.2 Process Capability Indices in Six Sigma, Lean Six Sigma, and Design for Six Sigma (DFSS) 5
1.3 Concept of Multivariate Process Capability Index (MPCI) . 7
1.4 Some Uses of Process Capability Indices 8
1.5 Some Applications of MPCIs 10
1.6 Overview of the Chapters 12

Bibliography — 15

2 Some Useful Concepts of Univariate and Multivariate Statistics — 19

2.1 Introduction 19
2.2 Univariate Statistics 20
    2.2.1 Normal Distribution 20
        2.2.1.1 Properties of Normal Distribution 21
    2.2.2 Radial Error Distribution 23
    2.2.3 Folded Normal Distribution 24
    2.2.4 Uniform Distribution 26
    2.2.5 Log-Normal Distribution 27
    2.2.6 Exponential Distribution 28
2.3 Estimation of Process Mean and Variance Using Control Chart Information 30
    2.3.1 Estimation of Process Mean and Variance Based on $\overline{X}-R$ Chart Information 31
    2.3.2 Estimation of Process Mean and Variance Based on $\overline{X}-S$ Chart Information 32
2.4 Some Bayesian Concepts 33

vii

Contents viii

2.5	Multivariate Statistics	34
	2.5.1 Multivariate Normal Distribution	35
	2.5.2 Multivariate Folded Normal Distribution	36
2.6	Principal Component Analysis (PCA)	38
2.7	Delta Method	39

Bibliography   **41**

3 Univariate Process Capability Indices   46

3.1 Introduction 46

3.2 Univariate Process Capability Indices for Symmetric Specification Limits 47

     3.2.1 Unification of Univariate PCIs for Symmetric Specification Limits 50

3.3 Univariate Process Capability Indices for Asymmetric Specification Limits 51

     3.3.1 Unification of Univariate PCIs for Asymmetric Specification Limits 53

3.4 Univariate Process Capability Indices for Unilateral (One-Sided) Specification Limits 56

     3.4.1 Unification of Univariate PCIs for Unilateral Specification Limits 58

3.5 Univariate Process Capability Indices for Non-Normal Distributions 63

3.6 Univariate Process Capability Indices PNC 67

3.7 Univariate Process Capability Assessments Using Bayesian Approach 68

3.8 Concluding Remarks 68

Bibliography   **70**

4 Bivariate Process Capability Indices (BPCIs)   78

4.1 Introduction 78

4.2 Bivariate Generalization of Univariate PCIs for Bilateral Specification Limits 79

4.3 Bivariate Generalization of Univariate PCIs for Unilateral Specification Limits 87

4.4 Bivariate PCIs for Circular Specification Region 88

4.5 Numerical Examples 105

     4.5.1 Example 1 105

     4.5.2 Example 2 106

4.6 Concluding Remarks 107

Bibliography   **108**

Contents

ix

5 Multivariate Process Capability Indices for Bilateral Specification Region Based on Principal Component Analysis (PCA) — **112**

5.1 Introduction 112

5.2 MPCIs Analogous to Univariate PCIs viz., C_p, C_{pk}, C_{pm}, and C_{pmk} 113

  5.2.1 Probability-Based MPCI Based on First Few Principal Components 115

5.3 PCA-Based MPCIs with Unequal Weighting 117

5.4 PCA-Based MPCIs Similar to Taam et al.'s [12] Ratio-Based MPCIs 118

5.5 MPCIs Based on First Principal Component Only 120

5.6 Some Other PCA-Based MPCIs 123

5.7 A Real-Life Example 123

5.8 Conclusion 125

Bibliography — **127**

6 Ratio-Based Multivariate Process Capability Indices for Symmetric Specification Region — **130**

6.1 Introduction 130

6.2 MPCIs Defined as Multivariate Analogue of C_p 131

6.3 MPCIs Defined as Multivariate Analogue of C_{pk} 142

6.4 MPCIs Defined as Multivariate Analogue of C_{pm} 147

6.5 $C_G(u, v)$ — A Super-structue of MPCIs 157

6.6 A Numerical Example 160

6.7 Concluding Remark 163

Bibliography — **164**

7 Multivariate Process Capability Indices for Asymmetric Specification Region — **168**

7.1 Introduction 168

7.2 MPCIs Generalizing $C_p''(u, v)$ for $u = 0, 1$ and $v = 0, 1$ — A Geometric Approach (Grau [11]) 169

7.3 Multivariate Analogue of $C_p''(u, v)$, for $u = 0, 1$ and $v = 0, 1$ — An Alternative Approach 174

  7.3.1 Interrelationships between the Member Indices of $C_M(u, v)$ for $u = 0, 1$ and $v = 0, 1$ 175

7.4 Threshold Value of $C_M(0, 0)$ 177

  7.4.1 For Bivariate Case 177

  7.4.2 For Multivariate Case 181

  7.4.3 Plug-in Estimators of the Member Indices of $C_M(u, v)$ for $u = 0, 1$ and $v = 0, 1$ and Their Estimation Procedures 182

7.5 A Real-Life Example 184

Contents

7.6 Concluding Remark 186

Bibliography   **188**

8 Multivariate Process Capability Indices for Unilateral Specification Region   **190**

8.1 Introduction 190

8.2 MPCI for Unilateral Specification Region Based on Proportion of Nonconformance 191

8.3 MPCI for Unilateral Specification Region Based on Principal Component Analysis 195

8.4 A Numerical Example 196

8.5 Concluding Remarks 199

Bibliography   **200**

9 Multivariate Process Capability Indices Based on Proportion of Nonconformance   **202**

9.1 Introduction 202

9.2 MPCIs Based on Location-Scale Family of Distributions . . . 203

9.3 Other MPCIs Based on Proportion of Conformance or Nonconformance 205

Bibliography   **211**

10 Multivariate Process Capability Indices for Quality Characteristics Having Nonnormal Statistical Distributions   **214**

10.1 Introduction 214

10.2 MPCIs for Nonnormal Data Using Principal Component Analysis 215

10.3 MPCIs for Multivariate Nonnormal Data Using Distance Approach 217

10.4 MPCIs Using Multivariate g and h Distribution 221

10.5 MPCIs for Multivariate Nonnormal Processes Using Skewness Reduction Approach 222

10.6 Nonparametric MPCIs for Nonnormal Processes 226

10.7 Numerical Example 230

10.8 Concluding Remark 231

Bibliography   **233**

11 Multivariate Process Capability Indices Based on Bayesian Approach   **236**

11.1 Introduction 236

11.2 $C_b(D)$: A Bayesian MPCI Analogous to C_{pk} 238

Contents

11.3 Vector Valued Multivariate Analogues of C_p and C_{pk} from Bayesian Perspective 240
11.4 A Numerical Example 243
11.5 Concluding Remark 245

Bibliography   **246**

12 Multivariate Process Capability Indices for Autocorrelated Data   **248**
12.1 Introduction 248
12.2 MPCIs Analogous to C_p for Autocorrelated Processes 249
12.3 MPCIs Analogous to C_{pm} for Autocorrelated Processes . . . 251
12.4 MPCIs for Autocorrelated Processes Having Unilateral Specification Region 251
12.5 Data Analysis 252
12.6 Concluding Remarks 253

Bibliography   **254**

13 Multivariate Process Capability Vectors   **256**
13.1 Introduction 256
13.2 Multivariate Process Capability Vectors for Bilateral Specification Region – A Modification of Traditional MPCIs 257
13.3 Multivariate Process Capability Vector Based on One-Sided Models 263
13.4 Multivariate Process Incapability Vector 268
13.5 An MPCV for Both the Unilateral and Bilateral Specification Regions 271
13.6 A Numerical Example 274
13.7 Concluding Remark 277

Bibliography   **278**

14 MPCIs Defined by Other Miscellaneous Approaches   **280**
14.1 Introduction 280
14.2 Priority-Based Multivariate Process Capability Indices (MPCIs) 280
14.3 MPCIs Based on Concepts of Linear Algebra 286
14.4 Viability Index 288
14.5 MPCIs Defined on Process-Oriented Basis 293
14.6 Multivariate Process Performance Analysis with Special Emphasis on Accuracy and Precision 295
14.7 Multivariate Process Capability Analysis Using Fuzzy Logic 298
    14.7.1 A Fuzzy Logic-Based MPCI 300
    14.7.2 Fuzzy Multivariate Process Capability Vector 302
14.8 MPCIs for Processes Having Linear and Nonlinear Profiles . 304

Contents

  14.8.1 MPCIs for Simple Linear Profile 304
  14.8.2 MPCIs for Multivariate Nonlinear Profiles 307
 14.9 Concluding Remark 310

Bibliography 311

15 Applications of MPCIs 314

 15.1 Introduction 314
 15.2 Supplier Selection Based on Multivariate Process Capability
   Analysis 314
  15.2.1 Supplier Selection Problem for Processes Having Symmetric Bilateral Specification Region 315
  15.2.2 Supplier Selection Problem for Processes Having Unilateral Specification Region 316
  15.2.3 Supplier Selection Problem for Processes Having Asymmetric Specification Region 319
 15.3 Assessing Process Capability of Multivariate Processes Affected
   by Gauge Measurement Error 319
  15.3.1 Impact of Gauge Measurement Error on MC_p 320
  15.3.2 MPCIs Based on Principal Component Analysis for Processes Affected by Measurement Error 321
 15.4 Multiresponse Optimization Using MPCIs 322
 15.5 Concluding Remark 324

Bibliography 325

Conclusion 328

Index 330

Preface

There are several books and papers on univariate process capability analysis. The subject of process capability indices (PCIs) became important for assessing a process with respect to cetain specification limits provided by the design or the customers. It is generally a unit-free measure. In real life, it is observed that the processes are not univariate in nature; rather, most of the time, they have multiple characteristics, which may or may not be correlated. Several authors subsequently worked on multivariate process capability analysis. However, there is no book, as of now, which discusses the multivariate process capability indices (MPCIs) in detail.

The authors felt that a book seperately on MPCIs will help the readers to understand the whole gamut of problems associated with MPCIs. Particularly, the second author felt such a need while doing her Ph.D. thesis. During that time itself, it was envisaged that, after completing the thesis, we will jointly write a book on MPCIs, so that future scholars and applied scientists will have a ready-made reference book to understand not only the theoretical aspects of MPCIs, but also its actual applications in different situations.

However, to understand MPCIs in proper perspective, the concept of PCIs in the univariate case needs to be understood thoroughly. The authors have provided an initial chapter discussing various PCIs in the univariate set-up.

The authors also noted that, in practice, there are several kinds of specifications. Some are bilateral, some unilateral, some may be symmetric, and some may be asymmetric with respect to target. Each of these kinds of specifications generates new PCIs. Unfortunately, many practitioners are not aware of the existence of different PCIs for different types of specifications. The problem becomes more interesting when there are several quality characteristics to be considered in a process. Researchers have taken up this challange whenever a new situation has arisen. MPCIs developed for a combination of different types of specification limits are of particular interest to the researchers. This field will need more development as and when different combinations of specification limits are required for a process to be said to be capable.

The authors themselves have worked on several such MPCIs and contributed toward their theoretical developments as well as practical applications. They also compared the performances of various MPCIs and showed which MPCI works better compared to others. It has been observed by the authors and a few other researchers that a PCI or a MPCI does not carry any

xiii

Preface

meaning unless its threshold value is known. The need for a threshold value for each and every MPCI has been stressed in this book.

Some new ideas from fuzzy set theory is used by some researchers to assess the capability of a process closer to reality. In many cases, the usual normality assumption of the quality characteristics are violated. Such cases need special attention. The authors have devoted one chapter on MPCIs for non-normal characteristics.

From the practitioner's point of view, this book is expected to be an important reference to understand the computational involvement for finding out MPCIs and also their interpretations. The book also will help the practitioners to decide which MPCI to be used under what circumstances. In many chapters of this book, examples with real life data are demonstrated which are expected to help the readers gain insight into the phenomenon from where data are obtained.

MPCIs based on a Bayesian approach and those involving variables which are auto-correlated are also discussed seperately. The developments in these fields are at present restricted to a few papers only. With new developments in the field of data analytics using a combination of statistics and machine learning, the authors expect challenging situations where more MPCIs need to be developed.

Ashis Kumar Chakraborty
Moutushi Chatterjee

Acknowledgements

The authors wish to acknowledge their respective family members who have encouraged and allowed sufficient time to write this book. The second author would particularly like to thank her husband, Soumen Adhikary, and sister, Dr. Moumita Chatterjee, for their help in the data analytical aspect. She is also thankful to her five-year old daughter, Aadtri, for being patient enough during her mother's long hours of study. Dr. Soumen Dey has greatly helped to go through Chapter 11 and provide critical comments. The authors are indebted to Ms. Aastha Sharma and Ms. Shikha Garg of CRC Press for having regular follow-up with the authors resulting in the timely publication of the book. There are numerous other persons who in some way or other helped the authors to complete this book.

Biography of First Author

Dr. Ashis Kumar Chakraborty completed his B.Stat. (Hons.) and M.Stat. in Statistics at the Indian Statistical Institute (ISI), Kolkata and his Ph.D. at the Indian Institute of Science, Bangalore, India. He has authored three books and contributed to several other books. His research interest is in Reliability, particularly in software reliability, process control, hybrid modelling, and similar areas. More than seventy articles were published by him in well-known peer-reviewed national and international journals. He has about 35 years of teaching, training, and consulting experience. He is a life member of the Operations Research Society of India and the Indian Association for Productivity, Quality, and Reliability. He served in the governing body of both. He is on the editorial Advisory Board of two journals and a regular reviewer of articles for several international journals. He has also served in the ISI council for two terms as the Head of the SQC & OR Division.

Address:

Ashis Kumar Chakraborty
SQC & OR Unit, Kolkata
Indian Statistical Institute,
203, B.T. Road,
Kolkata, India - 700108
email: akchakraborty123@rediffmail.com

Biography of Second Author

Dr. Moutushi Chatterjee received her B.Sc. (Hons.) degree in Statistics from the University of Calcutta, M. Sc. in Statistics from Kalyani University, and M. Tech. in Quality, Reliability, and Operations Research (QROR) from the Indian Statistical Institute, Kolkata, India. She has also completed her Ph.D. in QROR at the Indian Statistical Institute, Kolkata. At present, she is working as an assistant professor of Statistics at Lady Brabourne College (affiliated with the University of Calcutta). Her publications include 12 research articles in international journals and a chapter in an edited book. Her primary research interests are multivariate statistics, statistical quality control, reliability analysis, and supply chain management.

Chapter 1

Introduction

"In theory, theory and practice are the same. In practice, they are not."

Albert Einstein

Chapter Summary

In this chapter, basic concept of process capability analysis (PCA) is discussed along with the application of process capability indices (PCIs) in Six Sigma, Lean Six Sigma, and Design for Six Sigma (DFSS). The concept of univariate PCI is then generalized to the multivariate set-up, i.e., when there are more than one correlated quality characteristics, a phenomenon which is more likely to occur in practice. These indices are called Multivariate Process Capability Indices (MPCIs). Some practical applications of univariate PCIs are also briefly explained. Since the upcoming chapters of the book are primarily focused on multivariate process capability analysis, a few real-life datasets along with their backgrounds are discussed, which will be referred to in the next chapters, time and again, for quantitative analysis of the MPCIs.

Quality has always been the cutting-edge weapon for producers at all times. It appears that the only commonality between what customers want and what producers want is the quality (refer Chakraborty et al. [5]). Producing items with consistently good quality at reasonable cost is the key to survive in today's competitive world. It has long been established that in order to have consistent quality, the process through which the product is made has to be monitored properly. Consequently, in today's highly competitive market, importance of the correct assessment of the capability of a process to produce items within the pre-assigned specification limits is increasing day by day. Process capability analysis is the most used statistical quality control (SQC) methodology which is applied to carry out such assessment, especially in manufacturing processes. However, the concept has now been extended to measure capability of other processes like business processes as well. Such analysis is generally done through process capability indices (PCIs). A PCI measures the ability of a process to produce items within pre-assigned specification limit(s).

It is, generally, "the higher the better" type of index with the "higher than the threshold" value indicating that the process is capable of producing items that in all likelihood will meet customers' requirement.

Before computing the PCI of a process, one has to ensure that the process is under statistical control (refer Kotz and Johnson [26]). This is a very significant assumption because absence of stability in the process makes it unpredictable and hence, in that situation, PCI values may not be able to reflect the actual capability level of the process correctly. However, merely being in statistical control does not ensure that a process will be capable. For example, when

- the process is off-centered with respect to the stipulated target; or

- the process variability is too large relative to its specifications; or

- the process under consideration is both off-centered and has large variation.

In all such cases, the process will most likely produce products outside the specification limits, making the capability level of the process low. Thus, stability is a necessary condition of a capable process but not a sufficient one.

Kotz and Johnson [26] have also observed that most of the PCIs available in literature assume that the quality characteristic under consideration follows normal distribution. A possible explanation for this assumption may be that such assumption gives some computational advantages. In fact, by establishing stability of a process, through appropriate control charts, it is actually ensured that "the distribution does not change in the course of use of the PCI." This remains valid irrespective of whether the original distribution of the quality characteristic under consideration is normal or not (refer Kotz and Johnson [26]).

1.1 Concept of Process Capability Index

The necessity of quantifying capability of a process was felt long back. Feigenbaum [13] and Juran [16] proposed 6σ as a measure of process capability, where, σ is the standard deviation corresponding to the concerned quality characteristic. The logic behind this measure is that, under the assumption of normality of the underlying quality characteristic, 6σ represents the inherent variability of a process (refer Palmer and Tsui [30]). This metric is independent of the customer specification with the primary assumption that "the process does not know the specifications." However, with the increasing interfaces between the customers and producers, inclusion of customer specifications in the definition of PCIs became inevitable.

Introduction

In order to address this lacuna in the definition of a PCI, Juran [17] compared 6σ to the specification width and thereby established a stronger link between process variability and customer specification limits. Juran and Gryna [18] provided a metric that directly relates process variability to specification limits, by proposing the so called "Capability Ratio," given by

$$\text{Capability Ratio} = \frac{6\sigma}{\text{Specification Width}} \qquad (1.1)$$

Since this capability ratio explicitly links process variability to customer specifications, it puts emphasis on the producers' responsibility to satisfy those specifications (refer Anis [1]). Thus, the capability ratio, defined in equation (1.1), actually formed the background of process capability analysis.

Kane [19], in his seminal paper, first documented some of the PCIs which were already being used in industries for quite sometime, and discussed about the importance of using those PCIs for assessing capability of the process. Due to the unquestionable significance of the concept of PCIs, especially in the context of manufacturing industries, Kane's [19] paper motivated a huge number of statisticians as well as industrial engineers, working in the field of SQC, to carry out further research in this field. Kotz and Johnson [26] have reviewed about 170 of such high-quality research papers published within just 15 years of Kane's [19] paper. Yum and Kim [43] have enlisted the research articles and books written during 2000–2009 dealing with various aspects of PCIs.

According to Palmer and Tsui [30], almost all the PCIs available in literature owe their development to their common parent C_p, which is defined as

$$C_p = \frac{U - L}{6\sigma} \qquad (1.2)$$

where U is the upper specification limit (USL) and L is the lower specification limit (LSL). Note that we may use U or USL and L or LSL interchangeably throughout this book. From equations (1.1) and (1.2), it is evident that C_p is merely the reciprocal of the "capability ratio". C_p and, as a matter of fact, all the other PCIs have an added advantage over the capability ratio in a sense that the PCI values are, by definition, of higher the better type, i.e., PCIs increase in value as the process performance improves. Although this has limited analytical value, Palmer and Tsui [30] have rightly observed that this gives a psychological edge to the users of the PCIs as any increase in the capability level of a process is directly reflected by an increased value of the PCI – while the capability ratio has an inverse effect.

Most of the PCIs owe their developments to the basic need of assessing capability levels of processes corresponding to different quality characteristics having various types of specification limits. As has already been discussed, specification limits play a major role in process capability analysis.

Chakraborty and Chatterjee [9] discus several PCIs as applicable to different types of specifications that are normally encountered in practice. Generally, the quality characteristics, which are frequently encountered in practice, belong to either of the following three categories viz.,

1. Nominal the best, i.e., quality characteristics with both USL and LSL;

2. Smaller the better, i.e., quality characteristics with only USL; and

3. Larger the better, i.e., quality characteristics with only LSL.

The most common type of specification limits observed in manufacturing industries are of bi-lateral type corresponding to the nominal the best type of quality characteristics. Generally, for a quality characteristic corresponding to a particular item, a target or ideal value is decided and based on that target, lower and upper specification limits are suggested. Often, the target and the specification limits are set by customer or design engineer or other stake holders based on the specific use of the end product. The observed value of the quality characteristic corresponding to a produced item should not, ideally, fall beyond either of the specification limits as otherwise that item will be considered as non-conforming to the given specifications and hence will be either scrapped or sent for rework.

Even if the quality characteristics are of nominal the better type, the concerned specification limits may be symmetric or asymmetric with respect to the target. Symmetric bilateral specification limits, which are most common in manufacturing industries, are observed when the specification limits are at equal distance on either side of the target. Quality characteristics like height, length, and temperature, etc., generally, have symmetric bilateral specification limits.

On the contrary, asymmetric specification limits occur when the target value (T) differs from the specification mid-point ($M = (USL + LSL)/2$), i.e., when the USL and the LSL are not at equal distance from "T." Generally, specification limits become asymmetric when either due to various design aspects or to control production cost, either the customer or the producer or both are willing to allow more deviation from target on one side of the specification limits than toward the other. Even if a process initially starts with symmetric specification limits, asymmetry may be induced in the specifications afterwards to avoid increase in production cost. Thus, the quality characteristics of nominal the better type may have symmetric or asymmetric specification limits depending upon the design intent, production cost, area of application and so on. A detailed discussion on this topic is given in Chakraborty and Chatterjee [9].

Unilateral or one-sided specification limits are encountered when the quality characteristics are of larger the better or smaller the better types. For example, quality characteristics like surface roughness and flatness are of smaller the better type in a sense that their values should be as low as possible. Hence, only an *USL* is set for such quality characteristics. On the other hand, tensile strength and compressive strength are examples of larger the better type of quality characteristics, where the corresponding quality characteristic values should be as high as possible but should have at least a minimum value, decided by the *LSL*, for proper functioning of the concerned item.

Irrespective of the differences in the nature of specification limits, the basic commonality among most of the PCIs defined in literature is that they assume a single important quality characteristic in a manufactured item; while in reality, often an item has more than one inter-related quality characteristics. To deal with such problems of multiple quality characteristics, multivariate process capability indices (MPCIs) are used.

1.2 Process Capability Indices in Six Sigma, Lean Six Sigma, and Design for Six Sigma (DFSS)

Kane [19] has observed that as a consequence of the increasing effort poised by automotive industries to implement SPC in their plants and supply base, the usage of PCIs has also substantially increased–not only in process assessment but also in evaluation of purchasing decisions. In fact, quantifying the capability of a manufacturing process plays a major role in the context of the continual improvement of a process.

Due to the vast potential of PCIs, they are nowadays used in some of the modern age concepts like Six Sigma, Lean Six Sigma, and Design for Six Sigma (DFSS).

Six Sigma is a fact-based, data-driven philosophy of quality improvement that values defect prevention over defect detection. It aims at achieving customer satisfaction and bottom-line results by reducing variation and waste, and thereby promoting a competitive advantage. Six Sigma quality performance means no more than 3.4 defects per million opportunities. Six Sigma puts emphasis on the DMAIC (define, measure, analyze, improve, and control) approach to problem solving. It is often considered as a strategy, where Six Sigma experts use qualitative and quantitative techniques to drive process improvement through the entire set up and PCI plays an important role in this regard.

According to Box and Luceno [4], Six Sigma may be considered as the blueprint of quality improvement for both the present and the future production processes as well as business processes. Therefore, often Six Sigma initiatives use different types of tools of quality improvement to ensure production of very low proportion of nonconformance and this can be ascertained through the proper use of PCIs and setting high PCI values as target.

After the inherent problem is identified in the define phase, the measure phase is initiated when PCI values are calculated. The current defect level is expressed through either those PCI values or an appropriate sigma level.

The PCI values, as obtained in the measure phase, are then statistically investigated in the next phase, i.e., "analyze" phase in order to find out how the true health of a process can be improved. Based on the clues obtained from analyze phase, actions are taken to improve the process. This forms the improve phase.

In the "control" phase also, PCIs play an important role. During this time, when a Six Sigma project is being carried out, a process is likely to undergo some changes in the input parameters. For example, the number of arriving customers, the cycle time for a particular process and the amount of receivable out-standings, among others, are expected to get changed. These changes will be reflected once the PCI values of the improved processes are determined. Thus, the principal use for the process capability calculation in Six Sigma is to quantify the theoretical defect reduction after the Six Sigma project has been completed.

Any business process consists of a series of interconnected sub-processes. Six Sigma concentrates on fixing those sub-processes; while lean methodology focuses on the interconnections between those sub-processes (refer Muir [27]). In other words, lean reduces average cycle time and excess inventory and improves average response time.

An essential aspect of Lean Six Sigma is to understand how customer demand determines business process capability. In fact, a real business process frequently shows problems with customer expectations and process performance. This problem can be solved through the efficient use of process capability analysis as the PCIs, by definition, relate the "voice of the customer" to the "voice of the process".

PCIs become quite handy in the context of DFSS as well. DFSS is a systematic methodology which uses statistical tools, training and measurements to enable the designer to develop products, services, and processes that meet customer expectations at Six Sigma quality levels. DFSS optimizes the design process to achieve Six Sigma performance and integrates characteristics of Six Sigma methodology in product development.

A DFSS process consists of the following main steps (refer Kiemele [23]):

Identify: Identify customer needs and strategic intent;

Design: Deliver the detailed design by evaluating various design alternatives;

Optimize: Optimize the design from a productivity (business requirements) and quality (customer requirements) point of view and realize it;

Validate: Pilot the design, update as needed and prepare to launch the new design.

Thus, in order to apply DFSS, PCIs are used to establish baseline process capability and to determine final process capability.

Introduction 7

In a nut shell, PCIs find their applications in highly sophisticated modern age methodologies, like Six Sigma, Lean Six Sigma, and DFSS apart from the usual SQC.

1.3 Concept of Multivariate Process Capability Index (MPCI)

Most of the PCIs available in literature are designed for processes having single measurable quality characteristic. However, in reality, often, a process is seen to have more than one important quality characteristics which are inter-related among themselves. Some of these quality characteristics may be individually insignificant, but often when they are taken together, they influence the process to a large extent. For example (refer Taam et al. [39]), in an automated paint application process, there are more than one important quality characteristics viz., paint thickness, paint thinner levels, paint lot differences, and temperature, which are inter-related among themselves. To assess the capability level of such processes, the common industrial practice is to compute the capability value of the process based on any one of these quality characteristics or to compute PCI values for each of these characteristics separately using the available univariate PCIs and then summarizing the entire process capability by taking a function of these univariate PCIs or using statistical tools for summarization, like (i) minimum of the PCIs; (ii) arithmetic mean of the PCIs; and (iii) geometric mean of the PCIs. However, these approaches ignore the prevailing correlation structure among the quality characteristics and hence often fail to reflect the actual capability scenario of the process.

To address these problems, MPCIs were introduced. With the increase in the complexity of the production processes, processes with multiple correlated quality characteristics are becoming more common than those with single quality characteristics. However, the number of PCIs for univariate processes, available in literature, outnumber the MPCIs.

Following Shinde and Khadse [37], the MPCIs, available in literature, can be classified into either of the following groups:

1. MPCIs defined as the ratio of tolerance region to process region; refer Taam et al. [39];

2. MPCIs expressed as the probability of nonconforming products; refer Chen [12], Khadse and Shinde [21];

3. MPCIs based on principal component analysis; refer Wang and Chen [40], Wang and Du [41], Shinde and Khadse [37], and so on;

4. MPCIs based on Bayesian perspective; refer Bernardo and Irony [2] and Niverthi and Dey [28];

5. MPCIs based on the concept of nonparametric statistics; refer Polansky [34];

6. Other approaches like vector representation of MPCIs; refer Shahriari et al. [36]; Shahriari and Abdollahzadeh [35]; MPCIs based on lowner ordering; refer Kirmani and Polansky [24]; MPCIs defined based on proportion of nonconformance, refer Pearn et al. [32] and Wang et al. [42], and so on.

MPCIs can also be classified based on the respective specification regions (similar to univariate PCIs) as: (refer Chakraborty and Chatterjee [9])

1. MPCIs for symmetric specification regions; refer Taam et al. [39];

2. MPCIs for asymmetric specification region; refer Grau [14], Chatterjee and Chakraborty [10];

3. MPCIs for unilateral specification region; refer Jalili et al. [15].

Apart from these three types of quality characteristics having either an USL or LSL or both, there could be another type of quality characteristic which requires a special type of specification region viz., circular specification region. Circular specification regions can be seen in processes like hitting a target (in ballistics) and drilling a hole (in manufacturing industries). The uniqueness of the processes with circular tolerance region is that the USL or LSL does not exist corresponding to the concerned quality characteristics and hence classical PCIs or MPCIs are not applicable here (refer Karl et al. [20], Chatterjee and Chakraborty [6]).

Despite the presence of a number of mathematically sound MPCIs, Pearn and Kotz [31] have rightly observed that the methodology for evaluating capability in multivariate domain still lacks consistency. Moreover, besides defining MPCIs for different practical situations, a thorough study of the distributional and inferential properties is also of utmost importance for a better understanding of the capability level of a multivariate process. Although Pearn et al. [33] have done a substantial research work in this regard, there still remains more scope of study.

1.4 Some Uses of Process Capability Indices

From the very time of its inception, process capability analysis has been considered as a versatile statistical process control (SPC) tool to quantify the

Introduction 9

capability of a process. Kane [19] and Palmer and Tsui [30] have discussed a wide range of possible application areas of PCIs starting from the commencement of a process through its completion covering the entire production cycle. These uses are enlisted below:

1. **PCI as a Static Goal for Performance:** For various types of machine and process qualification trials, many a times it is required to establish a benchmark capability. Hence, often a minimal desirable PCI value is set to avoid unwarranted production of nonconforming items; to maintain customer satisfaction and to define and abide by certain contractual obligations. Thus, PCIs can be used to establish a healthy customer-manufacturer/supplier relationship.

2. **PCI as a Measure of Continuous Improvement:** PCI values can be monitored over time to keep an eye on the relative improvement of a process. Process, as the name suggests, is a continuous flow of pre-planned activities. Any improvement in the process is reflected in the corresponding PCI values as well.

3. **PCI as a Common Process Performance Language:** Since a PCI provides (mostly) a single-valued assessment of the overall capability of a process, its value can be used as a common process performance language among the stake holders like production engineers, design engineers, suppler and customer – some of whom may not even have a detailed knowledge of the process. This is due to the fact that PCIs provide consistent frames of reference regardless of the specific process which they describe.

4. **PCI as a Criterion for Prioritization:** Often, a process consists of several sub-processes which may or may not be dependent on each other. PCIs can be used to identify rooms for improvement in a process through identifying the priority sectors or prospects of investment.

5. **PCI as a Road-marker to Direct Process Improvement Activities:** A process may not perform satisfactorily either due to deviation from the stipulated target (off-centeredness) or due to increase in process variability or both. PCI values can be used to identify the actual problem and to determine the relative benefit of adjusting process location versus reducing process variability.

6. **PCI as an Audit Yardstick:** PCI values obtained as a part of quality system audits, like in ISO 9001:2015, can be compared to projected PCI values to identify deficiencies in sampling, measurement, process control, and so on.

7. **PCI as a Tool for Comparison:** PCIs are unitless, by definition. Hence they can be used to compare capability levels of two competitive processes or even to compare the same process at different time points.

Introduction 10

For example, PCIs can be used to compare performances of two processes producing similar items using different technologies. Therefore, it can be used to investigate whether purchase of costly machineries will indeed substantially increase the capability level of a process or not.

8. **MPCIs for More Complicated Processes:** Although univariate PCIs are more popular than MPCIs among practitioners due to their computational simplicity and ease of representation, use of MPCIs is still inevitable for complex processes. To be more precise, often in case of modern cutting edge processes, there exist more than one quality characteristics, which have moderate to high correlation among themselves. Therefore, while assessing the capability of the entire process, the general convention of computing process capability values of individual quality characteristics separately may yield misleading results.

For example, two very important quality characteristics of automobile paint are light reflective ability and adhesion ability, and these two are related among themselves through the chemical composition of the paint.

MPCIs come as savior in this case, because a good MPCI takes into account the underlying correlation structure, while computing the capability value of the process as a whole.

1.5 Some Applications of MPCIs

Since this book is written primarily to discuss about MPCIs, we now consider some real-life datasets, which are reffered later in different chapters to show applications of MPCIs.

Dataset 1: Tensile strength and Brinell hardness are often considered as two major quality characteristics in industries manufacturing steel, concrete, etc. For these type of processes, Sultan [38] has provided an interesting dataset. Although the data were originally given in the context of constructing acceptance charts for two correlated quality characteristics, later they have been used by many researchers in the literature of MPCIs.

The complete dataset is given in Table 1.1.

It is known that tensile strength and Brinell hardness are highly correlated.

Dataset 2: In a manufacturing industry, the items produced have two correlated characteristics coded as "7J" and "6J." A random sample of size $n = 39$ was drawn from the process to assess its capability level (refer Chakraborty and Chatterjee [11]). The data are presented in Table 1.2.

Introduction 11

TABLE 1.1: Dataset pertaining to a manufacturing industry with two correlated quality characteristics and 25 randomly selected sample observations (refer Sultan [38])

Characteristic / Sample No.	1	2	3	4	5	6	7	8	9	10
Brinell Hardness (H)	143	200	160	181	148	178	162	215	161	141
Tensile Strength (S)	34.2	57.0	47.5	53.4	47.8	51.5	45.9	59.1	48.4	47.3

Characteristic / Sample No.	11	12	13	14	15	16	17	18	19	20
Brinell Hardness (H)	175	187	187	186	172	182	177	204	178	196
Tensile Strength (S)	57.3	58.5	58.2	57.0	49.4	57.2	50.6	55.1	50.9	57.9

Characteristic / Sample No.	21	22	23	24	25	–	–	–	–	–
Brinell Hardness (H)	160	183	179	194	181	–	–	–	–	–
Tensile Strength (S)	45.5	53.9	51.2	57.5	55.6	–	–	–	–	–

It is observed that the quality characteristics are highly correlated with correlation coefficient -0.6433 (refer Chakraborty and Chatterjee [11]).

Dataset 3: The next dataset pertains to a product called striker used in making ammunitions (refer Chatterjee and Chakraborty [6]). These parts should be properly assembled to ensure perfect alignment of the parts resulting in satisfactory performance of the produced ammunitions. Under such circumstances, holes drilled in strikers are our subject of interest.

The data on the co-ordinates (X_1, X_2) of the centers of each of the 20 randomly selected drilled holes are collected. The data are given in Table 1.3.

Here also, Chatterjee and Chakraborty [6] have observed high correlation between (X_1, X_2).

In all the above cases, the quality characteristics are highly correlated among themselves and hence use of univariate PCIs for individual quality characteristics may yield misleading results. Therefore, for overall capability assessment of the process, use of suitable MPCIs is highly advocated.

In this context, a *suitable* MPCI may depend on a number of criteria. Some of them are:

1. Type of specification region (e.g., bilateral, unilateral, circular or among bilateral specification, symmetric or asymmetric about a stipulated target);

Introduction 12

TABLE 1.2: Dataset pertaining to a manufacturing industry with two correlated quality characteristics and 39 randomly selected sample observations

Name \ Sl. No.	1	2	3	4	5	6	7	8	9	10
7J	78.1	77.13	75.9	77.03	76.91	76.77	77.38	77.57	77.87	77.49
6J	1.82	1.97	2.39	1.59	1.87	1.93	1.92	1.95	1.91	1.84

Name \ Sl. No.	11	12	13	14	15	16	17	18	19	20
7J	77.36	78.27	78.02	76.49	77.21	78.27	78.27	78.07	77.40	77.30
6J	1.55	1.60	1.40	2.21	2.10	1.85	1.85	1.51	1.86	2.20

Name \ Sl. No.	21	22	23	24	25	26	27	28	29	30
7J	76.98	77.13	76.49	77.33	77.43	77.29	77.22	77.77	76.91	77.16
6J	1.89	2.26	2.45	2.03	2.19	1.98	2.01	1.86	2.06	2.23

Name \ Sl. No.	31	32	33	34	35	36	37	38	39	–
7J	76.82	76.78	77.57	78.19	77.64	76.81	77.74	75.43	77.38	–
6J	2.35	2.35	1.92	1.41	1.85	1.91	2.21	2.37	1.38	–

2. Underlying statistical distribution of the quality characteristics, viz. multivariate normal or non-normal;

3. Number of correlated quality characteristics; for example, if there are sufficiently large number of correlated quality characteristics, then one may have to take refuge to some dimension reduction technique like principal component analysis and the suitable MPCI will be selected accordingly.

1.6 Overview of the Chapters

Process capability analysis is a useful method for improving the level of performance in industrial processes provided it is applied in a statistically sound way. However, merely defining PCIs, which are theoretically sound but lack practical utility, should not be the ultimate objective of any researcher working in the field of SQC. Orchard [29] has aptly commented that *"Engineers struggle to come to terms with statistical issues that are relatively trivial and that statisticians have to learn a new vocabulary in order to talk about*

Introduction 13

TABLE 1.3: Co-ordinates of the centers of 20 drilled holes

Sl. No.	1	2	3	4	5	6	7	8	9	10
X_1	2.65	3.01	2.86	1.99	1.75	2.68	3.68	2.91	4.05	2.17
X_2	2.52	3.28	2.72	2.83	2.31	2.56	3.29	2.73	4.31	1.84

Sl. No.	11	12	13	14	15	16	17	18	19	20
X_1	2.98	3.03	1.67	3.53	2.29	3.43	2.19	2.97	2.41	3.07
X_2	2.94	3.08	1.79	3.02	2.51	3.31	2.09	2.94	2.73	2.72

bias, variation and confidence intervals." Thus, bridging the gap between theoreticians and practitioners is also of utmost importance. The overall aim of the research work presented in this book is to explore some of the existing PCIs in terms of their interpretational, inferential and distributional properties and also to define some new PCIs wherever necessary, to cater to the need of specific practical situations, where none of the existing PCIs deliver the goods.

Chapter 2 contains some useful concepts of univariate and multivariate statistics. These will be helpful for thorough understanding of the subsequent chapters.

In Chapter 3, we give a brief overview of the existing univariate PCIs especially designed for different types of specification limits. This will give a broad idea of the limitations of the existing methodologies as well as the future scopes of research.

Chapter 4 discusses some bivariate PCIs available in literature. This is actually the gateway for multivariate PCIs.

Chapter 5 deals with MPCIs based on principal component analysis (PCA). Being a popular statistical tool for dimension reduction, PCA-based MPCIs are easy to compute and interpret. We have discussed about some MPCIs, which are originally defined analogous to some popular PCIs under univariate set-up. Apart from this, PCA-based MPCIs defined from probabilistic approach are also discussed here.

In Chapters 6–8, MPCIs for different types of specification regions, viz symmetric, asymmetric, and unilateral, respectively, have been discussed.

Chapter 9 deals with MPCIs defined based on the notion of proportion of nonconformance.

Apart from the MPCIs defined based on the assumption of multivariate normality of the process distributions, there are a number of MPCIs which do not require such assumptions. Chapter 10 is dedicated to MPCIs for non-normal process distributions.

In Chapter 11, MPCIs based on a Bayesian approach are discussed.

A major problem in analyzing a real-life data could be the presence of auto-correlation in the data, due to various practical reasons. Chapter 12 presents a thorough discussion on how to deal with such data.

Introduction 14

Apart from single-valued MPCIs, which mostly dominate the literature, there are also a few vector-valued MPCIs. In Chapter 13, multivariate process capability vectors (MPCVs) are discussed.

After discussing all these different types of MPCIs, there still remain some MPCIs, which do not suit any of the above-mentioned categories. In Chapter 14, those MPCIs have been discussed.

Although there is no denial of the fact that theoretical knowledge about the multivariate process capability analysis is very much important, the ultimate objective is its application in industry. Chapter 15 deals with some very interesting applications of MPCIs.

The book concludes on with a general discussion on multivariate process capability analysis.

Many of the chapters contain numerical examples from actual process control situations and show how the theory is applied to the given dataset. Wherever possible, we have made comparative studies among the MPCIs based on real-life data. We have also discussed about some very interesting future research problems with immense potential application in practice.

Bibliography

[1] Anis, M. Z. (2008). Basic Process Capability Indices – An Expository Review. *International Statistical Review*, Vol. 76, No. 3, pp. 347–367.

[2] Bernardo, J. M., Irony, T. Z. (1996). A General Multivariate Bayesian Process Capability Index. *The Statistician*, Vol. 45, No. 3, pp. 487–502.

[3] Box, G. E. P., Cox, D. R. (1964). An Analysis of Transformations. *Journal of the Royal Statistical Society, Series B (Statistical Methodology)*, Vol. 26, No. 2, pp. 211–246.

[4] Box, G., Luceno, A. (2000). Six Sigma, Process Drift, Capability Indices and Feedback Adjustment. *Quality Engineering*, Vol. 12, No. 3, pp. 297–302.

[5] Chakraborty, A. K., Basu, P. K., Chakravarty, S. C. (2005). *Guide to ISO 9001:2000*. Asian Books Private Limited.

[6] Chatterjee, M., Chakraborty, A. K. (2015). A Super Structure of Process Capability Indices for Circular Specification Region. *Communications in Statistics – Theory and Methods*, Vol. 44, No. 6, pp. 1158–1181.

[7] Chatterjee, M., Chakraborty, A. K. (2015). Distributions and Process Capability Control Charts for C_{pu} and C_{pl} Using Subgroup Information. *Communications in Statistics – Theory and Methods*, Vol. 44, No. 20, pp. 4333–4353.

[8] Chatterjee, M., Chakraborty, A. K. (2016). Some Process Capability Indices for Unilateral Specification Limits – Their Properties and the Process Capability Control Charts. *Communications in Statistics – Theory and Methods*, Vol. 45, No. 24, pp. 7130–7160.

[9] Chakraborty, A. K., Chatterjee, M. (2016). Univariate and Multivariate Process Capability Analysis for Different Types of Specification Limits. *Quality and Reliability Management and Its Applications* edited by Prof. Hoang Pham. pp. 47–81. London: Springer.

[10] Chatterjee, M., Chakraborty, A. K. (2017). Unification of Some Multivariate Process Capability Indices for Asymmetric Specification Region. *Statistica Neerlandica*, Vol. 71, No. 4, pp. 286–306.

[11] Chakraborty, A. K., Chatterjee, M. (2020). Distributional and Inferential Properties of Some New Multivariate Process Capability Indices for Symmetric Specification Region. *Quality and Reliability Engineering International*, DOI:10.1002/qre.2783

[12] Chen, H. (1994). A Multivariate Process Capability Index Over a Rectangular Solid Tolerance Zone. *Statistica Sinica*, Vol. 4, No. 2, pp. 749–758.

[13] Feigenbaum, A.V. (1951). *Quality Control.* New York: McGraw Hill.

[14] Grau, D. (2007). Multivariate Capability Indices for Processes with Asymmetric Tolerances. *Quality Technology and Quantitative Management*, Vol. 4, No. 4, pp. 471–488.

[15] Jalili, M., Bashiri, M., Amiri, A. (2012). A New Multivariate Process Capability Index Under Both Unilateral and Bilateral Quality Characteristics. *Quality and Reliability Engineering International*, Vol. 28, No. 8, pp. 925–941.

[16] Juran, J. M. (1951). *Quality Control Handbook*, 1st ed., New York: McGraw Hill.

[17] Juran, J. M. (1962). *Quality Control Handbook*, 2nd ed., New York: McGraw Hill.

[18] Juran, J. M., Gryna, F. M. (1980). *Quality Planning and Analysis*, 2nd ed., New York: McGraw-Hill.

[19] Kane, V. E. (1986). Process Capability Index. *Journal of Quality Technology*, Vol. 18, No. 1, pp. 41–52.

[20] Karl, D. P., Morisette, J., Taam, W. (1994). Some Applications of a Multivariate Capability Index in Geometric Dimensioning and Tolerancing. *Quality Engineering*, Vol. 6, No. 4, pp. 649–665.

[21] Khadse, K. G., Shinde, R. L. (2006). Multivariate Process Capability Using Relative Importance of Quality Characteristics. *The Indian Association for Productivity, Quality and Reliability (IAPQR) Transactions*, Vol. 31, No. 2, pp. 85–97.

[22] Khadse, K. G., Shinde, R. L. (2009). Probability-Based Process Capability Indices. *Communications in Statistics – Simulation and Computation*, Vol. 38, No. 4, pp. 884–904.

[23] Kiemele, M. J. (2003). Using the Design for Six Sigma (DFSS) Approach to Design, Test, and Evaluate to Reduce Program Risk. *Air Academy Associates, NDIA Test and Evaluation Summit*, Victoria, British Columbia.
https://ndiastorage.blob.core.usgovcloudapi.net/ndia/2003/test/kiemele.pdf

Bibliography

[24] Kirmani, S., Polansky, A. M. (2009). Multivariate Process Capability Via Lowner Ordering. *Linear Algebra and Its Applications*, Vol. 430, No. 10, pp. 2681–2689.

[25] Kotz, S., Johnson, N. (1993). *Process Capability Indices*. London: Chapman & Hall.

[26] Kotz, S., Johnson, N. (2002). Process Capability Indices – A Review, 1992 - 2000. *Journal of Quality Technology*, Vol. 34, No. 1, pp. 2–19.

[27] Muir, A. (2006). *Lean Six Sigma Statistics – Calculating Process Efficiencies in Transactional Projects*, New York: McGraw-Hill.

[28] Niverthi, M., Dey, D. (2000). Multivariate Process Capability: A Bayesian Perspective. *Communications in Statistics – Simulation and Computation*, Vol. 29, No. 2, pp. 667–687.

[29] Orchard, T. (2000). Quality Improvement. *Royal Statistical Society News*, Vol. 27, p. 8.

[30] Palmer, K., Tsui, K. L. (1999). A Review and Interpretations of Process Capability Indices. *Annals of Operations Research*, Vol. 87, pp. 31–47.

[31] Pearn, W. L., Kotz, S. (2007). *Encyclopedia and Handbook of Process Capability Indices – Series on Quality, Reliability and Engineering Statistics*. Singapore: World Scientific.

[32] Pearn, W. L., Wang, F. K., Yen, C. H. (2006). Measuring Production Yield for Processes with Multiple Quality Characteristics. *International Journal of Production Research*, Vol. 44, No. 21, pp. 4649–4661.

[33] Pearn, W. L., Wang, F. K., Yen, C. H. (2007). Multivariate Capability Indices: Distributional and Inferential Properties. *Journal of Applied Statistics*, Vol. 34, No. 8, pp. 941–962.

[34] Polansky, A. (2001). A Smooth Nonparametric Approach to Multivariate Process Capability. *Technometrics*, Vol. 53, No. 2, pp. 199–211.

[35] Shahriari, H., Abdollahzadeh, M. (2009). A New Multivariate Process Capability Vector. *Quality Engineering*, Vol. 21, No. 3, pp. 290–299.

[36] Shahriari, H., Hubele, N. F., Lawrence, F. P. (1995). A Multivariate Process Capability Vector. *Proceedings of the 4th Industrial Engineering Research Conference*, Institute of Industrial Engineers, pp. 304–309.

[37] Shinde, R. L., Khadse, K. G. (2009). Multivariate Process Capability Using Principal Component Analysis. *Quality and Reliability Engineering International*, Vol. 25, No. 1, pp. 69–77.

[38] Sultan, T. L. (1986). An Acceptance Chart for Raw Materials of Two Correlated Properties. *Quality Assurance*, Vol. 12, pp. 70–72.

[39] Taam, W., Subbaiah, P., Liddy, W. (1993). A Note on Multivariate Capability Indices. *Journal of Applied Statistics*, Vol. 20, No. 3, pp. 339–351.

[40] Wang, F. K., Chen, J. C. (1998). Capability Index Using Principal Component Analysis. *Quality Engineering*, Vol. 11, No. 1, pp. 21–27.

[41] Wang, F. K., Du, T. C. T. (2000). Using Principal Component Analysis in Process Performance for Multivariate Data. *Omega*, Vol. 28, No. 2, pp. 185–194.

[42] Wang, D. -S., Koo, T. -Y., Chou, C. -Y. (2009). Yield Measure for the Process with Multiple Streams. *Quality and Quantity*, Vol. 43, No. 4, pp. 661–668.

[43] Yum, B. J., Kim, K. W. (2011). A Bibliography of the Literature on Process Capability Indices: 2000–20009. *Quality and Reliability Engineering International*, Vol. 27, No. 3, pp. 251–268.

Chapter 2

Some Useful Concepts of Univariate and Multivariate Statistics

Chapter Summary

After a brief introduction of process capability analysis (PCA) as a tool of statistical quality control (S.Q.C.), it becomes necessary to discuss some concepts of univariate and multivariate statistics, pertinent to PCA. This will help the reader to have an easy reading of the subsequent chapters. Some univariate and multivariate statistical distributions like univariate and multivariate normal distribution, radial error distribution, log-normal distribution, uniform distribution, exponential distribution, univariate and multivariate folded normal distribution and so on, along with some of their important properties, are discussed. Estimation procedure of unknown process parameters, using control chart information, is briefly explained. Some other important statistical methods like principal component analysis, Delta method of estimation among others, are also discussed. Apart from these so-called frequentist statistical tools, a brief discussion is also made on Bayesian way of statistical analysis.

2.1 Introduction

It is widely believed that, the word *"Statistics"* is derived from the Latin word *"statisticum collegium,"* which means "Council of State." In this context, the Roman census was established by the sixth king of Rome, Servius Tullius (534–578 B. C.). In fact, in ancient times, statistics evolved around providing information regarding population size, expected tax, prediction of forthcoming war and so on.

German scholar Gottfried Achenwall first use the word *"Statistics"* in mid-18th century. The scope of Statistics was broadened in 1800s, when it included the collection, summary and analysis of data of any type and also was conjoined with probability for the purpose of statistical inference.

Contributions of some legendary mathematicians and statisticians like De Moivre, Laplace, K. F. Gauss, Quetelet, Karl Pearson, R. A. Fisher, G. U.

Some Useful Concepts of Univariate and Multivariate Statistics   20

Yule, W. S. Gosset (more famous by his pseudonym "Student"), J. Neyman, E. S. Pearson, P. C Mahalanobis and many others (refer Gun et al. [19]) have shaped *"Statistics"*—the subject, in its present form.

In next few sections of this chapter, we shall discuss about some statistical concepts which will be useful, time and again, in the succeeding chapters.

In this context, since both univariate and multivariate process capability analysis mostly deal with quality characteristics which are characterized as continuous random variables, our discussion will primarily be for those variables only.

Note that this chapter does not provide extensive discussion on statistical theories. Rather, the primary intension of this chapter is to provide theoretical supplements for enabling smooth reading of the succeeding chapters. Relevant references are provided at each section for thorough discussion on these concepts.

2.2   Univariate Statistics

2.2.1   Normal Distribution

Normal distribution is the most important and widely used theoretical statistical distribution for continuous variables. It is also known as Gaussian distribution after the celebrated German mathematician, physicist and statistician Carl Friedrich Gauss.

Suppose X is a random variable which follows normal distribution with mean μ and variance σ^2, notationally, $X \sim N(\mu, \sigma^2)$, then the probability density function (p. d. f.) of X is defined as

$$f_X(x) = \frac{1}{\sigma\sqrt{2\pi}} \times e^{-\frac{(x-\mu)^2}{2\sigma^2}}, \quad -\infty < x < \infty; \ -\infty < \mu < \infty; \ \sigma > 0 \quad (2.1)$$

We will denote $f_X(x)$ by $f(x)$ in most of the cases for notational simplicity. The corresponding cumulative distribution function (c.d. f.) is given by

$$F_X(x) \ = \ \int_{-\infty}^{x} f(t)dt \tag{2.2}$$

$$= \ \frac{1}{\sigma\sqrt{2\pi}} \int_{-\infty}^{x} e^{-\frac{(t-\mu)^2}{2\sigma^2}} dt \tag{2.3}$$

A normal distribution with $\mu = 0$ and $\sigma = 1$ is called a *"Standard Normal*

Distribution." Suppose Z is a random variable, which follows standard normal distribution, notationally $Z \sim N(0,1)$. Then its p. d. f. is given by

$$\phi_Z(z) = \frac{1}{\sqrt{2\pi}} \times e^{-\frac{z^2}{2}}, \quad -\infty < z < \infty \tag{2.4}$$

Also, the corresponding c. d. f. is

$$\Phi_Z(z) = \int_{-\infty}^{z} \phi(t)dt \tag{2.5}$$

Note that, unlike other statistical distributions, p. d. f. of standard normal distribution is conventionally denoted by $\phi(.)$, instead of "f" and similarly, the cumulative distribution function (c.d. f.) is denoted by Φ, instead of "F."

Figure 2.1 depicts normal curves for various combinations of (μ, σ) values.

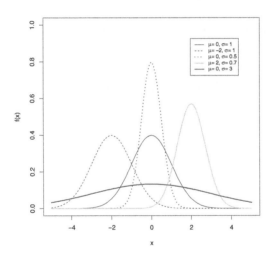

FIGURE 2.1: Shape of normal distribution for various combinations of (μ, σ) values.

For a given x, the values of $\Phi(x)$ have been tabulated in the so called "*Biometrika Table*" [44], "*RMM table*" [46] and "*Fisher - Yates Table*" [15]. These are of immense practical importance in statistical literature, though nowadays, one can compute the values using any standard statistical package.

2.2.1.1 Properties of Normal Distribution

Normal distribution being the single most popular statistical distribution, its properties have been studied thoroughly in literature (refer Gun et al. [19], Feller [14], Johnson et al. [22], and Patel and Read [41], among others).

Property 1: Normal distribution is symmetric about its mean μ, i.e.,

$$f(\mu + a) = f(\mu - a) = \frac{1}{\sigma\sqrt{2\pi}} \times e^{-\frac{a^2}{2\sigma^2}}, \qquad (2.6)$$

whatever the value of a may be.

Property 2: For normal distribution, mean = median = mode = μ.

Property 3: Since normal distribution is symmetric about its mean μ, its odd ordered central moments are zero, $E[X - \mu]^r = 0$, for $r = 2n + 1$, n being any positive integer.

Property 4: If X and Y are two independent random variables such that $X \sim N(\mu_1, \sigma_1^2)$ and $Y \sim N(\mu_2, \sigma_2^2)$, then $aX + bY \sim N(a\mu_1 + b\mu_2, a^2\sigma_1^2 + b^2\sigma_2^2)$, where a and b are any real numbers (both positive and negative).

Property 5: The point where a curve changes from convexity to concavity or concavity to convexity is known as its **point of inflection**. The curve of normal distribution has two points of inflection at $x = \mu \mp \sigma$.

The normal distribution curve is concave within the interval $(\mu - \sigma, \mu + \sigma)$ while outside this interval, the curve is convex.

Figure 2.2 shows effective range of standard normal, i.e., $N(0, 1)$ distribution.

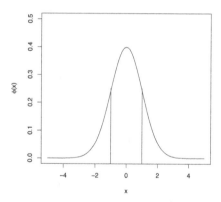

FIGURE 2.2: Points of inflection of standard normal distribution.

Property 6: As is evident from equation (2.1), theoretically, a normal variable can assume any value in $(-\infty, \infty)$. However, in practice, 99.73% of its values lie between $\mu \pm 3\sigma$. This is also known as **effective range of normal distribution**.

Figure 2.3 shows effective range of standard normal distribution.

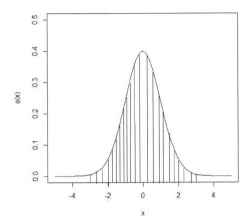

FIGURE 2.3: Effective range of standard normal distribution.

2.2.2 Radial Error Distribution

The distribution of radius of a circle is another interesting statistical distribution, which finds immense application in ballistics. In fact, Laurent [29] has observed that bombing problems (i.e., hitting a target) can be considered as the probability of hitting inside a circle centered at a stipulated target. Similar situations can be found in the study of turbulence in fluids (refer Frenkiel [16]). In the context of statistical quality control, the concept of radial error finds ample application in case of process capability analysis for quality characteristics with circular specification region, for example, in case of drilling a hole (refer Chatterjee and Chakraborty [7]).

Weil [55] was among the first to discuss about the distribution of radial error. Suppose X_i is a random variable, such that $X_i \sim N(\mu_i, \sigma_i^2)$, for $i = 1, 2$. Then radial error can be defined as $R = \sqrt{X_1^2 + X_2^2}$. Weil [55] has derived its p.d.f. as

$$f_R(r) = A r\, exp\left[\frac{-r^2(\sigma_1^2 + \sigma_2 2)}{4\sigma_1^2 + \sigma_2^2}\right]$$
$$\times \left[I_0(ar^r)I_0(dr) + 2\sum_{j=1}^{\infty} I_j(ar^2)I_{2j}(dr)\, cos\, 2j\psi\right] \quad (2.7)$$

where $A = \frac{1}{\sigma_1 \sigma_2} \times exp[-\frac{\mu_1^2 \sigma_2^2 + \mu_2^2 \sigma_1^2}{2\sigma_1^2 \sigma_2^2}]$, $a = \frac{\sigma_1^2 - \sigma_2^2}{4\sigma_1^2 \sigma_2^2}$, $b = \frac{\mu_1}{\sigma_1^2}$, $c = \frac{\mu_2}{\sigma_2^2}$, $d^2 = b^2 + c^2$, and $tan\psi = \frac{\mu_2 \sigma_1^2}{\mu_1 \sigma_2^2}$. Also, $I_j(w)$ is a Bessel function, whose values are tabulated by Abromoitz and Stegun [1].

Some Useful Concepts of Univariate and Multivariate Statistics   24

Scheuer [50] has derived the expressions for the moments of radial error distribution for a slightly modiified case.

Suppose $(Y_1, Y_2)' \sim N_2(0, 0, \sigma_1^2, \sigma_2^2, \rho = \frac{\sigma_{12}}{\sigma_1 \sigma_2})$, then for the radial error $\sqrt{Y_1^2 + Y_2^2}$, expected value will be $E[\sqrt{Y_1^2 + Y_2^2}] = \sqrt{\frac{2}{\pi}} \Im(K)\sigma_1^{*2}$ and $E[Y_1^2 + Y_2^2] = (2 - K^2)\sigma_1^{*2}$ (Scheur, 1962), where

- $\sigma_1^{*2} = \frac{1}{2}\left\{(\sigma_1^2 + \sigma_2^2) + [(\sigma_1^2 - \sigma_2^2)^2 + 4\sigma_{12}^2]^{\frac{1}{2}}\right\}$

- $\sigma_2^{*2} = \frac{1}{2}\left\{(\sigma_1^2 + \sigma_2^2) - [(\sigma_1^2 - \sigma_2^2)^2 + 4\sigma_{12}^2]^{\frac{1}{2}}\right\}$

- $K^2 = \frac{\sigma_1^2 - \sigma_2^2}{\sigma_1^2}$

- $\Im(K)$ is the complete elliptical integral of the second kind (Legendre [31]).

In general, the q raw moment is:

$$\mu_q' = (2\sigma_1^{*2})^{n/2}\Gamma\left(\frac{n}{2} + 1\right) F\left(-\frac{n}{2}, \frac{1}{2}; 1; K^2\right), \tag{2.8}$$

where, $F(a, b; c; z)$ is a hyper-geometric function (refer Abromoitz and Stegun [1]).

2.2.3   Folded Normal Distribution

Another very useful statistical distribution is folded normal distribution. It originates when, for example, the actual algebraic signs of the observations, coming from a normal distribution, are ignored or irretrievably lost. Leone [32] has enlisted the following examples of folded normal distribution:

1. When an object is placed convex side up and while measuring its flatness, a feeler gauge is used to find the difference between the surface plate and the object. The flatness, thus measured, follows folded normal distribution.

2. Measurement of straightness of miniature radio tube leads.

3. Distance between two objects.

   In all the above cases, the algebraic signs of the measurement become redundant. If the original measurement values follow normal distribution, then these absolute values will follow folded normal distribution;

Apart from these, folded normal distribution finds ample application in statistical quality control (S. Q. C.), in particular in process capability analysis. To be more precise, the statistical distribution of a very popular PCI, C_{pk} (refer Chapter 3 for more details) is based on folded normal distribution . Applications of folded normal distribution, in the context of univariate process capability indices has been made by Lin [34] and Lin [35]. Similarly, use of CUSUM control chart, under the folded normal set-up has been discussed by Johnson [21]. An economic tolerance design for folded normal data in manufacturing industries has been discussed by Liao [33].

Suppose Z is a random variable such that $Z \sim N(\mu, \sigma^2)$. Then, $X = |Z|$ follows folded normal distribution whose probability density function (p.d.f.) is given by

$$\begin{aligned} f_X(z) &= h_Z(z) + h_Z(-z) \\ &= \frac{1}{\sigma\sqrt{2\pi}} \left[\exp\left\{-\frac{1}{2}\left(\frac{z-\mu}{\sigma}\right)^2\right\} + \exp\left\{-\frac{1}{2}\left(\frac{z+\mu}{\sigma}\right)^2\right\} \right], \; z > 0, \end{aligned}$$
(2.9)

where "h" and "f" denote the p.d.f.s of the normal and the folded normal distributions, respectively.

Two dimensional and three dimensional density plots of folded normal distribution are given in Figures 2.4 and 2.5, respectively.

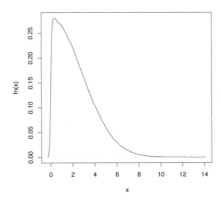

FIGURE 2.4: Two-dimensional density plot of folded normal distribution.

Leone et al. [32] have derived the expressions for the mean (μ_f) and variance (σ_f^2) of a folded normal distribution as

$$\mu_f = \sigma\sqrt{\frac{2}{\pi}} \exp\left(-\frac{\mu^2}{2\sigma^2}\right) + \mu\left[1 - 2\Phi\left(-\frac{\mu}{\sigma}\right)\right], \quad (2.10)$$

$$\sigma_f^2 = \mu^2 + \sigma^2 - \left\{\sigma\sqrt{\frac{2}{\pi}} \exp\left(-\frac{\mu^2}{2\sigma^2}\right) + \mu\left[1 - 2\Phi\left(-\frac{\mu}{\sigma}\right)\right]\right\}^2 \quad (2.11)$$

The subscript "f" is used here to distinguish the mean and variance of a folded normal distribution from that of a normal distribution.

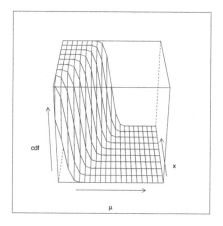

FIGURE 2.5: Three-dimensional density plot of folded normal distribution.

A general expression for the rth moment of folded normal distribution has been formulated by Elandt [13]. For this, the author has proposed two methods of estimating the parameters μ and σ of the *"parent"* normal distribution, viz., (i) based on the first and second raw and central moments of folded normal distribution and (ii) based on its third and fourth raw and central moments.

Chatterjee and Chakraborty [8] have discussed about a very simple step by step computer driven algorithm for having (μ, σ) values from the values of (μ_f, σ_f). They have also expressed the cdf of folded normal distribution as a function of two standard normal cdfs. Based on this algorithm and the expression for cdf, the areas of the folded normal distribution can easily be computed for any plausible combinations of (μ_f, σ_f) or (μ, σ). The statistical package "R" is used to execute the algorithms.

2.2.4 Uniform Distribution

This is also known as *Rectangular Distribution*. Suppose X is a random variable which follows uniform distribution on the interval $[a, b]$, where a and b are any two real numbers. Then the p.d.f. of X is given by

$$f_U(x) = \begin{cases} \frac{1}{b-a}, & -\infty < a \leq x \leq b < \infty \\ 0, & \text{Otherwise} \end{cases} \tag{2.12}$$

Notationally, this is represented as $X \sim U(a, b)$.

The density plot for uniform distribution with parameters 0 and 1 is given in Figure 2.6.

Some important properties of Uniform distribution are as follows:

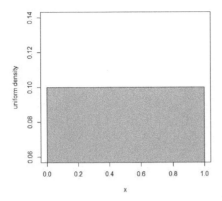

FIGURE 2.6: Density plot for uniform distribution.

[Unless otherwise stated, here we consider Uniform distribution with parameters a and b].

Property 1: $E(X) = \frac{b-a}{2}$.

Property 2: $Var(X) = \frac{(b-a)^2}{12}$.

Property 3: The kth order raw moment of X is given by $E(X^k) = \frac{b^{k+1} - a^{k+1}}{(k+1)(b-a)}$, where, $k > 0$ is an integer.

Property 4: Uniform distribution is symmetric about its mean and is highly platykurtic.

Property 5: Let W be any random variable with a continuous distribution function F. Then $F(w) \sim U(0, 1)$.

2.2.5 Log-Normal Distribution

A random variable Y is said to follow log-normal distribution with parameters μ and σ, if $X = \ln Y \sim N(ln\mu, \sigma^2)$. Its pdf is given by

$$f(y) = \begin{cases} \frac{1}{\sigma y \sqrt{2\pi}} exp\left[-\frac{(\ln y - \ln \mu)^2}{2\sigma^2}\right], & 0 < y < \infty, \ -\infty < \mu < \infty; \ \sigma > 0 \\ 0, & \text{Otherwise} \end{cases}$$

(2.13)

Note that, here μ and σ are originally the parameters of normal distribution.

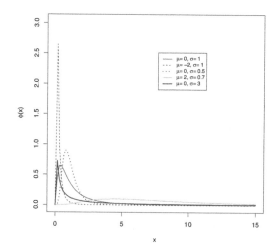

FIGURE 2.7: Density plot for log-normal distribution.

The density plot of log-normal distribution for various combinations of μ and σ are given in Figure 2.7.

Observe that in both the Figures 2.1 and 2.7, the values of (μ, σ) are kept intact to show the difference in shapes of the two distributions. While normal distribution is symmetric about μ, log-normal distribution is highly positively skewed.

Following are some important properties of log-normal distribution.

Property 1: $E(Y) = e^{\mu + \frac{\sigma^2}{2}}$.

Property 2: $V(Y) = \mu^2 e^{\sigma^2} \left(e^{\sigma^2} - 1 \right)$.

Property 3: The rth order raw moment of log-normal distribution is given by $E(Y^r) = \mu^r \, e^{\frac{r^2 \sigma^2}{2}}$, where, $r > 0$ is any integer.

Property 4: Since by Property 2 of Normal distribution, $\ln \mu$ is the median of $\ln Y$ and since $\ln Y$ is a monotonic function of Y, the median of Y is μ.

Property 5: Log-normal distribution is positively skewed and leptokurtic.

2.2.6 Exponential Distribution

Exponential distribution finds huge application in reliability theory and survival analysis. Examples could be the life time of a device or a component or a software etc. It is also used in the case of continuous time Markov chain. Because of its ability to model life time of machine components, exponential distribution is also being used in process capability analysis (refer Tong et al. [54] and the references therein).

If a continuous random variable X follows exponential distribution with parameter $\lambda(>0)$. Then the p.d.f. of X is given by

$$f(x) = \begin{cases} \lambda e^{-\lambda x}, x \geq 0 \\ 0, \text{ Otherwise} \end{cases} \qquad (2.14)$$

Notationally, this is represented as $X \sim EXP(\lambda)$.

Figure 2.8 shows density plot of exponential distribution for various values of λ.

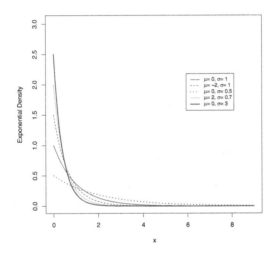

FIGURE 2.8: Density plot for exponential distribution.

c.d.f. of X is

$$F(x) = \begin{cases} 1 - e^{-\lambda x}, x \geq 0 \\ 0, \text{ Otherwise} \end{cases} \qquad (2.15)$$

Following are some important properties of Exponential distribution.

Property 1: $E[x] = \frac{1}{\lambda}$.

Property 2: $V[x] = \frac{1}{\lambda^2}$.

Some Useful Concepts of Univariate and Multivariate Statistics   30

Property 3: Let $X_1, X_2, \cdots, X_n$ be independent random variables with $X_i \sim Exp(\lambda_i)$, for $i = 1(1)n$. Then $\min(X_1, X_2, \cdots, X_n) \sim EXP(\lambda_1 + \lambda_2 + \cdots + \lambda_n)$ and the probability that the minimum is X_i is $\frac{\lambda_i}{\lambda_1 + \lambda_2 + \cdots + \lambda_n}$.

Property 4: "Memoryless" Property

Let X be a random variable denoting the life time (in hours) of certain component and $X \sim EXP(\lambda)$. Then for any positive t and t_0,

$$
\begin{aligned}
P(X \geq t + t_0 \mid X \geq t_0) &= \frac{P[\{X \geq t + t_0\} \cap \{X \geq t_0\}]}{P(X \geq t_0)} \\
&= \frac{P(X \geq t + t_0)}{P(X \geq t_0)} \\
&= \frac{1 - F(t + t_0; \lambda)}{F(t_0; \lambda)} \\
&= \frac{e^{-\lambda(t + t_0)}}{e^{-\lambda t_0}} \\
&= e^{-\lambda t} \qquad\qquad (2.16)
\end{aligned}
$$

Now from equation (2.15), $P(X \geq t) = e^{-\lambda t}$. Therefore, from equation (2.16),

$$
P(X \geq t) = P(X \geq t + t_0 \mid X \geq t_0) \qquad\qquad (2.17)
$$

This implies, the distribution of additional life time is exactly the same as the original life time, i.e., the distribution of remaining life time is independent of current age.

Life time of electric bulb also has similar property.

2.3   Estimation of Process Mean and Variance Using Control Chart Information

The expectations and variances of random variables, which have been discussed so far are based on single sample information only. However, in many industrial problems data is collected vide various subgroups each having either fixed or varying sample size. To make full utilization of such data, a diffferent approach needs to be adopted, which is discussed in detail now.

To start with, in conventional "one sample" approach, under normality assumption of the quality characteristic, generally two types of control charts

Some Useful Concepts of Univariate and Multivariate Statistics   31

are used to check stability of the process, viz., $\overline{X} - R$ chart and $\overline{X} - S$ chart, depending on the size of the sample. Accordingly, the estimators of the process parameters (μ, σ) also get changed.

Suppose the quality characteristic under consideration is normally distributed and the concerned process is under statistical control. Also, suppose, while checking stability of the process, we have "m" rational subgroups (refer Montgomery [47]) and from each rational subgroup, a sample of size "n" is drawn. Here we assume constant sample size for all the rational subgroups. So the total number of observations is $N = mn$. Let X_{ij} be the measured value of the quality characteristic for the jth sample from the ith rational subgroup, for $i = 1(1)m$ and $j = 1(1)n$. Then

1. $\overline{\overline{X}} = \frac{1}{N} \sum\limits_{i=1}^{m} \sum\limits_{j=1}^{n} X_{ij} = \frac{1}{m} \sum\limits_{i=1}^{m} \overline{X}_i$ is the average of subgroup averages;

2. $\overline{S} = \frac{1}{m} \sum\limits_{i=1}^{m} S_i$ is the average of the standard deviations over the sub-

   groups with $S_i = \sqrt{\frac{1}{n-1} \sum\limits_{j=1}^{n} (X_{ij} - \overline{X}_i)^2}$ being the standard deviation

   corresponding to the ith subgroup for $i = 1(1)m$.

3. $\overline{R} = \frac{1}{m} \sum\limits_{i=1}^{m} R_i$ is the average of the ranges over the subgroups with R_i

   being the range corresponding to the ith subgroup for $i = 1(1)m$.

2.3.1 Estimation of Process Mean and Variance Based on $\overline{X} - R$ Chart Information

In the context of statistical quality control (SQC), especially for control charting, generally, the sample size is considerably small, say 4 to 6 (refer Montgomery [47]). Hence often range is used as a measure of dispersion and consequently, $\overline{X} - R$ charts are the most commonly used control charts for checking the stability of a process. Woodall and Montgomery [56] have discussed two different estimators of σ, based on the average sample range $[\overline{R} = \frac{1}{m} \sum\limits_{i=1}^{m} R_i]$, given by

1. $\widehat{\sigma}_1 = \frac{\overline{R}}{d_2}$, which is generally used to design control chart and to analyze capability of a process;

2. $\widehat{\sigma}_2 = \frac{\overline{R}}{d_2^*}$, which is generally used in gauge repeatability and reproducibility study.

where $d_2^* = \sqrt{d_2^2 + \frac{d_3^2}{m}}$ and d_2 and d_3 are functions of "n" only. One may refer to Montgomery [47] for values of d_2, d_3, and so on for various values of "n."

Some Useful Concepts of Univariate and Multivariate Statistics 32

$\frac{\overline{R}}{d_2}$ will be more appropriate estimator of σ in the present context. Woodall and Montgomery [56] have made a thorough study of these two estimators of σ.

Following Patnaik [42] and Woodall and Montgomery [56], $\frac{\overline{R}}{\sigma} \sim \left(\frac{d_2^*}{\sqrt{v}}\right) \chi_v$ approximately, where v represents the fractional degrees of freedom for the $\chi-$distribution . Kuo [28] has formulated the mathematical expression for v as

$$v = \frac{1}{-2 + 2\sqrt{1 + \frac{2}{m} \times \left(\frac{d_3}{d_2}\right)^2}} \qquad (2.18)$$

Cox [11] also derived the distribution of $\frac{R}{\sigma}$ in terms of χ^2 distribution. While Patnaik's [42] derivation was from the view point of statistical quality control, Cox's [11] derivation was intended for sequential analysis. Pearson [43] made an extensive comparison of these two approaches and found that "more accurate results would be obtained with χ approximation when $n < 10$ and with χ^2 when $n > 10$ ". As such Patnaik's [42] approximate distribution of $\frac{R}{\sigma}$ will be more appropriate for our purpose.

Also, Lord [37] and Lin and Sheen [36] have shown that, $\overline{X}$ and $\overline{R}$ are mutually independent under the assumption of normality of the quality characteristic under consideration.

2.3.2 Estimation of Process Mean and Variance Based on $\overline{X} - S$ Chart Information

Due to the simplicity of computation and ease of interpretation, range is the most popular measure of dispersion among the practitioners. However, sometimes, despite these advantages, standard deviation outperforms range in measuring dispersion and consequently, $\overline{X} - S$ chart is used instead of $\overline{X} - R$ chart to check and establish stability of a process. According to Montgomery [47], when the sample size is moderately large, say, $n > 10$, standard deviation is preferred over range as a measure of dispersion.

Table 2.1 shows the tabulated values of the relative efficiency of range in comparison with standard deviation for various sample sizes (refer Montgomery [47]).

From Table 2.1 it is evident that, for $n > 10$ range does not perform satisfactorily.

Kirmani et al. [26] has also observed that distribution of $\overline{S}$ is mathematically intractable. He has suggested the use of the pooled variance $S_p^2 = \frac{1}{m(n-1)} \sum_{i=1}^{m} (n-1)S_i^2 = \frac{1}{m} \sum_{i=1}^{m} S_i^2$ instead, as $\frac{(n-1)S_p^2}{\sigma^2} \sim \chi^2_{m(n-1)}$ and hence is easier to handle in further applications. According to Kirmani et al. [26], $\overline{S} \overset{a}{\sim} N(c_4\sigma, \sigma^2 \left(\frac{1-c_4^2}{m}\right))$, where, " $\overset{a}{\sim}$ " denotes asymptotic distribution, m denotes the number of subgroups and c_4, a constant, is a function of the sample size n only.

Some Useful Concepts of Univariate and Multivariate Statistics 33

TABLE 2.1: Relative efficiency of range compared to that of standard deviation for different sample sizes

Sample size (n)	Relative efficiency
2	1.000
3	0.992
4	0.975
5	0.955
6	0.930
10	0.850

Chatterjee [4] has shown that

$$\frac{\overline{S}^2}{\sigma^2} \overset{a}{\sim} \left(\frac{1-c_4^2}{m}\right) \times \chi_1^2 \left(\delta_2 = \frac{mc_4^2}{1-c_4^2}\right) \tag{2.19}$$

where $\chi_1^2 (\delta_2)$ denotes non-central χ^2 distribution with 1 degree of freedom and non-centrality parameter $\delta_2 = \frac{mc_4^2}{1-c_4^2}$.

Lee and Amin [30] have observed that *the total sample size in a start-up control chart is mostly* ≥ 100 *(say 20 samples each of size 5)*. Therefore the asymptotic distribution of $\frac{\overline{S}^2}{\sigma^2}$ fits our purpose.

Chatterjee and Chakraborty [9, 10] have used $\overline{X} - R$ and $\overline{X} - S$ chart information to design process capability control charts which are useful in keeping constant vigil on process performance.

2.4 Some Bayesian Concepts

Bayes' theorem and Bayesian statistics gets its name from the celebrated theologian, philosopher, and mathematician Thomas Bayes. The famous Bayes' theorem is as follows:

Bayes' Theorem

Suppose $B_1, B_2, \cdots, B_m$ are m mutually exclusive and exhaustive events with $P(B_i) > 0$, $i = 1(1)m$. Also let A be an event which too has non-zero probability. Then According to Bayes' theorem,

$$P(B_i \mid A) = \frac{P(B_i)P(A|B_i)}{\sum\limits_{i=1}^{m} P(B_i)P(A|B_i)} \tag{2.20}$$

This formula can be used to reverse conditional probabilities, in a sense that, if one knows the probabilities of the events B_i and the conditional probabilities $P(A \mid B_i)$, $i = 1(1)m$, the formula can be used to compute the conditional probabilities $P(B_i \mid A)$.

On a simpler note, B_i denotes the statement about an unknown phenomenon and A denotes any information about the unknown phenomenon. Thus, according to Bayesian paradigm,

$$\text{posterior information} = \text{prior information}$$
$$+ \quad \text{information collected from relevant data} \tag{2.21}$$

Notationally,

$$p(\theta \mid y) \propto p(\theta)p(y \mid \theta) \tag{2.22}$$

where $\propto$ is a symbol for proportionality, θ is an unknown parameter, y is data, and $p(\theta)$, $p(\theta \mid y)$ and $p(y \mid \theta)$ are the density functions of the prior, posterior and sampling distributions, respectively.

In Bayesian inference, the unknown parameter θ is considered stochastic, unlike in classical inference. The distributions $p(\theta)$ and $p(\theta \mid y)$ express uncertainty about the exact value of θ. The density of data, $p(y \mid \theta)$, provides information from the data. It is called a likelihood function when considered a function of θ (refer Ghosh et al. [18]).

Thus, Bayesian analysis is parallel to frequentist approach for inference and other statistical analysis. Interested readers can refer to Gelman et al. [17], Koch [27], McElreath [39] and the references therein.

Although in statistical quality control, mostly frequentist approach is taken into consideration, nowadays, Bayesian analysis is also grabbing the attention of researchers.

Carter [3] has proposed a dynamic programming based approach to determine optimal sample size and optimal sampling interval in process control using Bayesian approach. Marcellus [38] has proposed a Bayesian process control chart. Tagaras and Nikolaidis [51] have made an extensive comparative study on effectiveness of various Bayesian $\overline{X}$ control charts. We have made a detail discussion on Bayesian approach based MPCIs in Chapter 11.

2.5 Multivariate Statistics

So far, we have discussed only about distributions considering one variable at a time. However, in practice, we often encounter situations where there are more than one inter related variables. The branch of statistics which deals with such problems is called *"Multivariate Statistics."*

Some Useful Concepts of Univariate and Multivariate Statistics 35

In the present section we shall discuss about some useful multivariate statistical distributions. We shall also discuss about two important statistical tools for multivariate analysis, viz., Principal component analysis (PCA) and multivariate δ method. Note that now onward, bold faced letters stand for vectors.

2.5.1 Multivariate Normal Distribution

A q - component random vector $\boldsymbol{X} = (X_1, X_2, \cdots, X_q)^{'}$ is said to follow a q-variate Normal distribution with parameters $\boldsymbol{\mu}$ and Σ if and only if their joint p.d.f. can be written as

$$f(\boldsymbol{x}) = \begin{cases} \dfrac{1}{(2\pi)^{p/2}\sqrt{|\Sigma|}} \, e^{-\frac{1}{2}(\boldsymbol{x}-\boldsymbol{\mu})^{'}\Sigma^{-1}(\boldsymbol{x}-\boldsymbol{\mu})}, & -\infty < x_i < \infty, \text{ for } i = 1(1)q; \\ \qquad\qquad -\infty < \mu_i < \infty; \; \Sigma \text{ is a positive definite matrix} \\[2mm] 0, \quad \text{Otherwise} \end{cases}$$

$$(2.23)$$

Notationally, this can be expressed as $\boldsymbol{X} \sim N_q(\boldsymbol{\mu}, \Sigma)$.
Following are some properties of multivariate normal distribution.

Property 1: If $\boldsymbol{X} \sim N_q(\boldsymbol{\mu}, \Sigma)$, then $E(\boldsymbol{X}) = \boldsymbol{\mu}$ and $Disp(\boldsymbol{X}) = \Sigma$, where, $Disp(\boldsymbol{X})$ implies dispersion matrix of $\boldsymbol{X}$.

Property 2: Moment generating function (m. g. f.) of $\boldsymbol{X}$ is

$$M_{\boldsymbol{X}} = E\left[e^{t^{'}\boldsymbol{X}}\right] = e^{t^{'}\boldsymbol{\mu}+\frac{1}{2}t^{'}\Sigma t} \qquad (2.24)$$

where $\boldsymbol{t} = (t_1, t_2, \cdots, t_q)^{'}$ is a vector of real numbers, i.e., $t_i \in \mathbb{R}$, for $i = 1(1)q$.

Property 3: Let $\boldsymbol{X}$ be a q component random vector. Then $\boldsymbol{X} \sim N_q(\boldsymbol{\mu}, \Sigma)$ if and only if every linear combination of $\boldsymbol{X}$ follows univariate normal distribution with suitable parameters, i.e., $\boldsymbol{l}^{'}\boldsymbol{X} \sim N(\boldsymbol{l}^{'}\boldsymbol{\mu}, \boldsymbol{l}^{'}\Sigma\boldsymbol{l})$, where, $\boldsymbol{l}$ is a vector of real numbers.

Interested readers may refer to Johnson et al. [22], Tong [53] and the references therein, for more detail discussion on multivariate normal distribution.

For multivariate process control and, in particular, for discussion on MPCIs, multivariate normal distribution is the single most important statistical distribution as most of the MPCIs defined so far are based on the assumption of multivariate normality of the underlying process distribution. Chatterjee [5] has made an extensive study on impact of multivariate normality assumption on performances of different MPCIs.

2.5.2 Multivariate Folded Normal Distribution

As has already been discussed in Section 2.2.3, univariate folded normal distribution was defined by Leone [32] in 1961 and it finds substantial amount of importance in statistical quality control. Its bivariate counter-part took forty long years to be defined, may be due to the computational complexity. We will, however, briefly discuss the pdf of a q-variate folded normal distribution with a focus on bivariate part.

The pdf of a bivariate folded normal (BVFN) distribution was developed by Psarakis and Panaretos [45] in the year 2001. Suppose that $\mathbf{Z} = (Z_1, Z_2)' \sim N_2(\boldsymbol{\mu}^{(2)}, \Sigma^{(2)})$ for $\boldsymbol{\mu}^{(2)} = (\mu_1, \mu_2)'$ and $\Sigma^{(2)} = \begin{pmatrix} \sigma_1^2 & \sigma_{12} \\ \sigma_{21} & \sigma_2^2 \end{pmatrix}$. Then, $(|Z_1|, |Z_2|)$ follows BVFN with mean vector $\boldsymbol{\mu}_f^{(2)}$ and dispersion matrix $\Sigma_f^{(2)}$, where the superscript "(2)" denotes the dimension of $\mathbf{Z}$. The pdf of $(|Z_1|, |Z_2|)$ can be derived as:

$$
\begin{aligned}
& f_{|Z_1|,|Z_2|}^{(2)}(z_1, z_2) \\
=\ & \sum_{\substack{u = z_1, -z_1 \\ v = z_2, -z_2}} h_{Z_1,Z_2}(u, v), \\
=\ & \frac{1}{2\pi\sigma_1\sigma_2\sqrt{1-\rho^2}} \\
\times\ & \left\{ \exp\left(-\frac{1}{2(1-\rho^2)}\left(\frac{(z_1-\mu_1)^2}{\sigma_1^2} - 2\rho\frac{(z_1-\mu_1)(z_2-\mu_2)}{\sigma_1\sigma_2} + \frac{(z_2-\mu_2)^2}{\sigma_2^2}\right)\right) \right. \\
+\ & \exp\left(-\frac{1}{2(1-\rho^2)}\left(\frac{(z_1+\mu_1)^2}{\sigma_1^2} - 2\rho\frac{(z_1+\mu_1)(z_2+\mu_2)}{\sigma_1\sigma_2} + \frac{(z_2+\mu_2)^2}{\sigma_2^2}\right)\right) \\
+\ & \exp\left(-\frac{1}{2(1-\rho^2)}\left(\frac{(z_1+\mu_1)^2}{\sigma_1^2} + 2\rho\frac{(z_1+\mu_1)(z_2-\mu_2)}{\sigma_1\sigma_2} + \frac{(z_2-\mu_2)^2}{\sigma_2^2}\right)\right) \\
+\ & \left. \exp\left(-\frac{1}{2(1-\rho^2)}\left(\frac{(z_1-\mu_1)^2}{\sigma_1^2} + 2\rho\frac{(z_1-\mu_1)(z_2+\mu_2)}{\sigma_1\sigma_2} + \frac{(z_2+\mu_2)^2}{\sigma_2^2}\right)\right) \right\}, \\
& \hspace{7cm} \text{for } z_1, z_2 > 0, \hspace{1cm} (2.25)
\end{aligned}
$$

where $h_{Z_1,Z_2}(.,.)$ denotes the pdf of bivariate normal(BVN) distribution with mean vector $\boldsymbol{\mu}^{(2)}$ and variance- covariance matrix $\Sigma^{(2)}$.

Psarakis and Panaretos [45] have derived the expression of the mgf for the bi-variate folded **standard** normal distribution, assuming $\boldsymbol{\mu}_f^{(2)} = \mathbf{0}$ and $\Sigma_f^{(2)} = I_2$ using Tallis' [52] formula for mgf of the truncated multi-normal distribution, where only the case of standard multivariate normal distribution is considered. It is to be noted that while deriving the mgf, Psarakis and Paneratos [45] have decomposed the exponent of the corresponding bivariate normal distribution and as a result, while generalizing the expression for higher dimensional cases, one has to undergo difficult computational procedure.

Some Useful Concepts of Univariate and Multivariate Statistics 37

According to Psarakis and Peneratos [45], the expression for the mgf of the bivariate folded standard normal distribution is

$$m = 2e^{T*}\Phi_2(\boldsymbol{b_s}; R^*) + 2e^{T}\Phi_2(\boldsymbol{b_s}; R) \qquad (2.26)$$

where $R^* = \begin{pmatrix} 1 & \rho \\ \rho & 1 \end{pmatrix} = \Sigma_1^{(2)}$, $R = \begin{pmatrix} 1 & -\rho \\ -\rho & 1 \end{pmatrix} = \Sigma_2^{(2)}$, and $\boldsymbol{b_s} = (b_1, b_2)' = -R^*\boldsymbol{t} = \begin{pmatrix} -t_1 - \rho t_2 \\ -\rho t_1 - t_2 \end{pmatrix}$ or $\boldsymbol{b_s} = -R\boldsymbol{t} = \begin{pmatrix} -t_1 + \rho t_2 \\ \rho t_1 - t_2 \end{pmatrix}$, depending upon the associated dispersion matrix.

Chakraborty and Chatterjee [6] have defined multivariate folded normal distribution (MVFN). Following Leone et al. [32], if $X \sim N(\mu, \sigma^2)$, then, $|X| \sim FN(\mu_f, \sigma_f^2)$. Also

$$|X| = \begin{cases} X, & \text{if } X > 0 \\ \\ -X, & \text{if } X < 0 \end{cases} \qquad (2.27)$$

Hence, proceeding similar to the constructions of the univariate and bivariate folded normal distributions, the p. d. f. of multivariate (say, q-variate) folded normal distribution can be defined as

$$f_{|\boldsymbol{X}|}^{(q)}(x_1, x_2, \cdots, x_q)$$
$$= \frac{1}{(2\pi)^{\frac{q}{2}}} \sum_{(s_1, s_2, \cdots, s_q) \in S(q)} \frac{1}{|\Sigma_s^{(q)}|} e^{-\frac{1}{2}(\boldsymbol{x}_s^{(q)} - \boldsymbol{\mu}_s^{(q)})'\Sigma_s^{(q)-1}(\boldsymbol{x}_s^{(q)} - \boldsymbol{\mu}_s^{(q)})}, \quad \boldsymbol{x}_s^{(q)} > \boldsymbol{0}$$

$$(2.28)$$

where $\boldsymbol{S(q)} = \{\mathbf{s} : \mathbf{s} = (s_1, s_2, \ldots, s_q), \text{ with } s_i = \pm 1, \forall 1 \leq i \leq q\}$, $\boldsymbol{x}_s^{(q)} = \Lambda_s^{(q)}\boldsymbol{x}^{(q)}$ and $\Lambda_s^{(q)} = \text{diag}(s_1, s_2, \ldots, s_q)$, such that

$$\begin{bmatrix} s_1 x_1 \\ s_2 x_2 \\ \vdots \\ s_q x_q \end{bmatrix} = \text{diag}(s_1, s_2, \ldots, s_q) \begin{bmatrix} x_1 \\ x_2 \\ \vdots \\ x_q \end{bmatrix} = \Lambda_s^{(q)}\boldsymbol{x}^{(q)}. \qquad (2.29)$$

As is evident from equation (2.27), X_i's may be positive or negative, as $X_i \sim N(\mu_i, \sigma_i^2)$, for $i = 1(1)q$. However, by definition, $X_{s_i} > 0$, for $i = 1(1)q$.

Kan and Robotti [25] have derived explicit expression for mgf of MVFN distribution and the corresponding product moments up to 4th order.

2.6 Principal Component Analysis (PCA)

Principal component analysis (PCA) is one of the most popular statistical techniques for dimension reduction. The central idea of principal component analysis (PCA) is to reduce the dimensionality of a dataset consisting of a large number of interrelated variables, while retaining as much as possible of the variation present in the data-set. This is achieved by transforming to a new set of variables called, the principal components (PCs), which are uncorrelated, and which are ordered so that the first few retain most of the variation present in all of the original variables (refer Jolliffe [24]).

Suppose X is a $q \times n$ sample data matrix, where q is the dimension of the process i.e., number of quality characteristics (often correlated) under consideration and n is the sample size. Suppose S is the sample dispersion matrix corresponding to this data. Therefore by definition, S is a non-singular square matrix of dimension $q \times q$.

A scalar λ is said to be an *eigen value* of a $q \times q$ matrix S if there is a non-trivial solution $\boldsymbol{u}$ for $S\boldsymbol{u} = \lambda\boldsymbol{u}$. Also, here $\boldsymbol{u}$ is called an *eigen vector* corresponding to λ. Thus, $\boldsymbol{u}$ is an eigen vector of S corresponding to eigen value λ if and only if $\boldsymbol{u}$ and λ satisfy $(S - \lambda I_q)\boldsymbol{u} = \boldsymbol{0}$, where I_q denotes identity matrix of order q.

Now, let us define the following:

1. D is a $q \times q$ diagonal matrix,

2. $\boldsymbol{u_i}$ is the q-component i^{th} eigen vector of S, for $i = 1(1)q$,

3. $\lambda_1, \lambda_2, \cdots, \lambda_q$ are q eigen values of S,

4. $U = (\boldsymbol{u_1}, \boldsymbol{u_2}, \cdots, \boldsymbol{u_q})'$ is the matrix of eigen vectors, corresponding to the above mentioned eigen values.

Then, using spectral decomposition, $D = U'SU$. Accordingly, the ith principal component (PC) is

$$Y_i = \boldsymbol{u_i}'\boldsymbol{x}, \quad \text{for } i = 1(1)q \tag{2.30}$$

where $\boldsymbol{x}$ is a $q \times 1$ vector of observations.

The ratio $\dfrac{\lambda_i}{\sum\limits_{i=1}^{q} \lambda_i}$ gives the proportion of variability explained by the ith PC, for $i = 1(1)q$.

Note that, although all the PCs, taken together, explain the total variation in the data, in practice, only the first few PCs (when all the PCs are arranged in descending order of their values) are sufficient to capture most of the variability, say $80 - 90\%$ (refer Jackson [20]).

Without loss of generality, let us assume that $\lambda_1 \geq \lambda_2 \geq \cdots \geq \lambda_q$.

Some Useful Concepts of Univariate and Multivariate Statistics   39

Jackson [20] has proposed a test for identifying significant PCs. The null and alternative hypotheses are

$$H_0 \quad : \quad \lambda_{k+1} = \lambda_{k+2} = \cdots = \lambda_q$$
$$H_1 \quad : \quad \text{At least one of these eigen values is different}$$

The test statistic for this test is

$$T = -(n-1) \sum_{j=k+1}^{q} \ln \lambda_j + (n-1)(q-k) \times \ln \left[\frac{\sum_{j=k+1}^{q} \ln \lambda_j}{q-k} \right] \qquad (2.31)$$

$T \sim \chi_r^2$ under H_0, where, χ_r^2 denotes χ^2 distribution with $r = (1/2)(q - k)(q - k + 1) - 1$ degrees of freedom.

Detailed discussion on PCA can be found in Johnson and Wicharn [23], Rencher [49] and the references therein.

PCA plays an important role in multivariate process capability analysis. Due to its dimension reduction ability, a number of PCA based MPCIs have been defined so far in literature. These have been discussed in detail in Chapter 5.

2.7   Delta Method

Delta method is a useful concept in the context of multivariate process capability analysis as it can be used to obtain asymptotic distribution and / or expressions for the mean and variance of estimators of some MPCIs, for which it is almost impossible to have an exact expression for the small sample scenario. Delta method is primarily based on *Taylor Series Expansion*.

Taylor Polynomial

If a function $g(x)$ has derivatives of order r, that is $g^{(r)}(x) = \frac{d^r}{dx^r} g(x)$ exists, then for any constant a, the *Taylor polynomial* of order r about a is

$$T_r(x) = \sum_{k=0}^{r} \frac{g^{(k)}(a)}{k!} (x-a)^k \qquad (2.32)$$

(refer Casella and Berger [2]) for more detail.

Furthermore, the so called Taylor's theorem is given as follows:

Taylor's Theorem

If $g^{(r)}(a) = \frac{d^r}{dx^r}g(x)\mid_{x=a}$ exists, then

$$\lim_{x \to a} \frac{g(x) - T_r(x)}{(x-a)^r} = 0 \qquad (2.33)$$

Delta Method

Let Y_n be a sequence of random variables that satisfies $\sqrt{n}(Y_n - \theta) \to N(0, \sigma^2)$ in distribution. For a given function g and a specific value θ, suppose that $g'(\theta)$ exists and is not 0. Then

$$\sqrt{n}\left[g(Y_n) - g(\theta)\right] \to N(0, \sigma^2[g'(\theta)]^2), \text{ as, } n \to \infty \qquad (2.34)$$

in distribution.

For the proof of this theorem, refer to Casella and Berger [2].

Multivariate Delta Method

Let $X_1, X_2, \cdots, X_n$ be a random sample with $E(X_{ij}) = \mu_i$ and $Cov(X_{ik}, X_{jk}) = \sigma_{ij}$. For a given function g with continuous partial derivative of first order and a specific value of $\boldsymbol{\mu} = (\mu_1, \mu_2, \cdots, \mu_q)$ for which $\tau^2 = \sum \sum \sigma_{ij} \frac{\delta g(\mu)}{\delta \mu_i} \times \frac{\delta g(\mu)}{\delta \mu_j} > 0,$

$$\sqrt{n}\left[g(\overline{X_1}, \overline{X_2}, \cdots, \overline{X_q}) - g(\mu_1, \mu_2, \cdots, \mu_q)\right] \to N(0, \tau^2), \; n \to \infty \qquad (2.35)$$

in distribution (refer Casella and Berger [2]).

These concepts are utilized in Chapters 6 and 7 for computing expectations of the estimators of some MPCIs.

Bibliography

[1] Abramoitz, M., Stegun, I. A. (1964). Handbook of Mathematical Functions. National Bureau of Standards Applied Mathematics Series 55, USA.

[2] Casella, G., Berger, R. L. (2007). *Statistical Inference*. New York: Thompson and Duxbury.

[3] Carter, P. L. (1972). A Bayesian Approach to Quality Control. *Management Science*, Vol. 18, No. 11, pp. 647–655.

[4] Chatterjee, M. (2017). On Some Univariate and Multivariate Process Capability Indices. Doctoral Thesis Under the guidance of Prof. Ashis Kumar Chakraborty. Indian Statistical Institute, Kolkata.

[5] Chatterjee, M. (2019). Impact of Multivariate Normality Assumption on Multivariate Process Capability Indices. *Communications in Statistics: Case Studies, Data Analysis and Applications*, Vol. 5, pp. 314–345.

[6] Chakraborty, A. K., Chatterjee, M. (2013). On Multivariate Folded Normal Distribution. *Sankhya : The Indian Journal of Statistics (Series B)*. Vol. 75, No. 1, pp. 1–15.

[7] Chatterjee, M., Chakraborty, A. K. (2015). A Super Structure of Process Capability Indices for Circular Specification Region. *Communications in Statistics—Theory and Methods*, Vol. 44, No. 6, pp. 1158–1181.

[8] Chatterjee, M., Chakraborty, A. K. (2016). A Simple Algorithm for Calculating Values for Folded Normal Distribution. *Journal of Statistical Computation and Simulation*, Vol. 86, No. 2, pp. 293–305.

[9] Chatterjee, M., Chakraborty, A. K. (2015). Distributions and Process Capability Control Charts for C_{pu} and C_{pl} Using Subgroup Information. *Communications in Statistics—Theory and Methods*, Vol. 44, No. 20, pp. 4333–4353. DOI http://dx.doi.org/10.1080/03610926.2013.851233.

[10] Chatterjee, M., Chakraborty, A. K. (2016). Some Process Capability Indices for Unilateral Specification Limits—Their Properties and the Process Capability Control Charts. *Communications in Statistics—Theory and Methods*, Vol. 45, No. 24, pp. 7130–7160.

Bibliography

[11] Cox, D.R. (1949). The Use of the Range in Sequential Analysis. *Journal of the Royal Statistical Society. Series B (Methodological)*, Vol. 11, No. 1, pp. 101–114 .

[12] Edmundson, H. P. (1961). The Distribution of Radial Error and Its Statistical Application in War Gaming. *Operations Research*, Vol. 9, No. 1, pp. 8–21.

[13] Elandt R. C. (1961) The Folded Normal Distribution: Two Methods of Estimating Parameters from Moments. *Technometrics*, Vol. 3, No. 4, pp. 551–562.

[14] Feller, W. (1968). An Introduction to Probability Theory and Its Applications. *Wiley Series in Probability and Mathematical Statistics*, Vol. 1.

[15] Fisher, R. A., Yates, F. (1963). Statistical Tables for Biological, Agricultural and Medical Research. London: Oliver and Boyd.

[16] Frenkiel, F. N. (1951). Frequency Distributions of Velocities in Turbulent Flow. *Journal of Meteorology*. Vol. 8, pp. 316–320.

[17] Gelman, A., Carlin, J. B., Stern, H. S., Dunson, D. B., Vehtari, A., Rubin, D. B. (2013). *Bayesian Data Analysis*, 3rd ed., CRC Press.

[18] Ghosh, J. K., Delampady, M., Samanta, T. (2006). *An Introduction to Bayesian Analysis – Theory and Methods*. Springer International Edition.

[19] Gun, A. M., Gupta, M. K., Dasgupta, B. (2005). *Fundamentals of Statistics*. Vol. 1. Kolkata, India: The World Press Private Limited.

[20] Jackson, J. E. (1980). Principal components and factor analysis: part I - principal components. *Journal of Quality Technology*, Vol. 12, pp. 201–213.

[21] Johnson, N. L. (1963). Cumulative Sum Control Charts for the Folded Normal Distribution. *Technometrics*, Vol. 5, 451–458.

[22] Johnson, N. L., Kotz, S., Balakrishnan, N. (1994). Continuous Univariate Distributions. Vol. 1, 2nd ed. *Wiley Series in Probability and Mathematical Statistics*.

[23] Johnson, R. A., Wicharn, D. W. (2007). *Applied Multivariate Statistical Analysis*, 6th ed. New Jersey: Pearson Education, Inc.

[24] Jolliffe, A. (2002). Principal Component Analysis. Springer Series in Statistics.

Bibliography

[25] Kan, R., Robotti, C. (2017). On Moments of Folded and Truncated Multivariate Normal Distributions. *Journal of Computational and Graphical Statistics*, Vol. 26, No. 4, pp. 930–934.

[26] Kirmani, S. N. U. A., Kocherlakota, A., Kocherlakota, S. (1991). Estimation of σ and the Process Capability Index Based on Sub-samples. *Communications in Statistics—Theory and Methods*, Vol. 20, No. 1, pp. 275–291.

[27] Koch, K. R. *Introduction to Bayesian Statistics*, 2nd ed Springer.

[28] Kuo, H. L. (2010). Approximate Tolerance Limits for Cp Capability Chart Based on Range. *ProbStat Forum*, Vol. 3, pp. 145–157.

[29] Laurent, A. G. (1957). Bombing Problems—A Statistical Approach. *Operations Research*, Vol. 5, No. 1, pp. 75–89.

[30] Lee, S. J., Amin, R. W. (2000). Process Tolerance Limits. *Total Quality Management*, Vol. 11, No. 3, pp. 267–280.

[31] Legendre, A. M. (1934). *Tables of the Complete and Incomplete Elliptic Integrals*. London: Biometric Office.

[32] Leone, F. C., Nelson, L. S.,Nottingham, R. B. (1961). The Folded Normal Distribution. *Technometrics*, Vol. 3, No. 4, pp. 543–550.

[33] Liao, M. Y. (2010). Economic Tolerance Design for Folded Normal Data. *International Journal of Production Research*, Vol. 18, No. 14: 4123–4137.

[34] Lin, H. C. (2004). The Measurement of a Process Capability for Folded Normal Process Data. *International Journal of Advanced Manufacturing Technology*, No. 24, 223–228.

[35] Lin, P. C. (2005). Application of the Generalized Folded-Normal Distribution to the Process Capability Measures. *International Journal Of Advanced Manufacturing Technology*, Vol. 26, 825–830.

[36] Lin H. C., Sheen, G. J. (2005). Practical Implementation of the Capability Index Cpk Based on the Control Chart Data. *Quality Engineering*, Vol. 17, No. 3, 371–390.

[37] Lord, E. (1947). The Use of Range in Place of Standard Deviation in the t-test. *Biometrika*, Vol. 41, No. 1, 41–67.

[38] Marcellus, R. L. (2007). Bayesian Statistical Process Control. *Quality Engineering*, Vol. 20, No. 1, pp. 113–127.

[39] McElreath, R. (2015). Statistical Rethinking: A Bayesian Course with Examples in R and Stan. CRC Press.

[40] Montgomery, D. C. (2000). Introduction to Statistical Quality Control, 5th ed., New York: John Wiley & Sons.

[41] Patel, J. K., Read, C. B. (1982). *Handbook of the Normal Distribution.* New York: Marcel and Dekker, INC.

[42] Patnaik, P. R. (1950). The Use of the Mean Range as an Estimator of Variance in Statistical Tests. *Biometrica.* Vol. 37, pp. 78–87.

[43] Pearson, E. S. (1952). Comparison of Two Approximations to the Distribution of the Range in Small Samples from Normal Populations. *Biometrika*, Vol. 39, No. 1, pp. 130–136.

[44] Pearson, E. S., Hartley, H. O. (1962). *Biometrika Tables for Statisticians.* Vols. 1 & 2. Cambridge, England: Cambridge University Press.

[45] Psarakis, S. and Panaretos, J. (2001). On Some Bivariate Extensions of the Folded Normal and the Folded T Distributions, *Journal of Applied Statistical Science*, Vol. 10, No. 2, 119–136

[46] Rao, C.R., Mitra, S. K.,Matthai, A. (1966). *Formulae and Tables for Statistical Work.* Calcutta, India: Statistical Publishing Company.

[47] Montgomery, D. C. (2000). *Introduction to Statistical Quality Control,* 5th ed., New York: John Wiley & Sons.

[48] Rencher, A. C. (1997). Multivariate Statistical Inference and Applications. *Wiley Series in Probability and Statistics.* John Wiley & Sons, INC.

[49] Rencher, A. C., Christensen, W. F. (2012). Methods of Multivariate Analysis, 3rd ed. *Wiley Series in Probability and Statistics.* John Wiley & Sons, INC.

[50] Scheuer, E. M. (1962). Moments of the Radial Error. *Journal of the American Statistical Association*, Vol. 57, No. 297, pp. 187–190.

[51] Tagaras, G., Nikolaidis. (2002). Comparing the Effectiveness of Various Bayesian $\overline{X}$ Control Charts. *Operations Research*, Vol. 50, No. 5, pp. 878–888.

[52] Tallis, G. M. (1961). The Moment Generating Function of the Truncated Multi-normal Distribution, *Journal of The Royal Statistical Society: Series B (Methodological)*, Vol. 23, No. 1, 223–229.

[53] Tong, Y. L. (1990). *The Multivariate Normal Distribution.* Springer - Verlag.

[54] Tong, L. I., Chen, K. S., Chen, H. T. (2002). Statistical Testing for Assessing the Performance of Lifetime Index of Electronic Components with Exponential Distribution. *International Journal of Quality & Reliability Management*, Vol. 19 Issue: 7, pp.812–824.

[55] Weil, H. (1954). The Distribution of Radial Error. *The Annals of Mathematical Statistics*, Vol. 25, No. 1. pp. 168–170.

[56] Woodall, W. H., Montgomery, D. C. (2000). Using Ranges to Estimate Variability. *Quality Engineering*, Vol. 13, No. 2, pp. 211–217.

Chapter 3

Univariate Process Capability Indices

Chapter Summary

Although this book primarily focuses on multivariate process capability indices (MPCIs), to become conversant with its background as well as its importance in Statistical Process Control (SPC), it is utmost necessary to have some basic idea about univariate process capability indices (PCI). In fact, many a times, MPCIs are defined as multivariate analogues of univariate PCIs. In the present chapter, brief literature survey is made on univariate PCIs for various types of specification limits, viz., bilateral (both symmetric and asymmetric about the stipulated target), and unilateral. Apart from the conventional univariate PCIs with normality assumption of the underlying process distribution, PCIs specially defined for non normal processes and those defined using other approaches are also discussed.

3.1 Introduction

The development of PCIs started with the capability ratio defined in equation (1.1). Subsequently, based on various needs, other univariate PCIs were defined and used. Further, when the need arose, various bivariate and multivariate PCIs were developed by researchers. Some authors also tried to unify the indices thus developed, in order to express all the indices in one particular format and studied statistical properties of the same.

3.2 Univariate Process Capability Indices for Symmetric Specification Limits

Kane [44], in his seminal paper, provided the first systematic documentation of PCIs which were being used by Japanese manufacturing industries for quite some times.

Suppose "X" is a random variable corresponding to the measurable quality characteristic under consideration such that $X \sim N(\mu, \sigma^2)$. Then, the four classical PCIs, for symmetric bilateral specification limits, which are most commonly used, are

$$
\begin{aligned}
C_p &= \frac{U - L}{6\sigma} \\
C_{pk} &= \frac{d - |\mu - M|}{3\sigma} \\
C_{pm} &= \frac{d}{3\sqrt{\sigma^2 + (\mu - T)^2}} \\
C_{pmk} &= \frac{d - |\mu - M|}{3\sqrt{\sigma^2 + (\mu - T)^2}}
\end{aligned}
\tag{3.1}
$$

where $d = \frac{U-L}{2}$, $M = \frac{U+L}{2}$ and "T" denotes the targeted value of the quality characteristic under consideration.

Among the four PCIs given in equation (3.1), C_p compares the allowable process spread (voice of the customer) to the actual process spread (voice of the process). However, since C_p incorporates only process dispersion (σ) in its definition but not the process centering (μ), it measures the actual capability of a process only when the said process is centered on target. Otherwise it measures the potential capability of that process (Palmer and Tsui [58]), i.e., the maximum level of capability that a process can attain under the present dispersion scenario, when mean of the process equals specification mid-point. To measure the actual capability of a process, C_{pk} was defined (refer Kane [44]).

C_p and C_{pk} are also known as yield based indices as they are directly related to the concept of proportion of nonconformance (PNC). Since in the literature of statistical quality control (SQC), process capability analysis and PNC are two parallel concepts of judging process performance, the ability to establish a relationship between them is considered as an added advantage of using that PCI as it makes the PCI value easier to interpret. When a process is centered on target, Kotz and Johnson [47] have established a one to one relationship between C_p and the corresponding PNC (say, p) as

$$
p = 2\Phi(-3C_p)
\tag{3.2}
$$

However, Kotz and Johnson [49] have observed that since C_p measures merely the potential capability of a process and "p," being a one-to-one function of C_p, it does not measure the actual PNC—rather, it gives the minimum observable PNC. When process mean is not equal to the mid-point of the speification limits, Kotz and Johnson [49] have established an exact relationship between C_p, C_{pk} and the PNC (say, p') as

$$p' = \Phi[-3(2C_p - C_{pk})] + \Phi[-3C_{pk}] \tag{3.3}$$

The concepts of PNC and PCI are two parallel concepts of judging the overall health of a process. Therefore, the basic intention behind equations (3.2) and (3.3) is not to derive formulae to compute PNC using PCI. Rather these are purely expressions that bridge these two concepts.

Another important factor of process capability analysis is the targeted value of the measurable quality characteristic. It should be noted that the target value "T" may not always be the mean of the two sided specification, particularly, when we have asymmetric specification limits. A good PCI should be able to capture the proximity of the process centering (i.e., μ) toward the target (T). However, both C_p and C_{pk} ignore this factor. Hsiang and Taguchi [41] and Chan et al. [9] studied the problem independently and C_{pm} was developed [refer equation (3.1)]. Boyles [7] has shown that although the motivation behind defining C_{pk} was to capture process centering, it often fails do so—rather it, along with C_p, assesses the process yield more satisfactorily. C_{pm}, on the other hand, actually measures the proximity of the process mean toward "T" and thus provides a measure of evaluating the capability of a process to center around the target properly.

Finally, C_{pmk} is defined by Pearn et al. [64] as a combination of both C_{pk} and C_{pm} and is often referred to as the "Third generation PCI." Kotz and Johnson [49] have later admitted that being a mixture of C_{pk} and C_{pm}, C_{pmk} is neither a yield based PCI like C_{pk} nor does it provide an assessment of process centering like C_{pm}. As a result, C_{pmk} values are not easily interpretable and hence the PCI finds very limited applications in practice. Moreover, if the PNC is regarded as the most important feature of a process, then the performances of C_{pm} and C_{pmk} are often found to be unreliable (refer Kotz and Johnson [49]).

Pearn and Kotz [63] have observed the following relationships to hold among these four PCIs:

$$\left. \begin{array}{l} C_p \geq C_{pk} \geq C_{pmk} \\ C_p \geq C_{pm} \geq C_{pmk} \end{array} \right\} \tag{3.4}$$

However, there does not exist any clear-cut relationship between C_{pk} and C_{pm} (refer Kotz and Johnson [47, 48]).

Threshold value of a PCI is another important aspect, especially from the interpretational point of view. The importance of a threshold value is that a PCI value greater than or equal to the threshold value is always preferable. For C_p, the threshold value is considered to be "1." We will see, in due course, that even the threshold values of the PCIs may change depending upon the type of the quality characteristics under consideration and the corresponding specification limits. This contradicts the general convention that, PCIs, irrespective of their type, should automatically be greater than one in order for the process to be capable.

From equation (3.1), it is easy to observe that, for $C_p = 1$ i.e., $U - L = 6\sigma$ which implies that when the process is centered on the middle of the specification limits, the current dispersion level of the concerned quality characteristic is such that the process spread is just coinciding with the specification spread and the process is said to be potentially just capable. Again, for a quality characteristic with $U - L < 6\sigma$ i.e., $C_p < 1$, the process spread is more than the allowable specification spread. This creates room for production of significantly large proportion of nonconforming items and hence the process will be considered as potentially incapable. Likewise, for $U - L > 6\sigma$, i.e., for $C_p > 1$ a process is considered to be potentially capable.

Interestingly, threshold value is generally computed for a PCI like C_p, which measures the potential capability of a process. Also, from equation (3.4), the other PCIs are always less than or equal to C_p and the equality attained when $\mu = T$. Thus, if C_p fails to attain its stipulated threshold value, there is no question of the other PCIs having better capability level.

It is interesting to note that all the PCIs, discussed so far, viz., C_p, C_{pk}, C_{pm}, and C_{pmk} are expressed as functions of the parameters μ and σ of the concerned quality characteristic and hence are often unobservable directly. The usual practice is to assess the capability of a process based on the estimated value of the corresponding plug-in estimator of the said PCI as obtained from one or more randomly drawn samples from the process. Therefore, such plug-in estimators are subject to sampling fluctuations. The distributional properties and the estimation procedures of the plug-in estimators of these basic PCIs are thoroughly studied by a number of researchers (refer Pearn et al. [64], Kotz and Johnson ([47], [49]), Vannman and Kotz [84], Pearn and Kotz [63], and the references therein).

To study the nature of the plug-in estimator of a PCI, it is not sufficient to carry out only the point estimation. One needs to explore the interval estimators and execute appropriate hypothesis testing. A substantial amount of research work has been carried out to design confidence intervals of the PCIs under various circumstances (refer Chou et al. [30], Hoffman [40], Kushlar and Hurley [51], Zimmer et al. [97], Pearn and Kotz [63], and the references there in). Many eminent researchers have also proposed several hypothesis testing procedures for C_p, C_{pk}, C_{pm}, and C_{pmk}. For instance, refer Hoffman [39], Lin and Pearn [54], Pearn and Lin [68], and Chen and Shu [24] among others.

3.2.1 Unification of Univariate PCIs for Symmetric Specification Limits

Vannman [81] unified these univariate PCIs and proposed the following super-structure of PCIs for symmetric bilateral specification limits:

$$C_p(u, v) = \frac{d - u|\mu - M|}{3\sqrt{\sigma^2 + v(\mu - T)^2}}, \quad u, v \geq 0. \tag{3.5}$$

For $u = 0, 1$ and $v = 0, 1$, $C_p(u, v)$ gives the four basic PCIs given in equation (3.1). For example, $C_p(0, 0) = C_p$, $C_p(1, 0) = C_{pk}$, $C_p(0, 1) = C_{pm}$, and $C_p(1, 1) = C_{pmk}$. Vannman and Kotz [84] have thoroughly studied the distributional properties of $C_p(u, v)$.

Most of the studies on the distributional and inferential properties of these PCIs make an inherent assumption that the estimated values of the parameters of the concerned quality characteristics are free from any measurement error. Therefore, the observed values of the plug-in estimators, based on the available data, are considered to be the desired estimated values of the PCIs. However, in industrial applications, despite the use of highly advanced measuring instruments, gauge measurement errors is considered as an indispensable part of measurement system analysis. Also, since PCIs are estimated based on sample observations, there are ample chances that their estimated values are contaminated by the sampling error. These aspects should be taken into consideration before reaching any conclusion regarding the overall health of a process. Bordignon and Scagliarini [3, 4, 5] have studied the impact of measurement error on the plug-in estimators of C_p, C_{pk}, and C_{pm}, respectively. For C_{pk}, Pearn and Liao [65] has also carried out similar study while Hsu et al. [42] studied it for C_{pmk}.

Besides the classical frequentist approach of studying the distributional and inferential properties of C_p, C_{pk}, C_{pm}, and C_{pmk}, substantial research work has also been done, from the Bayesian perspective as well. Singh and Saxena [77] have proposed a Bayesian-like estimator of C_p. Pearn and Wu [72] have used Bayesian approach while assessing capability of a process based on C_{pk}. Lin et al [55] have formulated lower confidence bound of C_{pm} from Bayesian perspective; while for C_{pmk}, Pearn and Lin [67] have proposed a Bayesian like estimator.

Apart from these four PCIs and their unification, a considerably large number of other PCIs are also available in literature to cater to the needs of different challenging situations encountered in practice. Pragmatic reviews of such PCIs have been given by Kotz and Johnson [49]; Palmer and Tsui [58] and Pearn and Kotz [63] among others.

3.3 Univariate Process Capability Indices for Asymmetric Specification Limits

The specification limits of a process are considered to be asymmetric with respect to the target, when there are lower and upper specification limits and the target value (T) differs from the specification mid-point (M). Usually the asymmetry in specification limits is not directly related to the shape of the underlying distribution of the quality characteristic (refer Chang [20]) i.e., asymmetry in specification limits may or may not arise due to the properties of the distribution of the quality characteristic. The PCIs discussed so far make an inherent assumption that the specification limits corresponding to the quality characteristic under consideration are symmetric about "T," which may not, always, be the case. For example, the free resonance of the speaker driver used in home theater sub-woofer speaker system often has asymmetric tolerances on either side of the target (refer Chen and Tsai [26]). Boyles [8] have enlisted the following situations where asymmetric specification limits are generally encountered in practice:

1. Often customers are willing to allow more deviation from target toward one side of the specification interval than the other.

2. Even if a process starts with symmetric specification interval, many a times it is observed that the manufacturer and/or the customer has to opt for asymmetric tolerance interval in order to avoid unnecessary increase in the production cost.

3. If the data on a quality characteristic, whose underlying distribution is nonnormal, is converted into a normal one using standard statistical transformations, like Box—Cox transformation (refer Box and Cox [6]), then the initial symmetric specification limits get automatically converted into asymmetric ones by virtue of the same transformation. An example of this phenomenon can be seen in case of Dataset 1 in Chapter 1, where originally the underlying distribution of the data is non-normal and the specification limits are symmetric about the target. However, as soon as normality transformation is applied to the data, the specification region becomes asymmetric owing to the same transformation.

There exist many other real life examples given by Boyles [8]; Choi and Owen [28]; Chen and Pearn [22]; Jessenberger and Weihs [43] and so on which motivated the researchers to define some indices specially for processes having quality characteristics with asymmetric specification limits.

Although the presence of asymmetry in specification limits is not at all a rare event, especially in manufacturing industries; the research work in this field are surprisingly fewer as compared to the case of symmetric specification limits.

To deal with the problem of asymmetric specification limits, Kane [44] and Chan et al. [9] suggested replacing the true specification limits viz., $(T-d_l, T+d_u)$ by $T \pm \min[d_l, d_u]$, where $d_u = USL - T$, $d_l = T - LSL$. This, eventually, makes the specification limits symmetric with respect to "T" (refer Boyles [8]). This approach shifts one of the specification limits, particularly the limit which is further away from the target, toward "T." Kane [44] modified C_p and C_{pk} for the cases where $USL - T \neq T - LSL$ as i) $C_p^* = \min \left(\frac{T-LSL}{3\sigma}, \frac{USL-T}{3\sigma} \right)$ and ii) $C_{pk}^* = \min (CPL^*, CPU^*)$, where $CPL^* = \frac{T-LSL}{3\sigma} (1 - \frac{|T-\mu|}{T-LSL})$ and $CPU^* = \frac{USL-T}{3\sigma} (1 - \frac{|T-\mu|}{USL-T})$.

Some similar proposals were given by Kushler and Hurley [51] and Franklin and Wasserman [34]. For asymmetric tolerances, they proposed to shift both the specification limits $(T - d_l, T + d_u)$ to obtain symmetric ones, viz., $(T \pm \frac{d_l+d_u}{2})$. However for both the cases of revised specification limits, new limits are different from the original ones and hence are often misleading. In fact, Boyles [8] has observed that these approaches of shifting at least one of the specification limits to make them symmetric, either over estimates or under estimates the true capability of a process depending upon the position of μ with respect to "T."

Jessenberger and Weihs [43] have extensively studied the behavior of C_{pmk} with asymmetric specification limits and have concluded that if for a process, proximity toward the target is more important than minimizing the PNC, then C_{pmk} may not be a good index, especially, when the process variation is large. In fact, the maximum value of C_{pmk} is obtained when the variable moves from near the target value toward the specification mid-point (M) if the process variation increases. This is not at all desirable, as a PCI should ideally be optimum on target.

Boyles [8] made a comprehensive study of process capability indices, defined so far, for processes with asymmetric tolerances. He observed that these indices attain their maximum values at some point between T and M, whereas for an ideal process the indices should be optimum on target. To overcome the deficiencies of these indices, he proposed a new PCI as

$$S_{pk} = S \left(\frac{USL - \mu}{\sigma}, \frac{\mu - LSL}{\sigma} \right) \tag{3.6}$$

where, S(x,y) is a smooth function which is defined as $S(x, y) = \frac{1}{3} \Phi^{-1} \{ \frac{\Phi(x)+\Phi(y)}{2} \}$. Chen and Pearn (2001) generalized this index as $S_p(v) = S \left(\frac{USL-\mu}{\sqrt{\sigma^2+v(\mu-T)^2}}, \frac{\mu-LSL}{\sqrt{\sigma^2+v(\mu-T)^2}} \right)$, where $v \geq 0$. Although the properties of S_{pk} were studied by Ho [38] and Pearn and Chuang [61], but due to its very complicated statistical as well as analytical properties, it has found very limited application in practice.

3.3.1 Unification of Univariate PCIs for Asymmetric Specification Limits

Vannman [82] proposed a superstructure of univariate process capability indices for asymmetric specification limits given by

$$C_{pv}(u,v) = \frac{d - |T - M| - u|\mu - T|}{3\sqrt{\sigma^2 + v(\mu - T)^2}} \tag{3.7}$$

where "u" and "v" can assume any non-negative real number. Although $C_{pv}(u,v)$ is optimum on target, it is symmetric around $\mu = T$ and hence fails to capture the asymmetry of the loss function. To address this problem, Vannman [82], herself, has introduced another superstructure as

$$C_{pa}(u,v) = \frac{d - |\mu - M| - u|\mu - T|}{3\sqrt{\sigma^2 + v(\mu - T)^2}}. \tag{3.8}$$

Although $C_{pa}(u,v)$ captures the asymmetry of loss function, it is no more optimum on target.

Since an ideal PCI for asymmetric specification limits should be able to capture the asymmetry in loss function while maintaining optimality on target, Pearn [59] proposed a new index analogous to C_{pk} for asymmetric tolerances which is given by

$$C_{pk}^* = \frac{d^* - F^*}{3\sigma} \tag{3.9}$$

where $d^* = min(d_l, d_u)$ and $F^* = max\{\frac{d^*(\mu-T)}{d_u}, \frac{d^*(T-\mu)}{d_l}\}$. Pearn and Lin [66] studied some properties of C_{pk}^* and proposed an estimator which is consistent, asymptotically unbiased and converges to a mixture of two normal distributions. As C_{pk}^* is analogous to C_{pk} of symmetric specification limits given in equation (3.1), Chen and Pearn [22] generalized this index to a superstructure, similar to $C_p(u,v)$ [refer equation (3.5)], which is defined as

$$C_p''(u,v) = \frac{d^* - uF^*}{3\sqrt{\sigma^2 + vF^2}} \tag{3.10}$$

where $F = max\{\frac{d(\mu-T)}{d_u}, \frac{d(T-\mu)}{d_l}\}$. For $u = 0, 1$ and $v = 0, 1$, $C_p''(0,0) = C_p''$, $C_p''(1,0) = C_{pk}''$, $C_p''(0,1) = C_{pm}''$, and $C_p''(1,1) = C_{pmk}''$ which are analogous to C_p, C_{pk}, C_{pm}, and C_{pmk} defined in equation (3.1).

Pearn et al. [69, 70] have made extensive studies on the various distributional aspects of C_{pmk}'' and C_{pk}'', respectively.

Pearn and Wu [71] also have explored relationships between PNC and C_{pk}'' based on four possible positions of μ with respect to U, L, and T. The authors have shown that, when the underlying distribution of the quality characteristic is normal and the concerned specification limits are asymmetric with respect to T, then for each of these four cases, a two-sided bound for PNC can be given as

$$1 - \Phi(3k^* C_{pk}'') \leq PNC \leq 2 - \Phi(3C_{pk}'') - \Phi(3k^* C_{pk}'') \tag{3.11}$$

where $k^* = \max\{d_u/d_l, d_l/d_u\}$. The bounds in equation (3.11) are similar to the bounds on PNC as expressed in terms of C_{pk} (refer Boyles [7]; Kotz and Johnson [47]) in the context of symmetric specification limits which is given by

$$\Phi(-3C_{pk}) \leq PNC \leq 2\Phi(-3C_{pk}) \tag{3.12}$$

Chatterjee and Chakraborty [13] have established exact relationship between C_p'', C_{pk}'', and the PNC. They have shown that PNC (say, P_{NC}) and C_p'' hold the following relationship, irrespective of the position of "T" with respect to USL and LSL:

$$
\begin{aligned}
P_{NC} &= \Phi(-3C_p'') + \Phi\left[3(C_p'' - 2C_p)\right] \\
&= 1 - \Phi\left(3C_p''\right) + \Phi\left[3(C_p'' - 2C_p)\right] \\
&= 2 - \Phi\left(3C_p''\right) - \Phi\left(3k^*C_p''\right) \tag{3.13}
\end{aligned}
$$

where, $k^* = \max\{\frac{d_u}{d_l}, \frac{d_l}{d_u}\}$.

Now, since C_p'' does not take into account the position of "μ" and measures the actual capability of a process only when $\mu = T$, equation (3.13) will provide the PNC only when the process is centered on target.

For the exact relationship(s) of PNC with C_p'' and C_{pk}'' for various positions of "T" with respect to "USL" and "LSL," let us consider the following:

Case I : For $d^* = d_u$ and $R_U < R_L$, i.e., $\mu < T$,

$$P_{NC}' = 2 - \Phi\left[3k^*C_{pk}''\right] - \Phi\left[3\left\{C_{pk}'' + (k^*+1)R_L C_p''\right\}\right] \tag{3.14}$$

where, $R_U = \frac{\mu-T}{d_u}$ and $R_L = \frac{T-\mu}{d_l}$;

Case II : $d^* = d_l$ and $R_U > R_L$, i.e. $\mu > T$;

$$P_{NC}' = 2 - \Phi\left[3k^*C_{pk}''\right] - \Phi\left[3\left\{C_{pk}'' + (k^*+1)R_U C_p''\right\}\right]. \tag{3.15}$$

Case III : $d^* = d_u$ and $R_U > R_L$, i.e., $\mu > T$,

$$P_{NC}' = 2 - \Phi\left[3C_{pk}''\right] - \Phi\left[3\left\{k^*C_{pk}'' + (k^*+1)R_U C_p''\right\}\right] \tag{3.16}$$

Case IV : $d^* = d_l$ and $R_U < R_L$, i.e., $\mu < T$

$$P_{NC}' = 2 - \Phi\left[3C_{pk}''\right] - \Phi\left[3\{kC_{pk}'' + 2(k^*+1)R_L C_p''\}\right] \tag{3.17}$$

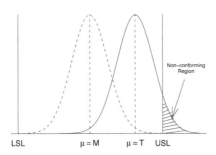

FIGURE 3.1: Asymmetric specification limits with quality characteristic having same variation but different centering.

It is easy to observe from Figure 3.1 that, contradicting the usual convention, P_{NC} is not always less than P'_{NC}; rather their relationship depends on the position of "μ" and "T" with respect to the specification limits. Consequently, it may so happen that between two processes with the same underlying variation of the quality characteristic under consideration, the process which is centered on the target is more likely to produce nonconforming items than the process for which $\mu \leq M$.

Following Chatterjee and Chakraborty [13], the inter-relationship between the member indices of $C_p''(u,v)$, for $u = 0, 1$ and $v = 0, 1$, can be given as

$$\left. \begin{array}{l} C_p'' \geq C_{pk}'' \geq C_{pmk}'' \\ C_p'' \geq C_{pm}'' \geq C_{pmk}'' \end{array} \right\} \tag{3.18}$$

However, there does not exist any clear-cut relationship between C_{pk}'' and C_{pm}''.

Again, suppose in terms of T and σ, the upper and lower specification limits can be expressed as $U = T + k_1\sigma$ and $L = T - k_2\sigma$, respectively, where, k_1 and k_2 are positive real numbers such that $k_1 \neq k_2$ capturing the asymmetry of the specification limits with respect to the target.

Then the threshold value of C_p'' can be formulated as (refer Chatterjee and Chakraborty [13]) as:

$$C_p''^{(T)}(0,0) = C_p''^{(T)} = \begin{cases} \frac{2k_1}{k_1+k_2} & \text{if } d_u < d_l \\ \frac{2k_2}{k_1+k_2} & \text{if } d_l < d_u \end{cases} \tag{3.19}$$

Thus, the threshold value of $C_p^{''(T)}$ is not unique—rather, it is a function of the degree of asymmetry of the specification limits based on the actual position of T and this is a highly desirable property of $C_p^{''(T)}(u, v)$. This also argues against the usual practice of considering one as the threshold value of any PCI without properly exploring its characteristics. In fact, the threshold value in this case will always be less than one and will be equal to one only when $k_1 = k_2$, that is, when we have a symmetric specification case.

3.4 Univariate Process Capability Indices for Unilateral (One-Sided) Specification Limits

Although most of the PCI's, available in literature, are designed for processes with bi-lateral specification limits i.e., processes where the concerned quality characteristic has both the upper and lower specification limits, it is often observed in practice that the design intent of a manufactured product provides information on either *USL* or *LSL*. This is true for quality characteristics of either smaller the better type or larger the better type respectively (refer Taguchi [79]). This necessitates the use of PCIs specially designed for processes with unilateral specifications.

Interestingly, most of the research works on PCIs for unilateral specification limits are based on C_{pu} and C_{pl} which are defined as follows:

$$\left. \begin{array}{c} C_{pu} = \frac{U - \mu}{3\sigma} \\ \text{and} \quad C_{pl} = \frac{\mu - L}{3\sigma} \end{array} \right\} \tag{3.20}$$

Like C_p, C_{pu}, and C_{pl} can also be expressed as one-to-one functions of the PNC, say "p," as, $p = \Phi(-3C_{pu}) = \Phi(-3C_{pl})$ respectively. Kane [44] has pointed out that C_{pu} (or C_{pl}) = 1.0 implies half as many nonconforming items (0.136%) compared to the case when $C_p = 1.0$ (in case of bilateral specification limits). Lin and Pearn [52] and Pearn et. al [62] have tabulated various values of C_I (where I stands for pu or pl as the case may be) corresponding to the proportion of nonconforming items in terms of nonconforming parts per million (NCPPM).

The distributional properties of the plug-in estimators of C_{pu} and C_{pl}, along with their uniformly minimum variance unbiased estimators (UMVUE), have been thoroughly studied by Kane [44], Chou and Owen [29], and Pearn and Chen [60], under the assumption of normality of the quality characteristic under consideration.

Univariate Process Capability Indices

However, despite being easy to compute and hence most widely used among the practitioners, C_{pu} and C_{pl} suffer from the following two major drawbacks:

1. Neither C_{pu} nor C_{pl} incorporate the concept of target in their definitions;

2. Unlike C_p, they cannot be considered as the PCIs measuring potential process capability either, as their definitions include μ.

Therefore, C_{pu} and C_{pl} are difficult to interpret as they measure neither the potential process capability; nor the actual one.

Kane [44], himself, modified C_{pu} and C_{pl} as follows:

$$C_{pu}^* = \frac{USL - T}{3\sigma} \left\{ 1 - \frac{|T - \mu|}{USL - T} \right\}$$

$$C_{pl}^* = \frac{T - LSL}{3\sigma} \left\{ 1 - \frac{|T - \mu|}{T - LSL} \right\} \tag{3.21}$$

However, these indices have found very limited application in industry compared to C_{pu} and C_{pl}.

Krishnamoorthy [50] addressed the problem of computing PCI's for processes with unilateral specifications from a different perspective. According to Krishnamoorthy [50], the *"ideal condition"* of a process with unilateral specification, changes with process variability. He defined $C_{PT} = \frac{\mu - T}{3\sigma}$ and suggested that for pushing a process to its ideal location, one should have $1.0 \le C_{PT} \le C_I$. But this keeps room for having high PCI value by merely changing "T," even if σ is considerably high.

To incorporate the loss theoretic approach in PCI's Chan et al. [9] generalized C_{pm} for unilateral specification limits as

$$C_{pmu}^* = \frac{USL - T}{3\sqrt{\sigma^2 + (\mu - T)^2}} \quad \text{and}$$

$$C_{pml}^* = \frac{T - LSL}{3\sqrt{\sigma^2 + (\mu - T)^2}} \tag{3.22}$$

Independent of this definition, Pillet et al. [74] have suggested another modification of C_{pm} for processes with unilateral specification limits based on the concept that a PCI should be inversely proportional to the average loss per piece (i.e., $\sigma^2 + \mu^2$). For this they have re-defined C_{pm} as

$$C_{pm}^* = \frac{\text{Tolerance}}{A\sqrt{\sigma^2 + \mu^2}} \tag{3.23}$$

For example, suppose for a process of smaller the better type, the tolerance is $(4 + \lambda)\sigma$ units wide, where $\lambda = \frac{\mu}{\sigma}$ is to be determined by the customer and / or the producer, according to the "expected level of quality." Then for

$C_{pm}^* = 1.33$, "A" can be expressed as $A = \frac{4+\lambda}{1.33\sqrt{1+\lambda^2}}$. Pillet et al. [74] have tabulated 'A' values for various values of "λ."

Similar to Chan et al.'s [9] modification of C_{pm} for unilateral specifications, Vannman [83] modified C_{pmk} as

$$C_{pmku} = \frac{USL - \mu}{3\sqrt{\sigma^2 + (\mu - T)^2}} \quad \text{and}$$

$$C_{pmkl} = \frac{\mu - LSL}{3\sqrt{\sigma^2 + (\mu - T)^2}} \qquad (3.24)$$

3.4.1 Unification of Univariate PCIs for Unilateral Specification Limits

Vannman [83] suggested the following two sets of superstructures of PCIs for unilateral specification limits:

$$\left.\begin{array}{l} C_{pvu}(u, v) = \frac{USL - T - u|\mu - T|}{3\sqrt{\sigma^2 + v(\mu - T)^2}} \\[2ex] C_{pvl}(u, v) = \frac{T - LSL - u|\mu - T|}{3\sqrt{\sigma^2 + v(\mu - T)^2}} \end{array}\right\} \qquad (3.25)$$

and

$$\left.\begin{array}{l} C_{pau}(u, v) = \frac{USL - \mu - u|\mu - T|}{3\sqrt{\sigma^2 + v(\mu - T)^2}} \\[2ex] C_{pal}(u, v) = \frac{\mu - LSL - u|\mu - T|}{3\sqrt{\sigma^2 + v(\mu - T)^2}} \end{array}\right\} \qquad (3.26)$$

where u and v are two non-negative parameters. Note that the superstructures of PCIs given in equations (3.26) and (3.25) are derived as special cases of $C_{pv}(u, v)$ and $C_{pa}(u, v)$, defined in equations (3.7) and (3.8) and hence inherit their drawbacks already discussed in Section 3.3.

The very existence of only one specification limit indicates that for processes with unilateral specification limits a shift of μ away from T toward the existing specification limit is more serious than a shift of μ toward the opposite side of T (refer Vannman [83]). Hence, $C_{pvu}(u, v)$ and $C_{pvl}(u, v)$ being symmetric around T, are of little interest (refer Grau [35]).

Moreover, Grau [35] has observed a number of drawbacks in the definitions of $C_{pau}(u, v)$ and $C_{pal}(u, v)$. Those are enlisted below, considering quality characteristics of, say, smaller the better type (i.e., processes with USL only). Similar observations are also true for quality characteristics of higher the better type.

1. For $u = 0$,

   (a) $C_{pau}(0, v)$ is not maximum on target.

Univariate Process Capability Indices

    (b) Even if μ shifts away from T toward the left, it never takes values close to 0 - rather its limit is $\frac{1}{3\sqrt{v}}$.

2. For $0 < u < 1$,

    (a) $C_{pau}(u,v)$ is not maximum on T.

    (b) The minimum value attainable by $C_{pau}(u,v)$ is $\frac{1-u}{3\sqrt{v}}$. Hence it never assumes 0 value even if μ differs significantly from T toward the left.

    (c) $C_{pau}(u,v)$ assumes negative value for $\mu > T + \frac{U-T}{1+u}$ which is well before μ reaches the USL.

3. For $u = 1$, $C_{pau}(u,v)$ assumes negative value for $\mu > \frac{U+T}{2}$.

4. For $u > 1$, $C_{pau}(u,v)$ assumes negative value for $\mu > T + \frac{U-T}{1+u}$, i.e., before μ reaches the USL.

Grau [35] defined the following superstructures of PCIs which are free from these drawbacks:

$$\left. \begin{array}{c} C_p^U(u,v) = \frac{U-T-uA_U^*}{3\sqrt{\sigma^2+vA_U^{*2}}} \\[3mm] C_p^L(u,v) = \frac{T-L-uA_L^*}{3\sqrt{\sigma^2+vA_L^{*2}}} \end{array} \right\} \qquad (3.27)$$

where $A_U^* = \max\{(\mu-T), \frac{T-\mu}{k}\}$, $A_L^* = \max\{\frac{\mu-T}{k}, (T-\mu)\}$ and u and v are two non-negative parameters and $k > 1$. The value of "k" quantifies the risk of deviation from the target in the direction opposite to the available specification limit with respect to "T." In fact, by introducing the concept of "k" Grau [35] addressed the problem of imposing equal amount of importance on deviation of μ toward either side of "T" which are inherent in Vannman's [83] superstructures of PCIs for unilateral specification limits given in equations (3.26) and (3.25).

    Interestingly, $C_p^U(0,0) = C_p^U, C_p^U(1,0) = C_{pk}^U, C_p^U(0,1) = C_{pm}^U$, and $C_p^U(1,1) = C_{pmk}^U$ are defined analogous to C_p, C_{pk}, C_{pm}, and C_{pmk}. Similar is the case for $C_p^L(u,v)$. To avoid notational ambiguity, let us define $C_p^I(u,v)$ which stands for $C_p^U(u,v)$ or $C_p^L(u,v)$ depending on the available specification limit.

    A thorough review of the PCIs for unilateral specification limits along with their relative merits and demerits have been carried out by Chatterjee and Chakraborty [11].

    Grau [35] did not provide any mathematical formulation of "k" and left it for the decision-making authority of the concerned industry to decide its value. This makes the choice of k rather subjective leaving room for favorable manipulation by the concerned stake holders. Chatterjee and Chakraborty [11] have given a formulation of k to address such ambiguity.

Univariate Process Capability Indices 60

In calculating $C_p^U(u, v)$, as per the design of the superstructure, "k" will have an impact only if μ deviates from T toward the left, i.e., toward the opposite side of USL. Hence, while formulating "k" as a function of the loss of profit, considering the characteristics of the produced items only from this region will be sufficient.

Suppose there are m^* stages through which the loss of profit is incurred. In general, a stage here, consists of a suitable unit of measurement, which may vary over the different quality characteristics. This suitable unit should be defined in such a way that, "loss of profit" or cost due to deviating one unit from target can be assessed properly.

Also let n denote the size of the sample randomly drawn from the process among which, n_1 are found to have the quality characteristic values deviated from "T" toward the left and the remaining n_2 are either on target or have values deviated from T toward USL such that $n = n_1 + n_2$ with $n_1 \neq 0$.

Let, C_i^U is the loss of profit corresponding to the ith stage, for $i = 1(1)m^*$ and C is the constant selling price per item. It may be noted that, even for a given quality characteristic, the 'loss of profit' per unit deviation from 'T' toward the opposite direction of the existing specification limit, may differ depending on the relative position of the quality characteristic with respect to its target.

Without loss of generality, let us define

$$I_{ij} = \begin{cases} 1 & \text{if } j^{th} \text{ item belongs to the } i^{th} \text{ stage of loss of profit,} \\ & \forall i = 1(1)m^*, \ j = 1(1)n^*, \\ 0 & \text{otherwise.} \end{cases} ,$$

where n^* stands for n_1 or n_2 depending upon the situation.

Then, for a quality characteristic of smaller the better type, the total loss of profit due to deviation from T toward left, can be defined as

$$C_{LP,U}^{Total} = \sum_{j=1}^{n_1} \sum_{i=1}^{m^*} C_i^U \, I_{ij} \tag{3.28}$$

with $n^* = n_1$.

Then "k" can be formulated as

$$\begin{aligned} k_U &= \frac{\text{Selling Price Per Item}}{\text{Average Loss of Profit Per Item}} \\ &= \frac{C}{\frac{1}{n_1} C_{LP,U}^{Total}} \end{aligned} \tag{3.29}$$

where k_U stands for "k" in the context of smaller the better type of quality characteristics.

Similarly, for quality characteristics of the larger-the-better type, "k" can be formulated as

$$k_L = \frac{C}{\frac{1}{n_2} C_{LP,L}^{Total}} \tag{3.30}$$

where k_L stands for "k" in the context of larger the better type of quality characteristics. Also, $C_{LP,L}^{Total} = \sum_{j=1}^{n_2} \sum_{i=1}^{m^*} C_i^L I_{ij}$ with $n^* = n_2$ and C_i^L is the loss of profit at the ith stage, where there exists m^* such stages through which loss of profit (due to deviation of process mean form T toward right i.e., toward the direction opposite to LSL with respect to "T") can be incurred.

Note that for any process that runs profitably, it is logical to expect that the loss per item will be less than the selling price and hence both k_U and k_L will be greater than one. This fulfils Grau's [35] criteria for the values of "k." Moreover, according to Grau [35], "k" should be such that the smaller the value of "k," the more serious is the shift of μ to the opposite direction of the available specification limit. k_U and k_L satisfy this criteria as the loss of profit being in their denominator, smaller values of k_U and k_L will signify more such deviation and thus more such loss of profit. To retain notational simplicity, from now onwards, we shall use "k" to denote k_U or k_L, depending upon the situation.

Also expression for threshold value for C_p^I, in general, can be given as (refer Chatterjee and Chakraborty [11])

$$C_p^{I(T)} = \frac{2}{1+k} \tag{3.31}$$

where C_p^I stands for C_p^U or C_p^L depending, respectively, upon whether USL or LSL is available.

The threshold values of C_p^I for various values of "k" are tabulated in Table 3.1.

TABLE 3.1: Threshold values of C_p^I for various values of "k"

k	1.00	1.5	2.0	2.5	3.0	3.5	4.0	4.5	5.0	5.5
$C_p^{I(T)}$	1	0.80	0.67	0.57	0.50	0.44	0.40	0.36	0.33	0.31
k	6.0	6.5	7.0	7.5	8.0	8.5	9.0	9.5	10.0	
$C_p^{I(T)}$	0.29	0.27	0.25	0.23	0.22	0.21	0.20	0.19	0.18	

Here it is evident that unlike the case of symmetric specification limits and contradicting the usual convention, for unilateral specification limits, the threshold value is not unique; rather it varies as a function of "k."

Grau [35] has established exact relationship between C_p^I and PNC. Suppose P_{NC}^U denotes the probability of producing nonconforming items when the process is centered at "T," i.e., $\mu = T$ and only USL exists. Similarly, P_{NC}^L is defined for the situation when only LSL exists. Then, $P_{NC}^U = \Phi(-3C_p^U)$ and $P_{NC}^L = \Phi(-3C_p^L)$ depending upon the availability of USL or LSL (refer Grau [35]). Thus in general, $P_{NC}^I = \Phi(-3C_p^I)$.

Grau [37] has also studied the relationship between PNC and $C_p^I(u,v)$ for $u \geq 0$ and $v \geq 0$ and provided the upper bounds on PNC based on the values of the member indices of $C_p^I(u,v)$.

The PCIs C_p^I and C_{pk}^I were defined analogous to C_p and C_{pk} of symmetric specification limits (refer Grau [35]) and hence they are supposed to be yield based indices having exact relationship with the corresponding PNC. The relationship between C_p^I and P_{NC}^I reflects the actual performance of a process only when the process is centered at T, i.e., $\mu = T$ (refer Grau [35]).

For quality characteristics of smaller the better type, Chatterjee and Chakraborty [17] have established exact relationship(s) between C_p^I, C_{pk}^I, and the PNC, viz., $P_{NC}^{'(I)}$, when $\mu \neq T$ as follows:

$$
P_{NC}^{'(U)} = \begin{cases} 1 - \Phi\left[3\{C_{pk}^U - (\frac{k+1}{k})R_U C_p^U\}\right], & \text{for } \mu < T \\ 1 - \Phi[3C_{pk}^U], & \text{for } \mu > T \end{cases}
\tag{3.32}
$$

where $R_U = \frac{\mu - T}{d_u}$ and $d_u = U - T$.

Similarly, for quality characteristics of larger the better type and for $\mu \neq T$, the relationship of the PNC, say $P_{NC}^{'(L)}$ with C_p^L and C_{pk}^L can be given as (refer Chatterjee and Chakraborty [17]),

$$
P_{NC}^{'(L)} = \begin{cases} 1 - \Phi[3C_{pk}^L], & \text{for } \mu < T \\ 1 - \Phi\left[3\{C_{pk}^L - (\frac{k+1}{k})R_L C_p^L\}\right], & \text{for } \mu > T \end{cases}
\tag{3.33}
$$

In Table 3.2, the $NCPPM^{'(I)} = P_{NC}^{'(I)} \times 10^6$ values are tabulated for different values of "k" and C_{pk}^U (or, C_{pk}^L) when $\mu > T$ (or, $\mu < T$), assuming that μ does not exceed the specification limits.

TABLE 3.2: $NCPPM^{'(I)}$ values corresponding to different C_{pk}^U (or, C_{pk}^L) values when $\mu > T$ (or, $\mu < T$)

C_{pk}^I	1.00	1.10	1.20	1.30	1.40	1.50	1.60	1.70	1.80	1.90	2.00
$NCPPM^{'(I)}$	158.66	135.67	125.07	115.07	96.80	80.76	54.80	44.57	35.93	28.72	22.75

Also, Table 3.3 gives the $NCPPM^{'(I)}$ values for different values of k_U (or k_L) and C_{pk}^U (or, C_{pk}^L) when $\mu < T$ (or, $\mu > T$) with $R_U C_p^U (or\ R_L C_p^L) = -0.3$. For other values of $R_U C_p^U (or\ R_L C_p^L)$, the corresponding values of $NCPPM^{'(I)}$ can be computed using the equation (3.32) or (3.33) depending upon the available specification limit.

Chatterjee and Chakraborty [17] have also studied some important inferential properties of $C_p^I(u, v)$, for $u = 0, 1$ and $v = 0, 1$.

Univariate Process Capability Indices

TABLE 3.3: $NCPPM'^{(I)}$ Values Corresponding to Different C_{pk}^{U} (or, C_{pk}^{L}) and k_U (or k_L) Values when $\mu < T$ (or, $\mu > T$) and $R_U C_p^{U}$ (or $R_L C_p^{L}$) = −0.3 $[x\ Ey = x \times 10^{-y}]$

C_{pk}^{I} \ k_I	1.5	2.0	2.5	3.0	3.5	4.0	4.5	5.0
1.00	3.3977	6.8069	10.2213	13.3457	16.1126	18.5367	20.6575	22.5178
1.05	1.6597	3.3977	5.1685	6.8069	8.2688	9.5569	10.6885	11.6846
1.10	0.7933	1.6597	2.5577	3.3977	4.1530	4.8221	5.4125	5.9340
1.15	0.3711	0.7933	1.2386	1.6597	2.0412	2.3811	2.6823	2.9492
1.20	0.1698	0.3711	0.5869	0.7933	0.9818	1.1506	1.3008	1.4344
1.25	0.0760	0.1698	0.2721	0.3711	0.4621	0.5440	0.6173	0.6827
1.30	0.0333	0.0760	0.1235	0.1698	0.2128	0.2517	0.2867	0.3179
1.35	0.0143	0.0333	0.0548	0.0760	0.0959	0.1140	0.1302	0.1449
1.40	0.0060	0.0143	0.0238	0.0333	0.0423	0.0505	0.0580	0.0646
1.45	0.0025	0.0060	0.0101	0.0143	0.0182	0.0219	0.0250	0.0282
1.50	0.0010	0.0025	0.0042	0.0060	0.0077	0.0093	0.0107	0.0120
1.55	0.0004	0.0010	0.0017	0.0025	0.0032	0.0038	0.0045	0.0050
1.60	0.0001	0.0004	0.0007	0.0010	0.0013	0.0016	0.0018	0.0020
1.65	5.95E5	0.0001	0.0003	0.0004	0.0005	0.0006	0.0007	0.0008
1.70	2.06E5	5.59E5	0.0001	0.0001	0.0002	0.0002	0.0003	0.0003
1.75	7.39E6	2.06E5	3.76E5	5.59E5	7.41E5	9.15E5	0.0001	0.0001
1.80	2.60E6	7.39E6	1.37E5	2.06E5	2.74E5	3.40E5	4.02E5	4.49E5
1.85	8.95E7	2.60E6	4.88E6	7.39E6	9.92E6	1.24E5	1.46E5	1.68E5
1.90	3.01E7	8.95E7	1.70E6	2.60E6	3.51E6	4.40E6	5.23E6	6.01E6
1.95	9.91E8	3.01E7	5.80E7	8.95E7	1.22E6	1.53E6	1.83E6	2.10E6
2.00	3.19E8	9.91E8	1.93G7	3.01E7	4.12E7	5.20E7	6.24E7	7.21E7

3.5 Univariate Process Capability Indices for Non-Normal Distributions

The PCIs discussed so far are based on the common assumption that the underlying distribution of the concerned quality characteristic is normally distributed. However, this may not always be the case in practice. The common industrial practice is to apply PCIs designed for normal distributions without checking the actual distribution of the quality characteristic under consideration. According to Pearn and Kotz [63], as a consequence of such indiscriminate use of PCIs, the values of the PCIs may, in majority of situations, be incorrect and quite likely to misrepresent the true health of the process. The ranking of the four basic PCIs, in terms of the sensitivity to departure from target, from the most sensitive one to the least sensitive are C_{pmk}, C_{pm}, C_{pk}, and C_p, respectively (refer Chen and Pearn [21]).

Moreover, for the normal distribution, the quantity 3σ is the distance of median (which is equal to mean, particularly for normal distribution) from both the upper 99.865 percentile and the lower 0.135 percentile. Therefore, for assessing the capability of a process with nonnormal distribution of the quality characteristic, the idea is to generalize the formulae for standard indices by replacing μ and 3σ with plausible alternatives like appropriate quantiles and so on.

While defining PCIs for nonnormally distributed quality characteristics, Clements [31] suggested replacing 6σ by the length of the interval between the upper and lower 0.135 percentile points of the actual distribution. The author defined PCIs analogous to C_p and C_{pk} for nonnormal distributions as follows:

$$C_p' = \frac{U - L}{\xi_{1-\alpha} - \xi_\alpha} \tag{3.34}$$

$$C_{pk}'' = \frac{d - |\xi_{0.5} - M|}{(\xi_{1-\alpha} - \xi_\alpha)/2} \tag{3.35}$$

where $\xi_{1-\alpha}$ and ξ_α are the upper and lower α percentiles of the distribution of the corresponding random variable X and $\xi_{0.5}$ is the corresponding median. Generally, $\alpha = 0.00135$ is considered for computational purposes.

Wright [88] proposed the following PCI which is sensitive to skewness:

$$C_s = \frac{\frac{d}{\sigma} - \frac{|\mu - M|}{\sigma}}{3\sqrt{1 + \left(\frac{\mu - T}{\sigma}\right)^2 + |\sqrt{\beta_1}|}} \tag{3.36}$$

where $\sqrt{\beta_1} = \frac{\mu_3}{\sigma^{3/2}}$ is a widely used measure of skewness and μ_3 is the third order raw moment of the corresponding random variate "X."

However, the quantile or percentile based approach of dealing with non-normality, while measuring capability of a process, suffers from a basic problem. Often these PCIs involve extreme percentiles viz., 99.87th or 0.27th percentiles. However, accurate estimation of these extreme percentiles require a huge amount of data, which is often difficult to obtain, especially for processes requiring destructive testing (refer Pearn et al. [64]).

It is interesting to note that "potential capability" means "possibility of achieving" rather than "actually achieving" (refer Kotz and Johnson [49]). Veevers [86] has used the term "viability" to represent "capability potential" and has proposed a viability index from a more general perspective, as compared to C_p, in a sense that the viability index is neither restricted to normal distribution of "X" nor even to univariate situations.

The univariate viability index is defined as

$$V_t = \frac{w}{2d} \tag{3.37}$$

where "w" is the "window of opportunity" measured by the length of interval of θ for which the distribution of $(X + \theta)$ would generate an expected PNC not greater than the conventional 0.27%.

Under the assumption of normality of the quality characteristic under consideration

$$M - (d - 3\sigma) \leq \mu \leq M + (d - 3\sigma) \tag{3.38}$$

i.e., the window of opportunity for μ can be defined as, $w = 2(d - 3\sigma)$ and the corresponding viability index will be

$$\begin{aligned} V_t &= \frac{2(d - 3\sigma)}{2d} \\ &= 1 - \frac{1}{C_p} \end{aligned} \tag{3.39}$$

Unlike most of the PCIs, V_t can assume negative values. If V_t is less than zero, there is no possibility of attaining a PNC value of 0.27% or lower and hence, the process is considered to be "nonviable."

Another approach to deal with the non-normality in the distribution of the quality characteristic is to transform the actual distribution into a normal one by virtue of the Box-Cox power transformation or Johnson transformation and then to apply PCIs for normal distributions. However, the computed PCI values corresponding to such transformed processes may often be difficult to interpret.

Families of distributions, like Pearson and Johnson, are also used sometimes to deal with non-normality of the distributions of the quality characteristics. Also, one can choose a process distribution from a smaller family of distributions such as gamma, lognormal or Weibull which in turn, simplifies the corresponding inferential problem. Rodriguez [75] have enlisted the following advantages of using families of distributions for computing PCIs of non-normal processes:

1. Method of maximum likelihood can be used to have stable and straight forward estimation of the concerned parameters.

2. Since the method of maximum likelihood yields asymptotic variances for estimates of the parameters, it can be used to construct confidence intervals for the plug-in estimators of the PCIs.

3. For various families of distributions like gamma, lognormal, and Weibull, goodness-of-fit tests based on empirical distribution functions are also available.

4. For standard families of distributions, estimated values of the percentiles and PNC, related to the plug-in estimators of the PCIs, can be easily computed using standard results.

For processes with unilateral specification limits also, substantial research work has been done to assess the capability of a process when the underlying statistical distribution is non-normal. Vannman and Albing [85] modified $C_{pvu}(u, v)$ [see equation (3.25)] for the case, where the quality characteristic has a skewed distribution with a long tail toward large values and a "USL" with target set at "0," i.e., the quality characteristic has a skewed zero - bound distribution. This superstructure is defined as

$$C_{MA}(\tau, v) = \frac{USL}{\sqrt{q_{1-\tau}^2 + v q_{0.5}^2}} \qquad (3.40)$$

where $v \geq 0$ and q_τ is the τth quantile of the quality characteristic. The parameter τ should be small and chosen in a suitable way, e.g., $\tau = 0.0027$.

However, we have observed the following drawbacks in this superstructure (refer Chatterjee and Chakraborty [11]):

1. Vannman and Albing [85] have modified only $C_{pvu}(u, v)$. Neither $C_{pau}(u, v)$ was modified nor any justification for omitting the same was given. However, as has been pointed out by Grau [35], $C_{pvu}(u, v)$ is not suitable for assessing capability of a process with unilateral specifications (refer Section 3.4).

2. There is room for studying whether considering $\tau = 0.0027$ is justified even if the underlying distribution of the quality characteristic is not normal.

3. Some constants of $C_{pvu}(u, v)$ were omitted just for simplicity without studying the impact of such omission.

4. $C_{MA}(\tau, v)$ fails to perform if the target is other than "0."

5. The ideal values of v have not been studied.

Albing [2] has modified the superstructure $C_{MA}(\tau, v)$ which is defined in Eq. (3.40) for the quality characteristic under Weibull distribution, as follows:

$$C_{MAW}(\tau, v) = \frac{USL}{a\sqrt{(ln(\frac{1}{\tau})^{\frac{2}{b}}) + v(ln2)^{\frac{2}{b}}}} \qquad (3.41)$$

where "a" is the scale parameter and "b" is the shape parameter of a two-parameter Weibull distribution. However, since this super-structure is an extension of $C_{MA}(\tau, v)$, it inherits the drawbacks of $C_{MA}(\tau, v)$ as listed above. Moreover, $C_{MAW}(\tau, v)$ is valid only when the underlying distribution of the quality characteristic is Weibull. It fails to perform in case of all the other types of statistical distributions.

Rodriguez [75] has also suggested other methods like goodness-of-fit, quantile-quantile plot, kernel density estimation and comparative histograms to assess capabilities of non-normal processes. For further review of the PCIs for nonnormal distributions, one can refer to Pearn and Kotz [63]; Tang and Than [80] and the references therein.

3.6   Univariate Process Capability Indices PNC

A parallel approach for assessing process performance, apart from using PCIs, is to compute PNC. Yeh and Bhattacharya [94] proposed use of the proportion p_0/p for the said purpose, where, p_0 is the desired (minimum allowable) PNC, while "p" is the actual PNC.

Again, to distinguish between nonconforming items exceeding either of the specification limits, Yeh and Chen [95] slightly modified the above index as follows:

$$C_f = \min\left\{\frac{p_0^L}{p^L}, \frac{p_0^U}{p^U}\right\} \tag{3.42}$$

where $\frac{p_0^L}{p^L}$ corresponds to items having quality characteristic value less than LSL and $\frac{p_0^U}{p^U}$ for those exceeding USL.

Khadse and Shinde [46] have proposed alternatives to traditional PCIs like C_p, C_{pk}, and C_{pm} based on the concept of PNC. Their formulation is valid for both the normal and non-normal distributions and also for symmetric as well as asymmetric specification limits.

Maiti et al. [57] have defined a generalized PCI, viz., C_{py}, defined as a ratio of the proportion of the observed process yield to desired process yield as follows:

$$C_{py} = \frac{P(L \leq X \leq U)}{P(LDL \leq X \leq UDL)} \tag{3.43}$$

where LDL and UDL are the lower and upper desired limits. The advantage of C_{py} is that it does not require normality assumption of the distribution of the concerned quality characteristics.

Moreover, the exact relationships between yield based PCIs and the corresponding PNCs can be utilized to compute the PNC values when the information on the respective PCIs are already available. For example, when the underlying distribution of the quality characteristic is normal, the relationships between C_p, C_{pk}, and PNC, as given in equations (3.2) and (3.3) can be used for the said purpose.

3.7 Univariate Process Capability Assessments Using Bayesian Approach

Apart from the process capability assessments based on the so called frequentist approach, some very interesting studies have also been carried out using Bayesian approach as well. This approach is more coherent than the frequentist approach, which we have discussed so far, particularly, when we have some relevant prior information regarding the said process and we should incorporate those information in our decision making.

Cheng and Spiring [27] were among the first to handle the problem of process capability analysis using Bayesian approach. They used uniform (noninformative) prior for this purpose. The Bayesian estimation procedures for the four classical univariate PCIs, viz., C_p, C_{pk}, C_{pm} and C_{pmk}, have been studied by Shiau, Hung and Chiang [76], Singh and Saxena [77], Pearn and Wu [72], Pearn and Lin [67], and Wu and Lin [90] among others. The Bayesian estimations of these PCIs based on multiple samples and subsamples have been studied by Pearn and Wu [73] and Wu [89], respectively. Shiau, Hung, and Chiang [76] have discussed the Bayesian approach of process capability analysis based on Bayes and empirical Bayes approaches by using noninformative and conjugate priors, respectively. Pearn and Wu [72] have discussed estimation and testing procedure of C_p based on multiple samples using Bayesian approach.

The corresponding hypothesis testing procedures and the confidence intervals, from Bayesian perspective, have been explored by Fan and Kao [32, 33], Karger, Mashinchi and parchami [45], Wu and Pearn [91], and so on.

Although, most of the studies on the Bayesian estimation of univariate PCIs are meant for quality characteristics having symmetric specification limits, there are some very interesting research works for quality characteristics with asymmetric and unilateral specification limits as well (refer Lin et al. [56], Wu and Shu [93] and Wu and Pearn [92]).

3.8 Concluding Remarks

The concept of process capability analysis is quite new compared to the other concepts like control chart techniques, acceptance sampling, various sampling inspection plans and so on. However due to its huge potential applications in practice, the theory has developed steadily over the time. Consequently, the literature of SQC is now enriched with many high quality research works on process capability analysis.

Spiring et al. [78] and Yum and Kim [96] have provided comprehensive bibliographies of books, book chapters, research articles, case studies, and reviews dealing with process capability analysis. These are of immense help to practitioners for ready references on PCIs pertaining to a specific problem and also to theoreticians for exploring future scopes of research.

Bibliography

[1] Albing, M. (2008). Contribution to Process Capability Indices and Plots. *Doctoral Thesis*. Department of Mathematics, Lulea University of Technology, Lulea, Sweden.

[2] Albing, M. (2009). Process Capability Indices for Weibull Distributions and Upper Specification Limits. *Quality and Reliability Engineering International*, Vol. 25, No. 3, pp. 317–334.

[3] Bordignon, S., Scagliarini, M. (2001). Statistical Analysis of Process Capability Indices with Measurement errors: The Case of C_p. *Statistical Methods and Applications*, Vol. 10, No. 1–3, pp. 273–285.

[4] Bordignon, S., Scagliarini, M. (2002). Statistical Analysis of Process Capability Indices with Measurement errors. *Quality and Reliability Engineering International*, Vol. 18, No. 4, pp. 321–332.

[5] Bordignon, S., Scagliarini, M. (2006). Estimation of C_{pm} When Measurement Error is Present. *Quality and Reliability Engineering International*, Vol. 22, No. 7, pp. 787–801.

[6] Box, G. E. P., Cox, D. R. (1964). An Analysis of Transformations. *Journal of the Royal Statitical Society, Series B (Statistical Methodology)*, Vol. 26, No. 2, pp. 211–46.

[7] Boyles, R. A. (1991). The Taguchi Capability Index. *Journal of Quality Technology*, Vol. 23, No. 1, pp. 17–26.

[8] Boyles, R. A. (1994). Process Capability with Asymmetric Tolerances. *Communications in Statistics—Simulation and Computation*, Vol. 23, No. 3, pp. 162–175.

[9] Chan, L. K., Cheng, S. W., Spring, F. A. (1988). A New Measure of Process Capability: C_{pm}. *Journal of Quality Technology*, Vol. 20, No. 3, pp. 162–175.

[10] Chatterjee, M., Chakraborty, A. K. (2011). Superstructure Of Multivariate Process Capability Indices for Asymmetric Tolerances. *Proceedings of International Congress on Productivity, Quality, Reliability, Optimization and Modelling*. Vol. 1, pp. 635–647, Allied Publishers PVT LTD, India.

Bibliography

[11] Chatterjee, M., Chakraborty, A. K. (2012). Univariate Process Capability Indices for Unilateral Specification Region: A Review & Some Modifications. *International Journal of Reliability, Quality and Safety Engineering*. Vol. 19, No. 4, pp. 1250020 (1–18).

[12] Chatterjee, M., Chakraborty, A. K. (2013). Distribution and Process Capability Control Chart of C_{pm}^{U}. *Proceedings of the International Conference on Quality, Reliability and Operations Research (ICONQROR 2013)*. pp. 1–8 , Excel India Publishers.

[13] Chatterjee, M., Chakraborty, A. K. (2014). Exact Relationship of $C_{pk}^{''}$ with Proportion of Non-conformance and Some Other Properties of $C_{p}^{''}(u,v)$. *Quality and Reliability Engineering International*, Vol. 30, pp. 1023–1034.

[14] Chatterjee, M., Chakraborty, A. K. (2015). A Super Structure of Process Capability Indices for Circular Specification Region. *Communications in Statistics—Theory and Methods*, Vol. 44, No. 6, pp. 1158–1181.

[15] Chatterjee, M., Chakraborty, A. K. (2015). Distributions and Process Capability Control Charts for C_{pu} and C_{pl} Using Subgroup Information. *Communications in Statistics—Theory and Methods*, Vol. 44,No. 20, pp. 4333–4353.

[16] Chatterjee, M., Chakraborty, A. K. (2016). Some Process Capability Indices for Unilateral Specification Limits - Their Properties and the Process Capability Control Charts. *Communications in Statistics—Theory and Methods*, Vol. 45, No. 24, pp. 7130–7160.

[17] Chatterjee, M., Chakraborty, A. K. (2016). Some Process Capability Indices for Unilateral Specification Limits - Their Properties and the Process Capability Control Charts. *Communications in Statistics - Theory and Methods*. Vol. 45, No. 24, pp. 7130–7160.

[18] Chakraborty, A. K., Chatterjee, M., (2016). Univariate and Multivariate Process Capability Analysis for Different Types of Specification Limits. *Quality and Reliability Management and Its Applications* edited by Prof. Hoang Pham. pp. 47–81, Springer London.

[19] Chatterjee, M., Chakraborty, A. K. (2017). Unification of Some Multivariate Process Capability Indices For Asymmetric Specification Region. *Statistica Neerlandica*, Vol. 71, No. 4, pp. 286–306.

[20] Chang, Y. C. (2009). Interval Estimation of Capability Index C_{pmk} for Manufacturing Processes With Asymmetric Tolerances. *Computers and Industrial Engineering*, Vol. 56, No. 1, pp. 312–322.

[21] Chen, K. S., Pearn, W. L. (1997). An Application of Non-normal Process Capability Indices. *Quality and Reliability Engineering International*, Vol. 13, No. 6, pp. 355–360.

[22] Chen, K. S., Pearn, W. L. (2001). Capability Indices For Process With Asymmetric Tolerances. *Journal of The Chinese Institute of Engineers*, Vol. 24, No. 5, pp. 559–568.

[23] Chen, K. S., Pearn, W. L., Lin, P. C. (1999). A New Generalization of C_{pm} for Processes with Asymmetric Tolerances. *International Journal of Reliability, Quality and Safety Engineering*, Vol. 6, No. 4, pp. 383–398.

[24] Chen, S. M., Hsu, Y. S. (2004). Uniformly Most Powerful Test for Process Capability Index C_{pk}. *Quality Technology and Quantitative Management*, Vol. 1, No. 2, pp. 257–269.

[25] Pearn, W. L. (1998). New Generalization of Process Capability Index C_{pk}. *Journal of Applied Statistics*, Vol. 25, No. 6, pp. 801–810.

[26] Chen, S. M., Tsai, T. J. (2012). Properties of Estimators of the Process Capability Index $C_{pk}^{''}$. *Communications in Statistics—Simulation and Computation*, Vol. 41, No. 8, pp. 1444–1462.

[27] Cheng, S. W., Spiring, F. A. (1989). Assessing Process Capability: A Bayesian Approach. *IIE Transactions*, Vol. 21, No.1, pp. 97–98.

[28] Choi, B. C., Owen, D. B. (1990). A Study of A New Process Capability Index. *Communications In Statistics—Theory and Methods*, Vol. 19, No. 4, pp. 1231–1245.

[29] Chou, Y. M., Owen, D. B. (1989). On the Distribution of the Estimated Process Capability Indices, *Communications in Statistics—Theory and Methods*, Vol. 18, No.2, pp. 4549–4560.

[30] Chou, Y. M., Owen, D. B., Borrego, S. A. (1990). Lower Confidence Limits on Process Capability Indices. *Journal of Quality Technology*, Vol. 22, No. 3, pp. 223–229.

[31] Clements, J. A. (1989). Process Capability Calculations for Non-normal Distributions. *Quality Progress*, Vol. 22, No. 9, pp. 95–100.

[32] Fan, S. -K. S., Kao, C. -K. (2004). Lower Bayesian Confidence Limits on the Process Capability Index C_{pm}: A Comparative Study. *Journal of the Chinese Institute of Industrial Engineers*, Vol. 21, No. 5, pp. 444–452.

[33] Fan, S. -K. S., Kao, C. -K. (2006). Development of Confidence Interval and Hypothesis Testing for Taguchi Capability Index Using a Bayesian Approach. *International Journal of Operations Research*, Vol. 3, No. 1, pp. 56–75.

[34] Franklin, L. A., Wasserman, G. (1992). Bootstrap Lower Confidence Limits For Capability Indices. *Journal of Quality Technology*, Vol. 24, No. 4, pp. 196–210.

[35] Grau, D. (2009). New Process Capability Indices for One-Sided Tolerances. *Quality Technology and Quantitative Management*, Vol. 6, No. 2, pp. 107–124.

[36] Grau, D. (2010). On the Choice of a Capability Index for Asymmetric Tolerances. *Quality Technology and Quantitative Management*, Vol. 7, No. 3, pp. 301–319.

[37] Grau, D. (2011). Process Yield and Capability Indices. *Communications in Statistics—Theory and Methods*, Vol. 40, No. 15, pp. 2751–2771.

[38] Ho, L. L. (2003). Statistical Inference from Boyles' Capability Index. *Economic Quality Control*, Vol. 18, No. 1, pp. 43–57.

[39] Hoffman, L. L. (1993). A General Approach for Testing the Process Capability Index. *Quality and Reliability Engineering International*, Vol. 9, No. 5, pp. 670–675.

[40] Hoffman, L. L. (2001). Obtaining Confidence Intervals for C_{pk} Using Percentiles of the Distribution of C_p. *Quality and Reliability Engineering International*, Vol. 17, No. 2, pp. 113–118.

[41] Hsiang, T. C., Taguchi, G. (1985). Tutorial on Quality Control and Assurance—The Taguchi Methods. *Joint Meetings of the American Statistical Association*, Las Vegas, Nevada, pp. 188.

[42] Hsu, B. M., Shu, M. H., Pearn, W. L. (2007). Measuring Process Capability Based on C_{pmk} with Gauge Measurement Errors. *Quality and Reliability Engineering International*, Vol. 23, No. 5, pp. 597–614.

[43] Jessenberger, J., Weihs, C. (2000). A Note on the Behavior of C_{pmk} with Asymmetric Specification Limits. *Journal of Quality Technology*, Vol. 32, No. 4, pp. 440–443.

[44] Kane, V. E. (1986). Process Capability Index. *Journal of Quality Technology*, Vol. 18, No. 1, pp. 41–52.

[45] Kargar, M., Mashinchi, M., Parchami, A. (2013). A Bayesian Approach to Capability Testing Based on C_{pk} with Multiple Samples. *Quality and Reliability Engineering International*, DOI: 10.1002/qre.1512.

[46] Khadse, K. G., Shinde, R. L. (2009). Probability-Based Process Capability Indices. *Communications in Statistics—Simulation and Computation*, Vol. 38, No. 4, pp. 884–904.

[47] Kotz, S., Johnson, N. (1993). *Process Capability Indices*. London: Chapman & Hall.

Bibliography

[48] Kotz, S., Johnson, N. (1999). Delicate Relations Among the Basic Process Capability Indices C_p, C_{pk}, and C_{pm} and Their Modifiactions. *Communications in Statistics—Simulation and Computation*, Vol. 28, No. 3, pp. 849–866.

[49] Kotz, S., Johnson, N. (2002). Process Capability Indices—A Review, 1992–2000. *Journal of Quality Technology* Vol. 34, No. 1, pp. 2–19.

[50] Krishnamoorthy, K. S. (1990). Capability Indices for Processes Subject to Unilateral and Positional Tolerances. *Quality Engineering*, Vol. 2, No. 4, pp. 461–471.

[51] Kushler, R. H., Hurley, P. (1992). Confidence Bounds for Capability Indices. *Journal of Quality Technology*, Vol. 24, No. 4, pp. 188–195.

[52] Lin, P. C., Pearn, W. L. (2002). Testing Process Capability for One-Sided Specification Limit with Application to the Voltage Level Translator. *Microelectronics Reliability*, Vol. 42, No. 12, pp. 1975–1983.

[53] Lin, P. C., Pearn, W. L. (2002). A Note on the Interval Estimation of C_{pk} with Asymmetric Tolerances. *Journal of Non-parametric Statistics*, Vol. 14, No. 6, pp. 647–654.

[54] Lin, P. C., Pearn, W. L. (2005). Testing Process Performance Based on the Capability Index C_{pm}. *International Journal of Advanced Manufacturing Technology*, Vol. 27, No. 3–4, pp. 351–358.

[55] Lin, G. H., Pearn, W. L., Yang, Y. S. (2005). A Bayesian Approach to Obtain a Lower Bound for the C_{pm} Capability Index. *Quality and Reliability Engineering International*, Vol. 21, No. 6, pp. 655–668.

[56] Lin, T. -Y., Wu, C. -W., Chen, J. C., Chiou, Y. H. (2011). Applying Bayesian Approach to Assess Process Capability for Asymmetric Tolerances Based on C''_{pmk} Index. *Applied Mathematical Modelling*, Vol. 35, pp. 4473–4489.

[57] Maiti, S. S., Saha, M., Nanda, A. K. (2010). On Generalizing Process Capability Indices. *Quality Technology and Quantitative Management*, Vol. 7, No. 3, pp. 279–300.

[58] Palmer, K., Tsui, K. L. (1999). A Review and Interpretations of Process Capability Indices. *Annals of Operations Research*, Vol. 87, pp. 31–47.

[59] Pearn, W. L. (1998). New Generalization of Process Capability Index C_{pk}. *Journal of Applied Statistics*, Vol. 25, No. 6, pp. 801–810.

[60] Pearn, W. L., Chen, K. S. (2002). One—Sided Capability Indices C_{pu} and C_{Pl} : Decision Making with Sample Information. *International Journal of Quality and Reliability Management*, Vol. 19, No. 3, pp. 221–245.

Bibliography

[61] Pearn, W. L., Chuang, C. C. (2004). Accuracy Analysis of the Estimated Process Yield Based on S_{pk}. *Quality and Reliability engineering International*, Vol. 20, No. 4, pp. 305–316.

[62] Pearn, W. L., Hung, H. N., Cheng, Y. C. (2009). Supplier Selection for One-Sided Processes With Unequal Sample Size. *European Journal of Operational Research*. Vol. 195, pp. 381–393.

[63] Pearn, W. L., Kotz, S. (2007). *Encyclopedia and Handbook of Process Capability Indices—Series on Quality, Reliability and Engineering Statistics*. Singapore: World Scientific.

[64] Pearn, W. L., Kotz, S., Johnson, N. L. (1992). Distributional and Inferential Properties of Process Capability Indices. *Journal of Quality Technology*, Vol. 24, No. 4, pp. 216–231.

[65] Pearn, W. L., Liao, M. Y. (2005). Measuring Process Capability Based on C_{pk} with Gauge Measurement Errors. *Microelectronics Reliability*, Vol. 45, No. 3–4, pp. 739–751.

[66] Pearn, W. L., Lin, P. C. (2000). Estimating Capability Index C_{pk} for Processes With Asymmetric Tolerances. *Communications in Statistics: Theory and Methods*, Vol. 29, No. 11, pp. 2593–2604.

[67] Pearn, W. L., Lin, G. H. (2003). A Bayesian-like Estimator of the Process Capability Index C_{pmk}. *Metrika*, Vol. 57, No. 3, pp. 303–312.

[68] Pearn, W. L., Lin, P. C. (2004). Testing Process Performance based on the Capability Index C_{pk} with Critical values. *Computers and Industrial engineering*, Vol. 47, pp. 351–369.

[69] Pearn, W. L., Lin, P. C., Chen, K. S. (2001). Estimating Process Capability Index C_{pmk}'' for Asymmetric Tolerances: Distributional Properties. *Metrika*, Vol. 54, No. 3, pp. 261–279.

[70] Pearn, W. L., Lin, P. C., Chen, K. S. (2004). The C_{pk}'' Index For Asymmetric Tolerances: Implications and Inferences. *Metrika*, Vol. 60, No. 2, pp. 119–136.

[71] Pearn, W. L., Wu, C. H. (2013). Measuring PPM Non-conformities for Processes with Asymmetric Tolerance. *Quality and Reliability Engineering International*, Vol. 29, No. 3, pp. 431–435.

[72] Pearn, W. L., Wu, C. -W. (2005). Process Capability Assessment for Index C_{pk} Based on Bayesian Approach. *Metrika*, Vol. 61, No. 2, pp. 221–234.

[73] Pearn, W. L., Wu, C. - W. (2005). A Bayesian Approach for Assessing process Precision Based on Multiple Samples. *European Journal of Operational Research*, Vol. 165, pp. 685–695.

Bibliography

[74] Pillet, M., Rochon, S., Duclos, E. (1997). SPC—Generalization of Capability Index C_{pm} : Case of Unilateral Tolerances. *Quality Engineering*, Vol. 10, No. 1, pp. 171–176.

[75] Rodriguez, R. N. (1992). Recent Developments in Process Capability Analysis. *Journal of Quality Technology*, Vol. 24, No. 4, pp. 176–187.

[76] Shiau, J. -J. H., Hung, H. -N., Chiang, C. -T. (1999). A Note on Bayesian Estimation of Process Capability Indices. *Statistics and Probability Letters*, Vol. 45, pp. 215–224.

[77] Singh, H. P., Sexena, S. (2005). Bayesian and Shrinkage Estimation of Process Capability Index C_p. *Communications in Statistics Theory and Methods*, Vol. 34, No. 1, pp. 205–228.

[78] Spiring, F., Leung, B., Cheng, S. and Yeung, A. (2003). A Bibliography of Process Capability Papers. *Quality and Reliability Engineering International*, Vol. 19, No. 5, pp. 445–460.

[79] Taguchi, G. (1986). *Introduction to Quality Engineering*, Asian Productivity Organization, UNIPUB, White Plains, New York.

[80] Tang, L. C., Than, S. E. (1999). Computing Process Capability Indices for Non-normal Data: A Review and Comparative Study. *Quality and Reliability Engineering International*, Vol. 35, No. 5, pp. 339–353.

[81] Vannman, K. (1995). A Unified Approach to Capability Indices. *Statistica Sinica*, Vol. 5, No. 2, pp. 805–820.

[82] Vannman, K. (1997). A General Class of Capability Indices in the Case of Asymmetric Tolerances. *Communications in Statistics—Theory and Methods*, Vol. 26, No. 8, pp. 2049–2072.

[83] Vannman, K. (1998). Families of Process Capability Indices for One—Sided Specification Limits. *Statistics*, Vol. 31, No. 1, pp. 43–66.

[84] Vannman, K. Kotz, S. (1995). A Superstructure of Capability Indices: Distributional Properties and Implications. *Scandinavian Journal of statistics*, Vol. 22, pp. 477–491.

[85] Vannman, K., Albing, M. (2007). Process Capability Indices for One—Sided Specification Intervals and Skewed Distributions. *Quality and Reliability Engineering International*, Vol. 23, No. 6, pp. 755–765.

[86] Veevers, A. (1998). Viability and Capability Indices for Multi-response Processes. *Journal of Applied Statistics*, Vol. 25, No. 4, pp. 545–558.

[87] Veevers, A. (1999). Capability indices for multiresponse processes. *Statistical Process Monitoring and Optimization*, Park, S. H. and Vining G. G. edited. New York, NY: Marcel Dekker: pp.241 - 256.

Bibliography

[88] Wright, P. A. (1995). A Process Capability Index Sensitive to Skewness. *Journal of Statistical Computation and Simulation*, Vol. 52, pp. 195–203.

[89] Wu, C. - W. (2008). Assessing Process Capability Based on Bayesian Approach with Subsamples. *European Journal of Operational Research*, Vol. 184, pp. 207–228.

[90] Wu, C. -W., Lin, T. Y. (2009). A Bayesian Procedure for Assessing Process Performance Based on the Third Generation Capability Index. *Journal of Applied Statistics*, Vol. 36, No. 11, pp. 1205–1223.

[91] Wu, C. -W., Pearn, W. L. (2005). Capability Testing Based on C_{pm} with Multiple samples. *Quality and Reliability International*, Vol. 21, pp. 29–42.

[92] Wu, C. -W., Pear, W. L. (2006). Bayesian Approach for Measuring EEP-ROM Process Capability Based on the One-sided Indices C_{pu} and C_{pl}. *International Journal of Advance Manufacturing Technology*, Vol. 31, pp. 135–144.

[93] Wu, C. -W., Shu, M. H. (2007). A Bayesian Procedure for Assessing Process Performance Based on Expected Relative Loss with Asymmetric Tolerance. *Journal of Applied Statistics*, Vol. 34, No. 9, pp. 1109–1123.

[94] Yeh, A. B., Bhattacharya, S. (1998). A Robust Capability Index. *Communications in Statistics—Simulation and Computation*, Vol. 27, No. 2, pp. 565–589.

[95] Yeh, A. B., Chen, H. (1999). A Non-parametric Multivariate Process Capability Index. *International Journal of Modelling and simulation*, Vol. 21, pp.218-223.

[96] Yum, B. J., Kim, K. W. (2011). A Bibliography of the Literature on Process Capability Indices: 2000–20009. *Quality and Reliability Engineering International*, Vol. 27, No. 3, pp. 251–268.

[97] Zimmer, L. S., Hubele, N. F., Zimmer, W. J. (2001). Confidence Intervals and Sample Size Determination for C_{pm}. *Quality and Reliability Engineering International*, Vol. 17, No. 1, pp. 51–68.

Chapter 4

Bivariate Process Capability Indices (BPCIs)

Chapter Summary

After having a brief idea about univariate process capability indices (PCI) in chapter 3, this Chapter actually takes the first step toward multivariate process capability indices (MPCIs). In most of the modern manufacturing or any other type of processes, often the assumption that, "there exists only one measurable quality characteristic or even if there are multiple quality characteristics, they are mutually independent and hence can be handled individually" is proven to be an unrealistic one. Often, one needs to consider all those quality characteristics together along with their prevailing correlation structure. In the present chapter, the simplest of such cases, viz., where only two correlated quality characteristics are available, are considered. Bivariate process capability indices (BPCIs) defined for various types of specification regions, viz., bilateral, unilateral, and circular, are discussed in detail. Finally, two numerical examples are given to show practical usage of these BPCIs.

4.1 Introduction

With the incorporation of cutting edge technologies and modern machineries in manufacturing industries, nowadays, it has become easier to asses performance of even highly complicated processes. In fact, in practice it is rare to have uncorrelated or single important quality characteristic(s) for a particular product. The quality characteristics, encountered in practice, are often highly correlated among themselves, so much so that considering their capabilities individually, may lead to misleading conclusion about the overall capability scenario of the process.

In many situations, the items produced in various manufacturing industries are found to have more than one measurable characteristics which are interrelated among themselves. Some of these quality characteristics may

Bivariate Process Capability Indices (BPCIs) 79

individually have insignificant impact on overall process capability, but often when they are taken together, they influence the process to a large extent.

Taam et al. [28] have given an interesting example in this regard. An automobile paint needs to have a range of light reflective ability and a range of adhesion ability. A paint that satisfies one criterion but not the other is undesirable. Moreover, these characteristics are related through the compositions of the paint. Therefore, to have a true picture about the overall capability of the process, one needs to consider both the quality characteristics together.

To assess the capability level of such processes, the common industrial practice is to compute the capability value of the process based on any one of these quality characteristics or to compute PCI values for each of these characteristics separately using the available univariate PCIs and then summarizing the capability of the entire process through arithmetic or geometric mean or any other measure of central tendency of these univariate PCIs. However, this approach ignores the prevailing correlation structure among the quality characteristics and hence often fails to reflect the actual capability scenario of a process.

In order to address these problems, multivariate process capability indices (MPCI) were introduced. With the increase in the complexity of the production processes, processes with multiple correlated quality characteristics are becoming more common than those with single quality characteristics.

Castagliola and Castellanos [4] have observed that, among the practical situations soliciting multivariate process capability analysis, the cases of "two correlated quality characteristics" are the most common ones. This necessitates the development of bivariate process capability indices (BPCIs).

Apart from this, BPCIs are also applicable for quality characteristics having circular or spherical specification regions (e.g., in case of hitting a target, drilling a hole and so on).

In this chapter, a number of BPCIs will be discussed along with their preambles and statistical properties.

4.2 Bivariate Generalization of Univariate PCIs for Bilateral Specification Limits

Kocherlakota and Kocherlakota [16] were probably among the first to conceptualize process capability analysis under bivariate set-up.

Suppose X is a random vector which follows bivariate normal distribution with parameters μ_1, μ_2, σ_1^2, σ_2^2 and ρ i.e., $X = (X_1, X_2)' \sim N_2(\mu_1, \mu_2, \sigma_1^2, \sigma_2^2, \rho)$. Also suppose here X_i stands for the ith quality characteristic, for $i = 1, 2$.

Bivariate Process Capability Indices (BPCIs)

Since, here one has to deal with two correlated quality characteristics simultaneously, therefore, this constitutes a bivariate process capability problem. At first, Kocherlakota and Kocherlakota [16] have considered bilateral specification limits, i.e., when for each quality characteristic, two specification limits, viz., upper specification limit (USL) and lower specification limit (LSL) are available.

Note that, although the two quality characteristics are correlated, Kocherlakota and Kocherlakota [16] have considered the PCI, $C_p = \frac{USL-LSL}{3\sigma}$ individually for each quality characteristic and then derived their joint probability density function (p.d.f.).

Thus, suppose for the two quality characteristics, the corresponding C_p values are given by $C_{p1} = \frac{USL_1-LSL_1}{3\sigma_1}$ and $C_{p2} = \frac{USL_2-LSL_2}{3\sigma_2}$, respectively.

Suppose $\overline{X}_i = \frac{1}{n}\sum_{j=1}^{n} X_{ij}$ $S_i^2 = \frac{1}{n-1}\sum_{j=1}^{n}(X_{ij} - \overline{X}_i)^2$ denote the mean (arithemetic mean) and variance , respectively, corresponding to the ith variable, for $i = 1, 2$. Then the plug-in estimator of C_{pi} is defined as

$$\hat{C}_{pi} = \frac{USL_i - LSL_i}{S_i} \tag{4.1}$$

for $i = 1, 2$.

Define $W_i = \frac{(n-1)S_i^2}{\sigma_i^2}$, for $i = 1, 2$. It is easy to observe that $W_i \sim \chi_{n-1}^2$, where χ_{n-1}^2 stands for χ^2 distribution with $(n-1)$ degrees of freedom.

Then (W_1, W_2) will jointly follow a bivariate chi-square distribution, whose joint p.d.f. is given by

$$
\begin{aligned}
f(w_1, w_2) &= \frac{1}{(1-\rho^2)^2} \sum_{j=0}^{\infty} nb\left(j; \frac{n-1}{2}, \rho^2\right) f_{n-1+2j}\left(\frac{w_1}{1-\rho^2}\right) \\
&\times f_{n-1+2j}\left(\frac{w_2}{1-\rho^2}\right)
\end{aligned} \tag{4.2}
$$

where

$$nb(j; \frac{n-1}{2}, \rho) = \frac{\Gamma\left(\frac{n-1}{2}+j\right)}{\Gamma\left(\frac{n-1}{2}\right)\Gamma(j+1)}(1-\rho)^{\frac{n-1}{2}}\rho^j, \quad j = 0, 1, 2, \cdots \tag{4.3}$$

Observe that this expression has close similarity with that of the p.d.f. of Beta distribution of type I, though not the exact one.

Also

$$f_{n-1+2j}(z) = \frac{e^{-\frac{z}{2}} z^{\frac{n-1+2j}{2}-1}}{2^{\frac{n-1+2j}{2}}\Gamma\left(\frac{n-1+2j}{2}\right)}, \quad z > 0 \tag{4.4}$$

Thus, the random variable Z follows chi-square distribution with $(n-1+2j)$ d.f., i.e., $Z \sim \chi_{(n-1+2j)}^2$.

Using expression in equation (4.2), Kocherlakota and Kocherlakota [16] have provided the expression for the joint p.d.f. of $(\hat{C}_{p1}, \hat{C}_{p2})$. This is discussed in detail now.

Suppose $\theta_i = C_{pi} \times \sqrt{\frac{n-1}{1-\rho^2}}$ and $Y_i = \frac{W_i}{1-\rho^2}$, for $i = 1, 2$. Then from equation (4.1), the plug-in estimator of C_{pi} can be re-written as

$$\hat{C}_{pi} = \frac{\theta_i}{\sqrt{Y_i}} = T_i, \quad \text{say} \tag{4.5}$$

for $i = 1, 2$.

Then using equation (4.2), the joint p.d.f. of $(\hat{C}_{p1}, \hat{C}_{pq})$ will be

$$g(t_1, t_2) = \sum_{r=0}^{\infty} nb\left(r, \frac{n-1}{2}, \rho^2\right) \times \left[\prod_{j=1}^{2} \left\{ \frac{2\theta_j^2}{t_j^3} \times f_{n-1+2r}\left(\frac{\theta_j}{t_j}\right)^2 \right\}\right] \tag{4.6}$$

Also under the assumption of statistical normality of the underlying distribution, Chou and Owen [10] have derived the expressions for the expectation and variance of $\hat{C}_{pi}$ as

$$E\left[\hat{C}_{pi}\right] = \left\{ \frac{\Gamma(\frac{n-2}{2})}{\Gamma(\frac{n-1}{2})} \times \sqrt{\frac{n-1}{2}} \right\} \times C_{pi} \tag{4.7}$$

$$V\left[\hat{C}_{pi}\right] = \left[\frac{n-1}{n-3} - \frac{n-1}{2} \times \left\{ \frac{\Gamma(\frac{n-2}{2})}{\Gamma(\frac{n-1}{2})} \right\}^2 \right] \times C_{pi}^2 \tag{4.8}$$

Therefore, using equations (4.6) and (4.7), Koccherlakota and Kocherlakota [16] have derived the expectation of $\hat{C}_{p1}\hat{C}_{p2}$ as

$$E\left(\hat{C}_{p1}\hat{C}_{p2}\right) = \left\{ \sum_{r=0}^{\infty} \frac{\Gamma\left(\frac{n-2}{2}+r\right)\Gamma\left(\frac{n-2}{2}+r\right)\Gamma\left(\frac{n-1}{2}+r\right)}{\Gamma\left(\frac{n-1}{2}+r\right)\Gamma\left(\frac{n-1}{2}+r\right)\Gamma\left(\frac{n-1}{2}\right)} \rho^{2r} \right\}$$
$$\times (1-\rho)^{\frac{n-1}{2}-1} \times \left(\frac{n-1}{2}\right) \times C_{p1}C_{p2} \tag{4.9}$$

Observe that, since the original random variables viz., X_1 and X_2, characterizing the quality characteristics under consideration, are correlated (the concerned correlation coefficient being ρ), $\hat{C}_{p1}$ and $\hat{C}_{p2}$ will also be correlated under the same bivariate set-up. Kocherlakota and Kocherlakota [16] have derived the expression for the corresponding covariance as

$$Cov\left(\hat{C}_{p1}, \hat{C}_{p2}\right) = C_{p1}C_{p2} \times b_{n-1}^2 \times {}_2F_1\left[\frac{1}{2}, \frac{1}{2}; \frac{n-1}{2}; \rho^2\right] \tag{4.10}$$

where

$$b_{n-1} = \sqrt{\frac{n-1}{2}} \times \frac{\Gamma\left(\frac{n-2}{2}\right)}{\Gamma\left(\frac{n-1}{2}\right)} \qquad (4.11)$$

and

$$_2F_1\left[\alpha, \beta; \gamma; z\right] = \sum_{r=0}^{\infty} \frac{\Gamma(\alpha+r)\,\Gamma(\beta+r)\,\Gamma(\gamma)}{\Gamma(\alpha)\,\Gamma(\beta)\,\Gamma(\gamma+r)} \times z^r \qquad (4.12)$$

for $|z| < 1$, is a hypergeometric function.

Since we now have the expressions for the variance of $\hat{C}_{pi}$, for $i = 1, 2$ [vide equation (4.8)] and covariance between $\hat{C}_{p1}$ and $\hat{C}_{p2}$ [vide equation (4.10)], the correlation coefficient between $\hat{C}_{p1}$ and $\hat{C}_{p2}$ can be obtained as

$$\rho_{\hat{C}_{p1},\ \hat{C}_{p2}} = \left[\frac{_2F_1\left[\alpha, \beta; \gamma; z\right]}{\frac{n-1}{n-3} - b_{n-1}^2}\right] \times b_{n-1}^2 \qquad (4.13)$$

Kocherlakota and Kocherlakota [16] have also discussed about testing the following hypotheses:

$$H_0 : \quad C_{p1} \le c_0 \text{ or } C_{p2} \le c_0 \quad \text{The process is not capable}$$
$$H_1 : \quad C_{p1} > c_0 \text{ and } C_{p2} > c_0 \quad \text{The process is capable}$$

where c_0 is the desired capability level (threshold), which must at least be attained by a process, in order to be capable.

To test this set of hypotheses, Kocherlakota and Kocherlakota [16] have defined the critical region as $\left[\hat{C}_{p1} > c, \hat{C}_{p2} > c\right]$. Observe that, c, which is generally different from c_0, is determined from the data itself, using bivariate χ^2 distribution, so that the probability of type I error is fixed at some small value α. Generally, α is fixed at 0.05 or 0.01.

Observe that, Kocherlakota and Kocherlakota [16] did not suggest any bivariate process capability index (BPCI). Rather, they have derived expression for the joint density of the plug-in estimators of C_p values for two individual quality characteristics. At the same time, they have not denied the existence of the correlation between these two quality characteristics either. Also, these expressions are very much computation-centric and hence certain amount of computer coding experience is a prerequisite to use this. Also, one needs to define BPCI(s) for easier representation of process performance.

Pal [23] first proposed a set of BPCIs, which are bivariate analogues of C_p, C_{pk}, and C_{pm}. It is evident that, being bivariate analogues of C_p, C_{pk}, and C_{pm}, these BPCIs are based on bivariate normality assumption of the underlying process distribution. Therefore, if X_1 and X_2 are two random variables characterizing two (correlated) quality characteristics, then $(Y_1, Y_2) \sim BN(\mu_1, \mu_2, \sigma_1^2, \sigma_2^2, \rho)$.

Following Taam et al. [28]'s approach, Pal [23] has defined bivariate analogue of C_p as

$$
\begin{aligned}
BC_p &= \frac{(USL_1 - LSL_1)(USL_2 - LSL_2)}{\pi \chi^2_{2,0.9973} \sqrt{\sigma_1^2 \sigma_2^2 - \sigma_{12}^2}} \\
&= \frac{(USL_1 - LSL_1)(USL_2 - LSL_2)}{37.1745 \sqrt{\sigma_1^2 \sigma_2^2 - \sigma_{12}^2}}
\end{aligned}
\tag{4.14}
$$

Recall that in the context of univariate peocess capability analysis, C_{pm} can be alternatively written as $C_{pm} = C_p \times \{\sigma^2 + (\mu - T)^2\}^{-1/2}$. Similarly, Pal [23] has defined a bivariate analogue of C_{pm} as

$$
BC_{pm} = \frac{BC_p}{\sqrt{1 + \frac{\tau^2}{n}}}
\tag{4.15}
$$

where n is the sample size,

$$
\begin{aligned}
\tau^2 &= \frac{n}{\sigma_1^2 \, \sigma_2^2 \, (1 - \rho^2)} \times \{\sigma_2^2(\mu_1 - T_1)^2 + \sigma_1^2(\mu_2 - T_2)^2 \\
&\quad -2\sigma_{12}(\mu_1 - T_1)(\mu_2 - T_2)\} \\
&= n \, (\boldsymbol{\mu} - \boldsymbol{T})^{'} \Sigma^{-1} (\boldsymbol{\mu} - \boldsymbol{T}),
\end{aligned}
\tag{4.16}
$$

$\boldsymbol{\mu} = \begin{pmatrix} \mu_1 \\ \mu_2 \end{pmatrix}$ is the mean vector and $\Sigma = \begin{pmatrix} \sigma_1^2 & \sigma_{12} \\ \sigma_{12} & \sigma_2^2 \end{pmatrix}$ is the dispersion matrix for the two correlated quality characteristics under consideration.

As has already been discussed, BC_p and BC_{pm} are defined similar to MC_p and MC_{pm} (defined by Taam ey al. [28]). However, it has been observed by several researchers that, MC_p and MC_{pm} grossly over-estimate process capability [refer Pan and Lee [24] and the references therein]. Accordingly, BC_p and BC_{pm} also suffer from the same problem of overestimation. Castagliola and Castellanos [4] have confirmed the same based on simulation study.

Next, Pal [23] defined bivariate analogue of C_{pk}, viz., BC_{pk}. For this, he explored relationship between C_{pk} and proportion of nonconformance (PNC). The logic behind this is, C_{pk} being an yield based PCI, i.e., a PCI having exact relationship with PNC, its bivariate analogue (BC_{pk}) should also have similar relationship with the corresponding PNC.

Now, for a process with two correlated quality characteristics and rectangular specification region (which is the most common type of specification region in practice), proportion of nonconformance (P) can be defined as

$$p = P \text{ [Probability of producing an item, which does not}$$
conform to at least one of the preassigned specification limits]
$$= 1 - P[L_1 \leq X_1 \leq U_1 \ \& \ L_2 \leq X_2 \leq U_2]$$
$$= 1 - [\{P(X_1 \leq U_1 \ \& \ X_2 \leq U_2) - P(X_1 \leq L_1 \ \& \ X_2 \leq U_2)\}$$
$$\qquad - \{P(X_1 \leq L_1 \ \& \ X_2 \leq L_2) - P(X_1 \leq U_1 \ \& \ X_2 \leq L_2)\}]$$
$$= 1 - [\Phi_2(c_1, d_1, \rho) - \Phi_2(c_2, d_1, \rho) + \Phi_2(c_2, d_2, \rho) - \Phi_2(c_1, d_2, \rho)]$$

$$(4.17)$$

where $c_1 = \frac{U_1 - \mu_1}{\sigma_1}$, $c_2 = \frac{\mu_1 - L_1}{\sigma_1}$, $d_1 = \frac{U_2 - \mu_2}{\sigma_2}$, $d_2 = \frac{\mu_2 - L_2}{\sigma_2}$, and Φ_2 is the joint cdf of bivariate standard normal distribution, the values of which are tabulated in [31].

Then following Wierda [30], BC_{pk} can then be defined as

$$BC_{pk} = -\frac{1}{3}\phi^{-1}(p) \qquad (4.18)$$

Now, for univariate processes, Kotz and Johnson [17] have shown that $p = 2\Phi(-3C_{pk})$, when $\mu = T$; otherwise $p \neq 2\Phi(-3C_{pk})$. Hence, under bivariate set-up, $BC_{pk} = -\frac{1}{3}\phi^{-1}(p)$ is true only when $\boldsymbol{\mu} = \boldsymbol{T}$, i.e., $\mu_i = T_i$, for $i = 1, 2$.

Pal [23] himself did not propose any bivariate analogue of C_{pmk}. However, similar to the bivariate generalization of C_{pm}, as given in equation (4.15), bivariate generalization of C_{pmk} can be given by

$$BC_{pmk} = \frac{BC_{pk}}{\sqrt{1 + \frac{\tau^2}{n}}} \qquad (4.19)$$

Observe that, since BC_{pmk} is a hybrid of BC_{pk} and BC_{pm}, it will inherit their drawbacks, as discussed above, as well.

Pal [23] suggested using the lower confidence bound (LCB) of the respective PCI to decide whether the process is capable or not. In this context, note that although the theoretical distributions of BC_p, BC_{pk}, and BC_{pm} are very complicated and hence are difficult to handle (particularly by the practitioner), one can opt for bootstrap method to obtain the empirical distribution of such BPCIs, using computer programming.

Apart from proportion of nonconformance, threshold value also plays an important role from the perspective of interpreting a PCI value. It is actually a value of the PCI itself below which the process is considered to be incapable. Usually, threshold value is computed for the PCIs measuring potential process capability, i.e., PCIs similar/analogous to C_p (refer Chatterjee and Chakraborty [8]), the idea being, if a process is not even potentially capable, then there is no point in computing its actual capability value.

Since threshold value plays an important role in deciding about the overall health of a process, it should be properly formulated in order to avoid any

Bivariate Process Capability Indices (BPCIs) 85

subjectivity and scope for manipulation induced thereby. Pal [23] did not propose any expression for the threshold value of BC_p. However, following Chatterjee and Chakraborty's [7] approach, this can be formulated as follows:

When a process, which is assumed to follow bivariate normal distribution, is just capable, then $U_i = \mu_i + 3\sigma_i$ and $L_i = \mu_i - 3\sigma_i$, for $i = 1, 2$. Note that since Pal [23] assumed the specification region to be rectangular, hence ρ (or σ_{12}) is not incorporated in these expressions. Thus, putting these expressions in equation (4.14), the expression for the threshold value of BC_p can be obtained as

$$
\begin{aligned}
BC_p^{(T)} &= \frac{(\mu_1 + 3\sigma_1 - \mu_1 + 3\sigma_1)(\mu_2 + 3\sigma_2 - \mu_2 + 3\sigma_2)}{37.1745\sqrt{\sigma_1^2\sigma_2^2 - \sigma_{12}^2}} \\
&= \frac{6\sigma_1 \times 6\sigma_2}{37.1745\sigma_1\sigma_2\sqrt{1 - \rho_{12}^2}} \\
&= \frac{0.9684}{\sqrt{1 - \rho_{12}^2}}
\end{aligned}
\tag{4.20}
$$

The threshold values of BC_p for various value of ρ are given in Table 4.1. Since the positive and negative values of ρ will lead to the same value of $BC_p^{(T)}$, absolute values of ρ are considered in the table.

TABLE 4.1: Threshold values of BC_p for various values of ρ

ρ	0	0.1	0.2	0.3	0.4	0.5	0.6	0.7	0.8	0.9	1.0
$BC_p^{(T)}$	0.968	0.973	0.988	1.015	1.057	1.118	1.211	1.356	1.614	2.222	∞

Interestingly, the contradicting common industrial practice of considering "1" as the threshold value, irrespective of the nature of the process or type of the specification limits, the expression of the threshold value of BC_p is found to vary positively with the correlation coefficient between the two quality characteristics, which is quite desirable in a sense that underlying correlation structure should play an important role in deciding capability level of a process.

To address the drawbacks of Pal's [23] BPCIs, Castagliola and Castellanos [4] have defined two BPCIs, analogous to C_p and C_{pk}, for processes following bivariate normal distribution, based on the concept of proportion of non-conformance (PNC).

Suppose the rectangular tolerance region is denoted by A. Also suppose, as before, $\boldsymbol{X} = (X_1, X_2)'$ is a random vector characterizing two quality characteristics under study, such that $\boldsymbol{X} \sim N_2(\boldsymbol{\mu}, \Sigma)$. Then, Σ can be alternatively expressed as $\Sigma = RVR'$, where $R = \Sigma = \begin{pmatrix} u_{11} & u_{21} \\ u_{12} & U_{22} \end{pmatrix}$ is a 2×2 matrix of the eigen vectors of Σ, such that $\boldsymbol{u_1} = (u_{11}, u_{12})'$ and $\boldsymbol{u_2} = (u_{21}, u_{22})'$ are the two corresponding eigen vectors and $v = \Sigma = \begin{pmatrix} \sigma_1^2 & 0 \\ 0 & \sigma_2^2 \end{pmatrix}$. Also, if θ is the rotation angle, then R can be alternatively written as $R = \begin{pmatrix} \cos\theta & -\sin\theta \\ \sin\theta & \cos\theta \end{pmatrix}$.

Suppose, D_1 and D_2 are two straight lines passing through the mean vector μ of X, such that they have the directions u_1 and u_2 in such a manner that the (X_1, X_2) plane gets divided into four equal regions A_1, A_2, A_3, A_4, i.e.,

$$P[\text{Any particular observation will lie in the region } A_i]$$
$$= P(X \in A_i) = \frac{1}{4} \tag{4.21}$$

Also suppose, the convex polygons generated by the intersections of A_1, A_2, A_3 and A_4 with A are denoted by Q_1, Q_2, Q_3, and Q_4. Let $q_i = P(X \in Q_i)$ and $p_i = \frac{1}{4} - q_i$, for $i = 1, 2$.

Then, using the concept of convex polygon, Castagliola and Castellanos [4] have defined a BPCI, analogous to C_{pk}, as

$$BC_{pk}^{(CC)} = \frac{1}{3} \min \left\{ -\Phi^{-1}(2p_1), -\Phi^{-1}(2p_2), -\Phi^{-1}(2p_3), -\Phi^{-1}(2p_4) \right\} \tag{4.22}$$

Castagliola and Castellanos [4] have also defined a bivariate counter part of C_p as

$$BC_p^{(CC)} = -\frac{1}{3}\Phi^{(-1)}\left(\frac{p}{2}\right) \tag{4.23}$$

where $p = p_1 + p_2 + p_3 + p_4$.

The authors have discussed a step-by-step methodology to obtain $BC_p^{(CC)}$ and $BC_{pk}^{(CC)}$ values from the sample observations.

As is evident from the above discussion, the basic drawback of $BC_p^{(CC)}$ and $BC_{pk}^{(CC)}$ is the complexity in their definitions and difficulties in interpreting their values. Since formulation of these BPCIs involve sophisticated mathematical theories, which the practitioners may not always be conversant with, they find very limited application in practice. Although nowadays, with the increasing application of various statistical packages, computation is not much an issue, still, in order to properly grasp the implication of a PCI value, its formulation should ideally be easily understood.

While making a simulation study to make a comparative performance analysis of some BPCIs (some of which are originally defined under multivariate set-up), it has been observed that the values of Castagliola and Castellanos [4]'s BPCIs are close to those of Bothe [1]. Interestingly, Bothe's [1] MPCI is based on independence of the quality characteristics (this will be discussed in detail in Chapter 9). This indicates that $BC_p^{(CC)}$ and $BC_{pk}^{(CC)}$

Bivariate Process Capability Indices (BPCIs) 87

may not capture the underlying correlation between two quality characteristics properly. However, this requires detailed investigation before arriving at any final conclusion regarding this. Threshold value of $BC_p^{(CC)}$ is also required to be formulated to avoid ambiguity in deciding whether a process is capable or not.

To have thorough insight about any PCI, one needs to have thorough knowledge about its statistical distribution (refer Vannman [29]). Although Kocherlakota and Kocherlakota [16] derived joint statistical distribution of two individual C_p values, they did not propose any closed-form BPCI for bivariate processes. On the other hand, the statistical distributions of none of the PCIs defined by Pal [23], and Castagliola and Castellanos [4] have been studied so far. This will be an interesting future problem to study.

4.3 Bivariate Generalization of Univariate PCIs for Unilateral Specification Limits

The BPCIs discussed so far are defined for processes for which both the quality characteristics have two specification limits, viz., USL and LSL. However in reality, there may exist bivariate processes for which both the quality characteristics have only USL or LSL, i.e., both the quality characteristics are either of higher the better type (i.e., having LSL only) or of lower the better type, i.e., having LSL only. A detailed discussion on univariate PCIs for unilateral specification limit is given in Chapter 3 (Section 3.3).

Similar to the joint pdf of two sample C_p values, Kocherlakota and Kocherlakota [16] have also derived expression for the joint pdf of two sample C_{pu} values or two sample C_{pl} values.

Without loss of generality, suppose, for two correlated quality characteristics, only USL exists. Then plug-in estimator of C_{pu} for the *ith* quality characteristic can be defined as

$$\hat{C}_{pui} = \frac{USL_i - \overline{X}_i}{3S_i}$$

$$= \frac{U_i - \mu_i - (\overline{X}_i - \mu_i)}{3S_i}$$

$$= \frac{3\sqrt{n}\, \frac{U_i - \mu_i}{3\sigma_i} - \frac{(\overline{X}_i - \mu_i)}{\frac{\sigma_i}{n_i}}}{3\sqrt{\frac{n}{n-1} \times \frac{(n-1)S_i^2}{\sigma_i^2}}}$$

$$= -\frac{Z_i + \delta_i}{3\sqrt{\frac{nW_i}{n-1}}} \qquad (4.24)$$

where $Z_i = \frac{(\overline{X}_i - \mu_i)}{\frac{\sigma_i}{n_i}}$ and $\delta = -3\sqrt{n}C_{pui}$, for $i = 1, 2$.

Bivariate Process Capability Indices (BPCIs) 88

Observe that, $(Z_1, Z_2) \sim N_2(0, 0, 1, 1, \rho)$ and $((n-1)S_1^2, (n-1)S_2^2)$ jointly follows bivariate χ^2 distribution with $(n-1)$ degrees of freedom (d.f.) and correlation coefficient ρ. Consequently, (W_1, W_2) follows bivariate χ^2 distribution. Let us now define $T_i = \frac{Z_i + \delta_i}{\sqrt{\frac{W_i}{n-1}}}$, for $i = 1, 2$.

Then, (T_1, T_2) jointly follow noncentral bivariate t distribution with $(n-1)$ d.f. and the corresponding noncentrality parameter is a function of $(\delta_1, \delta_2, \rho)$. Using this, the joint pdf of (T_1, T_2) and consequently, the joint pdf of $(\hat{C}_{pu1}, \hat{C}_{pu2})$ can be obtained.

However, similar to the case of bilateral specification limits, for unilateral specification limits also, Kocherlakota and Kocherlakota [16] did not propose any BPCI.

Apart from processes having quality characteristics with bilateral and unilateral specification limits, BPCIs also find ample application in cases where the corresponding specification region is circular. In fact this application of BPCI is more important than the other two types of specification regions in a sense that for bilateral and unilateral specification regions, BPCIs can be computed as special cases of multivariate process capability indices (MPCIs), taking the number of quality characteristics (q) as 2. However, for circular specification region, the problem is unique and hence requires specially designed BPCIs. This will be discussed in detail in the next section.

4.4 Bivariate PCIs for Circular Specification Region

Although, quality characteristics with bilateral (two-sided) and unilateral (one-sided) specification limits are mostly encountered in practice, there are still some parts which remain grossly unattended in literature. Computing capability of a process with quality characteristics having circular specification region is one of such cases.

Circularity is the condition of a surface where all points of the surface intersected by any plane perpendicular to a common axis are equidistant from that axis. Following the concept of *"Geometric dimensioning and tolerancing" (GD&T)*, circular specifications can be observed in processes engaging in drilling a hole or from ballistic point of view, hitting a target within a circular region (refer Laurent [19] and Davis et al. [12]).

The uniqueness of the quality characteristics with circular tolerance region is that the so called "USL" and/ or "LSL" does not exist and hence classical PCI's are not applicable here. Usually, the following steps are applied to construct the circular (positional) specification region:

1. Identify the target location (center) of the hole or the point to hit.

Bivariate Process Capability Indices (BPCIs)

2. Treat the location as origin, i.e., the (0,0) point of coordinate geometry and draw the X and Y axes from that point.

3. Draw a circle with center at this (0,0) point and radius as the preassigned tolerable distance from this point. This will give a circular specification region.

In this context, following Karl et al. [15], the problem of circular specification may also be designed as a multivariate (specifically, bivariate) process capability problem with X_1 and X_2 being the two correlated variables along the two axes of the specification region. Culpepper [11] has observed that, in the analysis of radial error for two dimensional case, X_1 measures the *azimuth or deflection error*, and X_2 measures the *range or pitch error*. Azimuth and range errors are associated with ground or horizontal targets, and deflection and pitch errors are associated with vertical targets.

Both Davis et al. [12] Phillips and Cho [26] discussed about various quality improvement issues for processes with circular or spherical specification regions.

Davis et al. [12] observed that, in case of shooting an object, its coordinates of impact are of particular importance. This makes the problem two dimensional with circular specification limits.

On the other hand, if the problem is to shoot an object in the sky (e.g., drone or any type of aircraft) or to launch a satellite in a prespecific orbit, the problem becomes three dimensional. This increase in dimension, as compared to the previous case, is due to the fact that here the target object is not fixed at a particular place. As a result, its positional coordinates also keep changing, although the target destination is known a priori (refer Davis et al. [12]).

Suppose in the two-dimensional case, the target location has the coordinates (x_0, y_0), while (X, Y) is its actual positional coordinates. Let $D_1 = x_0 - X$ and $D_2 = y_0 - Y$ denote the deviation from the target for the two coordinates. Then the radial distance between the original position and the target position will be

$$\Lambda = \sqrt{D_1^2 + D_2^2} \tag{4.25}$$

In order to define a BPCI for circular specification region, Davis et al. [12] have made the assumption that $D_i \overset{iid}{\sim} N(0, \sigma^2)$, for $i = 1, 2$. Therefore, the distribution of $\Lambda = \sqrt{D_1^2 + D_2^2}$ will be of interest.

Now, since $D_i \sim N(0, \sigma^2)$, $Y_i = \frac{D_i}{\sigma}$ is also normally distributed and hence $Y_i^2 \sim \chi_1^2$, for $i = 1, 2$, where χ_1^2 denotes chi-square distribution with one degree of freedom. Therefore, using additive property of chi-square distribution, $Y = Y_1^2 + Y_2^2 \sim \chi_2^2$.

In this context, if $Z \sim \chi_k^2$, then pdf of Z is given by

$$f_Z(z) = \frac{1}{2^{k/2}\Gamma(k/2)} \times z^{\frac{k}{2}-1} \times e^{-z/2}, \quad z > 0 \tag{4.26}$$

Similarly, pdf of Y will be

$$f_Y(y) = \frac{1}{2} e^{y/2}, \quad y \geq 0 \tag{4.27}$$

Recall that $D_i = \sigma Y_i$, for $i = 1, 2$ and the distribution, in which one is particularly interested, is that of

$$\Lambda = \sqrt{D_1^2 + D_2^2} = \sqrt{\sigma^2 Y_1^2 + \sigma^2 Y_2^2} = \sigma \sqrt{Y_1^2 + Y_2^2} = \sigma \sqrt{Y} \tag{4.28}$$

Therefore, $Y = \frac{\Lambda^2}{\sigma^2}$ and hence the Jacobian of transformation will be $J = \frac{2\Lambda}{\sigma^2}$. Therefore, from equation 4.27 the pdf of Λ will be

$$\begin{aligned} f_\Lambda(\lambda) &= \frac{1}{2} \times \frac{2\lambda}{\sigma^2} \times e^{-\frac{\lambda^2}{2\sigma^2}} \\ &= \frac{\lambda}{\sigma^2} e^{-\frac{\lambda^2}{2\sigma^2}}, \quad \lambda \geq 0 \end{aligned} \tag{4.29}$$

Suppose, the specification region under consideration is a circle with radius "U." In order to define a BPCI for circular specification region, Davis et al. [12] used the concept of "minimum fraction nonconforming" (mfn) items produced by a process. For the present purpose, mfn can be formulated as follows:

$$\begin{aligned} mfn &= \int_U^\infty f_\Lambda f(\lambda) d\lambda \tag{4.30} \\ &= \int_U^\infty \frac{\lambda}{\sigma^2} \times e^{-\frac{\lambda^2}{2\sigma^2}} \, d\lambda \tag{4.31} \\ &= \int_U^\infty e^{-\frac{\lambda^2}{2\sigma^2}} \, d\left(\frac{\lambda^2}{2\sigma^2}\right) \\ &= e^{-\frac{U^2}{2\sigma^2}} \tag{4.32} \end{aligned}$$

Davis et al. [12] have considered the expression for mfn itself as a BPCI with $\frac{U}{\sigma}$ being replaced by $R = \frac{U}{\sigma}$, the spread ratio. Therefore, the final expression for their proposed BPCI is

$$mfn = e^{-\frac{R^2}{2}} \tag{4.33}$$

Interestingly, mfn is not a BPCI in its true sense—rather it is the probability of nonconforming items produced by the process. Hence, unlike conventional BPCIs, mfn is of lower the better type.

Also observe that, this definition of BPCI is based on σ only and hence should be considered as a BPCI measuring potential process capability for processes with circular specification region. Therefore, expression for a threshold value is required in this case as well, so as to decide whether the concerned process is potentially capable or not.

Philips and Cho [26] handled the problem of quality assessment of a process with circular specification region from loss theoretic perspective. They adopted the same assumptions, as were made by Davis et al. [12].

If $x = (x_1, x_2, \cdots, x_q)'$ denotes a "q" component vector of the values of the quality characteristics, $T = (T_1, T_2, \cdots, T_q)'$ denotes the corresponding value of the target vector and C is a $q \times q$ positive definite (p.d.) matrix of loss coefficients, then for the nominal the best type of quality characteristics (as is the case here), the multivariate quality characteristic loss function (MQLF) will be defined as

$$L(x) = (x - T)' C (x - T) \tag{4.34}$$

Observe that, $L(x)$ is a quadratic loss function and since C is p.d., $L(x) > 0$ for all possible values of x and T.

Also, from equation (4.34), the expected loss can be computed as

$$E[L(X)] = (\mu - T)'C(\mu - T) + trace(C\Sigma) \tag{4.35}$$

Unlike general convention, Philips and Cho [26] opined that, although $X \sim N_q(\mu, \Sigma)$, since a specification limit is imposed on it, the actual underlying distribution of the set of quality characteristics should be truncated normal.

Thus, suppose, $\tilde{X}$ follows truncated normal distribution with truncated mean vector μ_T and truncated dispersion matrix Σ_T. Then similar to equation (4.35) we have,

$$E\left[L(\tilde{X})\right] = (\mu_T - T)'C(\mu_T - T) + trace(C\Sigma_T) \tag{4.36}$$

Suppose, R denotes the radius of the circular specification region. Philips and Cho [26] have considered the following three types of costs associated with the cost to quality model:

1. C_1 : Cost incurred due to rejecting an item, i.e., which falls outside the radius R;

2. C_2 : Cost of inspection per product;

3. Cost of loss in quality due to deviation from stipulated target.

Suppose (x_1, x_2) denotes the coordinates of a particular item and let us define $r = \sqrt{x_1^2 + x_2^2}$.

In the first case, the expected loss is

$$E[\text{Cost due to rejection of item}] = C_1[1 - P(r \leq R)] \qquad (4.37)$$

Similarly, for the second case

$$E[\text{Cost due to inspection}] = C_2 \qquad (4.38)$$

and hence total expected cost will be

$$
\begin{aligned}
& E[Total\ Cost] \\
=\ & E[\text{Cost due to loss of quality}] + E[\text{Cost due to rejection of item}] \\
+\ & E[\text{Cost due to inspection}] \\
=\ & E[L(\tilde{Y})] + C_1[1 - P(r \leq R)] + C_2 \\
=\ & (\boldsymbol{\mu_T} - \boldsymbol{T})'C(\boldsymbol{\mu_T} - \boldsymbol{T}) + trace(C\Sigma_T) + C_1[1 - P(r \leq R)] + C_2
\end{aligned}
$$
$$(4.39)$$

Since the expected total cost, as given in equation (4.39) is a function of R only, by minimizing this, the optimal value of R, say R^*, can be obtained, which in turn, will give the most economical screening process.

Note that, although Phillips and Cho [26] adopted a very pragmatic approach to propose a model for deriving optimum radius of the circular specification region, they did not define any process capability index to assess the performance of such processes.

Krishnamoorthi [18] was among the first to define a conventional PCI for circular specification region. He proposed the following two PCIs for this purpose:

$$PC_p = \frac{\frac{\pi}{4}D^2}{9\pi\sigma^2} = \frac{1}{36} \times \frac{D^2}{\sigma^2} \qquad (4.40)$$

$$PC_{pk} = \frac{D^2}{4\left[\sqrt{(\overline{X_1} - a)^2 + (\overline{X_2} - b)^2} + 3\sigma\right]^2} \qquad (4.41)$$

where D is the diameter of the circular tolerance region; σ is the (equal) standard deviation of the X_1 and X_2 coordinates and (a, b) is the target center. When the standard deviation of the X_1 and X_2 co-ordinates, say σ_1 and σ_2, are not equal, $\sigma = \max(\sigma_1, \sigma_2)$. Thus, Krishnamoorthi [18] considered the problem of assessing capability of a process with circular specification region as a univariate one.

Observe that PC_p provides the potential capability of a process and PC_{pk} measures its actual capability. Interestingly, although Krishnamoorthi [18] named the second PCI in equation (4.41) as PC_{pk}, it is actually analogous to the univariate PCI, C_{pm}, since it incorporates the criteria for quantifying deviation from the stipulated target (see denominator of PC_{pk} in equation 4.41). Also, despite being unitless, PC_p and PC_{pk} as basically, ratios of two areas, both of which are expressed in squared units. Hence, to follow the general convention, square-root of these PCIs should be used.

Unlike Krishnamoorthi [18], who considered actual coordinates of the points as the quality characteristic and hence used their arithemetic mean (a.m.) and standard deviation (s.d.) for defining PCI, Bothe [2] considered radial distance of the actual position of a point from its stipulated target as the quality characteristic. In this context, if (x_{1i}, x_{2i}) denotes the actual coordinates of the ith point and $(0, 0)$ is the target, then radial distance (or radial error) of the ith point is given by $r_i = \sqrt{x_{1i}^2 + x_{2i}^2}$, for $i = 1(1)n$.

Consider the following notations:

1. "n" is the sample size;

2. $\widehat{\mu_C} = \frac{\sum_{i=1}^{n} r_{C,i}}{n}$;

3. $r_{C,i} = \sqrt{(x_i - \overline{x})^2 + (y_i - \overline{y})^2}$;

4. $\overline{MR} = \frac{\sum_{i=2}^{n} MR_i}{n-1}$ where MR_is are obtained from moving range chart for $i = 1(1)n$;

5. $\widehat{\sigma_{ST}} = \frac{\overline{MR}}{1.128}$ is the short-term standard deviation with 1.28 being the value of d_2 for $n = 2$;

6. $\widehat{\sigma_{LT}} = \frac{1}{c_4} \sqrt{\frac{\sum_{i=1}^{n} (r_i - \overline{r})^2}{n-1}}$ is the long-term standard deviation;

7. $\widehat{\mu_r} = \frac{\sum_{i=1}^{n} r_i}{n}$;

8. c_4 is a constant expressed as a function of "n."

Using these notations, Bothe [2] has defined the following MPCIs:

$$\left. \begin{array}{l} \widehat{C}_P = \frac{USL - \widehat{\mu_C}}{3\widehat{\sigma}_{ST,C}} \\ \widehat{P}_P = \frac{USL - \widehat{\mu_C}}{3\widehat{\sigma}_{LT,C}} \\ \widehat{C}_{PK} = \frac{USL - \widehat{\mu_r}}{3\widehat{\sigma}_{ST}} \\ \widehat{P}_{PK} = \frac{USL - \widehat{\mu_r}}{3\widehat{\sigma}_{LT}} \end{array} \right\}$$

Interestingly, the BPCIs by Krishnamoorthi [18] and Bothe [2] are based on the following assumptions:

1. Variance along the two axes are equal (i.e., assumption of homoscedasticity). Even if these variances are not equal, maximum of these two

variances is considered as the representative variance. However, if values of these variances are widely apart, this assumption will not be a realistic one.

2. The random variables corresponding to the two axes are mutually independent. This assumption is not always feasible either, due to various practical constraints.

Violation of these two assumptions, which is often the case, leads to an elliptical specification region, rather than the originally assumed circular one.

Moreover, Bothe [2] defined PCIs similar to C_p and C_{pk}, for the quality characteristic "radial distance" between the actual center and the target center. Interestingly, even if the above mentioned assumptions are true, i.e., $(X_1, X_2) \sim N_2(\mu_1, \mu_2, \sigma^2, \sigma^2, \rho)$, distribution of $r = \sqrt{X_1^2 + X_2^2}$ does not follow normal distribution—rather it follows radial error distribution (refer Scheur [27] and Chew and Boyce [9]). Hence PCIs similar to C_p and C_{pk}, which are defined primarily for normally distributed quality characteristics, will not be applicable in the present scenario.

Observe that, both Krishnamoorthi [18] and Bothe [2] have considered the capability assessment problem of processes with circular specification region, as a univariate one. Following Davis et al. [12], Chatterjee and Chakraborty [6] have handled the said problem from bivariate perspective.

Ignoring the above mentioned assumptions, suppose

$$\boldsymbol{X} = (X_1, X_2) \quad \sim \quad N_2(\mu_1, \mu_2, \sigma_1^2, \sigma_2^2, \rho = \frac{\sigma_{12}}{\sigma_1 \sigma_2})$$

$$\text{i.e., } \boldsymbol{X} \quad \sim \quad N_2(\boldsymbol{\mu}, \Sigma)$$

where $\boldsymbol{\mu} = (\mu_1, \mu_2)'$ and $\Sigma = \begin{pmatrix} \sigma_1^2 & \sigma_{12} \\ \sigma_{12} & \sigma_2^2 \end{pmatrix}$.

Then following Chatterjee and Chakraborty [6], a BPCI, analogous to C_p, for measuring potential capability of a process, can be defined as the square root of the ratio of the area of circular specification region with diameter "D" units and center at $(0, 0)$; to the area of a constant contour ellipsoidal process region with dispersion matrix Σ and "α" proportion of right tail area.

In this context, for bivariate normal distribution the ellipses of the form $(\boldsymbol{X} - \boldsymbol{\mu})' \Sigma^{-1}(\boldsymbol{X} - \boldsymbol{\mu}) = \text{constant}$, are called "contours of the distribution" or "ellipses of equal concentrations" (refer Mardia et al. [22]).

Now, area of a circular specification region with diameter "D" units and center at $(0, 0)$ is

$$\text{Area of } \left\{ (x_1, x_2) : \frac{x_1^2}{\left(\frac{D}{2}\right)^2} + \frac{x_2^2}{\left(\frac{D}{2}\right)^2} \leq 1 \right\}$$

$$= \pi \times \left(\frac{D}{2}\right)^2 = \left(\frac{\pi}{4}\right) \times D^2 \qquad (4.42)$$

Also

Area of a $100(1 - \alpha)\%$ constant contour elliptical process region

$$= \chi^2_{\alpha,2} \pi \sigma_1 \sigma_2 \sqrt{1 - \rho^2} \qquad (4.43)$$

where $\chi^2_{\alpha,2}$ represents the value of a χ^2 distribution with 2 d.f. that has a right tail area of "α" units.

Hence using equations (4.42) and (4.43) , $C_{p,c}$ can be defined as

$$
\begin{aligned}
C_{p,c} &= \sqrt{\frac{\frac{\pi}{4} D^2}{\chi^2_{\alpha,2} \pi \sigma_1 \sigma_2 \sqrt{1 - \rho^2}}} \\
&= \frac{D}{2\sqrt{\chi^2_{\alpha,2} \sigma_1 \sigma_2 \sqrt{1 - \rho^2}}} \\
&= \frac{D}{2\sqrt{\chi^2_{\alpha,2} \sqrt{|\Sigma|}}} \qquad (4.44)
\end{aligned}
$$

where

$$|\Sigma| = \sigma_1^2 \sigma_2^2 (1 - \rho^2) \qquad (4.45)$$

Interestingly, similar to C_p, $C_{P,c}$ also does not include μ_1 and μ_2 in its definition and it is based only on process dispersion i.e., σ_1 and σ_2 and correlation coefficient (ρ). Therefore, $C_{p,c}$ measures potential process capability only and not the actual one.

Since $C_{p,c}$, by definition, measures process potential only, to quantify actual process capability for circular specification limits, one needs a BPCI analogous to C_{pk}. For this, Chatterjee and Chakraborty [6] defined the following BPCI:

$$C'_{pk,c} = \frac{\frac{D}{2} - \frac{\mu^*}{\sqrt{\pi}}}{\sqrt{\chi^2_{\alpha,2} \sigma_1 \sigma_2 \sqrt{1 - \rho^2}}}, \qquad (4.46)$$

where $\mu^* = \frac{1}{n} \sum_{i=1}^{n} d_i^*$, $d_i^* = \sqrt{(X_{1i} - \mu_1)^2 + (X_{2i} - \mu_2)^2}$ and $\boldsymbol{X}_i = (X_{1i}, X_{2i})'$ for $i = 1(1)n$ and "n" is the number of sample observations.

However, a major problem with indices like PC_{PK} [refer equation (4.41)], $C_P, C_{PK}, P_P,$ and P_{PK} [refer equation (4.42)] and $C'_{pk,c}$ [refer equation (4.46)] is that, all of their definitions include random variables and hence they can not be computed with certainty. In fact, the general convention is to define PCIs based on process parameters only and not based on any sort of estimates of these parameters.

To address this problem, Chatterjee [5] has slightly modified $C'_{pk,c}$.

According to Bothe [2], "a hole center is considered to be within specification region, when its radial distance from the target location is less than the radius of the true position circle". He used average radial distance of the

Bivariate Process Capability Indices (BPCIs)

observations from the target center as the measure of location [refer equation (4.42)].

In this context, Bothe [2] assumed both the specification and the process region to be circular and hence radial distance was appropriate. However, in our case, although the specification region is still circular, the process region is elliptical as here $\Sigma \neq I_2$, the (2×2) identity matrix.

Observe that, for quality characteristics with symmetric bilateral specification limits, C_{pk} can be re-written as

$$C_{pk} = \frac{d - |\mu - M|}{3\sigma} = C_p - \frac{|\mu - M|}{3\sigma}, \tag{4.47}$$

where $|\mu - M|$ measures the deviation of μ from the specification mid-point viz., $T = M = (U + L)/2$. Hence, analogous to the definition of C_{pk} as given in equation (4.47), a PCI for circular specification region can be defined as

$$
\begin{aligned}
C_{pk,c} &= C_{p,c} - \frac{\sqrt{\mu'\mu}}{\sqrt{\chi^2_{\alpha,2}\sigma_1\sigma_2\sqrt{1-\rho^2}}} \\
&= \frac{\frac{D}{2} - \sqrt{\mu'\mu}}{\sqrt{\chi^2_{\alpha,2}\sigma_1\sigma_2\sqrt{1-\rho^2}}}
\end{aligned} \tag{4.48}
$$

Note that, definition of $C_{pk,c}$ in equation (4.48) does not include any random variable and hence goes by the general convention.

Although $C_{pk,c}$ incorporates μ in its definition, it is basically a yield based index—defined similar to C_{pk}. Hence we are required to define a loss based PCI say $C_{pm,c}$ (analogous to C_{pm}), for circular specification region, which will take into account the proximity of the average center of the sample observations toward the target center. In this context, Boyles [3] has thoroughly discussed the advantages of C_{pm} over C_{pk} for bilateral specification limits, especially while computing the proximity of process centering toward the target and since $C_{pm,c}$ is defined analogous to C_{pm}, this is true for it as well.

Recall that C_{pm} can be written as

$$
\begin{aligned}
C_{pm} &= \frac{d}{3\sqrt{\sigma^2 + (\mu - T)^2}} \\
&= \frac{\frac{d}{3\sigma}}{\sqrt{1 + \left(\frac{\mu-T}{\sigma}\right)^2}} = C_p \times \frac{1}{\sqrt{1 + (\frac{\mu-T}{\sigma})^2}}
\end{aligned} \tag{4.49}
$$

Hence, for circular specification region, a loss based PCI, analogous to C_{pm}, can be defined as [refer Chatterjee and Chakraborty [6]],

$$
\begin{aligned}
C_{pm,c} &= C_{p,c} \times \frac{1}{\sqrt{1 + \mu'\Sigma^{-1}\mu}} \\
&= \frac{D}{2\sqrt{\chi^2_{\alpha,2}\sigma_1\sigma_2\sqrt{1-\rho^2}}} \times \frac{1}{\sqrt{1 + \mu'\Sigma^{-1}\mu}}
\end{aligned} \tag{4.50}
$$

Also, C_{pmk} can be redefined as

$$C_{pmk} = \frac{d - |\mu - M|}{3\sqrt{\sigma^2 + (\mu - T)^2}}$$

$$= \frac{\frac{d - |\mu - M|}{3\sigma}}{\sqrt{1 + \left(\frac{\mu - T}{\sigma}\right)^2}}$$

$$= C_{pk} \times \frac{1}{\sqrt{1 + \left(\frac{\mu - T}{\sigma}\right)^2}} \qquad (4.51)$$

Thus similar to C_{pmk} and from equations (4.48) and (4.50), a third generation PCI for circular specification region, can be defined as

$$C_{pmk,c} = \frac{\frac{D}{2} - \sqrt{\mu'\mu}}{\sqrt{\chi_{\alpha,2}^2 \sigma_1 \sigma_2 \sqrt{1 - \rho^2}}} \times \frac{1}{\sqrt{1 + \mu'\Sigma^{-1}\mu}} \qquad (4.52)$$

Finally, similar to Vannman's [29] $C_p(u, v)$, the BPCIs in equations (4.44), (4.48), (4.50), and (4.52) can be unified as

$$C_{p,c}(u, v) = \frac{\frac{D}{2} - u \times \sqrt{\mu'\mu}}{\sqrt{\chi_{\alpha,2}^2 \sigma_1 \sigma_2 \sqrt{1 - \rho^2}}} \times \frac{1}{\sqrt{1 + v\mu'\Sigma^{-1}\mu}} \qquad (4.53)$$

where u and v are two nonnegative parameters. Here, $C_{p,c}(0,0) = C_{p,c}$; $C_{p,c}(1,0) = C_{pk,c}$; $C_{p,c}(0,1) = C_{pm,c}$, and $C_{p,c}(1,1) = C_{pmk,c}$ are defined analogous to C_p, C_{pk}, C_{pm}, and C_{pmk} [refer Chatterjee and Chakraborty [6] and Chatterjee [5]].

Since by definition, $\mu'\mu \geq 0$ and $\mu\Sigma^{-1}\mu \geq 0$ and since Σ is a positive definite matrix, it is easy to observe that

$$\left.\begin{array}{l} C_{p,c}(u, v) \leq C_{p,c}(u, 0) \leq C_{p,c}(0, 0) \\ C_{p,c}(u, v) \leq C_{p,c}(0, v) \leq C_{p,c}(0, 0) \end{array}\right\},$$

for $u = 0, 1$ and $v = 0, 1$.

Note that for the above inequalities to hold good, $\frac{D^2}{4}$ should be greater than $\mu'\mu$ and this is always true provided $C_{pk,c} > 0$, which is generally the case. Hence, the above inequalities hold good in practice.

However, there is no clear-cut relationship between $C_{pk,c}$ and $C_{pmk,c}$. These observations regarding the interrelationships between the member PCI's of $C_{p,c}(u, v)$ are similar to the findings of Kotz and Johnson [17] for C_p, C_{pk}, C_{pm}, and C_{pmk}.

Chatterjee and Chakraborty [6] have also derived the expression for the threshold value of $C_{p,c}$ as

$$C_{p,c}^T = \sqrt{\frac{D}{2 \times \chi_{\alpha,2}^2 \times \sigma_{\min} \times \sqrt{1-\rho^2}}} \tag{4.54}$$

where $\sigma_{\min} = \min(\sigma_1, \sigma_2)$.

Interestingly, when $\rho = 0$ and $\sigma_1 = \sigma_2 = \frac{D}{2}$, the elliptical process region boils down to a circular one. Since the specification region is already a circular, in that case for "just capable" scenario, process region and specification region should coincide and hence threshold value should be one. However, substituting $\rho = 0$ and $\sigma_1 = \sigma_2 = \frac{D}{2}$ in equation (4.54), the threshold value of $C_{p,c}$ will be

$$C_{p,c}^{T*} = \sqrt{\frac{1}{\chi_{\alpha,2}^2}} = \frac{1}{\chi_{\alpha,2}} \tag{4.55}$$

Therefore, $C_{p,c}$ and in general $C_{p,c}(u,v)$ is not very suitable when there is zero or very low correlation between the two variables.

Finally, the threshold value of $C_{p,c}$ can be considered as the threshold value of $C_{pk,c}$, $C_{pm,c}$, and $C_{pmk,c}$ as well since for $\boldsymbol{\mu} = \mathbf{0}$, each of these indices boil down to $C_{p,c}$. Moreover, when $C_{p,c} \geq C_{p,c}^T$ but $C_{pm,c} < C_{p,c}^T$, the process is likely to be off-target. On the other hand, if $C_{pm,c} > C_{p,c}^T$, the process can be considered to be capable. Such observation is true for $C_{pk,c}$ and $C_{pmk,c}$ well.

Following Chatterjee [5], the plug-in estimator of $C_{p,c}(u,v)$ can be defined as

$$\begin{aligned}
\widehat{C}_{p,c}(u,v) &= \frac{\frac{D}{2} - u \times \sqrt{\overline{\boldsymbol{X}}'\overline{\boldsymbol{X}}}}{\sqrt{\chi_{\alpha,2}^2 s_1 s_2 \sqrt{1-r^2}}} \times \frac{1}{\sqrt{1 + v\overline{\boldsymbol{X}}' S^{-1} \overline{\boldsymbol{X}}}} \\
&= \frac{\frac{D}{2} - u \times \sqrt{\overline{\boldsymbol{X}}'\overline{\boldsymbol{X}}}}{\sqrt{\chi_{\alpha,2}^2 \sqrt{|S|}}} \times \frac{1}{\sqrt{1 + v\overline{\boldsymbol{X}}' S^{-1} \overline{\boldsymbol{X}}}}
\end{aligned} \tag{4.56}$$

where $\overline{\boldsymbol{X}} = (\overline{X_1}, \overline{X_2})'$ with $\overline{X_i}$ being the sample mean corresponding to ith axis, for $i = 1, 2$; s_1 and s_2 are the sample standard deviations corresponding to the variables "X_1" and "X_2" respectively, such that $s_i^2 = \frac{1}{n-1} \sum_{j=1}^{n} (X_{ij} - \overline{X}_i)^2$, $i = 1, 2$; "r" is the sample correlation coefficient between the two axes and "S" is the corresponding sample variance-covariance matrix such that $S = \begin{pmatrix} s_1^2 & s_{12} \\ s_{12} & s_2^2 \end{pmatrix}$ with $s_{12} = rs_1 s_2$.

Thus, $\widehat{C}_{p,c}(0,0) = \widehat{C}_{p,c}$, $\widehat{C}_{p,c}(1,0) = \widehat{C}_{pk,c}$, $\widehat{C}_{p,c}(0,1) = \widehat{C}_{pm,c}$, and $\widehat{C}_{p,c}(1,1) = \widehat{C}_{pmk,c}$ are the plug-in estimators of $C_{p,c}$, $C_{pk,c}$, $C_{pm,c}$, and $C_{pmk,c}$, respectively.

However, due to sampling fluctuations, mere computation of a PCI value using equation (4.56) may not, always, reveal the actual capability of the concerned process and hence the statistical properties of $\widehat{C}_{p,c}(u, v)$, especially, the expectations of its member indices, need to be studied. Chatterjee and Chakraborty [6] and Chatterjee [5] have derived the expressions for the expectations and variances (whereever possible) of the member indices of $\widehat{C}_{p,c}(u, v)$.

From equations (4.44) and (4.56), the plug-in estimator of $C_{p,c}$, viz., $\widehat{C}_{p,c}$, can be defined as

$$
\begin{aligned}
\widehat{C}_{p,c} &= \widehat{C}_{p,c}(0,0) = \frac{D}{2\sqrt{\chi^2_{\alpha,2}}\, s_1 s_2 \sqrt{1 - r^2}} \\
&= \frac{D}{2\sqrt{\chi^2_{\alpha,2}}} \times |S|^{-\frac{1}{4}}, \text{ since, } |S|^{\frac{1}{2}} = s_1 s_2 \sqrt{1 - r^2} \quad (4.57)
\end{aligned}
$$

$$
\text{i.e., } E[\widehat{C}_{p,c}] = E[\widehat{C}_{p,c}(0,0)] = \frac{D}{2\sqrt{\chi^2_{\alpha,2}}} \times E\left[|S|^{-\frac{1}{4}}\right] \quad (4.58)
$$

Before deriving the expressions for $E\left[\widehat{C}_{p,c}\right]$ and $V\left[\widehat{C}_{p,c}\right]$, we need to consider the following two lemmas:

Lemma 1

$$
E[|S|^{-\frac{1}{4}}] = \frac{\sqrt{n-1}}{|\Sigma|^{\frac{1}{4}}} \times \left[\frac{\Gamma\left(\frac{2n-5}{2}\right)}{\Gamma\left(n-2\right)}\right] \quad (4.59)
$$

Proof

Since $|S|$ is the determinant of the sample variance-covariance matrix (popularly known as sample generalized variance), $|S| \sim \frac{|\Sigma|}{(n-1)^2} \prod_{i=1}^{2} \chi^2_{n-i}$ (refer Giri [13]). Also, if χ^2_{n-1} and χ^2_{n-2} are independently distributed, then

$(\chi^2_{n-1} \times \chi^2_{n-2})$ is distributed as $\left\{ \frac{(\chi^2_{2n-4})^2}{4} \right\}$ (refer Pearn et al. [25]). Thus,

$$
\begin{aligned}
E[|S|^{-\frac{1}{4}}] &= E\left[\left\{ \frac{|\Sigma|}{(n-1)^2} \prod_{i=1}^{2} \chi^2_{n-i} \right\}^{-\frac{1}{4}} \right], \quad \text{refer Giri [13]} \\
&= \frac{\sqrt{n-1}}{|\Sigma|^{\frac{1}{4}}} \times E\left[\left\{ \chi^2_{n-1} \times \chi^2_{n-2} \right\}^{-\frac{1}{4}} \right] \\
&= \frac{\sqrt{n-1}}{|\Sigma|^{\frac{1}{4}}} \times E\left[\left\{ \frac{(\chi^2_{2n-4})^2}{4} \right\}^{-\frac{1}{4}} \right], \quad \text{refer Pearn et al. [25]} \\
&= \frac{\sqrt{2(n-1)}}{|\Sigma|^{\frac{1}{4}}} \times E\left[\left\{ \chi^2_{2n-4} \right\}^{-\frac{1}{2}} \right] \\
&= \frac{\sqrt{2(n-1)}}{|\Sigma|^{\frac{1}{4}}} \times \frac{1}{\sqrt{2}} \times \frac{\Gamma\left(\frac{2n-4}{2} - \frac{1}{2} \right)}{\Gamma\left(\frac{2n-4}{2} \right)} \\
&= \frac{\sqrt{n-1}}{|\Sigma|^{\frac{1}{4}}} \times \left[\frac{\Gamma\left(\frac{2n-5}{2} \right)}{\Gamma(n-2)} \right]
\end{aligned}
\tag{4.60}
$$

Hence the proof.

Lemma 2

$$
E[|S|^{-\frac{1}{2}}] = \frac{n-1}{(n-3) \times \sqrt{|\Sigma|}}
\tag{4.61}
$$

Proof

$$
\begin{aligned}
E\left[|S|^{-\frac{1}{2}} \mid |S| \sim \frac{|\Sigma|}{(n-1)^2} \prod_{i=1}^{2} \chi^2_{n-i} \right], \quad &\text{refer Giri [13]} \\
= \left\{ \frac{|\Sigma|}{(n-1)^2} \right\}^{-\frac{1}{2}} \times E\left[\left\{ \frac{\chi^2_{2n-4}}{4} \right\}^{-\frac{1}{2}} \right], \quad &\text{refer Pearn et al. [25]} \\
= \left(\frac{n-1}{\sqrt{|\Sigma|}} \right) \times \left(\frac{\Gamma(n-3)}{\Gamma(n-2)} \right) & \\
= \frac{n-1}{(n-3) \times \sqrt{|\Sigma|}}, \quad \text{since, } \Gamma(p+1) = p\,\Gamma(p). &
\end{aligned}
\tag{4.62}
$$

Hence the proof.

Theorem 1

$\tilde{C}_{p,c}^* = \frac{1}{k(n)} \, \widehat{C}_{p,c}$ is an unbiased estimator of $C_{p,c}$, where $k(n) = \frac{\sqrt{n-1} \, \Gamma(\frac{2n-5}{2})}{\Gamma(n-2)}$.

Proof

From equation (4.58) and equation 4.59,

$$
\begin{aligned}
E\left[\widehat{C}_{p,c}\right] &= \frac{D}{2\sqrt{\chi_{\alpha,2}^2}} \times E\left[|S|^{-\frac{1}{4}}\right] \\
&= \frac{D\sqrt{n-1}}{2\sqrt{\chi_{\alpha,2}^2 \times \sqrt{|\Sigma|}}} \times \left[\frac{\Gamma\left(\frac{2n-5}{2}\right)}{\Gamma(n-2)}\right] \\
&= \left\{\frac{\sqrt{n-1}\,\Gamma(\frac{2n-5}{2})}{\Gamma(n-2)}\right\} \times C_{p,c}(0,0) \qquad (4.63) \\
&= k(n) \times C_{p,c}, \ \text{say} \qquad (4.64) \\
\Rightarrow E[\frac{1}{k(n)}\,\widehat{C}_{p,c}] &= C_{p,c} \qquad (4.65)
\end{aligned}
$$

Hence the proof.

Theorem 2

$$
V\left[\widehat{C}_{p,c}\right] = (n-1)\left[\frac{1}{n-3} - \left(\frac{\Gamma\left(\frac{2n-5}{2}\right)}{\Gamma(n-2)}\right)^2\right] \times C_{p,c}^2(0,0) \qquad (4.66)
$$

Proof
From equation (4.58)

$$
E[\widehat{C}_{p,c}^2(0,0)] = \frac{D^2}{4\chi_{\alpha,2}^2} \times E[|S|^{-\frac{1}{2}}] \qquad (4.67)
$$

Therefore, from equation (4.67) and Lemma 2

$$
\begin{aligned}
E[\widehat{C}_{p,c}^2(0,0)] &= \frac{D^2}{4\chi_{\alpha,2}^2} \times \left\{\frac{n-1}{(n-3) \times \sqrt{|\Sigma|}}\right\} \\
&= \left(\frac{n-1}{n-3}\right) \times C_{p,c}^2(0,0) \qquad (4.68)
\end{aligned}
$$

Therefore, variance of $\widehat{C}_{p,c}$ can be obtained as

$$V[\widehat{C}_{p,c}(0,0)] = E\left[\widehat{C}_{p,c}^2(0,0)\right] - \left\{\widehat{C}_{p,c}(0,0)\right\}^2$$

$$= \left(\frac{n-1}{n-3}\right) \times C_{p,c}^2(0,0) - (n-1) \times \left[\frac{\Gamma\left(\frac{2n-5}{2}\right)}{\Gamma(n-2)}\right]^2 \times C_{p,c}^2(0,0),$$

from equations (4.63) and (4.68)

$$= (n-1)\left[\frac{1}{n-3} - \left(\frac{\Gamma\left(\frac{2n-5}{2}\right)}{\Gamma(n-2)}\right)^2\right] \times C_{p,c}^2(0,0) \tag{4.69}$$

This completes the proof of the theorem.

From equation (4.56), the plug-in estimator of $C_{p,c}(1,0)$, viz., $\widehat{C}_{p,c}(1,0)$, can be defined as

$$\widehat{C}_{p,c}(1,0) = \frac{\frac{D}{2} - \sqrt{\overline{X}'\overline{X}}}{\sqrt{\chi_{\alpha,2}^2\sqrt{|S|}}} \tag{4.70}$$

From equation (4.70)

$$E[\widehat{C}_{p,c}(1,0)] = \left\{\frac{D}{2} - \times E\left(\sqrt{\overline{X}'\overline{X}}\right)\right\} \times \frac{1}{\sqrt{\chi_{\alpha,2}^2}} \times E[|S|^{-\frac{1}{4}}], \tag{4.71}$$

since $|S|^{-\frac{1}{4}}$ is a function of "S" and hence is independent of $\overline{X}$.

Now, from equation 4.59

$$E[|S|^{-\frac{1}{4}}] = \frac{\sqrt{(n-1)}}{|\Sigma|^{\frac{1}{4}}} \times \left[\frac{\Gamma(\frac{2n-5}{2})}{\Gamma(n-2)}\right]. \tag{4.72}$$

Moreover, if $(Y_1, Y_2)' \sim N_2(0, 0, \sigma_1^2, \sigma_2^2, \rho = \frac{\sigma_{12}}{\sigma_1\sigma_2})$, then for the radial distance $\sqrt{Y_1^2 + Y_2^2}$, we have (refer Scheuer [27])

$$E[\sqrt{Y_1^2 + Y_2^2}] = \sqrt{\frac{2}{\pi}}\,\Im(\kappa)\sigma_1^* \tag{4.73}$$

and

$$E[Y_1^2 + Y_2^2] = (2 - \kappa^2)\sigma_1^{*2} \tag{4.74}$$

where

1. $\sigma_1^{*2} = \frac{1}{2}\left\{(\sigma_1^2 + \sigma_2^2) + \left[(\sigma_1^2 - \sigma_2^2)^2 + 4\sigma_{12}^2\right]^{\frac{1}{2}}\right\}$

2. $\sigma_2^{*2} = \frac{1}{2}\left\{(\sigma_1^2 + \sigma_2^2) - \left[(\sigma_1^2 - \sigma_2^2)^2 + 4\sigma_{12}^2\right]^{\frac{1}{2}}\right\}$

Bivariate Process Capability Indices (BPCIs)

3. $\kappa^2 = \frac{\sigma_1^{*2} - \sigma_2^{*2}}{\sigma_1^{*2}}$

4. $\Im(\kappa)$ is the complete elliptical integral of the second kind (refer Legendre [20]).

Thus, if $X \sim N_2(0, \Sigma)$, then $\overline{X} \sim N_2(0, \frac{1}{n} \times \Sigma = \Sigma^*)$, say and hence $E[\sqrt{\overline{X}'\overline{X}}] = \sqrt{\frac{2}{\pi}} \Im(\kappa) \frac{\sigma_1^*}{\sqrt{n}}$ and hence, from equations (4.71), (4.72), and (4.73),

$$E[\widehat{C}_{p,c}(1,0)] = \sqrt{\frac{n-1}{\chi_{\alpha,2}^2 \sqrt{|\Sigma|}}} \times \left[\frac{D}{2} - \frac{\sqrt{2}}{\sqrt{\pi}} \times \Im(\kappa) \frac{\sigma_1^*}{\sqrt{n}} \right] \times \frac{\Gamma(\frac{2n-5}{2})}{\Gamma(n-2)} \quad (4.75)$$

However, when $X \sim N_2(\boldsymbol{\mu}, \Sigma)$, with $\boldsymbol{\mu} \neq 0$, no closed-form expression for $E\left(\sqrt{\overline{X}'\overline{X}}\right)$ is available in literature. However, this problem can be solved numerically using standard statistical packages.

Again from equation (4.70)

$$E[\widehat{C}_{p,c}^2(1,0)] = \frac{1}{\chi_{\alpha,2}^2} \times E\left[\left\{ \frac{D}{2} - \sqrt{\overline{X}'\overline{X}} \right\}^2 \right] \times E\left(|S|^{-\frac{1}{2}} \right) \quad (4.76)$$

Now

$$E\left[\left\{ \frac{D}{2} - \sqrt{\overline{X}'\overline{X}} \right\}^2 \right] = \frac{D^2}{4} - D \times E(\sqrt{\overline{X}'\overline{X}}) + E(\overline{X}'\overline{X}) \quad (4.77)$$

Thus, for $X \sim N_2(0, \Sigma)$

$$\begin{aligned}
E&\left[\left\{ \frac{D}{2} - \sqrt{\overline{X}'\overline{X}} \right\}^2 \right] \\
&= \frac{D^2}{4} - \left(D \times \sqrt{\frac{2}{\pi}} \times \Im(\kappa) \times \frac{\sigma_1^*}{\sqrt{n}} \right) + \left((2 - \kappa^2) \times \frac{\sigma_1^{*2}}{n} \right) \\
&= \frac{D^2}{4} + \sigma_1^* \times \left[(2 - \kappa^2) \frac{\sigma_1^*}{n} - D\sqrt{\frac{2}{n\pi}} \Im(\kappa) \right] \quad (4.78)
\end{aligned}$$

Thus, substituting equations (4.78) and (4.61) in equation (4.76)

$$\begin{aligned}
E&[\widehat{C}_{p,c}^2(1,0)] \\
&= \frac{1}{\chi_{\alpha,2}^2} \times \left\{ \frac{D^2}{4} + \sigma_1^* \times \left[(2 - \kappa^2) \frac{\sigma_1^*}{n} - D\sqrt{\frac{2}{n\pi}} \Im(\kappa) \right] \right\} \times \frac{n-1}{(n-3)\sqrt{|\Sigma|}}
\end{aligned}$$
$$(4.79)$$

Therefore, from equations (4.75) and (4.79)

$$
V\left[\widehat{C}_{p,c}(1,0)\right]
$$

$$
= E[\widehat{C}_{p,c}^2(1,0)] - \left\{E\left[\widehat{C}_{p,c}(1,0)\right]\right\}^2
$$

$$
= \frac{1}{\chi_{\alpha,2}^2} \times \left\{\frac{D^2}{4} + \sigma_1^* \times \left[(2-\kappa^2)\frac{\sigma_1^*}{n} - D\sqrt{\frac{2}{n\pi}}\Im(\kappa)\right]\right\} \times \frac{n-1}{(n-3)\sqrt{|\Sigma|}}
$$

$$
- \left(\frac{n-1}{\chi_{\alpha,2}^2\sqrt{|\Sigma|}}\right) \times \left[\frac{D}{2} - \frac{\sqrt{2}}{\sqrt{n\pi}} \times \Im(\kappa)\sigma_1^*\right]^2 \times \left[\frac{\Gamma(\frac{2n-5}{2})}{\Gamma(n-2)}\right]^2 \qquad (4.80)
$$

$$
(4.81)
$$

However, when $X \sim N_2(\mu, \Sigma)$, with $\mu \neq 0$

$$
\begin{aligned}
E(\overline{X}'\overline{X}) &= E(\overline{X}_1^2 + \overline{X}_2^2) = E(\overline{X}_1^2) + E(\overline{X}_2^2) \\
&= [V(\overline{X}_1) + \{E(\overline{X}_1)\}^2] + [V(\overline{X}_2) + \{E(\overline{X}_2)\}^2] \\
&= (\mu_1^2 + \mu_2^2) + \frac{1}{n}(\sigma_1^2 + \sigma_2^2) \qquad (4.82)
\end{aligned}
$$

Thus, from equations (4.76), (4.77), and (4.82), the expressions for $E[\widehat{C}_{p,c}^2(1,0)]$ and hence for $V[\widehat{C}_{p,c}(1,0)]$ may be obtained.

From equation (4.56), the plug-in estimator of $C_{p,c}(0,1)$, viz., $\widehat{C}_{p,c}(0,1)$, can be defined as

$$
\begin{aligned}
\widehat{C}_{p,c}(0,1) &= \frac{\frac{D}{2}}{\sqrt{\chi_{\alpha,2}^2\sqrt{|S|}}} \times \frac{1}{\sqrt{1 + \overline{X}'S^{-1}\overline{X}}} \\
&= \widehat{C}_{p,c}(0,0) \times \frac{1}{\sqrt{1 + \overline{X}'S^{-1}\overline{X}}} \qquad (4.83)
\end{aligned}
$$

Now, following Lehman and Casella [21], since $\overline{X}$ and "S" are consistent estimators of μ and Σ, for a continuous function, say "h," $h(\overline{X}, S) \to h(\mu, \Sigma)$ almost surely. Thus, from equation (4.83)

$$
\widehat{C}_{p,c}(0,1) \to \frac{\frac{D}{2}}{\sqrt{\chi_{\alpha,2}^2\sqrt{|\Sigma|}}} \times \frac{1}{\sqrt{1 + \mu'\Sigma^{-1}\mu}} = C_{p,c}(0,1), \quad \text{almost surely} (4.84)
$$

Thus, $\widehat{C}_{p,c}(0,1)$ is a consistent estimator of $C_{p,c}(0,1)$.

From equation (4.56), the plug-in estimator of $C_{p,c}(1,1)$, viz., $\widehat{C}_{p,c}(1,1)$

Bivariate Process Capability Indices (BPCIs)

can be defined as

$$\widehat{C}_{p,c}(1,1) = \frac{\frac{D}{2} - \sqrt{\overline{\boldsymbol{X}}'\overline{\boldsymbol{X}}}}{\sqrt{\chi^2_{\alpha,2}\sqrt{|S|}}} \times \frac{1}{\sqrt{1 + \overline{\boldsymbol{X}}'S^{-1}\overline{\boldsymbol{X}}}} \tag{4.85}$$

$$= \widehat{C}_{p,c}(1,0) \times \frac{1}{\sqrt{1 + \overline{\boldsymbol{X}}'S^{-1}\overline{\boldsymbol{X}}}} \tag{4.86}$$

$$\tag{4.87}$$

It is difficult to obtain a closed-form expression for the expectation of $\widehat{C}_{p,c}(1,1)$. However, similar to the case of $\widehat{C}_{p,c}(0,1)$, here also it is easy to observe that $\widehat{C}_{p,c}(1,1)$ is a consistent estimator of $C_{p,c}(1,1)$.

4.5 Numerical Examples

In this chapter, two different types of BPCIs have been discussed, viz., (i) BPCIs for quality characteristics having bilateral or unilateral specification limits (as discussed in Sections 4.2 and 4.3) and (ii) BPCIs for circular specification limits (as discussed in Section 4.4). Two separate numerical examples will now be discussed for these two cases.

4.5.1 Example 1

Pal [23] has discussed about a dataset on a particular type of bobbin. Two major quality characteristics of bobbin are its height and weight. The specification region is assumed to be rectangular with the upper and lower specifiaction limits of bobbin height (BH) being 42.00 and 40.00, respectively; while the upper and lower specification limits of bobbin weight (BW) are 46.50 and 44.00, respectively.

Here, the number of sample observations $n = 100$. The summary statistics of the two variables are follows:

For BH, sample mean is $\overline{x_1} = 41.134$ and sample s.d. $s_1 = 0.27$. For BW, sample mean $\overline{x_2} = 45.428$ and sample s.d. $s_2 = 0.319$. Also, the sample correlation coefficient between x_1 and x_2 is $r = 0.57$, which is moderately high, indicating that the two quality characteristics are moderately positively correlated. Also, the underlying statistical distribution of the process is considered to be bivariate normal.

Based on the summary statistics, estimated values of BPCIs defined by Pal [23] are found to be $\hat{B}C_p = 1.903$, $\hat{B}C_{pk} = 0.976$, $\hat{B}C_{pm} = 1.634$, and $\hat{B}C_{pk} = 0.8381$; while using the newly proposed expression of threshold value, the threshold value of BC_p is computed as $BC_p^{(T)} = 1.1786$.

Also, the estimated values of the BPCIs proposed by Castagliola and Castellanos [4] are $\hat{BC}_p^{(CC)} = 1.198$ and $\hat{BC}_{pk}^{(CC)} = 1.005$.

Interestingly, values of PCIs proposed by Pal [23] are substantially higher than those by Castagliola and Castellanos [4]. In this context, Pal [23] considered 1.33 as the "minimum recommended value" for BC_p and based on this value, he considered the process to be potentially capable, but not actually capable (since $\hat{BC}_{pk} < 1.33$). However, 1.33 is the recommended threshold value only for univariate processes with normal process distribution. Using the newly proposed expression for threshold value of BC_p (vide equation (4.20)) also, $\hat{BC}_{pk} < BC_p^{(T)}$, indicating toward poor performance of the process.

On the other hand, as has been pointed out by Castagliola and Castellanos [4] themselves, estimated values of $BC_p^{(CC)}$ and $BC_{pk}^{(CC)}$ are close to the values of MPCIs proposed by Bothe [1] (this MPCI will be discussed in detail in Chapter). However, Bothe's [1] MPCIs are based on the assumption that the quality characteristics are mutually independent. Therefore, having values close to these MPCIs may indicate that $BC_p^{(CC)}$ and $BC_{pk}^{(CC)}$ are not efficient enough to capture the underlying correlation structure of the quality characteristics.

4.5.2 Example 2

Chatterjee and Chakraborty [6] have discussed a numerical example to make performance analysis of $C_{p,c}(u,v)$ for u = 0, 1 and v = 0, 1. The item under consideration is called "striker," which is used in making some ammunitions. These parts should be properly assembled to ensure perfect alignment of the parts resulting in satisfactory performance of the produced ammunitions. Hence, the quality characteristic under consideration is centers of the holes drilled in the strikers.

The data is given below [refer Chatterjee and Chakraborty [6]]:

TABLE 4.2: Data on the co-ordinates of the centers of 20 drilled holes

Sl. No.	1	2	3	4	5	6	7	8	9	10
X_1	2.65	3.01	2.86	1.99	1.75	2.68	3.68	2.91	4.05	2.17
X_2	2.52	3.28	2.72	2.83	2.31	2.56	3.29	2.73	4.31	1.84
Sl. No.	11	12	13	14	15	16	17	18	19	20
X_1	2.98	3.03	1.67	3.53	2.29	3.43	2.19	2.97	2.41	3.07
X_2	2.94	3.08	1.79	3.02	2.51	3.31	2.09	2.94	2.73	2.72

Summary statistics for the above data are as follows:
$\overline{X}_1 = 2.766$, $\overline{X}_2 = 2.776$, $\hat{\sigma}_1^2 = 0.408$, $\hat{\sigma}_2^2 = 0.321$, $\hat{\rho} = 0.856$. Also, the diameter of the circular specification region is considered to be 10 cm, i.e., $D = 10$.

The computed values of the member indices of the superstructure $C_{p,c}(u, v)$, with $\alpha = 0.0027$, and the existing PCIs for circular specification are as follows:

$\widehat{C}_{p,c} = 3.3617$, $\widehat{C}_{pk,c} = 0.7269$, $\widehat{C}_{pm,c} = 0.6711$, $\widehat{C}_{pmk,c} = 0.1451$, $\widehat{P}_p = 2.7992$, $\widehat{P}_{pk} = 0.4210$, $\widehat{PC}_p = 6.8152$, $\widehat{PC}_p^* = 2.6106$, $\widehat{PC}_{pk} = 0.7363$, $\widehat{PC}_{pk}^* = 0.8581$.

Observe that, here $C_{p,c}$ value is quite high and is even higher than $\widehat{C}_{p,c}^T = 1.20123$ — which indicates that the process is potentially capable. On the other hand, the low values of $C_{pk,c}$, $C_{pm,c}$, and $C_{pmk,c}$ imply that the process, at its present state, is not performing satisfactorily. Moreover, recall that although both $\widehat{P}_{pk}$ and $\widehat{PC}_{pk}$ rightly conclude the process to be incapable, they are based on some stringent assumptions, which may not always hold good in practice.

4.6 Concluding Remarks

In this chapter, a thorough discussion has been made on BPCIs, i.e., PCIs specially designed to assess capability of bivariate processes. These BPCIs can be broadly classified into two sectors, viz., (i) BPCIs for processes having bilateral or unilateral specification region and (ii) BPCIs for circular specification region.

Although a number of BPCIs are available in literature for each of these two sectors, statistical properties of the plug-in estimators of most of these BPCIs are not thoroughly studied yet. As a result, it becomes difficult to take any decision based on sample observations. Unavailability of statistically formulated expressions for threshold values of the BPCIs also make it difficult to take objective decision about the true health of a process. These will create some interesting future scopes of study.

In the following chapters, we shall discuss about more general form of PCIs, viz., multivariate process capability indices. To begin with, the very next chapter will deal with the most popular form of MPCIs, viz., ratio based MPCIs.

Bibliography

[1] Bothe, D. R. (1999) Composite Capability Index for Multiple Product Characteristics. *Quality Engineering*, Vol. 12, No. 2, pp. 253–258.

[2] Bothe, D. R. (2006). Assessing Capability for Hole Location. *Quality Engineering*, Vol. 18, No. 3, pp. 325–331.

[3] Boyles, R. A. (1991). The Taguchi Capability Index. *Journal of Quality Technology*, Vol. 23, No. 1, pp. 17–26.

[4] Castagliola, P., Castellanos, J. V. G. (2005). Capability Indices dedicated to the Two Quality Characteristics Case. *Quality Technology and Quantitative Management*, Vol. 2, No. 2, pp. 201–220.

[5] Chatterjee, M. (2017). On Some Univariate and Multivariate Process Capability Indices. *Ph.D. thesis submitted at Indian Statistical Institute.*

[6] Chatterjee, M., Chakraborty, A. K. (2015). A Super Structure of Process Capability Indices for Circular Specification Region. *Communications in Statistics—Theory and Methods*, Vol. 44, No. 6, pp. 1158–1181.

[7] Chatterjee, M., Chakraborty, A. K. (2014). Exact Relationship of $C_{pk}^{''}$ with Proportion of Non-conformance and Some Other Properties of $C_p^{''}(u, v)$. *Quality and Reliability Engineering International*, Vol. 30, pp. 1023–1034.

[8] Chatterjee, M., Chakraborty, A. K. (2017). Unification of Some Multivariate Process Capability Indices for Asymmetric Specification Region. *Statistica Neerlandica*, Vol. 71, No. 4, pp. 286–306.

[9] Chew, V., Boyce, R. (1962). Distribution of Radial Error in the Bivariate Elliptical Normal Distribution. *Technometrics*, Vol. 4, No. 1, pp. 138–140.

[10] Chou, Y. M., Owen, D. B. (1989). On the Distribution of the Estimated Process Capability Indices. *Communications in Statistics—Theory and Methods*, Vol. 18, pp. 4549–4560.

[11] Culpepper, G. A. (1978). Statistical Analysis of Radial Error in Two Dimensions. *Army Materiel Test And Evaluation Directorate*. Technical Report No. AD A059117. US Army White Sands Missile Range. New Mexico.

Bibliography 109

[12] Davis, R. D., Kaminsky, F. C., Saboo, S. (1992). Process Capability Analysis for Processes with Either a Circular or a Spherical Tolerance Zone. *Quality Engineering*, Vol. 5, No. 1, pp. 41–54.

[13] Giri, N. C. (2004). *Multivariate Statistical Analysis*. New York: Marcel & Dekker.

[14] Gunst, R. F., Webster, J. T. (1973). Density Functions of the Bivariate Chi-square Distribution. *Journal of Statistical Computation and Simulation*, Vol. 2, pp. 275–288.

[15] Karl, D. P., Morisette, J. and Taam, W. (1994). Some Applications of a Multivariate Capability Index in Geometric Dimensioning and Tolerancing. *Quality Engineering*, Vol. 6, No. 4, pp. 649–665.

[16] Kocherlakota, S., Kocherlakota, K. (1991). Process Capability Index: Bivariate Normal Distribution. *Communications in Statistics—Theory and Methods*, Vol. 20, No. 8, pp. 2529–2547.

[17] Kotz, S., Johnson, N. (2002). Process Capability Indices—A Review, 1992–2000. *Journal of Quality Technology* Vol. 34, No. 1, pp. 2–19.

[18] Krishnamoorthy, K. S. (1990). Capability Indices for Processes Subject to Unilateral and Positional Tolerances. *Quality Engineering*, Vol. 2, No. 4, pp. 461–471.

[19] Laurent, A. G. (1957). Bombing Problems—A Statistical Approach. *Operations Research*, Vol. 5, No. 1, pp. 75–89.

[20] Legendre, A. M. (1934). *Tables of the Complete and Incomplete Elliptic Integrals*. London: Biometric Office.

[21] Lehmann, E. L., Casella, G. (1998). *The Theory of Point Estimation*, 2nd ed., Springer.

[22] Mardia, K. V., Kent, J. T., Bibby, J. M. (1995). *Multivariate Analysis*. London: Academic Press 10th reprint.

[23] Pal, S. (1999). Performance Evaluation of a Bivariate Normal Process. *Quality Engineering*, Vol. 11, No. 3, pp. 379–386.

[24] Pan, J. N., Lee, C. Y. (2010). New Capability Indices for Evaluating the Performance of Multivariate Manufacturing Processes. *Quality and Reliability engineering International*, Vol. 26, No. 1, pp. 3–15.

[25] Pearn, W. L., Wang, F. K., Yen, C. H. (2007). Multivariate Capability Indices: Distributional and Inferential Properties. *Journal of Applied Statistics*, Vol. 34, No. 8, pp. 941–962.

[26] Phillips, M. D., Cho, B. R. (1998). Quality Improvement for Processes with Circular and Spherical Specification Regions. *Quality Engineering*, Vol. 11, No. 2, pp. 235–243.

[27] Scheur, E. M. (1962). Moments of the Radial Error. *Journal of the American Statistical Association*, Vol.57, No. 297, pp. 187–190.

[28] Taam, W., Subbaiah, P., Liddy, W. (1993). A Note on Multivariate Capability Indices. *Journal of Applied Statistics*, Vol. 20, No. 3, pp. 339–351.

[29] Vannman, K. (1995). A Unified Approach to Capability Indices. *Statistica Sinica*, Vol. 5, No. 2, pp. 805–820.

[30] Wierda, S. J. (1992). A multivariate Process Capability Index. *Proceedings of* 9th *International Conference of Israel Society for Quality Assurance*.

[31] National Bureau of Standards (1959). *Tables of the Bivariate Normal Distribution Function and Related Functions*, Applied Mathematics Series, Vol. 50.

Chapter 5

Multivariate Process Capability Indices for Bilateral Specification Region Based on Principal Component Analysis (PCA)

Chapter Summary

One of the effective ways of handling multidimensional data, i.e., data having more than one (mostly correlated) variables, is to use a dimension reduction technique. Principal component analysis (PCA) is one of the most effective as well as popular measures of dimension reduction. In Chapter 5, some PCA-based multivariate process capability indices (MPCIs) are discussed in detail, along with an example using real-life data.

5.1 Introduction

Among all the multivariate process capability indices (MPCIs) available in literature, principal component analysis (PCA)-based MPCIs are one of the most popular ones due to their simplicity of computation and ease of representation. Since by virtue of PCA, the dimension of the original data gets reduced (refer to Chapter 2 for more detail), the original process capability assessment problem for correlated multi-dimensional quality characteristics often becomes easier to handle. We shall now discuss some important MPCIs, which are defined using the concept of PCA.

5.2 MPCIs Analogous to Univariate PCIs viz., C_p, C_{pk}, C_{pm}, and C_{pmk}

Wang and Chen [15] were the first to define MPCIs based on the concept of PCA. Since the four PCIs viz. C_p, C_{pk}, C_{pm}, and C_{pmk}, for univariate processes having symmetric specification limits with respect to the stipulated target, are widely accepted by the practitioners, the authors chose to suggest some multivariate analogues of those PCIs. Moreover, since by definition, principal components are mutually independent, the authors have considered them as new variables and consequently have computed MPCIs for them.

Suppose there are "q" quality characteristics measured on a part. Let the underlying distribution of the quality characteristics $(\boldsymbol{X})$ is multivariate normal, i.e., $\boldsymbol{X} \sim N_q(\boldsymbol{\mu}, \Sigma)$. Also,

$$
\begin{aligned}
\boldsymbol{T}^{'} &= (T_1, T_2, \cdots, T_q)^{'} : \text{ Target vector for } \boldsymbol{X} \\
\boldsymbol{LSL}^{'} &= (LSL_1, LSL_2, \cdots, LSL_q)^{'} : \text{ Lower specification vector for } \boldsymbol{X} \\
\boldsymbol{USL}^{'} &= (USL_1, USL_2, \cdots, USL_q)^{'} : \text{ Upper specification vector for } \boldsymbol{X} \\
S &= \{\boldsymbol{x} | \boldsymbol{LSL} \le \boldsymbol{x} \le \boldsymbol{USL}\} : \text{Hyper-rectangular specification of } \boldsymbol{X}
\end{aligned}
$$

$$(5.1)$$

Without loss of generality, let $\lambda_1, \lambda_2, \cdots, \lambda_q$ be "q" eigen values of the dispersion matrix Σ, arranged in descending order, i.e., $\lambda_1 \ge \lambda_2 \ge \cdots \ge \lambda_q$ and let $\boldsymbol{U} = (\boldsymbol{U}_1, \boldsymbol{U}_2, \cdots, \boldsymbol{U}_q)^{'}$: eigen vector of Σ. Then, $\boldsymbol{Y} = \boldsymbol{U}^{'} \boldsymbol{X}$ is the vector of principal components. Also, the proportion of total variability explained by the ith principal component is given by $\frac{\lambda_i}{\sum_{i=1}^{q} \lambda_i}$, for $i = 1(1)q$.

Wang and Chen [15] have defined multivariate analogues of C_p, C_{pk}, C_{pm}, and C_{pmk}, respectively, (refer equation (3.1)) as follows:

$$
\left.
\begin{aligned}
MC_p^{(\text{Wang})} &= \left(\prod_{i=1}^{q} C_{p;PC_i} \right)^{1/q} \\[2ex]
MC_{pk}^{(\text{Wang})} &= \left(\prod_{i=1}^{q} C_{pk;PC_i} \right)^{1/q} \\[2ex]
MC_{pm}^{(\text{Wang})} &= \left(\prod_{i=1}^{q} C_{pm;PC_i} \right)^{1/q} \\[2ex]
MC_{pmk}^{(\text{Wang})} &= \left(\prod_{i=1}^{q} C_{pmk;PC_i} \right)^{1/q}
\end{aligned}
\right\}
$$

$$(5.2)$$

PCA-Based MPCIs for Bilateral Specification

where PC_i stands for the ith principal component and $C_{p;PC_i}$, $C_{pk;PC_i}$, $C_{pm;PC_i}$, and $C_{pmk;PC_i}$ represent the univariate PCIs C_p, C_{pk}, C_{pm}, and C_{pmk}, respectively, corresponding to the ith principal component, for $i = 1(1)q$. For example,

$$C_{p;PC_i} = \frac{USL_{PC_i} + LSL_{PC_i}}{6\sigma_{PC_i}} \tag{5.3}$$

where $USL_{PC_i} = \boldsymbol{u}_i' \boldsymbol{USL}$, $LSL_{PC_i} = \boldsymbol{u}_i' \boldsymbol{LSL}$, $\boldsymbol{u}_1, \boldsymbol{u}_2, \cdots, \boldsymbol{u}_q$ are "q" eigen vectors of the dispersion matrix Σ, $\boldsymbol{USL} = (USL_1, USL_2, \cdots, USL_q)'$ is the q component vector of upper specification limits and $\boldsymbol{LSL} = (LSL_1, LSL_2, \cdots, LSL_q)'$ is the q component vector of lower specification limits.

$MC_{pk}^{(\text{Wang})}$, $MC_{pm}^{(\text{Wang})}$, and $MC_{pmk}^{(\text{Wang})}$ can be defined accordingly.

Similar to Vannman's unification of univariate PCIs viz., $C_p(u,v)$ (refer equation (3.5)), Dharmasena and Zeephongsekul [1] have unified these MPCIs for the ith principal component as

$$C_{p;PC_i}(u,v) = \frac{d_{PC_i} - u|\mu_{PC_i} - T_{PC_i}|}{3\sqrt{\sigma_{PC_i} + v(\mu_{PC_i} - T_{PC_i})^2}} \tag{5.4}$$

where $d_{PC_i} = \frac{USL_{PC_i} - LSL_{PC_i}}{2}$, $T_{PC_i} = \boldsymbol{u}_i' \boldsymbol{T}$, and $\mu_{PC_i} = \boldsymbol{u}_i' \boldsymbol{\mu}$.

Now, since the MPCIs defined in equation (5.2) involve process parameters, which are hardly observable, Wang and Du [16] defined plug-in estimator of MC_p as

$$\hat{M}C_p^{(\text{Wang})} = \left(\prod_{i=1}^{q} \hat{C}_{p;PC_i} \right)^{1/q} \tag{5.5}$$

where $\hat{C}_{p;PC_i} = \frac{USL_{PC_i} - LSL_{PC_i}}{6S_{PC_i}}$, S_{PC_i} is the sample standard deviation corresponding to the ith principal component. Plug-in estimators of $MC_{pk}^{(\text{Wang})}$, $MC_{pm}^{(\text{Wang})}$ and $MC_{pmk}^{(\text{Wang})}$ can be defined accordingly.

Based on the assumption of multivariate normality of the underlying process distribution, Wang and Du [16] have derived expression for an $100(1-\alpha)\%$ approximate confidence interval as

$$\left(\prod_{i=1}^{q} \hat{C}_{p;PC_i} \sqrt{\frac{\chi_{1-\alpha/2,n-1}^2}{n-1}} \right)^{1/q} \leq MC_p^{(\text{Wang})}$$

$$\leq \left(\prod_{i=1}^{q} \hat{C}_{p;PC_i} \sqrt{\frac{\chi_{\alpha/2,n-1}^2}{n-1}} \right)^{1/q} \tag{5.6}$$

Note that both Wang and Chen [15] and Wang and Du [16] have considered all the principal components (PC). However, by definition, the proportion of variability associated with the PCs gradually decreases with the order of the principal component. Hence, in practice, by merely retaining only a few PCs, one can capture, say $90 - -95\%$ of the total process variability (refer Johnson and Wichern [3]). Hence, one can replace "q" by "v" in equation (5.2), where "v" represents the first "v" PCs, without losing too much information (refer Shinde and Khadse [11]).

Shinde and Khadse [11] have observed that although USL_{PC_i} and LSL_{PC_i}, for $i = 1(1)q$ are defined assuming the specification limits of different PCs to be mutually independent, in reality, only the distributions of PCs are independent, but not the specification limits. They have formulated the specification region as

$$V = \left\{ y | LSL \leq U^{'} y \leq USL \right\} \tag{5.7}$$

which is a set of $2q$ linear inequalities in q variables. Based on this specification region, Shinde and Khadse [11] have suggested the following approaches for assessing process capability.

5.2.1 Probability-Based MPCI Based on First Few Principal Components

Shinde and Khadse [11] have assumed that $Y_i = E(Yi)$ for $i = v+1, \cdots, q$, since by definition $Y_{v+1}, Y_{v+2}, \cdots, Y_q$ have very less variation as compared to $Y_1, Y_2, \cdots, Y_v$. Then the revised specification region for the first v principal components will be

$$V^{'} = \left\{ y^* = (y_1, y_2, \cdots, y_v)^{'} | LSL \leq U^{'} y \leq USL, \right.$$
$$\left. \text{such that } y_i = E(Y_i), \ i = \overline{v+1}, \cdots, q \right\}$$

For the specification region $V^{'}$, Shinde and Khadse [11] have defined probability-based MPCIs as

1.

$$MP_1 = P \left\{ Y = (Y_1, Y_2, \cdots, Y_v)^{'} \in V^{'} | \right.$$
$$\left. Y \sim N_v(T_Y, \Sigma_Y = diag(\lambda_1, \lambda_2, \cdots, \lambda_v)) \right\} \tag{5.8}$$

where T_Y is the target vector corresponding to the first v principal components and Σ_Y is the corresponding dispersion matrix.

Observe that MP_1 is a multivariate analogue of C_p as it assumes the process to be perfectly centered on target and therefore measures potential process capability $-$ rather than the absolute one. Thus, MP_1

can be considered as an alternative to $MC_p^{(\text{Wang})}$, defined by Wang and Chen [15], without requiring independence of the specification limits for the principal components.

2.

$$
\begin{aligned}
MP_2 \;=\; & P\Big\{ \boldsymbol{Y} = (Y_1, Y_2, \cdots, Y_v)^{'} \in V^{'} \,| \\
& \boldsymbol{Y} \sim N_v(\boldsymbol{\mu}_Y, \Sigma_Y = diag(\lambda_1, \lambda_2, \cdots, \lambda_v)) \Big\}
\end{aligned}
\tag{5.9}
$$

Since MP_2 assumes the process to be centered on process mean vector $\boldsymbol{\mu}_Y$, it can be considered as a multivariate analogue of C_{pk} and hence provides an alternative to $MC_{pk}^{(\text{Wang})}$.

Since the principal components are assumed to be multivariate normal, $MP_1 \geq 0.9973$ implies that the process is potentially capable, i.e., even if the process is not capable at present, it has the potential to be so, provided it is perfectly centered on target. On the other hand, $MP_2 \geq 0.9973$ implies that the process is actually capable.

Although the formulations of MP_1 and MP_2 is simple, the associated computation is difficult owing to the complicated form of $V^{'}$. To address this problem, Shinde and Khadse [11] proposed an empirical approach.

To understand this approach, recall that MP_1 and MP_2 requires two different mean vectors viz., $\boldsymbol{T}_Y$ and $\boldsymbol{\mu}_Y$, which are used for defining multivariate analogues of C_P and C_{pk}, respectively.

For satisfactory performance of the empirical approach, one requires a sufficiently large sample size (n), say $n \geq 20000$. At first, one has to draw two random samples of size n from the distribution of the first v principal components:

1. one with mean vector $\boldsymbol{T}_Y$ (say, Sample I) − required for empirical version of MP_1;

2. the other with mean vector $\boldsymbol{\mu}_Y$ (say, Sample II) − required for empirical version of MP_2.

Once these samples are drawn, empirical version of MP_1 can be defined as

$$
\begin{aligned}
& MP_1^{(\text{emp})} \\
& = \frac{\text{No. of observations in Sample } I \text{ with } \boldsymbol{y} = (y_1, y_2, \cdots, y_v)^{'} \in V^{'}}{n}.
\end{aligned}
\tag{5.10}
$$

Similarly, empirical version of MP_2 can be defined as

$$MP_2^{(\text{emp})}$$

$$= \frac{\text{No. of observations in Sample } II \text{ with } \boldsymbol{y} = (y_1, y_2, \cdots, y_v)^{'} \in V^{'}}{n}.$$

(5.11)

Thus, $MP_1^{(\text{emp})}$ and $MP_2^{(\text{emp})}$ are easier to handle than MP_1 and MP_2 and hence are more suitable for practitioners.

5.3 PCA-Based MPCIs with Unequal Weighting

The MPCIs defined by Wang and Chen [15] and Wang and Du [16] are basically geometric means of univariate PCIs for the retained PCs. However, this assigns same importance to all the significant PCs irrespective of their individual ability to capture overall process variation. In fact, when arranged in the ascending order, the first PC (viz., λ_1) captures the highest amount of process variability, the second PC captures the next highest amount of variability and so on. Moreover, these amounts of variability captured by different PCs are generally not equispaced, i.e., there may be significant differences between the variabilities captured by two consecutive PCs. Hence, instead of using simple geometric mean of these PCIs, one should assign appropriate weightage.

One possible solution to this problem is to assign weights to the individual PCIs, where the weights are some suitably chosen functions of the amount of variability captured by the respective PCs. Xekalaki and Perakis [14] have suggested the following new MPCIs in this regard, which are the weighted arithmetic means of the univariate PCIs for significant PCs.

$$\left.\begin{aligned}
MC_p^{(XP)} &= \tfrac{1}{\Lambda} \times \sum_{i=1}^{v} \lambda_i |C_{p;PC_i}| \\
MC_{pk}^{(XP)} &= \tfrac{1}{\Lambda} \times \sum_{i=1}^{v} \lambda_i |C_{pk;PC_i}| \\
MC_{pm}^{(XP)} &= \tfrac{1}{\Lambda} \times \sum_{i=1}^{v} \lambda_i |C_{pm;PC_i}| \\
MC_{pmk}^{(XP)} &= \tfrac{1}{\Lambda} \times \sum_{i=1}^{v} \lambda_i |C_{pmk;PC_i}|
\end{aligned}\right\}$$

(5.12)

where $\Lambda = \sum_{i=1}^{v} \lambda_i$ is the total process variation explained by the first "v" PCs. It is interesting to observe that instead of following the general convention of considering PCIs for different PCs as it is, Xekalaki and Perakis [14] have considered their absolute values. This is due to the fact that sometimes while using PCA, LSL of a PC may become larger than the corresponding USL, owing to the rotation of axis. This, in turn, will make the corresponding PCI value negative. Since by definition, PCIs are considered to be nonnegative (refer Kotz and Johnson [6]), Xekalaki and Perakis [14] have used "modulus function" to restrict their proposed MPCI values from being negative. Infact, they have argued for using this function in other similar PCA-based MPCIs as well, including those suggested by Wang and Chen [15].

Perakis and Xakalaki [8] have rightly observed that a process, which is centered close to the target, should ideally have small variation, since the chances of producing nonconformig items will be less. On the other hand, an off-target process is expected to have high process variability. Although substantial amount of non-conforming items will be produced as a result, it will also provide enhanced scope for improvement.

Perakis and Xakalaki [8] have made an extensive simulation study to compare performances of their proposed MPCIs with those proposed by Wang and Chen [15]. Through this study, they have shown that their proposed MPCIs, in particular MC_{pm}^{XP} and MC_{pmk}^{XP}, possess the above mentioned property, but Wang and Chen's [15] MPCIs do not have such property.

Perakis and Xakalaki [8] have also studied the standard errors associated with the plug-in estimators of MC_p^{XP}, MC_{pk}^{XP}, MC_{pm}^{XP}, and MC_{pmk}^{XP} through simulation study using parametric bootstrap technique (refer Efron and Tibsirani [2]). Perakis and Xakalaki [8] have observed that standard error of MC_p^{XP}, MC_{pk}^{XP}, MC_{pm}^{XP} and MC_{pmk}^{XP} decreases with the increase in sample size. Also, except for MC_p^{XP}, estimated values of all the other MPCIs decrease with the proximity of the process center toward the target. Since, by definition, MC_p^{XP} assumes the process to be centered on target, such property is not applicable to it.

5.4   PCA-Based MPCIs Similar to Taam et al.'s [12] Ratio-Based MPCIs

Min et al. [7] have observed that Shinde and Khadse's [11] probability-based MPCIs, given in equations (5.8) and (5.9), may give infeasible result, when more than one PCs are found to be significant. This is mainly due to the fact that, often in manufacturing processes involving several quality characteristics, the scales of engineering specifications are different. Moreover, one should not use PCs on a covariance matrix, when the variables have different units of measurements and their variances are also widely different (refer Jolliffe [4]).

PCA-Based MPCIs for Bilateral Specification

Min et al. [7] have proposed standardizing the variables prior to applying PCA. Suppose, $\boldsymbol{X} = (X_1, X_2, \cdots, X_q)^{'}$ be the original random vector representing "q" correlated quality characteristics such that $\boldsymbol{X} \sim N_q(\boldsymbol{\mu}, \Sigma)$. Also let $\boldsymbol{Z} = (Z_1, Z_2, \cdots, Z_q)^{'}$ be the vector of standardized variables, with its ith component being defined as $Z_i = \frac{X_i - \mu_i}{\sigma_i}$, for $i = 1(1)q$. Therefore, $\boldsymbol{Z} \sim N_q(\boldsymbol{0}, 1)$ and this is unit free.

Let us define the vectors of upper specification limits, lower specification limits and target values of $\boldsymbol{Z}$ as $\boldsymbol{USL_Z}$, $\boldsymbol{LSL_Z}$, and $\boldsymbol{T_Z}$, respectively, with their ith component being given by $USL_{Z_i} = \frac{USL_{X_i} - \mu_i}{\sigma_i}$, $LSL_{Z_i} = \frac{\mu_i - LSL_{X_i}}{\sigma_i}$, and $T_{Z_i} = \frac{T_{X_i} - \mu_i}{\sigma_i}$.

Then similar to Shinde and Khadse [11], Min et al. [7] have defined the modified specification region V^* for the first "v" PCs of $\boldsymbol{Z}$ as

$$V^* = \left\{ (Y_1, Y_2, \cdots, Y_v) \mid \boldsymbol{LSL_Z} \leq \boldsymbol{U}^{'} \boldsymbol{Y} \leq \boldsymbol{USL_Z}, \right.$$
$$\left. \boldsymbol{Y}^{'} = (Y_1, Y_2, \cdots, Y_v), Y_r = E(Y_r) = 0, \text{ for } r = v+1, v+2, \cdots, q \right\}$$
(5.13)

For this modified specification region, Min et al. [7] have defined two new ratio-based MPCIs using PCA-analogous to univariate indices C_p and C_{pm} and similar to those defined by Taam et al. [12]. Taam et al. [12] are among the first to define MPCIs in literature. A through discussion on their MPCIs will be made in Chapter 6.

Following Taam et al.'s [12] approach, Min et al [7] have defined the following MPCIs analogous to the univariate PCIs C_p and C_{pm} as:

$$MC_p^{MWSZ} = \frac{\text{Volume of modified tolerance region of the first '}v\text{' PCs}}{(\pi \, \chi_{v,0.9973}^2)^{v/2} \times |\Sigma_{PC}|^{1/2} \times \left[\Gamma \left(\frac{v}{2} + 1 \right) \right]^{-1}}$$
(5.14)

$$MC_{pm}^{MWSZ} = \frac{MC_p^{MWSZ}}{D_{PC}}$$
(5.15)

where $\boldsymbol{\mu}_{PC}$, $\boldsymbol{T}_{PC}$, and Σ_{PC} are the mean vector, target vector, and dispersion matrix for the first "v" significant PCs and

$$D_{PC} = \left[1 + (\boldsymbol{\mu}_{PC} - \boldsymbol{T}_{PC})^{'} \Sigma_{PC}^{-1} (\boldsymbol{\mu}_{PC} - \boldsymbol{T}_{PC}) \right].$$

For a random sample of size "n" drawn from a $N_q(\boldsymbol{\mu}, \Sigma)$ distribution, Min et al. [7] have also derived the expressions for the confidence intervals of MC_p^{MWSZ} and MC_{pm}^{MWSZ} for bivariate (i.e., $q = 2$) and trivariate processes (i.e., $q = 3$).

For a bivariate process, the $100(1 - \alpha)\%$ confidence interval of MC_p^{MWSZ} is

$$\left[\hat{MC}_p^{MWSZ} \times \sqrt{\frac{(\chi_{2n-4,\alpha/2}^2)^2}{4(n-1)^2}}, \hat{MC}_p^{MWSZ} \times \sqrt{\frac{(\chi_{2n-4,1-\alpha/2}^2)^2}{4(n-1)^2}} \right] \text{ and the } 100(1-$$

$\alpha)\%$ confidence interval for MC_{pm}^{MWSZ} is

$$\left[\hat{MC}_{pm}^{MWSZ}\sqrt{\frac{\hat{F}_W^{-1}(\alpha/2)}{(n-1)^2\hat{D}_{PC}^2}},\ \hat{MC}_{pm}^{MWSZ}\sqrt{\frac{\hat{F}_W^{-1}(1-\alpha/2)}{(n-1)^2\hat{D}_{PC}^2}}\right],\text{ where }\hat{MC}_p^{MWSZ}\text{ and}$$

$\hat{MC}_{pm}^{MWSZ}$ are the plug-in estimators of MC_p^{MWSZ} and MC_{pm}^{MWSZ}, respectively. Also,

$$\hat{F}_W(w)$$
$$= \int_0^w \int_1^\infty \frac{\frac{1}{2}e^{\hat{\tau}^2/2}}{t\Gamma(n-2)\Gamma\left(\frac{n-2}{2}\right)} \times e^{-\sqrt{w/t}} \times \sum_{i=0}^\infty \frac{\left(\hat{\tau}^2/2\right)^i (t-1)^i \Gamma\left(n/2+i\right)}{i!\Gamma(i+1)t^{n/2+i}} dtdw,$$

$$(5.16)$$

where $\hat{\tau}^2 = n(\overline{Y}-T_{PC})'S_{PC}^{-1}(\overline{Y}-T_{PC})$, $\overline{Y}$ being the mean vector corresponding to the PCs, viz., Y.

For trivariate process, the expressions are more complicated.

5.5 MPCIs Based on First Principal Component Only

Although the concept of process capability analysis is there in literature for quite sometimes now (the first seminal paper on this topic being published way back in the year 1986 (refer Kane [5])), the MPCIs find very limited application in practice owing to the complicated conceptual ideas − which are often difficult to visualize and also due to computational complexities.

One way to handle this problem is to use PCA-based MPCIs. However, this does not address the problem completely, as, even then, one may have more than one principal component (PC) at a time. A slight improvization to this can be to retain only the first PC and thereby convert the multivariate process capability problem to a univariate one, which is more acceptable among practitioners.

Tano and Vannman [13] have proposed one such MPCI. Often, it has been observed that although the variability with respect to a quality characteristic may apparently look like moderate or small, the same amount of variability, when considered with respect to the respective specification limits, may be quite high – so much so that it may exceed the specification span altogether. This motivated Tano and Vannman [13] to standardize the variables before applying the so-called PCA.

If there exists q correlated quality characteristics represented by q random variables $X_1, X_2, \cdots, X_q$, then for the ith random variable, they suggested the transformation $X_{T_{V_i}} = \frac{X_i-M_i}{d_i}$, for $i = 1(1)q$, where $M_i = \frac{USL_i+LSL_i}{2}$ and $d_i = \frac{USL_i-LSL_i}{2}$.

It is easy to observe that each $X_{T_{V_i}}$, for $i = 1(1)q$, has the same specification interval $[-1, 1]$, making the transformed tolerance region a hyper-cube.

Thus, if $\boldsymbol{X} \sim N_q(\boldsymbol{\mu}, \Sigma)$, $\boldsymbol{X}_{Tv} \sim N_q(\boldsymbol{\mu}_{Tv}, \Sigma_{Tv})$ with $\Sigma_{Tv} = D'\Sigma D$, where, D is a diagonal $q \times q$ matrix whose ith diagonal element is given by $\frac{1}{d_i}$, for $i = 1(1)q$. This is due to the fact that variance is affected only by change of scale (di) but not by change of origin $(M_i, \quad i = 1(1)q)$. Also, since Tano and Vannman [13] intended to propose an MPCI measuring only the potential capability of a process (analogous to C_p), they have assumed $\boldsymbol{\mu}_{Tv} = \boldsymbol{0}$, which in turn implies that each original random variable (X_i) has its expected value equal to the specification mid-point (Mi), i.e., $E(X_i) = M_i$ for $i = 1(1)q$.

Due to the very nature of the transformation proposed by the authors, the original variable having the maximum variability with respect to its respective specification limits, will have the largest contribution in the first principal component (PC_1). Therefore, if a process is found to be capable, by considering PC_1 only, then it will be considered so by the other PCs as well. However, the converse is not true.

Now by definition, $-1 < X_{Tv_i} < 1$ and since PCs are mutually orthogonal, we have

$$
\begin{aligned}
-1 \quad &< \quad X_{Tv_1} = U_{11}PC_1 + U_{21}PC_2 + \cdots + U_{q1}PC_q < 1 \\
-1 \quad &< \quad X_{Tv_2} = U_{12}PC_1 + U_{22}PC_2 + \cdots + U_{q2}PC_q < 1 \\
&\vdots \\
-1 \quad &< \quad X_{Tv_q} = U_{1q}PC_1 + U_{2q}PC_2 + \cdots + U_{qq}PC_q < 1
\end{aligned}
$$

From this, Tano and Vannman [13] have obtained the specification interval for PC_1 as $USL_{PC_1} = \frac{1}{\max_i |U_{1i}|}$ and $LSL_{PC_1} = -\frac{1}{\max_i |U_{1i}|}$, where U_{1i} is the ith component of the first eigen vector, for $i = 1(1)q$ and $\max_i |U_{1i}|$ is the maximum absolute value of the components of the first PC.

Thus, based on PC_1 and analogous to $C_p = \frac{USL - LSL}{6\sigma}$, the authors have defined a new MPCI as

$$
\begin{aligned}
C_{p,TV} \quad &= \quad \frac{USL_{PC_1} - LSL_{PC_1}}{6\sigma_{PC_1}} \\
&= \quad \frac{\frac{1}{\max_i |U_{1i}| - \left(-\max_i |U_{1i}|\right)}}{6\sqrt{\lambda_1}} \\
&= \quad \frac{1}{\max_i |U_{1i}| 3\sqrt{\lambda_1}},
\end{aligned}
\qquad (5.17)
$$

where λ_1 is the largest eigen value representing the variance of PC_1.

It has been argued many a times in literature that mere defining an MPCI will not deliver the good until its computed values can be properly interpreted [refer Kotz and Johnson [6] and Roddriguez [9]]. In the case of PCA-based

MPCIs, it becomes difficult, as it is, to interpret the value obtained from $C_{p,TV}$. Since PCs are linear combinations of the original variables and $C_{p,TV}$ is calculated from PCs, it becomes difficult to relate the value directly to the health of the process. Hence, for any such new measures, a threshold value should be suggested for better interpretation of the results obtained. It may be noted that in the case of C_p for the univariate case, where the threshold value is 1 and hence C_p values more than 1 are always preferable with higher the value of C_p, the better is the health of the process. Threshold values of other PCIs, including MPCIs, need to be derived properly.

Thus, threshold value plays a fundamental role in interpreting the computed values of a PCI in a sense that a PCI value exceeding this threshold value implies that the process is performing satisfactorily, whereas a PCI value below this signals toward poor process performance.

For processes having two correlated (i.e., for which $\rho \neq 0$) quality characteristics, let k_0 be the threshold value of $C_{p,TV}$ such that if $C_{p,TV} > k_0$, the proportion of nonconformance (PNC) is less than 0.0027. Then Tano and Vannman [13] have formulated

$$k_0 = \frac{\sqrt{1 + \frac{(C-1+B)^2}{4C\rho^2}}}{3\sqrt{\frac{\sigma_{22}}{2}(C+1+B)}}$$

where $B = \sqrt{(1-C)^2 + 4C\rho^2}$ and $0 < C = \frac{\sigma_{11}}{\sigma_{22}} < 1$.

Observe that when $\rho = 0$, $k_0 = \frac{1}{3\sqrt{\sigma_{22}}}$. Tano and Vannman [13] have also shown (graphically) that, for $C_{p,TV} = 1$, PNC is not constant – rather, it depends on two of the three parameters viz., (B, C, ρ).

Since $C_{p,TV}$, defined in equation (5.17), involves process parameters, through λ_1 and U_{1i} for $i = 1(1)q$, which is often unforeseen, the plug-in estimator of $C_{p,TV}$ can be defined as

$$\hat{C}_{p,TV} = \frac{1}{\max_i |\hat{U}_{1i}| 3\sqrt{\hat{\lambda}_1}}, \tag{5.18}$$

where $\hat{\lambda}_1$ is the first eigen value of the sample dispersion matrix S_{TV} and U_1 is the first eigen vector.

Note that since $\hat{C}_{p,TV}$ is based on sample observations only, it is subject to sampling fluctuations and hence computed values of $\hat{C}_{p,TV}$ may not reflect the true capability scenario. To address this problem, it is necessary to study certain inferential properties of $\hat{C}_{p,TV}$.

In this regard, Tano and Vannman [13] have suggested a hypothesis testing based decision rule for $C_{p,TV}$. For this, let us first consider the following hypotheses

$$H_0 : C_{p,TV} = k_0$$
$$\text{against} \quad H_1 : C_{p,TV} > k_0 \tag{5.19}$$

Interestingly, $C_{p,TV}$ is defined in such a manner that in order to estimate it, one has to estimate the specification limits of the first PC as well and hence, although $C_{p,TV}$ is defined analogous to C_p, the lower confidence bound of C_p (at confidence level $1 - \alpha$) viz., $\hat{C}_p\sqrt{\frac{\chi^2_{n-1,\alpha}}{n-1}}$ cannot be used as it is, as the lower confidence bound of $C_{p,TV}$.

Rather, the lower confidence bound of $C_{p,TV}$ will be $\hat{C}_{p,TV}\sqrt{\frac{\chi^2_{n-1,\alpha}}{n-1}}$ with an **approximate** confidence level $(1 - \alpha)$.

5.6 Some Other PCA-Based MPCIs

Apart from those discussed so far, there are some other PCA-based MP-CIs, which will be discussed in detail in subsequent chapters. For example, Wang and Du [16] defined a new MPCI analogous to the univariate PCI, C_p, for processes, which do not follow multivariate normal distribution (see Chapter 10 for more details). Perakis and Xekalaki [8] defined MPCIs for unilateral processes, i.e., when each of the quality characteristics has only one specification limit (see Chapter 8). Scagliarini [10] discussed about impact of measurement error on PCA-based MPCIs and also how to deal with them (Chapter 15).

5.7 A Real-Life Example

Let us consider Dataset 2 given in Chapter 1. Suppose, X_1 and X_2 denote the random variables corresponding to $7J$ and $6J$, respectively. For these two quality characteristics, the USLs and LSLs are $(USL_1, LSL_1) = (85, 75)$ and $(USL_2, LSL_2) = (3, 0)$, respectively. Thus, $\boldsymbol{M} = \boldsymbol{T} = (80.0, 1.5)'$ and $\boldsymbol{d} = (5.0, 1.5)'$. Based on the data in Chapter 1, sample size $n = 39$, $\overline{\boldsymbol{X}} = (77.3046, 1.9495)'$, $\widehat{\Sigma} = \begin{pmatrix} 0.3897 & -0.1134 \\ -0.1134 & 0.0798 \end{pmatrix}$ and hence the observed correlation coefficient is $\hat{\rho} = -0.6433$. Thus, there exists considerably high amount of negative correlation between the two quality characteristics and this nullifies the possibility of assessing the capability of the process with respect to individual quality characteristics.

For these data, eigen values are $\lambda_1 = 0.4268$ and $\lambda_2 = 0.0427$ and eigen vectors are $U_1 = \begin{pmatrix} -0.9505 \\ 0.3107 \end{pmatrix}$ and $U_2 = \begin{pmatrix} -0.3107 \\ 0.9505 \end{pmatrix}$.

PCA-Based MPCIs for Bilateral Specification

Thus, the variation explained by the first PC is 90.91% of the total process variation and hence we only retain the first PC.

Also, the first PC is given by

$$Y_1 = -0.9505X_1 + 0.3107X_2 \qquad (5.20)$$

Based on these information, Wang and Chen's [15] MPCIs can be computed as $\hat{M}C_p^{Wang} = -2.1272$, $\hat{M}C_{pk}^{Wang} = -3.5657$, $\hat{M}C_{pm}^{Wang} = -0.5140$ and $\hat{M}C_{pmk}^{Wang} = -0.8381$. Note that here we have used " ^ " since all the MPCI values are computed from sample information.

It is interesting to observe here that the conventional inequalities between these MPCIs (similar to those given in equation (3.4) of Chapter 3) is violated. This is due to the fact that, for Y_1, the USL is $USL_{Y_1} = -79.8620$ and LSL is $LSL_{Y_1} = -71.28888$, i.e., $LSL_{Y_1} > USL_{Y_1}$. Similar observation was also made by Xekalaki and Perakis [14]. However, they suggested only taking modulus of the existing MPCI values, which does not deliver the good as well, particularly for MC_{pk}^{Wang}, as then $MC_{pk}^{Wang} > MC_p^{Wang}$, which still violates the inequality.

To deal with this problem, one can consider the following modification:

$$MC_{pk}^{(\text{Wang}^*)} = \left(\prod_{i=1}^{v} C_{pk;PC_i}^* \right)^{1/v} \qquad (5.21)$$

where $C_{pk;PC_i}^* = \frac{|d_{PC_i}| - |\mu_{PC_i} - M_{PC_i}|}{3\sigma_{PC_i}}$ with $d_{PC_i} = \frac{USL_{PC_i} - LSL_{PC_i}}{2}$ and $M_{PC_i} = \frac{USL_{PC_i} + LSL_{PC_i}}{2}$, for $i = 1(1)v$.

Thus, based on Xekalaki and Parakis' [14] suggestion and our proposed further modification, the corrected MPCI values are $\hat{M}C_p^{(\text{Wang}^*)} = 2.1872$, $\hat{M}C_{pk}^{(\text{Wang}^*)} = 0.8087$, $\hat{M}C_{pm}^{(\text{Wang}^*)} = 0.5140$, and $\hat{M}C_{pmk}^{(\text{Wang}^*)} = 0.1901$.

Similarly, for unequal weighting (Xekalaki and Parakis' [14]), $\hat{M}C_p^{(\text{XP})} = 1.9884$, $\hat{M}C_{pk}^{(\text{XP})} = 0.7352$, $\hat{M}C_{pm}^{(\text{XP})} = 0.4673$, and $\hat{M}C_{pmk}^{(\text{XP})} = 0.1728$.

Also, computed value of Tano and Vannman's [13] MPCI, $C_{P,TV}$ is $\hat{C}_{P,TV} = 1.3609$ whose threshold value 0.8009, is lower than $\hat{C}_{P,TV}$.

Therefore, except Wang and Chen's [15] MPCIs (which are not technically correct suitable for this data), in all the other cases, computed values of MPCIs analogous to C_p, viz., $\hat{M}C_p^{(\text{Wang}^*)}$, $\hat{M}C_p^{(\text{XP})}$, and $C_{P,TV}$ are substantially high. This indicates toward high level of potential capability of the process. However, all the other MPCI values are quite low, which shows poor level of the actual capability of the process.

Let us now consider the plot of the data as given in Figure 5.1.

From Figure 5.1, it is evident that the process is highly off-centered and this is reflected in the MPCI values, which have just been computed.

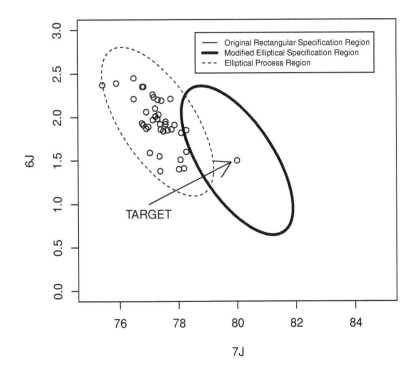

FIGURE 5.1: Plot for data with the actual and modified specification regions and the process region

5.8 Conclusion

PCA, being an efficient statistical tool for dimension reduction, plays an important role in multivariate process capability analysis. However, the success of such MPCIs is subject to proper selection of the number of principal components to be retained. Such choice becomes crucial when scree plot fails to show few significant PCs, say two to four as then PCA fails to reduce dimension of the data effectively.

Again MPCIs based only on first PC (e.g., Tano and Vannman's [13] MPCI) may not perform satisfactorily, if there exists large number of correlated quality characteristics, as then the first PC may not be able to capture substantial amount of variability.

Despite these drawbacks, PCA-based MPCIs are attracting researchers day by day due their computational simplicity.

It may be of interest to know what action is to be taken to improve the present level of $C_{p,TV}$ to higher level. This may be a very difficult question to answer since the PCA-based indices do not reflect the connectivity with the original process parameters. Sometimes, one may have to prioritize the action plan due the usual constraints that one faces in an industrial scenario. This also becomes difficult due to non-existence of clarity with respect to which original variable is to be experimented with.

Bibliography

[1] Dharmasena, L. S., Zeephongsekul, P. (2016). A New Process Capability Index for Multiple Quality Characteristics Based on Principal Components. *International Journal of Production Research*, Vol. 54, No. 15, pp. 4617–4633.

[2] Efron, B. Tibsirani, R.J. (1993). *An Introduction to the bootstrap*, New York: Chapman & Hall.

[3] Johnson, R. A., Wichern, D. A.(2007). *Applied Multivariate Statistical Analysis*, New Jersey: Prentice Hall.

[4] Joliffe, I. T. (2002). *Principal Component Analysis*, New York: Springer.

[5] Kane, V. E. (1986). Process Capability Index. *Journal of Quality Technology*, Vol. 18, No. 1, pp. 41–52.

[6] Kotz, S., Johnson, N. (2002). Process Capability Indices—a Review, 1992–2000. *Journal of Quality Technology*, Vol. 34, No. 1, pp. 2–19.

[7] Min, Z., Wang, G. A., Shuguang, H. E., Zhen, H. E. (2014). Modified Multivariate process capability index Using Principal Component Analysis. *Chinese Journal of Mechanical Engineering*, Vol. 27, No. 2, pp. 249–259.

[8] Perakis, M. Xekalaki, E. (2012). On the Implementation of the Principal Component Analysis—Based Approach in Measuring Process Capability. *Quality and Reliability Engineering International*, Vol. 28, pp. 467–480.

[9] Rodriguez, R. N. (1992). Recent Developments in Process Capability Analysis. *Journal of Quality Technology*, Vol. 24, No. 4, pp. 176–187.

[10] Scagliarini, M. (2011). Multivariate Process Capability Using Principal Component Analysis in the Presence of Measurement Errors. *Advanced Statistical Analysis*, Vol. 95, pp. 113–118.

[11] Shinde, R. L., Khadse, K. G. (2009). Multivariate Process Capability Using Principal Component Analysis. *Quality and Reliability Engineering International*, Vol. 25, No. 1, pp. 69–77.

[12] Taam, W., Subbaiah, P., Liddy, W. (1993). A Note on Multivariate Capability Indices. *Journal of Applied Statistics*, Vol. 20, No. 3, pp. 339–351.

[13] Tano, I., Vannman, K. (2012). A Multivariate Process Capability Index Based on the First Principal Component Only. *Quality and Reliability Engineering International*, Vol. 29, No. 7, pp. 987–1003.

[14] Xekalaki, E., Perakis, M. (2002). The Use of Principal Components Analysis in the Assessment of Process Capability Indices. Proceedings of the Joint Statistical Meetings of the American Statistical Association - Section on Physical and Engineering Sciences (SPES), New York, pp. 3819–3823.

[15] Wang, F. K., Chen, J. C. (1998). Capability Index Using Principal Component Analysis. *Quality Engineering*, Vol. 11, No. 1, pp. 21–27.

[16] Wang, F. K., Du, T. C. T. (2000). Using Principal Component Analysis in Process Performance for Multivariate Data. *Omega*, Vol. 28, No. 2, pp. 185–194.

Chapter 6

Ratio-Based Multivariate Process Capability Indices for Symmetric Specification Region

Chapter Summary

Ratio-based multivariate process capability indices (MPCIs) grossly outnumber other approaches of defining MPCIs. Most of these MPCIs are defined as multivariate analogues of some univariate process capability index (PCI) or the other. As a result, these indices often find ready acceptance among practitioners. In Chapter 6, such ratio-based MPCIs are discussed for bilateral and symmetric (with respect to the stipulated target vector) specification regions along with some of their important statistical properties. A real life example is discussed to supplement the applications of the MPCIs discussed.

6.1 Introduction

Like in the case of univariate process capability indices, ratio-based indices out-number other approaches for multivariate process capability indices (MPCIs) as well. Ease of representation and comparative simplicity of representation are two of the key contributors behind this.

Recall (vide Chapter 3) that, if "X" is a random variable corresponding to the measurable quality characteristic under consideration such that $X \sim N(\mu, \sigma^2)$, then, the four classical process capability indices (PCIs), for symmetric bilateral specification limits, which are most commonly used, are

$$C_p = \frac{U - L}{6\sigma}$$

$$C_{pk} = \frac{d - |\mu - M|}{3\sigma}$$

$$C_{pm} = \frac{d}{3\sqrt{\sigma^2 + (\mu - T)^2}}$$

$$C_{pmk} = \frac{d - |\mu - M|}{3\sqrt{\sigma^2 + (\mu - T)^2}} \tag{6.1}$$

where $d = \frac{U-L}{2}$, $M = \frac{U+L}{2}$ and "T" denotes the targeted value of the quality characteristic under consideration.

Among the four PCIs given in equation (6.1), C_p measures potential process capability. C_{pk} measures process capability taking both process centering μ and process dispersion σ into account. C_{pm} is a target-focused PCI, in a sense that C_{pm} incorporates the concept of "squared error loss" in its definition and finally, C_{pmk} is a "third generation PCI" hybridized from C_{pk} and C_{pm}.

Vannman [25] unified these univariate PCIs and proposed the following super-structure of PCIs for symmetric bi-lateral specification limits:

$$C_p(u, v) = \frac{d - u|\mu - M|}{3\sqrt{\sigma^2 + v(\mu - T)^2}}, \quad u, v \geq 0. \tag{6.2}$$

For $u = 0, 1$ and $v = 0, 1$, $C_p(u, v)$ gives the four basic PCIs given in equation (6.1). For example, $C_p(0, 0) = C_p$, $C_p(1, 0) = C_{pk}$, $C_p(0, 1) = C_{pm}$, and $C_p(1, 1) = C_{pmk}$.

Since the PCIs given in equation (6.1), viz., C_p, $C_{[pk]}$, C_{pm}, and C_{pmk} are widely used in industries, their multivariate analogs have been interesting research area for many eminent statisticians and quality engineers. In the present chapter, we shall discuss some of these MPCI as well as some other ratio-based MPCIs defined so far.

6.2 MPCIs Defined as Multivariate Analogue of C_p

Although Chan et al. [4] were the first to define an MPCI, they had given a multivariate analogue of C_{pm}, whereas. Pearn, Kotz, and Johnson [17] first defined a multivariate analogue of C_p.

Recall that, C_p is the ratio of specification spread and process spread. Now, under multivariate set-up, for correlated characteristics, the specification region becomes elliptical.

Suppose, $\boldsymbol{X}$ is a q-component random vector characterizing the quality characteristics, such that, $\boldsymbol{X} \sim N_q(\boldsymbol{\mu}, \Sigma)$, where q is the number of correlated quality characteristics and $T = (T_1, T_2, \cdots, T_q)$ is the corresponding qcomponent target vector. Then the elliptical specification region will be

$$(\boldsymbol{X} - \boldsymbol{T})' A^{-1}(\boldsymbol{X} - \boldsymbol{T}) \le c^2 \tag{6.3}$$

where c determines the coverage of the ellipse, such that any point lying on or within this region will be considered as being within specification region. Also, A is a $q \times q$ positive definite matrix.

Thus, having information on $\boldsymbol{T}$, Σ, and c is sufficient for setting the specification region.

Recall that, the present objective is to define a multivariate analogue of C_p. Moreover, C_p, in univariate case, is defined as the ratio of specification spread to the process spread and since the underlying process distribution is multivariate normal, using $\boldsymbol{T} = \boldsymbol{\mu}$ and $A = \Sigma$ in equation (6.3), the value of c^2 which will lead to 0.27% proportion of non-conformance is $c_q^2 = \chi_{q,0.9973}^2$.

Based on these information, Pearn et al. [17] defined a multivariate analogue of C_p as

$$_qC_p^2 = \frac{c^2}{c_q^2} \tag{6.4}$$

For $\boldsymbol{\mu} = \boldsymbol{T}$ and $\Sigma = A$, numerator of equation (6.4) coincides with its denominator and consequently, $_qC_p^2 = 1$. Also, similar to the case of C_p, here also

$$P[(\boldsymbol{X} - \boldsymbol{\mu})' \Sigma^{-1}(\boldsymbol{X} - \boldsymbol{\mu}) \le c_q^2] = 0.0027 \tag{6.5}$$

However, if at least one of the conditions viz., $\boldsymbol{\mu} = \boldsymbol{T}$ and $\Sigma = A$ is not satisfied, then it becomes computationally complicated to have a closed-form expression of c_q as it will then depend upon $\boldsymbol{\mu}$, $\boldsymbol{T}$, Σ, and A (refer Pearn and Kotz [16]).

Starting from the basic definition of C_p, Taam et al. [23] have proposed a multivariate analogue of C_p as

$$MC_p = \frac{\text{Volume of } R_1}{\text{Volume of } R_3} \tag{6.6}$$

where R_1 is the modified elliptical tolerance region, i.e., the largest ellipsoid centered at the target vector and placed completely within the original tolerance region and R_3 is the region which includes 99.73% of the process spread. Note that, although in most of the practical situations, the original specification region is rectangular, since for multivariate normal process distribution, the process region is elliptical, the specification region has been modified here into an elliptical one, so as to define MPCIs analogous to C_p and C_{pm}.

Also, under multivariate normal set-up, the volume of a q-component sphere with dispersion matrix Σ and coverage k_q can be given by $|\Sigma|^{1/2} \times (\pi k_q)^{q/2} \times [\Gamma(q/2 + 1)]^{-1}$.

Accordingly

$$
\begin{aligned}
\text{Volume of } R_3 &= Vol. \left[(\boldsymbol{X} - \boldsymbol{\mu})' \Sigma^{-1} (\boldsymbol{X} - \boldsymbol{\mu}) \leq k_q \right] \\
&= |\Sigma|^{1/2} \times (\pi k_q)^{q/2} \times [\Gamma(q/2 + 1)]^{-1} \qquad (6.7)
\end{aligned}
$$

Thus

$$
MC_p = \frac{(\prod_{i=1}^{q} d_i) \times \pi^{q/2} \times [\Gamma\left(\frac{q}{2}\right) + 1]^{-1}}{|\Sigma|^{1/2} \times (\pi k_q)^{q/2} \times [\Gamma(q/2 + 1)]^{-1}} \qquad (6.8)
$$

As has been discussed before, definition of a PCI involves process parameters, which are often unobservable in practice and MC_p is no exception. For practical computational purpose, its plug-in estimator can be defined as follows (refer Pearn et al. [19]):

Suppose n random samples are drawn from q-variate normal distribution, such that $\boldsymbol{X_i} \sim N_q(\boldsymbol{\mu}, \Sigma)$, for $i = 1(1)n$. Then plug-in estimator of MC_p, viz., $\hat{MC}_p$ will be

$$
\begin{aligned}
\hat{MC}_p &= \frac{Vol. \text{ (Modified tolerance region)}}{|S|^{1/2} \times (\pi k_q)^{q/2} \times [\Gamma(q/2 + 1)]^{-1}} \\
&= \frac{(\prod_{i=1}^{q} d_i) \times \pi^{q/2} \times [\Gamma\left(\frac{q}{2}\right) + 1]^{-1}}{|\Sigma|^{1/2} \times (\pi k_q)^{q/2} \times [\Gamma(q/2 + 1)]^{-1}} \times \left(\frac{|S|}{|\Sigma|}\right)^{-1/2} \\
&= MC_p \times \left(\frac{|S|}{|\Sigma|}\right)^{-1/2} \qquad (6.9)
\end{aligned}
$$

where $|S|$ is the determinant of the sample dispersion matrix S and is known as "*Generalized Variance.*"

Pearn et al. [19] have made a detailed discussion regarding the statistical distribution of $\hat{MC}_p$. Following Anderson [1]

$$
|S| \sim \frac{|\Sigma|}{(n-1)^q} \times \prod_{i=1}^{q} \chi_{n-i}^2 \qquad (6.10)
$$

Using this result, the pdf of $\hat{MC}_p$ can be obtained as

$$
\begin{aligned}
f(x) &= \frac{(n-1)^3 \times \left(\frac{1}{2}\right)^{(n-3)/2}}{MC_p \Gamma(n-2) \Gamma(n-3/2)} \times \left(\frac{MC_p}{x}\right)^{n-2} \\
&\times \int_0^{\infty} q^{-1/2} \times e^{-\left[\sqrt{q} + \frac{(n-1)^3 \times (MC_p/x)^2}{2q}\right]} dq, \quad x > 0 \qquad (6.11)
\end{aligned}
$$

From this p.d.f, Pearn et al. [19] have obtained expressions for the rth order raw moment, expectation, and variance of $\hat{M}C_p$ as follows:

$$E\left(\hat{M}C_p^r\right) \;=\; MC_p^r \times \frac{2^{-qr/2}\prod\limits_{i=1}^{q}\Gamma\left[\frac{1}{2(n-i)}-r/2\right]}{(n-1)^{-qr/2}\prod\limits_{i=1}^{q}\Gamma\left[\frac{1}{2(n-i)}\right]} \tag{6.12}$$

and in particular, for $r = 1$

$$E\left(\hat{M}C_p\right) \;=\; MC_p \times \frac{2^{-q/2}\prod\limits_{i=1}^{q}\Gamma\left[\frac{1}{2(n-i)}-1/2\right]}{(n-1)^{-q/2}\prod\limits_{i=1}^{q}\Gamma\left[\frac{1}{2(n-i)}\right]}$$

$$\;=\; \frac{1}{b_q} \times MC_p, \tag{6.13}$$

$$\Rightarrow E\left(b_q\hat{M}C_p\right) \;=\; MC_p \tag{6.14}$$

where $b_q = \left(\frac{2}{n-1}\right)^{q/2}\frac{\Gamma\left[\frac{1}{2(n-1)}\right]}{\Gamma\left[\frac{1}{2(n-q)}-\frac{1}{2}\right]}$. Thus, $b_q\hat{M}C_p$ is an unbiased estimator of MC_p.

Also

$$E\left(\hat{M}C_p^2\right) \;=\; MC_p^2 \times \frac{2^{-q}\prod\limits_{i=1}^{q}\Gamma\left[\frac{1}{2(n-i)}-1\right]}{(n-1)^{-q}\prod\limits_{i=1}^{q}\Gamma\left[\frac{1}{2(n-i)}\right]} \tag{6.15}$$

Therefore, using equations (6.13) and (6.15)

$$V\left[\hat{M}C_p\right] \;=\; MC_p^2 \times \frac{2^{-q}\prod\limits_{i=1}^{q}\Gamma\left[\frac{1}{2(n-i)}-1\right]}{(n-1)^{-q}\prod\limits_{i=1}^{q}\Gamma\left[\frac{1}{2(n-i)}\right]} - \frac{1}{b_q^2} \times MC_p^2 \tag{6.16}$$

Apart from the point estimation of $\hat{M}C_p$, Pearn et al. [19] have also discussed interval estimation and hypothesis testing procedure regarding $\hat{M}C_p$.

Recall from equation (6.9) that, $\hat{M}C_p = MC_p \times \left(\frac{|S|}{|\Sigma|}\right)^{-1/2}$ and also $|S| \sim \frac{|\Sigma|}{(n-1)^q} \times \prod\limits_{i=1}^{q}\chi^2_{n-i}$. Based on these, Pearn et al. [19] have derived expression for the $100 \times (1-\alpha)\%$ confidence interval. Suppose

$$P\left[L_{MC_p} \leq MC_p \leq U_{MC_p}\right] = 1 - \alpha$$

$$\Rightarrow P\left[L_{MC_p} \leq \hat{MC}_p \times \left(\frac{|S|}{|\Sigma|}\right)^{1/2} \leq U_{MC_p}\right] = 1 - \alpha$$

$$(6.17)$$

where L_{MC_p} and U_{MC_p} are, respectively, the $100 \times (1 - \alpha)\%$ lower and upper confidence bounds of MC_p.

Let Y be a random variable such that $Y \sim \prod_{i=1}^{q} \chi^2_{n-i}$ and also let its cumulative distribution function (CDF) be given by $F_Y(.)$. Then the $100 \times (1 - \alpha)\%$ confidence interval can be obtained as

$$\left[\hat{MC}_p\sqrt{\frac{F_Y^{-1}(\alpha/2)}{(n-1)^q}}, \hat{MC}_p\sqrt{\frac{F_Y^{-1}(1-\alpha/2)}{(n-1)^q}}\right]$$

$$(6.18)$$

For a particular dataset, explicit form of this confidence interval can be obtained using numerical integration.

To carry out a hypothesis testing procedure based on MC_p, Pearn et al. [19] considered-following hypotheses:

$$H_0 \quad : \quad MC_p \leq c_0$$
$$\text{Against } H_1 \quad : \quad MC_p > c_0$$

Pearn et al. [19] referred to c_0 as "standard minimal criteria for MC_p." To be more precise, c_0 acts like some sort of a threshold, in a sense that if H_0 is accepted, the process is considered to be potentially incapable and otherwise it is considered to be potentially capable.

Now, as has already been discussed, since MC_p is a function of process parameters and hence is mostly unobservable, some critical value, say c, is required for $\hat{MC}_p$, which will play similar role as that of c_0, for $\hat{MC}_p$. This critical value c can be formulated as

$$c = c_0\sqrt{\frac{(n-1)^q}{F_Y^{-1}(\alpha)}}$$

$$(6.19)$$

Corresponding power of test $\beta(MC_p)$ is given by

$$\beta(MC_p) = P\left[\hat{MC}_p > c \mid MC_p\right]$$

$$= P\left[\frac{(n-1)^q MC_p^2}{c^2} > f_Y(y) \mid MC_p\right]$$

$$(6.20)$$

where $f_Y(y)$ is the probability density function (p. d. f.) of $Y = \prod_{i=1}^{q} \chi_{n-i}^2$.

Pearn et al. [19] have shown that the chance of incorrectly concluding that a process is not capable decreases with an increasing value of c_0, while the situation is just the opposite with c. Thus, statistical properties of MC_p have been thoroughly explored by several eminent statisticians and quality engineers and this is highly desirable for a PCI.

Although, MC_p is one of the most widely accepted MPCIs among the practitioners, it suffers from some serious drawbacks. Pan and Lee [15] have shown that

$$MC_p = |R|^{-1/2}, \qquad (6.21)$$

where R is the correlation matrix of the process. Interestingly, similar to C_p, here also the simplified form of MC_p is independent of the mean vector, viz., $\boldsymbol{\mu}$.

They have also observed that, since the simplified expression for MC_p, as given in equation (6.21) is merely the reciprocal of the square-root of correlation matrix of the process, MC_p will assume a value more than one, whenever the quality characteristics are correlated among themselves. Consequently, it tends to over-estimate the capability level of a process.

Following Shahriari and Abdollahzadeh [22], this tendency of MC_p to over-estimate process capability can be geometrically explained as follows:

Consider Figure 6.1 depicting relative positions of original tolerance region, modified tolerance region and elliptical process region for a presumed process.

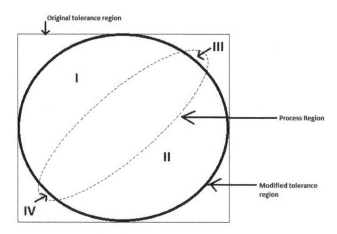

FIGURE 6.1: Relative positions of original tolerance region, modified tolerance region and elliptical process region.

From Figure 6.1, it can be easily seen that, observations seldom occur in areas I and II. These observations are not covered by the elliptical process region, though both the original rectangular as well as the modified elliptical tolerance regions cover them. Situation is just the opposite for areas labeled as III and IV. The observations which may fall in these areas are covered by both the process region and the original rectangular tolerance region but not by the modified tolerance region.

Note that, the observations which fall in these areas I, II, III, and IV may be countably rare, but feasible. In fact, being inside the original tolerance region, such observations should not be ideally considered as nonconforming ones.

Recall that, the formula for MC_p is the ratio of the volume of the modified tolerance region to the volume of the process region. As Figure 6.1 suggests, inclusion of areas I and II in the modified tolerance region, and not in the process region, will inflate numerator of MC_p, resulting in over-estimation of the process capability.

On the contrary, inclusion of areas III and IV in the process region, and not in the modified tolerance region, will inflate denominator of MC_p, resulting in under-estimation of the process capability.

It is also evident from Figure 6.1 that, contributions of regions labeled I and II may out-number contributions of regions labeled III and IV and hence MC_p will end up over-estimating the process capability.

Interestingly, Pan and Lee [15] and Shahriari et al. [22] have also observed that this problem of over-estimation is caused by the modified tolerance region defined by Taam et al. [23]. In fact, their proposed modified tolerance region does not take into account the prevailing correlation structure among the process variables, due to the fact that, while it is inscribed to the original rectangular engineering tolerance region, its two axes remain parallel to the co-ordinate axes (refer Pan and Lee [15] and Wang et al. [27]).

To prove this, note that if

$$E_{c,A,\boldsymbol{X}_0} = \left\{ \boldsymbol{X} \in \mathbb{R}^q | \ (\boldsymbol{X} - \boldsymbol{X}_0)^{'} A(\boldsymbol{X} - \boldsymbol{X}_0) = c^2 \right\} \qquad (6.22)$$

is an ellipsoid having center at $\boldsymbol{X}_0 \in \mathbb{R}^q$, A is a positive definite matrix and c is a constant, then the rectangle circumscribing the ellipsoid can be defined by

$$X_{0i} - \sqrt{c^2 a^{ii}} \leq X_i \leq X_{0i} + \sqrt{c^2 a^{ii}}, \ i = 1(1)q, \qquad (6.23)$$

where, a^{ii} is the $(i, i)^{\text{th}}$ element of A^{-1} and X_{0i} is the ith element of $\boldsymbol{X}_0$ (refer Hardle and Simar [8]).

Thus, using similar notations, for $d^2 = \chi^2_{1-\alpha,q}$, Taam's [23] modified tolerance region can be defined as

$$E_{\chi^2_{1-\alpha,q},A,\boldsymbol{T}}$$
$$= \left\{ \boldsymbol{X} \in \mathbb{R}^q | \ (\boldsymbol{X} - \boldsymbol{T})^{'} A^{-1}(\boldsymbol{X} - \boldsymbol{X_0}) \leq \chi^2_{1-\alpha,q} \right\} \qquad (6.24)$$

where ith diagonal element of A is given by $\frac{(USL_i - LSL_i)^2}{\left(2\sqrt{\chi^2_{1-\alpha,q}}\right)^2}$, $i = 1(1)q$ (refer Pan and Lee [15]).

Thus, similar to equation (6.23), the rectangle circumscribed to the ellipsoid $E_{\chi^2_{1-\alpha,q}, \Sigma^*, T}$ is given by

$$T_i - \sqrt{\chi^2_{1-\alpha,q} \times \left(\frac{USL_i - LSL_i}{2^2\chi^2_{1-\alpha,q}}\right)^2} \leq X_i$$

$$\leq T_i + \sqrt{\chi^2_{1-\alpha,q} \times \left(\frac{USL_i - LSL_i}{2^2\chi^2_{1-\alpha,q}}\right)^2}$$

i.e., $\quad T_i - \dfrac{USL_i - LSL_i}{2} \leq X_i \leq T_i + \dfrac{USL_i - LSL_i}{2}$

i.e., $\quad \dfrac{USL_i + LSL_i}{2} - \dfrac{USL_i - LSL_i}{2} \leq X_i$

$$\leq \dfrac{USL_i + LSL_i}{2} - \dfrac{USL_i - LSL_i}{2}$$

Therefore, $\quad LSL_i \leq X_i \leq USL_i$ $\hfill (6.25)$

This implies that, equation (6.24) truly represents modified specification region as defined by Taam et al. [23]. Also observe that A is indeed independent of the correlation structure of the process.

To address this problem, Pan and Lee [15] have proposed a correction to this modified specification region. For this, the authors have assumed that, the underlying correlation structure is consistent with the correlation among the specification limits. This is quite a viable assumption in a sense that, although at design level, often prior to commencement of production, the specifications are set individually for the quality characteristics, since the quality characteristics are correlated among themselves, ideally, their combined specification region should also have the same correlation structure.

Recall that, Pan and Lee [15] have shown that for Taam et al.'s [23] modified specification region (vide equation (6.24)), the ith diagonal element of A is given by $\frac{(USL_i - LSL_i)^2}{\left(2\sqrt{\chi^2_{1-\alpha,q}}\right)^2}$, $i = 1(1)q$. Similar to this, Pan and Lee's [15] revised engineering tolerance region can be defined as

$$E_{\chi^2_{1-\alpha,q}, A^*, T} = \left\{ \boldsymbol{X} \in \mathbb{R}^q \mid (\boldsymbol{X} - \boldsymbol{T})^{'} A^{-*1} (\boldsymbol{X} - \boldsymbol{T}) \leq \chi^2_{1-\alpha,q} \right\} \qquad (6.26)$$

where ith element of A^*, viz., a^*_{ij}, is given by

$$a^*_{ij} = \rho_{ij} \left(\frac{USL_i - LSL_i}{2c}\right) \times \left(\frac{USL_j - LSL_j}{2c}\right), \qquad (6.27)$$

for $i = 1(1)q$, $j = 1(1)q$ with $c = \sqrt{\chi^2_{1-\alpha,q}}$.

Observe that, since the problem of over estimation of MC_p is primarily caused by the definition of modified tolerance region, Pan and Lee [15] have retained the expression for the process region, as defined by Taam et al. [23] as it is. Thus, keeping symmetry with the notation of revised tolerance region as given in equation (6.26), the process region may be given by

$$E_{\chi^2_{1-\alpha,q},\Sigma,\mu} = \left\{ \boldsymbol{X} \in \mathbb{R}^q \mid (\boldsymbol{X} - \boldsymbol{\mu})' \Sigma^{-1} (\boldsymbol{X} - \boldsymbol{\mu}) \leq \chi^2_{1-\alpha,q} \right\} \qquad (6.28)$$

Based on these information Pan and Lee [15] have defined a multivariate analogue of C_p as

$$\begin{aligned}
NMC_p &= \frac{E_{\chi^2_{1-\alpha,q},A^*,\boldsymbol{T}}}{E_{\chi^2_{1-\alpha,q},\Sigma,\mu}} \\
&= \frac{|A^*|^{1/2}(\pi\chi^2_{1-\alpha,q})^{q/2}[\Gamma\left(\frac{q}{2}+1\right)]^{-1}}{|\Sigma|^{1/2}(\pi\chi^2_{1-\alpha,q})^{q/2}[\Gamma\left(\frac{q}{2}+1\right)]^{-1}} \\
&= \left(\frac{|A^*|}{|\Sigma|}\right)^{1/2} \qquad (6.29)
\end{aligned}$$

Note that, the expression for NMC_p does not incorporate $\boldsymbol{\mu}$ in its definition and hence it can be considered as an MPCI measuring potential capability of a process.

Observe that in the definition of NMC_p, as given in equation (6.29), the numerator is solely based on the specifications of the concerned quality characteristics and hence is fully observable. On the contrary, its denominator is the determinant of the dispersion matrix, which is seldom known in practice and hence needs to be estimated. Therefore, the plug-in estimator of NMC_p can be defined as

$$\widehat{NMC}_p = \left(\frac{|A^*|}{|S|}\right)^{1/2} \qquad (6.30)$$

where, $S = \frac{1}{n-1}\sum_{i=1}^{q}(\boldsymbol{X}_i - \overline{\boldsymbol{X}})(\boldsymbol{X}_i - \overline{\boldsymbol{X}})'$ is the sample dispersion matrix and

$\overline{\boldsymbol{X}} = \frac{1}{n}\sum_{i=1}^{q} \boldsymbol{X}_i$ is the sample mean vector. Note that the denominator of $\widehat{NMC}_p$, viz., $|S|$ is nothing but the generalized variance corresponding to Σ.

Note that the denominator of $\widehat{NMC}_p$, viz., $|S|$ is nothing but the generalized variance corresponding to Σ. Using its statistical properties, Pan and Lee [15] have derived expression for the rth moment of $\widehat{NMC}_p$ as

$$E\left[\widehat{NMC}_p^r\right] \;=\; \frac{1}{b_r} \times NMC_p^r \tag{6.31}$$

where $b_r = \left(\frac{2}{n-1}\right)^{qr/2} \prod\limits_{i=1}^{q} \left(\frac{\Gamma\left(\frac{n-i}{2}\right)}{\Gamma\left(\frac{n-i-r}{2}\right)}\right)$.

Accordingly from equation (6.31), expectation and variance of $\widehat{NMC}_p$ can be obtained as

$$E\left[\widehat{NMC}_p\right] \;=\; \frac{1}{b_1} \times NMC_p \tag{6.32}$$

$$V\left[\widehat{NMC}_p\right] \;=\; \left(\frac{1}{b_2} - \frac{1}{b_1^2}\right) NMC_p^2 \tag{6.33}$$

where $b_1 = \left(\frac{2}{n-1}\right)^{q/2} \prod\limits_{i=1}^{q}\left(\frac{\Gamma\left(\frac{n-i}{2}\right)}{\Gamma\left(\frac{n-i-1}{2}\right)}\right)$ and $b_2 = \left(\frac{2}{n-1}\right)^{q} \prod\limits_{i=1}^{q}\left(\frac{\Gamma\left(\frac{n-i}{2}\right)}{\Gamma\left(\frac{n-i-2}{2}\right)}\right)$.

Thus, $b_1 \times \widehat{NMC}_p$ is an unbiased estimator of NMC_p.

Recall from equation 6.10 that, $|S| \sim \frac{|\Sigma|}{(n-1)^q} \times \prod\limits_{i=1}^{q} \chi_{n-i}^2$. Using this, Pan and Lee [15] have derived expression for the $100(1-\alpha)\%$ confidence interval of NMC_p as

$$\left[\widehat{NMC}_p\sqrt{\frac{w_\alpha}{2}}, \;\; \widehat{NMC}_p\sqrt{\frac{w_{1-\alpha}}{2}}\right] \tag{6.34}$$

where w_α is the αth percentile of $\frac{1}{(n-1)^q} \times \prod\limits_{i=1}^{q} \chi_{n-i}^2$.

However, Tano and Vannman [24] have shown that for the interval estimate of NMC_p, the estimated significance level exceeds the nominal level irrespective of the sample size and therefore the problem of overestimation of process capability is still not resolved.

Jessenberger and Weih [10] have proposed another multivariate analogue of C_p as follows:

$$
\begin{aligned}
MVC_p^* \;&=\; \frac{(\boldsymbol{X}-\boldsymbol{\mu})'\Sigma^{-1}(\boldsymbol{X}-\boldsymbol{\mu}) \le k^2}{(\boldsymbol{X}-\boldsymbol{\mu})'\Sigma^{-1}(\boldsymbol{X}-\boldsymbol{\mu}) \le \chi_{1-\alpha,q}^2} \\[2mm]
&=\; \frac{(\pi k^2)^{q/2}|\Sigma|^{1/2}[\Gamma(q/2+1)^{-1}]}{(\pi\chi_{1-\alpha,q}^2)^{q/2}|\Sigma|^{1/2}[\Gamma(q/2+1)^{-1}]} \\[2mm]
&=\; \left(\frac{k^2}{\chi_{1-\alpha,q}^2}\right)^{q/2} \tag{6.35}
\end{aligned}
$$

where k^2 is so chosen that, the resulting ellipsoidal specification region has the greatest volume, while being inside the original rectangular specification region.

Jessenberger and Weih [10] have further shown that

$$k = \min_{i=1,2,\cdots,q} \left(\frac{USL_i - T_i}{\sigma_i}, \frac{T_i - LSL_i}{\sigma_i} \right) \tag{6.36}$$

Thus, substituting the value of k from equation (6.36) in equation (6.35),

$$MVC_p^* = \min_{i=1,2,\cdots,q} \left(\left[\frac{USL_i - T_i}{\sigma_i \sqrt{\chi_{1-\alpha,q}^2}} \right]^q, \left[\frac{T_i - LSL_i}{\sigma_i \sqrt{\chi_{1-\alpha,q}^2}} \right]^q \right) \tag{6.37}$$

Now, since here it is assumed that the specification limits for the ith quality characteristic to be symmetric about the stipulated target T_i, i.e., $T_i = \frac{USL_i + LSL_i}{2}$, for $i = 1(1)q$

$$\min_{i=1,2,\cdots,q} (USL_i - T_i, T_i - LSL_i)$$

$$= \frac{1}{2} [USL_i - T_i + T_i - LSL_i + |USL_i - T_i - T_i + LSL_i|]$$

$$= \frac{1}{2} [USL_i - LSL_i + USL_i + LSL_i - 2T_i]$$

$$= \frac{1}{2} \left[USL_i - LSL_i + USL_i + LSL_i - 2\frac{USL_i + LSL_i}{2} \right]$$

$$= \frac{USL_i - LSL_i}{2}$$

$$= 3C_{pi} \tag{6.38}$$

Therefore, from equation (6.37)

$$MVC_p^* = \min_{i=1,2,\cdots,q} \left\{ \left(\frac{3}{\sqrt{\chi_{1-\alpha,q}^2}} \times C_{pi} \right)^q \right\} \tag{6.39}$$

As such, MVC_p^* is nothing but a constant (viz., $\frac{3}{\sqrt{\chi_{1-\alpha,q}^2}}$) times minimum C_{pi} value raised to qth power, where q is the number of quality characteristics under consideration. Clearly, MVC_p^*, by its definition, fails to capture correlation structure prevailing in the process.

6.3 MPCIs Defined as Multivariate Analogue of C_{pk}

Recall that, since C_p is independent of process centering, it measures potential capability only. To incorporate the concept of process centering in the definition of PCI, Kane [11] defined C_{pk}, whose expression is given as below:

$$C_{pk} = \frac{d - |\mu - M|}{3\sigma}, \tag{6.40}$$

where $d = \frac{USL-LSL}{2}$ and $M = \frac{USL+LSL}{2}$.

Kotz and Johnson [12] have shown that

$$p = \Phi\left(-3(2C_p - C_{pk})\right) + \Phi(-3C_{pk}) \tag{6.41}$$

where p denotes proportion of nonconformance.

Since C_{pk} measures exact process capability and is a yield based PCI, i.e., having exact relationship with p, it finds ample application in practice.

However, from multidimensional perspective, MPCIs analogous to C_{pk} are outnumbered by those analogous to C_p and C_{pm}.

Pearn et al. [18] proposed a multivariate analogue of C_{pk}, based on the concept of proportion of nonconformance. Suppose there are q correlated quality characteristics and their underlying distribution is q component multivariate normal distribution, i.e., $\boldsymbol{X} \sim N_q(\boldsymbol{\mu}, \Sigma)$. Then Pearn et al. [18] proposed a multivariate analogue of C_{pk} as

$$C_{pk}^T = \frac{1}{3}\Phi^{-1}\left[\frac{\prod_{i=1}^{q}\{2\Phi(3C_{pki}) - 1\} + 1}{2}\right] \tag{6.42}$$

where C_{pki} is the C_{pk} value for ith quality characteristic, for $i = 1, 2, \cdots, q$ and $\Phi(.)$ is the c.d.f. of univariate normal distribution.

As is evident from equation (6.42), the definition of C_{pk}^T is based on the assumption that all the quality characteristics are mutually independent. Note that, since C_{pk} is a yield based PCI, C_{pk}^T, being its multivariate analogue, should possess similar property. Also, Boyles [3] have established-following relationship between C_{pk} and the corresponding proportion of nonconformance (say, p):

$$2\Phi(3C_{pk}) - 1 \leq p \leq \Phi(3C_{pk}) \tag{6.43}$$

Interestingly, while defining C_{pk}^T, Pearn et al. [18] have used left hand side of the inequality given in equation (6.43). One possible reason behind this

Ratio-based MPCIs for symmetric specification region   143

choice may be, this part of the inequality gives a lower bound to the proportion of nonconformance (now onwards abbreviated as "PNC") and hence is practically more useful.

Now, since Pearn et al. [18] have considered mutual independence of the concerned quality characteristics, the corresponding PNC, say P_T, can be defined as

$$
\begin{aligned}
P_T &= \prod_{i=1}^{q} p_i \\
&\geq \prod_{i=1}^{q} \{2\Phi(3C_{pki}) - 1\}
\end{aligned}
\tag{6.44}
$$

where p_i is the PNC corresponding to the ith quality characteristic, for $i = 1(1)q$.

Again, from equation (6.42)

$$
C_{pk}^{T} = \frac{1}{3}\Phi^{-1}\left[\frac{\prod\limits_{i=1}^{q} \{2\Phi(3C_{pki}) - 1\} + 1}{2}\right]
$$

$$
\Rightarrow \quad \prod_{i=1}^{q} \{2\Phi(3C_{pki}) - 1\} = 2\Phi(3C_{pk}^{T}) - 1
\tag{6.45}
$$

Hence from equations (6.44) and (6.45)

$$
P_T \geq 2\Phi(3C_{pk}^{T}) - 1
\tag{6.46}
$$

Replacing μ_i by $\overline{X}_i = \frac{1}{n}\sum\limits_{k=1}^{n} X_{ik}$ and σ_i^2 by $S_i^2 = \frac{1}{n-1}\sum\limits_{k=1}^{n}(X_{ik} - \overline{X}_i)^2$, Pearn et al. [18] have defined a plug-in estimator of C_{pk}^{T} as

$$
\hat{C}_{pk}^{T} = \frac{1}{3}\Phi^{-1}\left[\frac{\prod\limits_{i=1}^{q} \left\{2\Phi(3\hat{C}_{pki}) - 1\right\} + 1}{2}\right]
\tag{6.47}
$$

where $\hat{C}_{pki} = \frac{d - |\overline{X} - M|}{3S_i}$ is the plug-in estimator of the C_{pk} value for ith quality characteristic, for $i = 1, 2, \cdots, q$.

Observe that $\hat{C}_{pk}^{T}$ is merely a function of $\overline{X}_i$ and S_i^2, for $i = 1(1)q$, i.e., notationally, $\hat{C}_{pk}^{T} = f(\overline{X}_1, \overline{X}_2, \cdots, \overline{X}_q, S_1^2, S_2^2, \cdots, S_q^2)$. Then, using first order Taylor series expansion of this function with respect to $\mu_1, \mu_2, \cdots, \mu_q$, and $\sigma_1^2, \sigma_2^2, \cdots, \sigma_q^2$, Pearn et al. [18] have derived expression for the approximate distribution of $\hat{C}_{pk}^{T}$ as follows:

The first order derivative of $\hat{C}_{pk}^T = f(\overline{X}_1, \overline{X}_2, \cdots, \overline{X}_q, S_1^2, S_2^2, \cdots, S_q^2)$ with respect to $\hat{\mu}_i$, for $i = 1(1)q$ is

$$
\begin{aligned}
\frac{\delta f}{\delta \hat{\mu}_i} &= \frac{\delta}{\delta \hat{\mu}_i} \frac{1}{3} \Phi^{-1} \left[\frac{\prod\limits_{i=1}^{q} \left\{ 2\Phi(3\hat{C}_{pki}) - 1 \right\} + 1}{2} \right] \\
&= \frac{\delta}{\delta \hat{\mu}_i} \frac{1}{3} \Phi^{-1} \left[g(\overline{X}_1, \overline{X}_2, \cdots, \overline{X}_q, S_1^2, S_2^2, \cdots, S_q^2) \right], \quad \text{say}
\end{aligned}
$$

$$(6.48)$$

where $g(\overline{X}_1, \overline{X}_2, \cdots, \overline{X}_q, S_1^2, S_2^2, \cdots, S_q^2) = \dfrac{\prod\limits_{i=1}^{q} \left\{ 2\Phi(3\hat{C}_{pki}) - 1 \right\} + 1}{2}$. Therefore

$$
\begin{aligned}
&\frac{\delta f}{\delta \hat{\mu}_i} \bigg|_{\hat{\mu}_i = \mu_i, \hat{\sigma}_i = \sigma_i, \ i=1(1)q} \\[2mm]
&= \frac{-1}{3\phi \left[\dfrac{\prod\limits_{i=1}^{q} \left\{ 2\Phi(3\hat{C}_{pki}) - 1 \right\} + 1}{2} \right]} \\[2mm]
&\times \frac{\delta}{\delta \hat{\mu}_i} g(\overline{X}_1, \overline{X}_2, \cdots, \overline{X}_q, S_1^2, S_2^2, \cdots, S_q^2) \big|_{\hat{\mu}_i = \mu_i, \hat{\sigma}_i = \sigma_i, \ i=1(1)q} \\[2mm]
&= \frac{-1}{3\phi \left[3\hat{C}_{pk}^T \right]} \times \frac{\prod\limits_{i=1}^{q} \left\{ 2\Phi(3\hat{C}_{pki}) - 1 \right\}}{2} \times 2\left\{ \phi(3\hat{C}_{pki}) \right\} \\[2mm]
&\quad \times 3 \frac{\delta}{\delta \hat{\mu}_i} \left\{ \frac{d - |\hat{\mu}_i - M|}{3\hat{\sigma}_i} \right\} \bigg|_{\hat{\mu}_i = \mu_i, \hat{\sigma}_i = \sigma_i, \ i=1(1)q} \\[2mm]
&= -\frac{1}{3\phi(\Phi(3\hat{C}_{pk}^T))} \\[2mm]
&\quad \times \frac{1}{\hat{\sigma}_i} \left\{ \left[\prod\limits_{j=1, j \neq i}^{q} \left(2\Phi(3\hat{C}_{pkj}) - 1 \right) \right] \phi(3\hat{C}_{pki})\delta_i \right\} \bigg|_{\hat{\mu}_i = \mu_i, \hat{\sigma}_i = \sigma_i, \ i=1(1)q} \\[2mm]
&= -\frac{1}{3\phi(\Phi(3C_{pk}^T))} \times \frac{1}{\sigma_i} \left\{ \left[\prod\limits_{j=1, j \neq i}^{q} \left(2\Phi(3C_{pkj}) - 1 \right) \right] \phi(3C_{pki})\delta_i \right\}
\end{aligned}
$$

$$(6.49)$$

where $\delta_i = \begin{cases} 1, & \text{for } \mu \geq M_i \\ -1, & \text{for } \mu < M_i \end{cases}$, i.e., the indicator variable δ_i takes care of the modulus function in the numerator of C_{pk}^T.

Similarly, the first order derivative of

$$\hat{C}_{pk}^T = f(\overline{X}_1, \overline{X}_2, \cdots, \overline{X}_q, S_1^2, S_2^2, \cdots, S_q^2)$$

with respect to $\hat{\sigma}_i^2$, for $i = 1(1)q$ is

$$\frac{\delta f}{\delta \hat{\sigma}_i}\bigg|_{\hat{\mu}_i=\mu_i, \hat{\sigma}_i=\sigma_i, \ i=1(1)q}$$

$$= -\frac{1}{3\phi(\Phi(3C_{pk}^T))} \times \left\{ \frac{3C_{pki}}{2\sigma_i^2} \left[\prod_{j=1, j\neq i}^{q} (2\Phi(3C_{pkj}) - 1) \right] \phi(3C_{pki}) \right\}$$

$$(6.50)$$

Thereore, the first order Taylor Series expansion of $\hat{C}_{pk}^T = f(\overline{X}_1, \overline{X}_2, \cdots, \overline{X}_q, S_1^2, S_2^2, \cdots, S_q^2)$ with respect to $\mu_1, \mu_2, \cdots, \mu_q, \sigma_1^2, \sigma_2^2, \cdots, \sigma_q^2$ will be

$$\hat{C}_{pk}^T \approx f(\mu_1, \mu_2, \cdots, \mu_q, \sigma_1^2, \sigma_2^2, \cdots, \sigma_q^2) + \sum_{i=1}^{q} \frac{\delta f}{\delta \hat{\mu}_i}\bigg|_{\hat{\mu}_i=\mu_i, \hat{\sigma}_i=\sigma_i, \ i=1(1)q}$$

$$+ \sum_{i=1}^{q} \frac{\delta f}{\delta \hat{\sigma}_i^2}\bigg|_{\hat{\mu}_i=\mu_i, \hat{\sigma}_i=\sigma_i, \ i=1(1)q},$$

retaining partial derivatives up to first order only

$$= C_{pk}^T - \frac{1}{3\phi(\Phi(3C_{pk}^T))} \sum_{i=1}^{q} (W_i + G_i) \qquad (6.51)$$

where

$$W_i = \frac{1}{\sigma_i} \left[\prod_{j=1, j\neq i}^{q} (2\Phi(3C_{pkj}) - 1) \right] \times (\overline{X}_i - \mu_i) \times \phi(3C_{pki}) \qquad (6.52)$$

and

$$G_i = \frac{3C_{pki}}{2\sigma_i^2} \left[\prod_{j=1, j\neq i}^{q} (2\Phi(3C_{pkj}) - 1) \right] \times (S_i^2 - \sigma_i^2) \times \phi(3C_{pki}) \qquad (6.53)$$

Also, using central limit theorem, Pearn et al. [18] have derived approximate statistical distribution of $\hat{C}_{pk}^T$ as

$$\hat{C}_{pk}^T \sim N\left(C_{pk}^T, \frac{1}{9n[\phi(\Phi(3C_{pk}^T))]^2} \sum_{i=1}^{q} \{a_i^2 + b_i^2\}\right), \qquad (6.54)$$

where $a_i = \left[\prod_{j=1, j \neq i}^{q} (2\Phi(3C_{pkj}) - 1) \right] \phi(\Phi(3C_{pki}))$ and $b_i = \frac{3C_{pki}}{\sqrt{2}} \times a_i$, for $i = 1(1)q$.

Pearn et al. [18] have derived an expression for the lower confidence bound of C_{pk}^{T} and have also discussed about a hypothesis testing procedure related to C_{pk}^{T}. Consider the following set of hypotheses:

$$H_0 : C_{pk}^{T} \leq c$$
$$\text{against} \quad H_1 : C_{pk}^{T} > c \tag{6.55}$$

To test this, Pearn et al [18] have considered the following test statistic:

$$T = \frac{3\sqrt{n} \left(\hat{C}_{pk}^{T} - c \right) \phi(\Phi(3\hat{C}_{pk}^{T}))}{\sqrt{\sum_{i=1}^{q} \left\{ \hat{a}_i^2 + \hat{b}_i^2 \right\}}} \tag{6.56}$$

where, $\hat{a}_i$ and $\hat{b}$ are obtained by replacing C_{pk}^{T} with its plug-in estimator $\hat{C}_{pk}^{T}$ in their respective definitions.

Now, if $\overline{X} \sim N(\mu, \frac{\sigma^2}{\sqrt{n}})$, then $\frac{\sqrt{n}(\overline{X} - \mu)}{\sigma} \sim N(0, 1)$ and a $100(1 - \alpha)\%$ lower confidence bound of μ will be $\overline{X} - \frac{\sigma}{\sqrt{n}}\tau_\alpha$.

Similarly, $T \overset{H_0}{\sim} N(0, 1)$ approximately. Thus, if $T < \tau_\alpha$, H_0 is accepted and otherwise it is rejected. Here, τ_α denotes upper $100\alpha\%$ point of standard normal distribution. Accordingly, the approximate $100(1 - \alpha)\%$ lower confidence bound of C_{pk}^{T} will be

$$C_{pk}^{T(LB)} = \hat{C}_{pk}^{T} - \left[\frac{1}{9n[\phi(\Phi(3C_{pk}^{T}))]^2} \sum_{i=1}^{q} \left\{ a_i^2 + b_i^2 \right\} \right]^{1/2} \times \tau_\alpha \tag{6.57}$$

Note that, here the lower confidence bound (LCB) is considered to be approximate since the statistical distribution of $\hat{C}_{pk}^{T}$ is not exact but an approximate one.

Interestingly, apart from the multivariate normality assumption, another strong assumption is made while defining C_{pk}^{T}, viz., Pearn et al. [18] considered component PCIs, i.e., C_{pk} values for individual quality characteristics, to be independent and merely multiplied them to have the final expression of C_{pk}^{T}. Recall that, the very essence of studying multivariate process capability is to consider the underlying correlation structure prevailing among the quality characteristics. Therefore, the assumption of independence of the concerned quality characteristics, falls short of the original motivation.

6.4 MPCIs Defined as Multivariate Analogue of C_{pm}

When the question of generalizing univariate PCIs for multivariate set-up arises, C_{pm} is the most popular index among the practitioners. One of the reasons behind this sheer popularity may be that, C_p, although the easiest to define, does not even measure actual process capability; while defining a multivariate analogue of C_{pk} is somewhat mathematically intensive (due to the involvement of modulus in its definition), unless any strong assumption, like independence of the quality characteristics, is made.

Recall that, under univariate set-up, C_{pm} can be defined as

$$
\begin{aligned}
C_{pm} &= \frac{d}{3\sqrt{\sigma^2 + (\mu - T)^2}} \\
&= \frac{USL - LSL}{6\sigma} \Big/ \sqrt{1 + \frac{(\mu - T)^2}{\sigma^2}} \\
&= \frac{C_p}{\sqrt{1 + \frac{(\mu - T)^2}{\sigma^2}}}
\end{aligned}
\tag{6.58}
$$

To the best of our knowledge, Chan et al. [4] first defined a multivariate analogue of C_{pm} as

$$
C_{pm}^{(CCS)} = \sqrt{\frac{q}{E\left[(\boldsymbol{X}_i - \boldsymbol{T}_i)' A^{-1} (\boldsymbol{X}_i - \boldsymbol{T}_i)\right]}},
\tag{6.59}
$$

where A is a $q \times q$ positive definite matrix, such that

$$
(\boldsymbol{X}_i - \boldsymbol{T}_i)' A^{-1} (\boldsymbol{X}_i - \boldsymbol{T}_i) \le c^2
\tag{6.60}
$$

is the elliptical specification region. Observe that, when $A = \Sigma$, in the denominator of equation (6.59), $(\boldsymbol{X}_i - \boldsymbol{T}_i)' A^{-1} (\boldsymbol{X}_i - \boldsymbol{T}_i)$ is nothing but the Mahalanobis distance of the actual observations from the stipulated target vector. Therefore, when the observed values of the quality characteristics lie close to their stipulated targets, then the denominator of equation (6.59) is likely to assume small value as compared to the situation when the observed values are far away from their targets. This leads the MPCI to be a higher the better one.

Pearn et al. [19] have proposed another multivariate analogue of C_{pm}, which is considered to be of more natural generalization than $C_{pm}^{(CCS)}$ (refer Pearn and Kotz [16]). Recall from equation (6.4) that Pearn et al. [19] have defined a multivariate analogue of C_p as $_qC_p^2 = \frac{c^2}{c_q^2}$. From this, a multivariate analogue of C_{pm} can be defined as

$$_qC_{pm} = \frac{_qC_p}{\sqrt{1 + \frac{(\mu-T)'\Sigma^{-1}(\mu-T)'}{q}}} \tag{6.61}$$

We have already discussed that Taam et al. [23] have defined a multivariate analogue of C_p, viz., MC_p (vide equation (6.6)). They have further extended this definition of MC_p to that of MC_{pm}, a multivariate analogue of C_{pm}, keeping analogy with the definition of C_{pm} as given in equation (6.58).

Now from equation (6.6) and similar to equation (6.58)

$$MC_{pm}$$

$$= \frac{\text{Volume of modified tolerance region}}{\text{Volume of 99.73 \% process region scaled by the process mean square error}}$$

$$= \frac{\text{Volume of modified tolerance region}}{\text{Volume of } (\boldsymbol{X} - \boldsymbol{\mu})'\Sigma_T^{-1}(\boldsymbol{X} - \boldsymbol{\mu}) \leq k(q)}$$

$$= \frac{\text{Volume of modified tolerance region}}{|\Sigma_T|^{1/2}(\pi k(q))^{q/2}\left[\Gamma(q/2+1)\right]^{-1} \times \sqrt{1 + (\boldsymbol{\mu} - \boldsymbol{T})'\Sigma^{-1}(\boldsymbol{\mu} - \boldsymbol{T})}}$$

$$= MC_p/D \tag{6.62}$$

where $\Sigma_T = E\left[(\boldsymbol{X} - \boldsymbol{T})(\boldsymbol{X} - \boldsymbol{T})'\right]$ is the mean squared error matrix of the process and

$$D^{-1} = \sqrt{1 + (\boldsymbol{\mu} - \boldsymbol{T})'\Sigma^{-1}(\boldsymbol{\mu} - \boldsymbol{T})} \tag{6.63}$$

Observe that, D^{-1} is the multivariate counterpart of $\sqrt{1 + \frac{(\mu-T)^2}{\sigma^2}}$, the multiplier of C_p space the definition of C_{pm} [vide equation (6.58)].

Taam et al. [23] have defined the plug-in estimator of MC_{pm} as,

$$\hat{M}C_{pm} = \hat{M}C_p/\hat{D}, \tag{6.64}$$

where $\hat{M}C_p$ is the plug-in estimator of MC_p, as defined in equation (6.9) and

$$\hat{D}^{-1} = \sqrt{1 + \frac{n}{n-1}(\overline{\boldsymbol{X}} - \boldsymbol{T})'S^{-1}(\overline{\boldsymbol{X}} - \boldsymbol{T})} \tag{6.65}$$

It is evident from equation (6.64) that the statistical distribution of $\hat{M}C_p$ is not easily tractable. Consequently, it is very difficult to obtain closed-form expressions for its expectation and variance. Pearn et al. [19] have proposed an approximate $100(1 - \alpha)\%$ confidence interval for MC_{pm} as

$$\left[\hat{M}C_p \frac{\hat{F}_Z^{-1}(\alpha/2)}{(n-1)^q \hat{D}^2}, \quad \hat{M}C_p \frac{\hat{F}_Z^{-1}(1-\alpha/2)}{(n-1)^q \hat{D}^2} \right] \tag{6.66}$$

where, $Z = \hat{D} \times Y$ is a random variable, whose cdf is given by $F_Z(.)$. Similar to the case of MC_p, here also for a given data, $100(1-\alpha)\%$ approximate confidence interval of MC_{pm} can be obtained using numerical methods.

Although MC_{pm} is one of the most accepted MPCIs among practitioners, since by definition, it is expressed in terms of MC_p, which, as has already been discussed in detail, over-estimates process capability, consequently, MC_{pm} also over-estimates process capability [refer Pan and Lee [15]].

Apart from the so called problem of over estimation, Scagliarini [21] have observed an ambiguity in the definition of MC_{pm}, which may not necessarily be considered as drawback of the MPCI, but may cause confusion while comparing performances of two or more processes using MC_{pm}.

As has already been observed, MC_{pm} consists of two parts, viz., MC_p and D. Scagliarini [21] has shown that, for two or more processes with the same target value, specification limits, process variability (as measured by MC_p), and proximity of process mean toward the target (as measured by D), the increase of the same amount of variability will result in different values of MC_{pm}.

Suppose $D = \sqrt{1+\delta}$, where $\delta = (\boldsymbol{\mu} - \boldsymbol{T})' \Sigma^{-1} (\boldsymbol{\mu} - \boldsymbol{T})$. Then for $\boldsymbol{\mu} \neq \boldsymbol{T}$, let δ_F is such that it satisfies

$$\left\{ \boldsymbol{\mu} : (\boldsymbol{\mu} - \boldsymbol{T})' \Sigma^{-1} (\boldsymbol{\mu} - \boldsymbol{T}) = \delta_F \right\} \tag{6.67}$$

Also suppose, after increase in the process variability, the dispersion matrix Σ changes to Σ_W, such that $(\Sigma_W - \Sigma)$ is a p.d. matrix. Thus, the process performance has deteriorated in terms of its dispersion. Let the changed value of MC_{pm}, in accordance with Σ_W, is $MC_{pm(W)}$. Then it is logical to expect that for a particular Σ_W, $MC_{pm(W)}$ should be unique. However, Scagliarini has shown that, this is not the case in reality. Let us discuss this in detail.

Suppose, due to the change of Σ to Σ_W, MC_p has changed to $MC_{p(W)}$ and D has changed to

$$D_{(W)} = \sqrt{1 + (\boldsymbol{\mu} - \boldsymbol{T})' \Sigma_W^{-1} (\boldsymbol{\mu} - \boldsymbol{T})} = \sqrt{1 + \delta_W}, \text{ say.}$$

Although $MC_{p(W)}$ is unique for a particular Σ_W, when $\boldsymbol{\mu}$, $\boldsymbol{T}$, $\boldsymbol{USL}$, and $\boldsymbol{LSL}$ are constant, $D_{(W)}$ is not unique. This is due to the fact that, for $\boldsymbol{\mu}$ satisfying $\delta = \delta_F$, δ_W is not unique. Rather, following Mardia et al. [14] it can be shown that, δ_W ranges between

$$\min(\delta_W) = \delta_F, \quad [\text{Minimum eigen value of } \Sigma\Sigma_W^{-1}] \tag{6.68}$$

$$\max(\delta_W) = \delta_F^*, \quad [\text{Maximum eigen value of } \Sigma\Sigma_W^{-1}] \tag{6.69}$$

Accordingly, $MC_{pm(W)}$ ranges between $MC_{pm(W, \text{ min})} = \frac{MC_{p(W)}}{\max(D_W)}$ and $MC_{pm(W, \text{ max})} = \frac{MC_{p(W)}}{\min(D_W)}$, where, $\max(D_W) = \sqrt{1 + \max(\delta_W)}$ and $\min(D_W) = \sqrt{1 + \min(\delta_W)}$.

To explain this phenomenon, Scagliarini [21] has used the concept of polar coordinates under bivariate set-up. Suppose θ, which varies in the range 0 and 2π, both inclusive, is the azimuthal angle related to $(\boldsymbol{\mu} - \boldsymbol{T})$, i.e., θ (measured in radian) is the angle between $(\boldsymbol{\mu} - \boldsymbol{T})$ and the abscissa axis. Then Scagliarini has shown that δ_W depends on θ and consequently, MC_{pm} depends on θ. Thus, while comparing two processes, if there is a change in the value of dispersion matrix, then it is not sufficient to compare their values only. One should also note the corresponding angular change to make a fair comparison between the processes under the changed circumstances.

Holmes and Mergen [9] have proposed a univariate PCI and an MPCI analogous to C_{pm}, or to be more precise, reciprocal of it.

Recall from equation (6.58) that

$$C_{pm} = \frac{USL - LSL}{6\sqrt{\sigma^2 + (T - \mu)^2}}$$

$$\Rightarrow \frac{1}{6C_{pm}^2} = \frac{\sigma^2}{(USL - LSL)^2} + \frac{(T - \mu)^2}{(USL - LSL)^2} \tag{6.70}$$

Interestingly, equation (6.70) is the equation of a circle with radius $\frac{1}{6C_{pm}}$. Moreover, the first term in the right hand side of the equation is $\left(\frac{1}{6C_p}\right)^2$, while the second part, viz., $\frac{(T-\mu)^2}{(USL-LSL)^2}$ measures the squared distance between target and average value of the concerned quality characteristic, standardized by square of specification span (i.e., $USL - LSL$).

Accordingly, Holmes and Mergen [9] have proposed a univariate PCI as

$$C_{rm} = \frac{6\sqrt{\sigma^2 + (T - \mu)^2}}{USL - LSL}$$

$$= \frac{6\sigma_T}{USL - LSL}, \tag{6.71}$$

where $\sigma_T = \sqrt{\sigma^2 + (T - \mu)^2}$.

Observe that, C_{rm} is essentially reciprocal of C_{pm}.

Interestingly, C_{pk} can be written, in terms of C_p, as

$$C_{pk} = \frac{d - |\mu - M|}{3\sigma} = C_p - \frac{|\mu - T|}{3\sigma} \tag{6.72}$$

assuming $T = M = \frac{USL + LSL}{2}$.

Holmes and Mergen [9] have argued that in the above definition of C_{pk}, the first part, viz., C_p is of larger the better type, while the second part, viz.,

$\frac{|\mu - T|}{3\sigma}$ is of smaller the better type. Due to this contrast, one may encounter a situation, where C_{pk} is higher than its stipulated threshold, while the customer does not get an item close to its target. However, this argument is not quite correct in a sense that the said contrast is well taken care of by the *minus* operator lying between the two parts in the expression of C_{pk} as given in equation (6.72).

Nonetheless, C_{rm} can be alternatively written as, $C_{rm} = \frac{1}{C_p} + \frac{|T-\mu|}{6(USL-LSL)}$ and both the parts in its definition are of smaller the better type. Consequently, C_{rm}, which is the reciprocal of C_{pm}, is of smaller the better type, which is just opposite to the general convention of PCIs being of higher the better type. This may create confusion among practitioners, particularly, when values of two or more PCIs are being compared based on a given set of data.

Holmes and Morgan [9] have generalized their proposed PCI, C_{rm}, under multivariate set-up as follows:

$$C_{rm}^{*2} = 36\left[\left(\frac{1}{\boldsymbol{W}}\right)' \Sigma \left(\frac{1}{\boldsymbol{W}}\right) + \left(\frac{1}{\boldsymbol{W}}\right)' Q \left(\frac{1}{\boldsymbol{W}}\right)\right]$$

$$\Rightarrow C_{rm}^{*} = 6\left[\sum_{i=1}^{q}\sum_{j=1}^{q}\frac{\sigma_{ij}}{(USL_i - LSL_i)(USL_j - LSL_j)}\right.$$

$$+ \left.\sum_{i=1}^{q}\left(\frac{T_i - \mu_i}{USL_i - LSL_i}\right)^2\right]^{\frac{1}{2}},$$

$$(6.73)$$

where $\left(\frac{1}{\boldsymbol{W}}\right)$ is q component vector whose ith element is given by $\frac{1}{USL_i - LSL_i}$, i.e., reciprocal of the length of the specification span of the ith quality characteristic; Σ is the dispersion matrix and Q is a diagonal matrix whose ith diagonal element is given by $(T_i - \mu_i)^2$, for $i = 1(1)q$.

With increase in the number of quality characteristics, viz. q, C_{rm}^{*} tends to decrease, i.e., the process performance is supposed to get better. To remove this subjectivity, the authors suggested taking some sort of an average of it by dividing C_{rm}^{*} with q. However, there are ample chances that this may overlook some important contribution of one or more quality characteristics on the overall quality of the process.

Pan and Lee [15], proposed another multivariate analogue of C_{pm}. Recall that, the authors have already proposed a multivariate analogue of C_p, viz., NMC_p, to address the problem of over estimation as is done by MC_p. Then, following Taam et al.'s [23] approach, the authors have extended the definition of NMC_p to define multivariate C_{pm} as

$$NMC_{pm} = NMC_p/D \qquad (6.74)$$

where NMC_p and D have already been defined in equations (6.29) and (6.63), respectively.

Since NMC_{pm} involves process parameters, which are mostly unobservable, its plug-in estimator needs to be defined and its statistical properties have to be studied for all practical purposes. The plug-in estimator of NMC_{pm} can be defined as

$$
\begin{aligned}
\widehat{NMC}_{pm} &= \widehat{NMC}_p / \widehat{D} \\
&= \left(\frac{|A^*|}{|S^*|} \right)^{1/2}
\end{aligned}
\tag{6.75}
$$

where $\widehat{NMC}_p$ and $\widehat{D}^{-1}$ are already defined in equations (6.30) and (6.65), respectively, and $|S^*| = \frac{1}{n-1} \sum_{i=1}^{n} (\boldsymbol{X}_i - \overline{\boldsymbol{X}})(\boldsymbol{X}_i - \overline{\boldsymbol{X}})'$. Pan and Lee [15] have derived expression for the rth moment of $\widehat{NMC}_{pm}$ as

$$
E\left[\widehat{NMC}_{pm}^{\,r} \right] = \frac{1}{b_r^*} (NMC_{pm})^r
\tag{6.76}
$$

where

$$
\begin{aligned}
b_r^* &= \left(\frac{2^{q-1}}{(n-1)^q (1 + \frac{\lambda}{n})} \right) \times e^{\frac{\lambda}{2}} \left(\sum_{j=0}^{\infty} \frac{(\frac{\lambda}{2})^j \Gamma\left(\frac{n+2j-r}{2} \right)}{j! \Gamma\left(\frac{n+2j}{2} \right)} \right) \\
&\quad \times \prod_{i=1}^{q-1} \left(\frac{\Gamma(\frac{n-i}{2})}{\Gamma(\frac{n-i-r}{2})} \right)
\end{aligned}
\tag{6.77}
$$

Thus, from equation (6.76), expressions for expectation and variance of $\widehat{NMC}_{pm}$ can be obtained as

$$
E\left[\widehat{NMC}_{pm} \right] = \frac{1}{b_1^*} (NMC_{pm})
\tag{6.78}
$$

$$
V\left[\widehat{NMC}_{pm} \right] = \left(\frac{1}{b_2^*} - \frac{1}{b_1^{*2}} \right) NMC_{pm}^2
\tag{6.79}
$$

where b_1^* and b_2^* are obtained by substituting $r = 1$ and $r = 2$, respectively, in equation (6.77). Thus, $b_1^* \times \widehat{NMC}_{pm}$ is an unbiased estimator of NMC_{pm}. Pan and Lee [15] have derived expression for the $100(1 - \alpha)\%$ confidence interval of NMC_{pm} as

$$
\left[\widehat{NMC}_{pm} \times \sqrt{\frac{w_{\alpha/2}^*}{1 + \frac{\hat{\lambda}}{n}}}, \ \ \widehat{NMC}_{pm} \times \sqrt{\frac{w_{1-\alpha/2}^*}{1 + \frac{\hat{\lambda}}{n}}} \right]
\tag{6.80}
$$

where, w_α^* is the αth percentile of the distribution $\frac{1}{(n-1)^q} \times \chi_n^2(\lambda) \prod_{i=1}^{q-1} \chi_{n-i}^2$, $\chi_n^2(\lambda)$ is the non-central chi-square distribution with degrees of freedom n and noncentrality parameter $\lambda = n(\mu - T)\Sigma^{-1}(\mu - T)$.

The multivariate analogues of C_{pm} discussed so far, suffer from a very unique problem. For almost all those MPCIs, it is inherently assumed that impact of deviation from target remains the same for all quality characteristics— while in reality, this is seldom the case. For any production, there must be some quality characteristics which are key to its overall quality, while the other characteristics are not so important, as compared to them, though cannot be ignored altogether either. Interestingly, this problem does not exist for univariate C_{pm}, as in that case, there is only one quality characteristic to deal with. One of the plausible way to handle this problem is to redefine the associated loss function incorporating this criterion.

Goethals and Cho [7] have defined a multivariate analogue of C_{pm} which takes into account the fact that loss incurred due to deviation of process centering from target may vary for different quality characteristics.

As has just been discussed, while defining most of the multivariate analogues of C_{pm}, it is inherently assumed that the deviation from target results in equal amount of loss irrespective of the nature of the corresponding quality characteristics. Goethals and Cho [7] considered this approach as pro-producer. Also, while defining a new MPCI, often specification region is modified solely to avoid computational complications, while in reality, those modifications are seldom pragmatic.

Suppose $DL(T)$ is the first order differentiation of $L(X)$ at $X = T$. This is also known as gradient of L evaluated at $X = T$. Also suppose $D^2L(T)$ is the second order differentiation of $L(X)$ at $X = T$. This is also known as Hessian matrix of L evaluated at $X = T$. In general, let $D^iL(T)$ is the ith order differentiation of $L(X)$ at $X = T$, for $i = 1(1)q$.

Then based on the concept of Taylor series expansion, the authors have defined a loss function $L(X)$ in the neighborhood of the target vector T, as follows:

$$
\begin{aligned}
L(X) &\approx L(T) + \frac{[DL(T)]'}{1!}(X - T) \\
&\quad + (X - T)'\frac{[D^2L(T)]'}{2!}(X - T),
\end{aligned}
$$

discarding higher order terms

$$
= \frac{1}{2}(X - T)'[D^2L(T)]'(X - T) \tag{6.81}
$$

since when on target, no loss should be incurred, i.e., for $(X - T) = 0$, $L(T) = 0$. Also by convention, an ideal loss function should attain its minimum value, when on target and hence, $[DL(T)]'(X - T) = 0$.

Ratio-based MPCIs for symmetric specification region 154

Goethals and Cho [7] have further simplified this loss function as

$$L(\boldsymbol{X}) \approx \sum_{i=1}^{q} \sum_{j=1}^{i} \delta_{ij}(X_i - T_i)(X_j - T_j) \tag{6.82}$$

where $\delta_{ii} = \frac{1}{2}\left(\frac{\delta^2 L}{\delta X_i \delta X_i} \mid \boldsymbol{X=T}\right)$ is the quality loss due to deviation of the ith quality characteristic from its stipulated target and $\delta_{ij} = \left(\frac{\delta^2 L}{\delta X_i \delta X_j} \mid \boldsymbol{X=T}\right)$, $\forall i \neq j = 1(1)q$, where δ_{ij} is the deviation of target for the ith and jth quality characteristics taken together, from their respective targets. Observe that δ_{ii} and δ_{ij} can be directly obtained from the Hessian matrix discussed above.

Now suppose the underlying statistical distribution of the quality characteristics is normal, i.e., $\boldsymbol{X} \sim N_q(\boldsymbol{\mu}, \Sigma)$. Then volume of the 99.73% region will be

$$PR = \left(\pi \times \chi^2_{q,0.0027}\right)^{q/2} \times \left\{\Gamma\left(\frac{q}{2} + 1\right)\right\}^{-1} \times |\Sigma|^{1/2} \tag{6.83}$$

Let us now slightly modify the definition of Σ as

$$\Sigma_L = E\left[\sum_{i=1}^{q} \sum_{j=1}^{i} \delta_{ij}(X_i - T_i)(X_j - T_j)\right]$$

i.e., the process dispersion matrix is now modified by including the information on quality loss in its definition and also, the usual $(X_i - \overline{X})$ is replaced by $(X_i - T_i)$, for $i = 1(1)q$. Then volume of the 99.73% process region will be

$$\left(\pi \times \chi^2_{q,0.0027}\right)^{q/2} \times \left\{\Gamma\left(\frac{q}{2} + 1\right)\right\}^{-1} \times |\Sigma_L|^{1/2}$$

Also, volume of the hyper-rectangular process region will be, $\prod_{i=1}^{q}(USL_i - LSL_i)$.

Using these information, ratio of the volumes of tolerance region and process region can be obtained as

$$\frac{\text{Volume of Tolerance Region}}{\text{Volume of Process Region}}$$

$$= \frac{\prod_{i=1}^{q}(USL_i - LSL_i)}{\left(\pi \times \chi^2_{q,0.0027}\right)^{q/2} \times \left\{\Gamma\left(\frac{q}{2}+1\right)\right\}^{-1} \times |\Sigma_L|^{1/2}}$$

$$= \frac{\prod_{i=1}^{q}(USL_i - LSL_i)}{\left(\pi \times \chi^2_{q,0.0027}\right)^{q/2} \times \left\{\Gamma\left(\frac{q}{2}+1\right)\right\}^{-1}}$$

$$\times \frac{1}{\left[\sum_{i=1}^{q}\sum_{j=1}^{i}\delta_{ij}\left\{\Sigma_{ij}+(\mu_i - T_i)(\mu_j - T_j)\right\}\right]^{1/2}}$$

$$= \frac{\prod_{i=1}^{q}(USL_i - LSL_i)}{PR} \times \frac{1}{D_{GC}} \qquad (6.84)$$

[from equation (6.83)]

where

$$D_{GC}$$
$$= \left[\delta_{ii}\left\{1+\sum_{i=1}^{q}(\mu_i - T_i)\Sigma_{ii}^{-1}(\mu_i - T_i)\right\}\right.$$
$$\left. +\delta_{ij}\left\{1+\sum_{i=2}^{q}\sum_{i=1}^{i-1}(\mu_i - T_i)\Sigma_{ij}^{-1}(\mu_j - T_j)\right\}\right]^{1/2} \qquad (6.85)$$

Based on this ratio, Goethals and Cho [7] defined a multivariate analogue of C_{pm} as

$$MC_{pmC} = \left[\frac{\prod_{i=1}^{q}(USL_i - LSL_i)}{PR}\right]^{1/q} \times \frac{1}{D_{GC}} \qquad (6.86)$$

$$= MC_{pC} \times \frac{1}{D_{GC}} \qquad (6.87)$$

Note that, Goethals and Cho [7] did not name MC_{pC}. However, in their definition of MC_{pmC}, the first part is nothing but a multivariate analogue of C_p, that is MCpC.

Interestingly, while defining MC_{pmC}, the authors took qth root of $\frac{\prod_{i=1}^{q}(USL_i - LSL_i)}{PR}$, while only square root in case of $\frac{1}{D_{GC}}$. To keep parity in both the cases, D_{GC} should also involve qth root. Then the modified version of MC_{pmC} will be

$$MC^*_{pmC} = \left[\frac{\prod\limits_{i=1}^{q}(USL_i - LSL_i)}{PR}\right]^{1/q} \times \frac{1}{D^*_{GC}} \qquad (6.88)$$

where

$$
\begin{aligned}
D^*_{GC} = &\left[\delta_{ii}\left\{1 + \sum_{i=1}^{q}(\mu_i - T_i)\Sigma_{ii}^{-1}(\mu_i - T_i)\right\}\right.\\
&\left. + \delta_{ij}\left\{1 + \sum_{i=2}^{q}\sum_{j=1}^{i-1}(\mu_i - T_i)\Sigma_{ij}^{-1}(\mu_j - T_j)\right\}\right]^{1/q}
\end{aligned}
\qquad (6.89)
$$

The authors themselves have admitted that MC_{pmC} slightly overestimates process capability. MC^*_{pmC} addresses the problem to a large extent.

Suppose for sample observations, the unbiased estimator of the dispersion matrix is given by $\widehat{\Sigma} = \frac{1}{n-1}\sum\limits_{i=1}^{n}(X_i - \overline{X})(X_i - \overline{X})'$ and the plug-in estimator of D^*_{GC} be defined as

$$
\begin{aligned}
\widehat{D^*_{GC}} = &\left[\delta_{ii}\left\{1 + \left(\frac{n}{n-1}\right) \times \sum_{i=1}^{q}(\overline{X_i} - T_i)\widehat{\Sigma}_{ii}^{-1}(\overline{X_i} - T_i)\right\}\right.\\
&\left. + \delta_{ij}\left\{1 + \left(\frac{n}{n-1}\right) \times \sum_{i=2}^{q}\sum_{j=1}^{i-1}(\overline{X_j} - T_i)\widehat{\Sigma}_{ij}^{-1}(\overline{X_j} - T_j)\right\}\right]^{1/q}
\end{aligned}
$$

$$(6.90)$$

Substituting the values of $\widehat{\Sigma}$ and $\widehat{D^*_{GC}}$ in equation (6.88), the plug-in estimator of MC^*_{pmC} can be obtained as

$$\widehat{MC^*_{pmC}} = \left[\frac{\prod\limits_{i=1}^{q}(USL_i - LSL_i)}{\widehat{PR}}\right]^{1/q} \times \frac{1}{\widehat{D^*_{GC}}}$$

$$= \left[\frac{\prod\limits_{i=1}^{q}(USL_i - LSL_i)}{\left(\pi \times \chi^2_{q,0.0027}\right)^{q/2} \times \left\{\Gamma\left(\frac{q}{2}+1\right)\right\}^{-1} \times |\widehat{\Sigma}|^{1/2}}\right]^{1/q} \times \frac{1}{\widehat{D^*_{GC}}},$$

$$(6.91)$$

from equation (6.83).

Goethals and Cho [7] did not derive expression for $E\left[\widehat{MC^*_{pmC}}\right]$, which may be mathematically complicated, but can be handled using numerical methods. The authors have however derived an expression for the lower bound of MC_{pC} as

$$MC_{pC} \geq \left[\frac{q \prod\limits_{i=1}^{q}(USL_i - LSL_i)}{2\pi^{q/2}\Gamma\left(\frac{q}{2}\right)|\Sigma|^{1/2}k^q}\right] \qquad (6.92)$$

where $k = \min\left\{\frac{|LSL_i - T_i|}{\Sigma_{ii}}, \frac{|USL_i - T_i|}{\Sigma_{ii}}\right\}$.

Here, the lower bound has been obtained by replacing the volume of the actual process region by the volume of the largest elliptical contour within the rectangular specification region which is given by $\pi^{q/2}\Gamma\left(\frac{q}{2}+1\right)|\Sigma|^{1/2}k^q$. For unknown values of process parameters, Σ should be replaced by $|\widehat{\Sigma}|$ in the above lower bound.

6.5 $C_G(u, v) -$ A Super-structue of MPCIs

It has been pointed out time and again by many eminent statisticians and quality engineers (refer Kotz and Johnson [12], Rodriguez [20] and the references therein) that, statistical quality control (SQC) being a branch of applied statistics, should have balance between mathematical statistics and practical application, so as to "bridge the gap" between theoreticians and practitioners. As such one should adopt a pragmatic approach when defining a new PCI irrespective of the dimension of the process. The situation worsens for multivariate processes, because one has to deal with complicated mathematical formulations without making the expressions for the newly defined MPCI(s) too much complicated, as finally the practitioners or shop floor people, who are going to be the end users of these indices, may not be conversant with higher mathematics/ mathematical statistics.

As has been discussed in detail in Chapter 3, the four classical PCIs, viz., C_p, C_{pk}, C_{pm}, and C_{pmk} and their super-structure viz., $C_p(u,v)$, defined by Vannman [25], are very popular among practitioners due to their simplicity of computation and ease of representation and interpretation.

Keeping this in mind, Chakraborty and Das [5] have defined a multivariate analogue of $C_p(u,v)$, under multivariate normality assumption of the process distribution, as follows:

$$C_G(u,v) = \frac{1}{3}\sqrt{\frac{(\boldsymbol{d} - u\boldsymbol{D})'\Sigma^{-1}(\boldsymbol{d} - u\boldsymbol{D})}{1 + v(\boldsymbol{\mu} - \boldsymbol{T})'\Sigma^{-1}(\boldsymbol{\mu} - \boldsymbol{T})}} \quad (6.93)$$

where, $\boldsymbol{D} = (|\mu_1 - M_1|, |\mu_2 - M_2|, \cdots, |\mu_q - M_q|)'$;
$\boldsymbol{d} = ((USL_1 - LSL_1)/2, ((USL_2 - LSL_2)/2, \cdots, ((USL_q - LSL_q)/2)'$;
$\boldsymbol{T} = (T_1, T_2, \cdots, T_q)'$;
$\boldsymbol{M} = (M_1, M_2, \cdots, M_q)'$; $\boldsymbol{\mu} = (\mu_1, \mu_2, \cdots, \mu_q)'$.
T_i is the target value , M_i is the nominal value for the ith characteristic of the item, for $i = 1(1)q$;
"q" denotes the number of characteristics under consideration and
$\boldsymbol{X} = (X_1, X_2, \cdots, X_q)'$ represents the set of measurable quality characteristics;
Σ = Variance - covariance matrix of the random vector $\boldsymbol{X}$;
μ_i = Mean of the ith characteristic of the variable X , for $i = 1, 2, \ldots, q$;
$\boldsymbol{\mu}$ = The mean vector of the random vector $\boldsymbol{X}$;
u and v are the scalar constants that can take any non-negative integer value, though in practice these are mostly restricted to $u = 0, 1$ and $v = 0, 1$ to avoid computational complexities.

For $q = 1$, i.e., when there is only one measurable quality characteristic, $C_G(u,v)$ boils down to $C_p(u,v)$. Also, in that case, $C_G(0,0) = C_p(0,0) = C_p$, $C_G(1,0) = C_p(1,0) = C_{pk}$, $C_G(0,1) = C_p(0,1) = C_{pm}$, and $C_G(1,1) = C_p(1,1) = C_{pmk}$. Also observe that, putting $u = 0$, $v = 0$ in equation (6.93),

$$C_G(0,0) = \frac{1}{3}\sqrt{\boldsymbol{d}'\Sigma^{-1}\boldsymbol{d}} \quad (6.94)$$

which is independent of $\boldsymbol{\mu}$ and hence, similar to C_p of univariate processes, can be considered as MPCI measuring potential process capability.

Since $C_G(u,v)$ was defined as multivariate analogue of $C_p(u,v)$, it should have statistical properties similar to the later. In this context, Kotz and Johnson [12] have established the following inter-relationships between C_p, C_{pk}, C_{pm}, and C_{pmk}:

$$\left.\begin{array}{c} C_{pmk} \leq C_{pk} \leq C_p \\[2mm] C_{pmk} \leq C_{pm} \leq C_p \end{array}\right\}. \tag{6.95}$$

However, there does not exist any clear-cut relationship between C_{pk} and C_{pm}. Kotz and Johnson [13] have made a detail discussion on it.

Similar to this, Chakraborty and Chatterjee [6] have established inter-relationships between $C_G(0,0)$, $C_G(1,0)$, $C_G(0,1)$, and $C_G(1,1)$ as follows:

$$\left.\begin{array}{c} C_G(1,1) \leq C_G(1,0) \leq C_G(0,0) \\[2mm] C_G(1,1) \leq C_G(0,1) \leq C_G(0,0) \end{array}\right\}, \tag{6.96}$$

while no exact relationship exists between $C_G(1,0)$ and $C_G(0,1)$. Chatterjee and Chakraborty [6] have also computed expressions for the threshold value of $C_G(0,0)$.

Let us first consider a bivariate process with the correlation coefficient between the two quality characteristics being ρ. Then the threshold value of $C_G(0,0)$ can be computed as

$$C_G^{T^{(2)}}(0,0) = \sqrt{\frac{2}{1+\rho}} \tag{6.97}$$

provided $\sigma_1 \sigma_2 \neq \sigma_{12}$, i.e., $\rho \neq \pm 1$, since for $\rho = \pm 1$, Σ is a singular matrix and hence the corresponding Σ^{-1} does not exist and consequently, $C_G^{T^{(2)}}(0,0)$ is also mathematically undefined.

Observe that, unlike univariate C_p, for $C_G(0,0)$, the threshold value is not unique rather it depends on ρ and lies between 1 and ∞, since for $0 \leq \rho < 1$, $1 < C_G^{T^{(2)}}(0,0) \leq \sqrt{2}$ and for $-1 < \rho < 0$, $C_G^{T^{(2)}}(0,0) > \sqrt{2}$. Also the threshold value $C_G^{T^{(2)}}(0,0) \downarrow \rho$.

For a trivariate process, i.e., for $q = 3$

$$\begin{aligned} C_G^{T^{(3)}}(0,0) &= \frac{1}{\sqrt{1 - \rho_{12}^2 - \rho_{13}^2 - \rho_{23}^2 + 2\rho_{12}\rho_{13}\rho_{23}}} \\ &\quad \times \quad [(1+\rho_{12})^2 + (1+\rho_{13})^2 + (1+\rho_{23})^2 \\ &\quad - \quad 2\rho_{12}(\rho_{12}+\rho_{13}) - 2\rho_{13}(\rho_{13}+\rho_{23}) \\ &\quad - \quad 2\rho_{23}(\rho_{23}+\rho_{12})]^{\frac{1}{2}} \end{aligned} \tag{6.98}$$

For higher order processes, it is difficult to have any close form expression for $C_G^{T^{(2)}}(0,0)$.

The plug-in estimator of $C_G(u,v)$ can be defined as

$$\hat{C}_G(u,v) = \frac{1}{3}\sqrt{\frac{(\boldsymbol{d} - u\hat{\boldsymbol{D}})'\hat{\Sigma}^{-1}(\boldsymbol{d} - u\hat{\boldsymbol{D}})}{1 + v(\overline{\boldsymbol{X}} - \boldsymbol{T})'\hat{\Sigma}^{-1}(\overline{\boldsymbol{X}} - \boldsymbol{T})}}, \tag{6.99}$$

where $\hat{D} = (|\overline{X}_1 - M_1|, |\overline{X}_2 - M_2|, \cdots, |\overline{X}_q - M_q|)'$; $\overline{X} = \begin{pmatrix} \overline{X}_1 \\ \overline{X}_2 \\ \vdots \\ \overline{X}_q \end{pmatrix}$; $\overline{X}_i = $

$\frac{1}{n} \sum_{j=1}^{n} X_{ij}$ is the average of the sample observations corresponding to the ith quality characteristic, for $i = 1(1)q$; X_{ij} is the random variable characterizing the jth random sample observation corresponding to the ith quality characteristic, for $i = 1(1)q$ and $j = 1(1)n$; $\widehat{\Sigma} = \frac{1}{n-1} S^*$ with $S^* = (X - \overline{X})(X - \overline{X})'$ and hence $\widehat{\Sigma}^{-1} = (n-1)S^{*-1}$.

Chakraborty and Chatterjee [6] have studied properties of $C_G(0,0)$ for $u = 0, 1$ and $v = 0, 1$.

$$
\begin{aligned}
E[\widehat{C}_G(0,0)] &= \left[\sqrt{\frac{n-1}{2}} \times \frac{\Gamma\left(\frac{n-q-1}{2}\right)}{\Gamma\left(\frac{n-q}{2}\right)} \right] \times C_G(0,0) \\
&= b_{n-q}^{-1} C_G(0,0) \qquad (6.100)
\end{aligned}
$$

where $b_{n-q} = \sqrt{\frac{2}{n-1}} \times \frac{\Gamma\left(\frac{n-q}{2}\right)}{\Gamma\left(\frac{n-q-1}{2}\right)}$. Then $\widetilde{C}_G(0,0) = b_{n-q} \widehat{C}_G(0,0)$ is an unbiased estimator of $C_G(0,0)$.

Also

$$
E\left[\widehat{C}_G(1,0)\right] = \frac{\sqrt{n-1}}{3\sqrt{2}} \times \frac{\Gamma\left(\frac{n-q-1}{2}\right)}{\Gamma\left(\frac{n-q}{2}\right)} \times E\left[\sqrt{H'\Sigma^{-1}H}\right] \qquad (6.101)
$$

where $(d - \hat{D}) = H$ is a random vector. The expression for $\sqrt{H'\Sigma^{-1}H}$ involves the "square-root" and "modulus" operators and hence derivation of the exact expression of its expectation will be complicated. However, it can be solved numerically.

Chatterjee and Chakraborty [6] have also shown that $\widehat{C}_G(0,1)$ and $\widehat{C}_G(1,1)$ are consistent estimators of $CG(0,1)$ and $C_G(1,1)$, respectively.

6.6   A Numerical Example

Consider a numerical example to have more understanding of the MPCIs discussed so far. The data was originally used by Chakraborty and Chatterjee [6]. The data pertains to a chemical industry, where two correlated quality characteristics are of particular interest, which are coded as "7J" and "6J." A random sample of size $n = 39$ was drawn, shown in Table 6.1.

TABLE 6.1: Data set pertaining to a manufacturing industry with two correlated quality characteristics and 39 randomly selected sample observations

Name \ Sl. No.	1	2	3	4	5	6	7	8	9	10
7J	78.1	77.13	75.9	77.03	76.91	76.77	77.38	77.57	77.87	77.49
6J	1.82	1.97	2.39	1.59	1.87	1.93	1.92	1.95	1.91	1.84

Name \ Sl. No.	11	12	13	14	15	16	17	18	19	20
7J	77.36	78.27	78.02	76.49	77.21	78.27	78.27	78.07	77.40	77.30
6J	1.55	1.60	1.40	2.21	2.10	1.85	1.85	1.51	1.86	2.20

Name \ Sl. No.	21	22	23	24	25	26	27	28	29	30
7J	76.98	77.13	76.49	77.33	77.43	77.29	77.22	77.77	76.91	77.16
6J	1.89	2.26	2.45	2.03	2.19	1.98	2.01	1.86	2.06	2.23

Name \ Sl. No.	31	32	33	34	35	36	37	38	39	-
7J	76.82	76.78	77.57	78.19	77.64	76.81	77.74	75.43	77.38	-
6J	2.35	2.35	1.92	1.41	1.85	1.91	2.21	2.37	1.38	-

Suppose X_1 and X_2 are two random variables characterizing the quality characteristics "7J" and "6J" respectively. Vector of specification limits for the quality characteristic "7J" is $(USL_1, LSL_1) = (85, 75)$ and that corresponding to the quality characteristic "6J" is $(USL_2, LSL_2) = (3, 0)$. Also, $\boldsymbol{M} = \boldsymbol{T} = (80.0, 1.5)'$ and $\boldsymbol{d} = (5.0, 1.5)'$.

From the data given in Table 6.1, sample size $n = 39$, observed mean vector is $\overline{\boldsymbol{X}} = (77.3046, 1.9495)'$

observed dispersion matrix is $\widehat{\Sigma} = \begin{pmatrix} 0.3897 & -0.1134 \\ -0.1134 & 0.0798 \end{pmatrix}$ and therefore, $\hat{\rho} = -0.6433$. Thus the two quality characteristics have moderately high negative correlation among themselves and hence computing univariate PCI values for the individual quality characteristics and combining them to judge overall capability level of the process will not deliver the good. Rather one needs to use MPCIs.

For the data given in Table 6.1, following computations have been based on the ratio-based MPCIs discussed in this chapter.

$\widehat{MC}_p = 4.6972$, $\widehat{MC}_{pm} = 1.0005$, $\widehat{NMC}_p = 3.5962$, $\widehat{NMC}_{pm} = 5.8011$, $\widehat{MC}_{pC} = 2.4455$, $\widehat{MC}_{pmC} = 0.5533$, $\widehat{C}^*_{rm} = 0.4326$, and $\widehat{C}_{pkT} = 1.9712$. Note that, here the number of quality characteristics, i.e., $q = 2$, hence $\widehat{MC}_{pmC}$

and $\widehat{MC}^*_{pmC}$ both will have the same value and therefore the original notation viz., $\widehat{MC}_{pmC}$ have been retained.

Now, observe that all these MPCI values are estimated values and may be subjected to sampling fluctuations of various degrees.

Following Pearn et al. [19], $\widehat{MC}_p \times b_q$ is an unbiased estimator of MC_p [refer equation (6.13)]. For $n = 39$ and $q = 2$, $b_q = 2.1803$ and hence $\widehat{MC}_p \times b_q = 10.2415$ and $\widehat{MC}_{pm} \times b_q = 2.1814$ are unbiasedly estimated values of MC_p and MC_{pm}, respectively. Also, from equation (6.32), $b_1 = 0.49474$ and hence $b_1 \times \widehat{NMC}_p = 3.4069$ and $b_1 \times \widehat{NMC}_{pm} = 0.7256$ are unbiasedly estimated values of NMC_p and NMC_{pm}, respectively. From equation (6.54), $\widehat{C}^T_{pk}$ is asymptotically unbiased estimator of C^T_{pk} and hence, $\widehat{C}^T_{pk} = 1.9712$ is asymptotically unbiasedly estimated value of C^T_{pk}.

$\widehat{C}_G(0,0) = 5.2804$, $\widehat{C}_G(1,0) = 2.9249$, $\widehat{C}_G(0,1) = 1.1247$, and $\widehat{C}_G(1,1) = 0.6230$. Also, $\widetilde{C}_G(0,0) = 5.1040$ which is the unbiasedly estimated value of $C_G(0,0)$. The threshold value of $\widehat{C}_G(0,0)$ is $\widehat{C}^T_G(0,0) = 2.3679$. While $\widehat{C}_G(0,0)$ and $\widehat{C}_G(1,0)$ are greater than this threshold value, $\widehat{C}_G(0,1)$ and $\widehat{C}_G(1,1)$ are less than this.

Since for MC_{pC}, MC_{pmC}, and C^*_{rm}, no expression for the unbiased estimators are available, we have to consider their estimated values only.

From the above computations, following can be observed:

1. As can be seen from Figure 5.1 of Chapter 5, the process is highly off centred, though the process dispersion is alright. This has been reflected by almost all the multivariate analogues of C_p and C_{pm}.

2. Taam et al.'s [23] MCIs, viz., MC_p and MC_{pm} indeed over-estimate process capability. Though the situation is somewhat better for NMC_p and NMC_{pm}, still they over-estimate process capability, especially the potential process capability to some extent. C^T_{pk} too over-estimates process capability.

3. C^T_{pk}, however, fails to capture the poor performance of the process. This may be due to the fact that the quality characteristics needed to be independent, while in the present case, they are moderately correlated.

4. Although, apparently $C_G(u,v)$ values, for $u = 0, 1$ and $v = 0, 1$, are quite high, compared to the other MPCIs; when compared to the threshold value of $C_G(0,0)$, the situation becomes clearer. In fact, despite having a visibly high value, $C_G(0,1)$ and $C_G(1,1)$ are still less than the threshold.

   This reinstates the importance of threshold value from interpretational perspective of both univariate and multivariate process capability analysis in a sense that even if an MPCI assumes very small or very high value, it cannot be decided with certainty that the process performance is below or above satisfactory, respectively, until these are compared to the corresponding threshold values.

5. $C_G(1,0)$, as a multivariate analogue of C_{pk}, still over-estimates process capability.

6.7 Concluding Remark

Although the literature of multivariate process capability analysis is comparatively younger than other branches of statistical quality control, including univariate process capability analysis, still ratio-based MPCIs outnumber other varieties of MPCIs. One possible reason for this may be that, univariate PCIs, which are used in practice, are mostly ratio-based and hence adopting a generalized approach of that may render interpretational advantage. The ratio-based MPCIs for symmetric specification region, available in literature, are thus mostly multivariate analogues of the four classical PCIs, viz., C_p, C_{pk}, C_{pm}, and C_{pmk}.

Almost all the MPCIs discussed in this chapter are defined from practical view point and the statistical properties have been extensively studied for many of them. Still there remains some room for future study, which are enlisted below for interested readers:

1. The concept of MPCI was born from the fact that there may be more than one correlated quality characteristics corresponding to a process which are required to be studied simultaneously. Hence, computing univariate PCIs for individual quality characteristics and combining them to have overall process capability (e.g., as is done in case of c_{PK}^t), may not give exact result.

   In fact, both the multivariate analogues of C_{pk}, viz., C_{pk}^T and $C_G(1,0)$ tend to over-estimate process capability. Therefore making correction to these MPCIs or defining new index will be of special interest.

2. For none of the MPCIs defined so far, exact relationship between the MPCI and the corresponding proportion of non-conformance has been established.

3. Threshold value is computed for very few of the indices, discussed in this chapter. Formulating these will help to make decision about process performance unambiguously.

4. For many of these MPCIs, closed form expressions of the expectations of the plug-in estimators are unavailable. Extensive simulation studies can be made for these to have thorough knowledge about these indices.

Bibliography

[1] Anderson, T. W. (2003). An Introduction to Multivariate Statistical Analysis, 3rd edn., New York: Wiley.

[2] Bothe, D. R. (1999) Composite Capability Index for Multiple Product Characteristics. *Quality Engineering*, Vol. 12, No. 2, pp. 253–258.

[3] Boyles, R. A. (1991). The Taguchi Capability Index. *Journal of Quality Technology*, Vol. 23, No. 1, pp. 17–26.

[4] Chan, L. K., Cheng, S. W., Spiring, F. A. (1991). A Multivariate Measure of Process Capability. *International Journal of Modeling and Simulation*, Vol. 11, pp. 1–6.

[5] Chakraborty, A. K., Das, A. (2007). Statistical Analysis of Multivariate Process Capability Indices. *Private Communication*, Indian Statistical Institute, Kolkata, India.

[6] Chakraborty, A. K., Chatterjee, M. (2020). Distributional and Inferential Properties of Some New Multivariate Process Capability Indices for Symmetric Specification Region. Quality and Reliability Engineering International, DOI:10.1002/qre.2783.

[7] Goethals, P. L., Cho, B. R. (2011). The Development of a Target Focused Process Capability Index with Multiple Characteristics. *Quality and Reliability Engineering International*, Vol. 27, No. 3, pp. 297–311.

[8] Hardle, W., Simar, L. (2003). *Applied Multivariate Statistical Analysis*. Springer: Berlin, UA, pp. 73–74.

[9] Homes, D. S., Mergen, A. E. (1998). Measuring Process Performance for Multiple Variables. *Quality Engineering*, Vol. 11, No. 1, pp. 55 –59.

[10] Jessenberger, J., Claus, W. (1998). A Note on a Multivariate Analogue of the Process Capability index C_p. *Technical report, SFB 475: Universitat Dortmund, No. 1998, 7.*

[11] Kane, V. E. (1986). Process Capability Index. *Journal of Quality Technology*, Vol. 18, No. 1, pp. 41–52.

[12] Kotz, S., Johnson, N. (2002). Process Capability Indices—a Review, 1992–2000. *Journal of Quality Technology* Vol. 34, No. 1, pp. 2–19.

Bibliography

[13] Kotz, S., Johnson, N. (1999). Delicate Relations Among the Basic Process Capability Indices C_p, C_{pk} and C_{pm} and Their Modifiactions. *Communications in Statistics—Simulation and Computation*, Vol. 28, No. 3, pp. 849–866.

[14] Mardia, K. V., Kent, J. T., Bibby, J. M. (1979). Multivariate Analysis. Academic Press: San Diego.

[15] Pan, J. N., Lee, C. Y. (2010). New Capability Indices for Evaluating the Performance of Multivariate Manufacturing Processes. *Quality and Reliability engineering International*, Vol. 26, No. 1, pp. 3–15.

[16] Pearn, W. L., Kotz, S. (2007). *Encyclopedia and Handbook of Process Capability Indices—Series on Quality, Reliability and Engineering Statistics.* World Scientific, Singapore.

[17] Pearn, W. L., Kotz, S., Johnson, N. L. (1992). *Journal of Quality Technology*, Vol. 24 (4), pp. 2016–231.

[18] Pearn, W. L., Shiau, J. -J. H., Tai, Y. T, Li, M. Y. (2011). Capability Assessment for Processes with Multiple Characteristics: a Generalization of the Popular index C_{pk}. *Quality and Reliability Engineering International*, Vol. 27, pp. 1119–1129.

[19] Pearn, W. L., Wang, F. K., Yen, C. H. (2007). Multivariate Capability Indices: Distributional and Inferential Properties. *Journal of Applied Statistics*, Vol. 34, No. 8, pp. 941–962.

[20] Rodriguez, R. N. (1992). Recent Developments in Process Capability Analysis. *Journal of Quality Technology*, Vol. 24, No. 4, pp. 176–187.

[21] Scagliarini, M. (2015). A Note on the Multivariate Process Capability Index MC_{pm}. *Quality and Reliability Engineering International*, Vol. 31, No. 2, pp. 329–339.

[22] Shahriari, H., Abdollahzadeh, M. (2009). A New Multivariate Process Capability Vector. *Quality Engineering*, Vol. 21, No. 3, pp. 290–299.

[23] Taam, W., Subbaiah, P., Liddy, W. (1993). A Note on Multivariate Capability Indices. *Journal of Applied Statistics*, Vol. 20, No. 3, pp. 339–351.

[24] Tano, I., Vannman, K. (2012). A multivariate Process Capability Index based on the First Principal Component Only. *Quality and Reliability Engineering International*, Vol. 29, No. 7, pp. 987–1003.

[25] Vannman, K. (1995). A Unified Approach to Capability Indices. *Statistica Sinica*, Vol. 5, No. 2, pp. 805–820.

[26] Wang, F. K. (2006). Quality Evaluation of a Manufactured Product with Multiple Characteristics. *Quality and Reliability Engineering International*, Vol. 22, pp. 225–236.

[27] Wang, F. K., Hubele, N. F., Lawrence, F. P., Maskulin, J. D., Shahriari, H. (2000). Comparison of Three Multivariate Process Capability Indices. *Journal of Quality Technology*. Vol. 32, pp. 263–275.

Chapter 7

Multivariate Process Capability Indices for Asymmetric Specification Region

Chapter Summary

After a thorough discussion on ratio-based multivariate process capability indices (MPCIs) for symmetric specification region in Chapter 6, Chapter 7 discusses about those for asymmetric specification region. It has been observed time and again that, often the specification region deviates from symmetry due to various practical problems. This necessitates use of MPCIs specially designed for asymmetric specification region. In Chapter 7, these MPCIs are discussed along with some of their important applications. A numerical example has also been discussed to explain their usage.

7.1 Introduction

The specification limits of a process are considered to be asymmetric with respect to the target, when mid-point of the specification difffers from the target value (T).

Most of the indices available in literature make an inherent assumption that the quality characteristic under consideration is symmetric about the target. However, in practice, it has been found over and again that it may not be realistic to have the specification limits corresponding to a quality characteristic symmetric about the target always.

Asymmetry of the specification may arise due to engineering drawing requirements, process conditions, or transformation of data.

In practice, often customers are willing to allow more deviation from target on one side of the specification interval than the other. Even if a process starts with symmetric specification limits, many a times it is observed that the manufacturer and/or the customer has to opt for asymmetric tolerance interval in order to avoid unnecessary increase in the production cost. Boyles [1] has discussed such situations in a very lucid manner. He has also observed that

168

if data on a process parameter, whose initial underlying distribution is non-normal, is converted into a normal one, using standard transformations like Johnson's transformation or Box-Cox transformation, then the initial symmetric specification limits get automatically converted into asymmetric ones for the transformed data, by virtue of the same transformation. There exist many other real-life examples discussed by Boyles [1]; Chen and Pearn [7]; Jessenberger and Weihs [12] and so on, which motivated the researchers to define some indices especially for processes having quality characteristics with asymmetric specification limits.

A detailed review of the univariate PCIs for asymmetric specification limits is given in Chapter 3.

Although the presence of asymmetry in specification limits is not at all a rare event, specially in manufacturing industries; the research work in this field are surprisingly fewer as compared to the case of symmetric specification limits. The situation worsens for multivariate processes. To the best of our knowledge, only two research articles are available in this field, given by Grau [11] and Chatterjee and Chakraborty [5]. Both of them generalized the superstructure of univariate PCIs viz., $C_p^{''}(u,v)$ [vide equation (3.10) of Chapter 3] for $u = 0, 1$ and $v = 0, 1$.

One of the reasons behind choosing $C_p^{''}(u,v)$ for multivariate generalization, may be that, the member indices of $C_p^{''}(u,v)$, for $u = 0, 1$ and $v = 0, 1$ are analogous to univariate PCIs for symmetric specifiaction limits, viz., C_p, C_{pk}, C_{pm}, and C_{pmk}, which are the most popular among practitioners. Hence a multivariate generalization of $C_p^{''}(u,v)$, should be easy to accept by the practitioners and may be easy to interpret as well.

7.2 MPCIs Generalizing $C_p^{''}(u,v)$ for $u = 0, 1$ and $v = 0, 1$ – A Geometric Approach (Grau [11])

In order to develop an MPCI for asymmetric specification limits, one may need to understand its univariate counterpart properly, including its geometric interpretation.

For the sake of ease of discussion, let us recall (vide Section 3.2.1) the expressions for $C_p^{''}(u,v)$ and four of its member indices, viz., $C_p^{''}$, $C_{pk}^{''}$, $C_{pm}^{''}$, and $C_{pmk}^{''}$.

$$C_p''(u,v) = \frac{d^* - uF^*}{3\sqrt{\sigma^2 + vF^2}} \tag{7.1}$$

$$C_p'' = C_p''(0,0) = \frac{d^*}{3\sigma} \tag{7.2}$$

$$C_{pk}'' = C_p''(1,0) = \frac{d^* - F^*}{3\sigma} \tag{7.3}$$

$$C_{pm}'' = C_p''(0,1) = \frac{d^*}{3\sqrt{\sigma^2 + F^2}} \tag{7.4}$$

$$C_{pmk}'' = C_p''(1,1) = \frac{d^* - F^*}{3\sqrt{\sigma^2 + F^2}} \tag{7.5}$$

$$\tag{7.6}$$

where $d = \frac{U-L}{2}$, $d^* = min(d_l, d_u)$, $d_u = U - T$, $d_l = T - L$, $F^* = max\{\frac{d^*(\mu-T)}{d_u}, \frac{d^*(T-\mu)}{d_l}\}$, and $F = max\{\frac{d(\mu-T)}{d_u}, \frac{d(T-\mu)}{d_l}\}$.

Let us define the following:

1. $VN = 6\sigma$: This is the natural variation of a process, which includes 99.73% of the observations, under normality assumption.

2. $VN' = 6\sqrt{\sigma^2 + F^2}$: This is the modified natural variation of a process;

3. $VA_T = 2d^*$: This is the allowable process variation centering T.

   Note that, if $d_u < d_l$, i.e., if T is closer to U as compared to L, then $d^* = d_u$ and consequently, $2d^*$ denotes the length of the largest interval centered at T and fully included in the original specification interval. Grau [11] has named it allowable variation around T.

4.
$$VA_\mu^* = \begin{cases} 2(U - \mu) & \text{if } \mu > T \\ 2(\mu - L) & \text{if } \mu < T \end{cases}$$

   Observe that, when $\mu > T$, then $L < T < \mu < U$ and if $\mu < T$, then $L < \mu < T < U$. Hence μ, VA_μ^* is the largest interval centered at μ and fully included in the original specification interval. Grau [11] has named it allowable variation around μ.

5.
$$VA_T^* = \begin{cases} 2d_u & \text{if } \mu > T \\ 2d_l & \text{if } \mu < T \end{cases}$$

   This is defined similar to VA_μ^*, the only difference being here the interval is centered around T.

Using these notations, Grau [11] has redefined C_p'', C_{pk}'', C_{pm}'', and C_{pmk}'' as follows:

$$C_p'' = \frac{d^*}{3\sigma} = \frac{VA_T}{VN} \tag{7.7}$$

Now

$$
\begin{aligned}
F^* &= max\{\frac{d^*(\mu - T)}{d_u}, \frac{d^*(T - \mu)}{d_l}\} \\
&= (\mu - T)\left\{\frac{d^*}{U - T} I_{[\mu>T]} - \frac{d^*}{T - L} I_{[\mu<T]}\right\} \\
&= d^*(\mu - T)\left\{\frac{1}{U - T} I_{[\mu>T]} - \frac{1}{T - L} I_{[\mu<T]}\right\} \tag{7.8}
\end{aligned}
$$

where

$$I_{[\mu>T]} = \left\{ \begin{array}{ll} 1 & \text{if } \mu > T \\ 0 & \text{if } \mu < T \end{array} \right.$$

and

$$I_{[\mu<T]} = \left\{ \begin{array}{ll} 1 & \text{if } \mu < T \\ 0 & \text{if } \mu > T \end{array} \right.$$

Similarly

$$
\begin{aligned}
F &= max\{\frac{d(\mu - T)}{d_u}, \frac{d(T - \mu)}{d_l}\} \\
&= d(\mu - T)\left\{\frac{1}{U - T} I_{[\mu>T]} - \frac{1}{T - L} I_{[\mu<T]}\right\} \tag{7.9}
\end{aligned}
$$

Therefore

$$
\begin{aligned}
C_{pk}'' &= \frac{d^* - F^*}{3\sigma} = \frac{d^*}{3\sigma}\left(1 - \frac{F^*}{d^*}\right) \\
&= \left(1 - \frac{F^*}{d^*}\right) C_p'' \\
&= \left[1 - (\mu - T)\left\{\frac{1}{U - T} I_{[\mu>T]} - \frac{1}{T - L} I_{[\mu<T]}\right\}\right] C_p''
\end{aligned}
\tag{7.10}
$$

Observe that, if $\mu > T$, then from equation (7.10)

$$
\begin{aligned}
C_{pk}'' &= C_p''\left[1 - \frac{\mu - T}{U - T}\right] = C_p'' \times \frac{U - \mu}{d_u} \\
&= C_p'' \times \frac{VA_\mu^*}{VA_T^*} \tag{7.11}
\end{aligned}
$$

Similarly, if $\mu < T$, then from equation (7.10)

$$
\begin{aligned}
C_{pk}'' &= C_p'' \left[1 + \frac{\mu - T}{T - L} \right] = C_p'' \times \frac{\mu - L}{d_l} \\
&= C_p'' \times \frac{VA_\mu^*}{VA_T^*}
\end{aligned}
\tag{7.12}
$$

Also,

$$
C_{pm}'' = \frac{d^*}{3\sqrt{\sigma^2 + F^2}} = \frac{VA_T}{VN'}
$$

Finally,

$$
\begin{aligned}
C_{pmk}'' &= \frac{d^* - F^*}{3\sqrt{\sigma^2 + F^2}} = \frac{d^* - F^*}{d^*} \times \frac{d^*}{\sqrt{\sigma^2 + F^2}} \\
&= \left(1 - \frac{F^*}{d^*} \right) \times C_{pm}^*
\end{aligned}
\tag{7.13}
$$

Now, from equations (7.10), (7.11), and (7.12)

$$
1 - \frac{F^*}{d^*} = 1 - (\mu - T) \left\{ \frac{1}{U - T} \, I_{[\mu > T]} - \frac{1}{T - L} \, I_{[\mu < T]} \right\} = \frac{VA_\mu^*}{VA_T^*}
\tag{7.14}
$$

Hence from equation (7.13),

$$
C_{pmk}'' = \frac{VA_\mu^*}{VA_T^*} \times C_{pm}''
\tag{7.15}
$$

Therefore, following Grau's [11] notations, the alternative expressions for C_p'', C_{pk}'', C_{pm}'', and C_{pmk}'' can be consolidated as follows:

$$
\left.
\begin{aligned}
C_p'' &= \frac{VA_T}{VN} \\[4pt]
C_{pk}'' &= \frac{VA_\mu^*}{VA_T^*} \times C_{pm}'' \\[4pt]
C_{pm}'' &= \frac{VA_T}{VN'} \\[4pt]
C_{pmk}'' &= \frac{VA_\mu^*}{VA_T^*} \times C_{pm}''
\end{aligned}
\right\}
\tag{7.16}
$$

Grau [11] has, then, defined MPCIs analogous to C_p'', C_{pk}'', C_{pm}'', and C_{pmk}''. Suppose there are q quality characteristics, which are correlated among themselves and are having the mean vector μ and dispersion matrix Σ. Then Grau's [11] MPCIs can be defined as:

$$\underline{C}_p^{''} = \frac{3}{\sqrt{\chi_{p,0.9973}^2}} \times \inf_i(C_{p,i}^{''}) \tag{7.17}$$

$$\underline{C}_{pk}^{''} = \left(1 - \sup_i \left(\sup \left(\frac{\mu_i - T_i}{U_i - T_i}, \frac{T_i - \mu_i}{T_i - L_i}\right)\right)\right) \times \underline{C}_p^{''}$$

$$\tag{7.18}$$

$$\underline{C}_{pm}^{''} = \left\{1 + Q(\boldsymbol{\mu})'\Sigma^{-1}Q(\boldsymbol{\mu})\right\}^{-\frac{1}{2q}} \times \underline{C}_p^{''} \tag{7.19}$$

$$\underline{C}_{pmk}^{''} = \left\{1 + (\boldsymbol{\mu} - \boldsymbol{T})'\Sigma^{-1}(\boldsymbol{\mu} - \boldsymbol{T})\right\}^{-\frac{1}{2q}} \times \underline{C}_{pk}^{''} \tag{7.20}$$

where $C_{p,i}^{''}$ is the $C_p^{''}$ value corresponding to the ith variable, for $i = 1(1)q$ and $Q(\boldsymbol{\mu})$, the multivariate analogue of F, is a q component vector whose ith element is defined as

$$Q(\boldsymbol{\mu})_i = (\mu_i - T_i) \times \left(\frac{d}{U_i - T_i} \ I_{[\mu_i > T_i]} + \frac{d}{T_i - L_i} \ I_{[\mu_i < T_i]}\right), \ i = 1(1)q$$

with $I_{[\mu \in A]} = \begin{cases} 1, & \text{if } \mu \in A \\ 0, & \text{otherwise} \end{cases}$

Note that, although, while defining $Q(\boldsymbol{\mu})_i$, Grau [11] did not consider the situation where, $\mu_i = T_i$, for $i = 1(1)q$, it may be noted that, for that particular "i," $Q(\boldsymbol{\mu})_i = 0$ and hence, $C_{pm,i}^{''}$ boils down to $C_{p,i}^{''}$, for $i = 1(1)q$.

Grau [11] has shown that similar to the interrelationships between $C_p^{''}$, $C_{pk}^{''}$, $C_{pm}^{''}$ and $C_{pmk}^{''}$, as discussed in equation (3.18) (vide Section 3.2.1); $\underline{C}_p^{''}$, $\underline{C}_{pk}^{''}$, $\underline{C}_{pm}^{''}$ and $\underline{C}_{pmk}^{''}$ also have the following interrelationship:

$$\left. \begin{array}{l} \underline{C}_p^{''} \geq \underline{C}_{pk}^{''} \geq \underline{C}_{pmk}^{''} \\ \underline{C}_p^{''} \geq \underline{C}_{pm}^{''} \geq \underline{C}_{pmk}^{''} \end{array} \right\} \tag{7.21}$$

Grau [11] has shown the relationship between proportion of non-conformance and these MPCIs as follows:

$$yield \ \geq \ \Phi_{\chi_q^2} \left(\chi_{q,0.9973}^2 \times \underline{C}_p^{''2}\right), \tag{7.22}$$

$$yield \ \geq \ \Phi_{\chi_q^2} \left(\chi_{q,0.9973}^2 \times \underline{C}_{pk}^{''2}\right) \tag{7.23}$$

$$yield \ \geq \ \Phi_{\chi_q^2} \left(\chi_{q,0.9973}^2 \times \underline{C}_{pmk}^{''2}\right) \tag{7.24}$$

$$\tag{7.25}$$

where $\Phi_{\chi_q^2}$ is the cumulative distribution function of χ^2 distribution with q degrees of freedom. However, similar relationship is not available for $\underline{C}_{pm}^{''}$. Also, any exact relationship between the PNC and the MPCI's defined in this chapter is yet to be established.

7.3 Multivariate Analogue of $C_p''(u, v)$, for $u = 0, 1$ and $v = 0, 1$ – An Alternative Approach

Kotz and Johnson [13] and Rodriguez [16] have rightly opined that, a PCI should bridge the gap between theoreticians and practitioners – in a sense that it should be easy to compute and even easier to interpret.

Therefore, an ideal process capability index should have simple interpretation and properties similar to those of the classical indices C_p, C_{pk}, C_{pm}, and C_{pmk} so as to get higher degree of acceptability among the practitioners, especially, the shop floor personnel. We may recall that the very idea of defining C_p'', C_{pk}'', C_{pm}'', and C_{pmk}'' was to have some analogues of those indices for univariate processes with asymmetric specification regions.

Under such circumstances and with the assumption of multivariate normality of the underlying process distribution, Chatterjee and Chakraborty [3] have suggested a superstructure of process capability indices for asymmetric specification region which is given by

$$C_M(u, v) = \frac{1}{3} \sqrt{\frac{(\mathbf{d}^* - u\mathbf{G}^*)'\Sigma^{-1}(\mathbf{d}^* - u\mathbf{G}^*)}{1 + v\mathbf{G}'\Sigma^{-1}\mathbf{G}}} \tag{7.26}$$

where u and v are two nonnegative real numbers,

$\mathbf{d}^* = (\min(d_{l1}, d_{u1}), \min(d_{l2}, d_{u2}), \cdots, \min(d_{lq}, D_{uq}))'$, i.e., $d_i^* = min(d_{li}, d_{ui})$, for $i = 1(1)q$ with $\mathbf{d}_u = (d_{u1}, d_{u2}, \cdots, d_{uq})'$ and $\mathbf{d}_l = (d_{l1}, d_{l2}, \cdot, d_{lq})'$.

For multivariate case, "$\mathbf{G}$" can be defined as

$\mathbf{G} = (a_1 d_1, a_2 d_2, \cdots, a_q d_q)'$, where, $a_i = \left[\max\{\frac{\mu_i - T_i}{d_{ui}}, \frac{T_i - \mu_i}{d_{li}}\}\right]$ and $d_i = \frac{U_i - L_i}{2}$, for $i = 1(1)q$, such that, $A = [diag(a_1, a_2, \cdots, a_q)]$ is a $(q \times q)$ diagonal matrix with $a_i = \left[\max\{\frac{\mu_i - T_i}{d_{ui}}, \frac{T_i - \mu_i}{d_{li}}\}\right]$ and $\mathbf{d} = (d_1, d_2, \cdots, d_q)'$ is a "q" -component vector.

Thus, $\mathbf{G} = [diag(a_1, a_2, \cdots, a_q)] \times \mathbf{d} = A\mathbf{d}$ and its univariate counterpart is defined as $F = \max\left\{\frac{d(\mu - T)}{d_u}, \frac{d(T - \mu)}{d_l}\right\}$.

Similarly, $F^* = \max\left(\frac{d^*(\mu - T)}{d_u}, \frac{d^*(T - \mu)}{d_l}\right)$ can be generalized as $\mathbf{G}^* = A\mathbf{d}^*$ for the multivariate case.

Note that for $q = 1$, $C_M(u, v)$ boils down to $C_p''(u, v)$, which is defined in equation (7.1).

Moreover, similar to C_p, $C_M(0, 0)$ does not incorporate the process mean vector $\boldsymbol{\mu}$ in its definition. Hence, it measures the true capability of a process only when it is centered on its target and fails to detect any deviation of process centering from target. Therefore, $C_M(0, 0)$ should be treated as the potential capability index rather than an MPCI measuring the expected process capability.

MPCIs for asymmetric specification region

Chatterjee and Chakraborty [5] studied some of the very crucial statistical properties of $C_M(u,v)$, which do have immense interpretational importance as well. Some of these properties are,

1. interrelationships between the member indices of $C_M(u,v)$, for $u = 0,1$ and $v = 0,1$;

2. threshold value of $C_M(0,0)$;

7.3.1 Interrelationships between the Member Indices of $C_M(u,v)$ for $u = 0,1$ and $v = 0,1$

interrelationships between the various member indices of $C_M(u,v)$, particularly for $u = 0,1$ and $v = 0,1$ are discussed in detail below:

Relationship between $C_M(0,0)$ and $C_M(1,0)$

From equation (7.26),

$$C_M^2(0,0) = \frac{1}{9} \times \boldsymbol{d^{*'}} \Sigma^{-1} \boldsymbol{d^*} \tag{7.27}$$

and

$$C_M^2(1,0) = \frac{1}{9} \times (\boldsymbol{d^*} - \boldsymbol{G^*})' \Sigma^{-1} (\boldsymbol{d^*} - \boldsymbol{G^*}) \tag{7.28}$$

Now, to explore the relationship between $C_M(0,0)$ and $C_M(1,0)$, we have to study the behavior of $\boldsymbol{G^*}$ for different positions of $\boldsymbol{T}$ with respect to $\boldsymbol{\mu}$.

Let, $\boldsymbol{\mu} \leq \boldsymbol{T}$, i.e., $(\boldsymbol{T} - \boldsymbol{\mu}) \geq \boldsymbol{0}$, i.e., $T_i - \mu_i \geq 0$, for $i = 1(1)q$. Hence, $a_i = \frac{T_i - \mu_i}{d_{li}}$, for $i = 1(1)q$.

Moreover, for $\boldsymbol{\mu} \leq \boldsymbol{T}$, $0 \leq a_i \leq 1$, for $i = 1(1)q$. Hence, $\boldsymbol{d^*} \geq A\boldsymbol{d^*} = \boldsymbol{G^*}$.

Note that, $(\boldsymbol{d^*} - \boldsymbol{G^*})' \Sigma^{-1} (\boldsymbol{d^*} - \boldsymbol{G^*}) \lesseqgtr \boldsymbol{d^{*'}} \Sigma^{-1} \boldsymbol{d^*}$, based on the form of the dispersion matrix, viz., Σ. Since $C_M(0,0)$ and $C_M(1,0)$ are defined analogous to C_p'' and C_{pk}'' of univariate process capability analysis, one would expect $C_M(1,0) \leq C_M(0,0)$ as $C_M(0,0)$ is defined to measure the potential process capability and hence should have the highest index value among all the member indices of $C_M(u,v)$, for $u = 0,1$ and $v = 0,1$. Now

$$(\boldsymbol{d^*} - \boldsymbol{G^*})' \Sigma^{-1} (\boldsymbol{d^*} - \boldsymbol{G^*}) \leq \boldsymbol{d^{*'}} \Sigma^{-1} \boldsymbol{d^*}$$
$$\Rightarrow \boldsymbol{d^{*'}} \Sigma^{-1} \boldsymbol{d^*} + \boldsymbol{D^{*'}} \Sigma^{-1} \boldsymbol{G^*} - 2\boldsymbol{d^{*'}} \Sigma^{-1} \boldsymbol{G^*} \leq \boldsymbol{d^{*'}} \Sigma^{-1} \boldsymbol{d^*}$$
$$\Rightarrow \boldsymbol{G^{*'}} \Sigma^{-1} \boldsymbol{G^*} \leq 2\boldsymbol{d^{*'}} \Sigma^{-1} \boldsymbol{G^*} \tag{7.29}$$

Thus, for $\boldsymbol{G^{*'}} \Sigma^{-1} \boldsymbol{G^*} \leq 2\boldsymbol{d^{*'}} \Sigma^{-1} \boldsymbol{G^*}$, we have

$$C_M(0,0) \geq C_M(1,0) \tag{7.30}$$

Also, for $\mu_i \geq T_i$, $0 \leq a_i = \frac{\mu_i - T_i}{d_{ui}} \leq 1$. Thus, for $\boldsymbol{\mu} \geq \boldsymbol{T}$, $\boldsymbol{d}^* \geq A\boldsymbol{d}^*$ and hence, in this case also, $C_M(0,0) \geq C_M(1,0)$.

Finally suppose, for some "i," $\mu_i < T_i$, while for the others, $\mu_i \geq T_i$, for $i = 1(1)q$. Then also, by virtue of the definition of a_i, $0 \leq a_i \leq 1$, for $i = 1(1)q$ and hence, $C_M(0,0) \geq C_M(1,0)$.

Relationship between $C_M(1,0)$ and $C_M(1,1)$

From equation (7.26),

$$
\begin{aligned}
C_M^2(1,1) &= \frac{1}{9} \times \frac{(\boldsymbol{d}^* - \boldsymbol{G}^*)'\Sigma^{-1}(\boldsymbol{d}^* - \boldsymbol{G}^*)}{1 + \boldsymbol{G}\Sigma^{-1}\boldsymbol{G}} \\
&= \frac{C_M^2(1,0)}{1 + \boldsymbol{G}\Sigma^{-1}\boldsymbol{G}} \\
&\leq C_M^2(1,0),
\end{aligned}
\tag{7.31}
$$

since Σ is positive definite and $\boldsymbol{G}\Sigma^{-1}\boldsymbol{G}$ is a quadratic form and hence is always nonnegative. Thus, from equations (7.30) and (7.31) and for $\boldsymbol{G}^{*'}\Sigma^{-1}\boldsymbol{G}^* \leq 2\boldsymbol{d}^{*'}\Sigma^{-1}\boldsymbol{G}^*$,

$$
C_M(0,0) \geq C_M(1,0) \geq C_M(1,1)
\tag{7.32}
$$

Relationship between $C_M(0,0)$ and $C_M(0,1)$

From equation (7.26),

$$
C_M^2(0,1) = \frac{1}{9} \times \frac{\boldsymbol{d}^{*'}\Sigma^{-1}\boldsymbol{d}^*}{1 + \boldsymbol{G}\Sigma^{-1}\boldsymbol{G}} = \frac{C_M^2(0,0)}{1 + \boldsymbol{G}\Sigma^{-1}\boldsymbol{G}} \leq C_M^2(0,0)
\tag{7.33}
$$

Also, for $\boldsymbol{G}^{*'}\Sigma^{-1}\boldsymbol{G}^* \leq 2\boldsymbol{d}^{*'}\Sigma^{-1}\boldsymbol{G}^*$,

$$
\begin{aligned}
C_M^2(1,1) &= \frac{1}{9} \times \left\{ \frac{(\boldsymbol{d}^* - \boldsymbol{G}^*)'\Sigma^{-1}(\boldsymbol{d}^* - \boldsymbol{G}^*)}{1 + \boldsymbol{G}'\Sigma^{-1}\boldsymbol{G}} \right\} \\
&\leq \frac{1}{9} \times \left\{ \frac{\boldsymbol{d}^{*'}\Sigma^{-1}\boldsymbol{d}^*}{1 + \boldsymbol{G}'\Sigma^{-1}\boldsymbol{G}} \right\} = C_M^2(0,1)
\end{aligned}
\tag{7.34}
$$

Thus, from equations (7.33) and (7.34) and for $\boldsymbol{G}^{*'}\Sigma^{-1}\boldsymbol{G}^* \leq 2\boldsymbol{d}^{*'}\Sigma^{-1}\boldsymbol{G}^*$

$$
C_M(0,0) \geq C_M(0,1) \geq C_M(1,1)
\tag{7.35}
$$

Therefore, combining equations (7.32) and (7.35), and for $\boldsymbol{G}^{*'}\Sigma^{-1}\boldsymbol{G}^* \leq 2\boldsymbol{d}^{*'}\Sigma^{-1}\boldsymbol{G}^*$,

$$
\left.
\begin{aligned}
C_M(1,1) \leq C_M(1,0) \leq C_M(0,0) \\
C_M(1,1) \leq C_M(0,1) \leq C_M(0,0)
\end{aligned}
\right\}
\tag{7.36}
$$

It is to be noted that, (vide Chapter 3), here also, no clear-cut relationship exists between $C_M(1,0)$ and $C_M(0,1)$, as is the case of C_{pk}'' and C_{pm}'' (refer Chapter 3).

7.4 Threshold Value of $C_M(0,0)$

Threshold value plays an important role in interpreting a PCI (both univariate and multivariate), particularly, for a PCI measuring potential process capability (refer Chapter 3 for more detail). Chatterjee and Chakraborty [5] have developed expression for threshold value of $C_M(0,0)$, which is discussed in detail now.

Recall that threshold value of C_p'' depends upon the position of T with respect to U and L (refer Chapter 3). Also, Chatterjee and Chakraborty [5] have derived expression for the threshold value of $C_M(0,0)$ for bivariate processes only, since it is difficult to get a closed-form expression for its multivariate counterpart. Though some bounds for it can be obtained under some stringent assumptions.

7.4.1 For Bivariate Case

Let $USL_1 = T_1 + k_{U_1}\sigma_1$ and $USL_2 = T_2 + k_{U_2}\sigma_2$ such that $\boldsymbol{USL} = \boldsymbol{T} + K_U \times \boldsymbol{\sigma}$, where, $K_U = diag(k_{U_1}, k_{U_2})$ and $\boldsymbol{\sigma} = (\sigma_1, \sigma_2)'$.

Similarly, $LSL_1 = T_1 - k_{L_1}\sigma_1$ and $LSL_2 = T_2 - k_{L_2}\sigma_2$ such that $\boldsymbol{LSL} = \boldsymbol{T} - K_L \times \boldsymbol{\sigma}$, where $K_L = diag(k_{L_1}, k_{L_2})$ with $K_U \neq K_L$ as otherwise the specification region will become symmetric. Also for $i = 1, 2$, k_{U_i} is the distance of USL_i from T_i in terms of the corresponding sigma unit (σ_i). The elements of the matrices K_L may be similarly defined. Thus $d_{u1} = k_{U_1}\sigma_1; d_{u2} = k_{U_2}\sigma_2$.

For deriving the expression for the threshold value, consider the following cases:

Case I: $\boldsymbol{d}^* = \boldsymbol{d_u}$:

Here, $\boldsymbol{d}^* = \min\{\boldsymbol{d_u}, \boldsymbol{d_l}\} = \boldsymbol{d_u} < \boldsymbol{d_l}$. Then, from equation (7.26)

$$C_M(0,0) = \frac{1}{3}\sqrt{\boldsymbol{d}^{*'}\Sigma^{-1}\boldsymbol{d}^*} = \frac{1}{3}\sqrt{\boldsymbol{d_u'}\Sigma^{-1}\boldsymbol{d_u}}$$

$$\text{i.e., } C_M^2(0,0) = \frac{1}{9} \times (d_{u1}\ d_{u2})\Sigma^{-1}\begin{pmatrix} d_{u1} \\ d_{u2} \end{pmatrix} \tag{7.37}$$

Now, $\Sigma^{-1} = \frac{1}{(\sigma_1\sigma_2)^2 - \sigma_{12}^2} \times \begin{pmatrix} \sigma_2^2 & -\sigma_{12} \\ -\sigma_{12} & \sigma_1^2 \end{pmatrix}$. Hence, from equation (7.37),

$$C_M^2(0,0) = \frac{1}{9(1-\rho_{12}^2)} \times \left(\frac{d_{u2}^2}{\sigma_2^2} + \frac{d_{u1}^2}{\sigma_1^2} - \frac{2\rho_{12}d_{u1}d_{u2}}{\sigma_1\sigma_2}\right) \tag{7.38}$$

Substituting the values of d_u in equation (7.38), the threshold value of $C_M^{(T)}(0,0)$ can be obtained as

$$C_M^{(T)^2}(0,0) \;=\; \frac{1}{9\,(1-\rho_{12}^2)} \times \left(k_{U_1}^2 + k_{U_2}^2 - 2\rho_{12}k_{U_1}k_{U_2}\right)$$

$$\text{i.e., } C_M^{(T)}(0,0) \;=\; \frac{1}{3}\sqrt{\frac{k_{U_1}^2 + k_{U_2}^2 - 2\rho_{12}k_{U_1}k_{U_2}}{1-\rho_{12}^2}} \tag{7.39}$$

Special Case:

For $k_{U_1} = k_{U_2} = k_U$, say, i.e., when both the *USLs* are at equal distances from their respective targets in terms of the corresponding sigma units, equation (7.39) simplifies to

$$C_M^{(T)}(0,0) = \frac{k_U}{3}\sqrt{\frac{2}{1+\rho_{12}}} \tag{7.40}$$

<u>Case II: $d^* = d_l$:</u>

Here, $d^* = \min\{d_u, d_l\} = d_l < d_u$. Then, from equation (7.26) and similar to equation (7.38),

$$\begin{aligned}
C_M^2(0,0) &= \frac{1}{9} \times d_l' \Sigma^{-1} d_l \\
&= \frac{1}{9(1-\rho_{12}^2)} \times \left(\frac{d_{l2}^2}{\sigma_2^2} + \frac{d_{l1}^2}{\sigma_1^2} - \frac{2\rho_{12}d_{l1}d_{l2}}{\sigma_1\sigma_2}\right)
\end{aligned} \tag{7.41}$$

Thus, similar to equation (7.39) and substituting the expression of $d^* = d_l$ in equation (7.41), the expression for the threshold value will be

$$C_M^{(T)}(0,0) = \frac{1}{3}\sqrt{\frac{k_{L_1}^2 + k_{L_2}^2 - 2\rho_{12}k_{L_1}k_{L_2}}{1-\rho_{12}^2}} \tag{7.42}$$

Special Case:

When both the *LSLs* are at equal distances from their respective targets in terms of the corresponding sigma units, then, substituting $k_{L_1} = k_{L_2} = k_L$, in equation (7.42), the expression for $C_M^{(T)}(0,0)$ simplifies to

$$C_M^{(T)}(0,0) = \frac{k_L}{3}\sqrt{\frac{2}{1+\rho_{12}}} \tag{7.43}$$

Case III : $d_{u1} < d_{l1}$ and $d_{u2} > d_{l2}$

Here $d^* = \begin{pmatrix} d_{u1} \\ d_{l2} \end{pmatrix}$. Thus, from equation (7.26),

$$C_M^2(0,0) = \frac{1}{9(1-\rho_{12}^2)} \times \left(\frac{d_{u1}^2}{\sigma_1^2} + \frac{d_{l2}^2}{\sigma_2^2} - \frac{2\rho_{12}d_{u1}d_{l2}}{\sigma_1\sigma_2} \right) \tag{7.44}$$

Hence, substituting the values of d_{u1} and d_{l2} in equation (7.44), the threshold value of $C_M^{(T)}(0,0)$ can be obtained as

$$C_M^{(T)}(0,0) = \frac{1}{3} \sqrt{\frac{k_{L_1}^2 + k_{U_2}^2 - 2\rho_{12}k_{L_1}k_{U_2}}{1-\rho_{12}^2}} \tag{7.45}$$

Note that, the expressions of $C_M^T(0,0)$ for all the three cases, as obtained from equations (7.39), (7.42), and (7.45), can be generalized as :

$$C_M^{(T)}(0,0) = \frac{1}{3} \sqrt{\frac{k_{.1}^2 + k_{.2}^2 - 2\rho_{12}k_{.1}k_{.2}}{1-\rho_{12}^2}} \tag{7.46}$$

where, $k_{.1} = \min(k_{U_1}, k_{L_1})$ and $k_{.2} = \min(k_{U_2}, k_{L_2})$.

Hence from equation (7.46), $C_M^{(T)}(0,0)$, being a function of ρ_{12}, is not unique. Such relationship between $C_M^T(0,0)$ and ρ_{12} is quite reasonable, as unlike a univariate process, for a bivariate (or in general, multivariate) process, the variables are interrelated and hence influence the process performance according to their strength of correlation.

Also, for $k_{.1} = k_{.2} = k_{.}$, the general expression of the threshold value of $C_M(0,0)$, as given in equation (7.46) boils down to

$$C_M^{(T)}(0,0) = \frac{k_.}{3} \times \sqrt{\frac{2}{1+\rho_{12}}} \tag{7.47}$$

Note that, when $-1 \leq \rho_{12} \leq 0$, for a just capable process, threshold value of $C_M(0,0)$ will lie within the interval $[\frac{k_.\sqrt{2}}{3}, \infty)$, depending upon the position of T with respect to tolerance region. Also, for $0 \leq \rho_{12} \leq 1$, the threshold value of $C_M(0,0)$ will lie within the interval $[\frac{k_.}{3}, \frac{k_.\sqrt{2}}{3}]$. Hence, considering these two cases together, for $-1 \leq \rho_{12} \leq 1$, the threshold value of $C_M(0,0)$ varies between $[\frac{k_.}{3}, \infty)$.

Moreover, in many cases, at first, the target is fixed and then as per requirement, upper and lower specification limits are established. As such our formulations of **USL** and **LSL** are more realistic than the existing concept of $T = (3\,USL + LSL)/4$ proposed by Boyles [1].

The threshold values of $C_M(0,0)$, corresponding to various combinations of $(k_{.1}, k_{.2})$ and $\rho_{12} = -1(0.05)1$, are presented in Table 7.1.

A wide range of $(k_{.1}, k_{.2})$ values have been covered in this table in a sense that a $k_{.i}, i = 1, 2$, value less than "2" will make the specification design too conservative, while the value greater than "4" may overlook some serious problems present in the process.

TABLE 7.1: Threshold values of $C_M(0,0)$ for $\rho_{12} = -1(0.1)1$, & p = 2

ρ_{12}	$(2, 2)$	$(2, 2.5)$	$(2, 3)$	$(2, 3.5)$	$(2, 4)$	$(2.5, 2.5)$	$(2.5, 3)$	$(2.5, 3.5)$	$(2.5, 4)$	$(3, 3)$	$(3, 3.5)$	$(3, 4)$	$(3.5, 3.5)$	$(3.5, 4)$	$(4, 4)$
-1.00	∞	∞	∞	∞	∞	∞	∞	∞	∞	∞	∞	∞	∞	∞	∞
-0.95	4.2164	4.7442	5.2732	5.8030	6.3336	5.2705	5.7981	6.3268	6.8563	6.3246	6.8521	7.3806	7.3786	7.9061	8.4327
-0.90	2.9814	3.3552	3.7307	4.1075	4.4852	3.7268	4.1003	4.4754	4.8516	4.4721	4.8456	5.2203	5.2175	5.5908	5.9628
-0.85	2.4343	2.7400	3.0478	3.3573	3.6679	3.0429	3.3483	3.6556	3.9643	3.6515	3.9567	4.2636	4.2601	4.5652	4.8686
-0.80	2.1082	2.3733	2.6411	2.9107	3.1817	2.6352	2.9001	3.1672	3.4359	3.1623	3.4269	3.6935	3.6893	3.9538	4.2164
-0.75	1.8856	2.1232	2.3637	2.6065	2.8508	2.3570	2.5943	2.8340	3.0758	2.8284	3.0654	3.3046	3.2998	3.5367	3.7712
-0.70	1.7213	1.9386	2.1592	2.3823	2.6072	2.1517	2.3685	2.5883	2.8103	2.5820	2.7986	3.0177	3.0123	3.2288	3.4427
-0.65	1.5936	1.7952	2.0005	2.2085	2.4185	1.9920	2.1932	2.3975	2.6042	2.3905	2.5913	2.7949	2.7889	2.9895	3.1873
-0.60	1.4907	1.6796	1.8727	2.0687	2.2669	1.8634	2.0518	2.2438	2.4385	2.2361	2.4242	2.6154	2.6087	2.7966	2.9814
-0.55	1.4055	1.5840	1.7670	1.9533	2.1419	1.7568	1.9348	2.1167	2.3015	2.1082	2.2858	2.4668	2.4595	2.6369	2.8109
-0.50	1.3333	1.5031	1.6777	1.8559	2.0367	1.6667	1.8359	2.0092	2.1858	2.0000	2.1688	2.3413	2.3333	2.5019	2.6667
-0.45	1.2713	1.4335	1.6011	1.7725	1.9467	1.5891	1.7508	1.9169	2.0866	1.9069	2.0682	2.2333	2.2247	2.3857	2.5426
-0.40	1.2172	1.3729	1.5344	1.7001	1.8687	1.5215	1.6766	1.8366	2.0003	1.8257	1.9804	2.1393	2.1300	2.2843	2.4343
-0.35	1.1694	1.3195	1.4758	1.6365	1.8004	1.4618	1.6111	1.7658	1.9245	1.7541	1.9030	2.0565	2.0465	2.1950	2.3388
-0.30	1.1269	1.2719	1.4237	1.5802	1.7401	1.4086	1.5529	1.7029	1.8572	1.6903	1.8341	1.9828	1.9720	2.1154	2.2537
-0.25	1.0887	1.2293	1.3771	1.5299	1.6865	1.3608	1.5006	1.6465	1.7971	1.6330	1.7722	1.9168	1.9052	2.0440	2.1773
-0.20	1.0541	1.1907	1.3351	1.4849	1.6387	1.3176	1.4534	1.5957	1.7430	1.5811	1.7163	1.8572	1.8447	1.9793	2.1082
-0.15	1.0226	1.1557	1.2970	1.4442	1.5957	1.2783	1.4104	1.5496	1.6941	1.5339	1.6654	1.8030	1.7896	1.9206	2.0452
-0.10	0.9938	1.1237	1.2624	1.4075	1.5570	1.2423	1.3711	1.5076	1.6497	1.4907	1.6188	1.7536	1.7392	1.8668	1.9876
-0.05	0.9673	1.0943	1.2308	1.3741	1.5221	1.2091	1.3350	1.4691	1.6093	1.4510	1.5761	1.7083	1.6928	1.8173	1.9346
0.00	0.9428	1.0672	1.2019	1.3437	1.4907	1.1785	1.3017	1.4337	1.5723	1.4142	1.5366	1.6667	1.6499	1.7717	1.8856
0.05	0.9201	1.0421	1.1753	1.3161	1.4624	1.1501	1.2709	1.4012	1.5385	1.3801	1.5000	1.6282	1.6102	1.7294	1.8402
0.10	0.8989	1.0189	1.1508	1.2910	1.4370	1.1237	1.2423	1.3711	1.5076	1.3484	1.4660	1.5926	1.5731	1.6901	1.7979
0.15	0.8792	0.9973	1.1283	1.2682	1.4144	1.0990	1.2156	1.3433	1.4792	1.3188	1.4344	1.5597	1.5386	1.6534	1.7583
0.20	0.8607	0.9772	1.1076	1.2477	1.3944	1.0758	1.1907	1.3176	1.4534	1.2910	1.4048	1.5290	1.5062	1.6191	1.7213
0.25	0.8433	0.9584	1.0887	1.2293	1.3771	1.0541	1.1675	1.2939	1.4298	1.2649	1.3771	1.5006	1.4757	1.5870	1.6865
0.30	0.8269	0.9409	1.0713	1.2130	1.3623	1.0336	1.1457	1.2719	1.4086	1.2403	1.3511	1.4742	1.4471	1.5568	1.6538
0.35	0.8114	0.9245	1.0556	1.1988	1.3503	1.0143	1.1253	1.2518	1.3896	1.2172	1.3267	1.4498	1.4200	1.5285	1.6229
0.40	0.7968	0.9092	1.0415	1.1869	1.3412	0.9960	1.1061	1.2334	1.3729	1.1952	1.3037	1.4272	1.3944	1.5018	1.5936
0.45	0.7830	0.8951	1.0290	1.1774	1.3354	0.9787	1.0882	1.2167	1.3587	1.1744	1.2822	1.4066	1.3702	1.4766	1.5659
0.50	0.7698	0.8819	1.0184	1.1706	1.3333	0.9623	1.0715	1.2019	1.3472	1.1547	1.2620	1.3878	1.3472	1.4530	1.5396
0.55	0.7573	0.8699	1.0097	1.1671	1.3357	0.9466	1.0560	1.1890	1.3387	1.1359	1.2431	1.3710	1.3252	1.4307	1.5146
0.60	0.7454	0.8590	1.0035	1.1674	1.3437	0.9317	1.0417	1.1785	1.3340	1.1180	1.2255	1.3566	1.3044	1.4099	1.4907
0.65	0.7340	0.8494	1.0002	1.1729	1.3591	0.9175	1.0287	1.1708	1.3341	1.1010	1.2092	1.3448	1.2845	1.3905	1.4680
0.70	0.7231	0.8415	1.0011	1.1854	1.3846	0.9039	1.0173	1.1669	1.3407	1.0847	1.1946	1.3366	1.2654	1.3728	1.4462
0.75	0.7127	0.8357	1.0079	1.2084	1.4254	0.8909	1.0079	1.1684	1.3569	1.0690	1.1819	1.3333	1.2472	1.3569	1.4254
0.80	0.7027	0.8333	1.0244	1.2485	1.4907	0.8784	1.0015	1.1785	1.3889	1.0541	1.1719	1.3380	1.2298	1.3437	1.4055
0.85	0.6932	0.8371	1.0588	1.3198	1.6008	0.8665	1.0005	1.2048	1.4499	1.0398	1.1668	1.3571	1.2130	1.3348	1.3863
0.90	0.6840	0.8550	1.1343	1.4610	1.8097	0.8550	1.0116	1.2681	1.5765	1.0260	1.1723	1.4101	1.1970	1.3355	1.3680
0.95	0.6752	0.9245	1.3503	1.8335	2.3388	0.8439	1.0675	1.4618	1.9245	1.0127	1.2172	1.5834	1.1815	1.3713	1.3503
1.00	∞	∞	∞	∞	∞	∞	∞	∞	∞	∞	∞	∞	∞	∞	∞

A graphical representation of a part of Table 7.1 with $k_{.1} = 2.0$ and $k_{.2} = 2.0, 2.5, 3.0, 3.5, 4.0$ is given in Figure 7.1. Figures for other combinations of $(k_{.1}, k_{.2})$ can be generated accordingly.

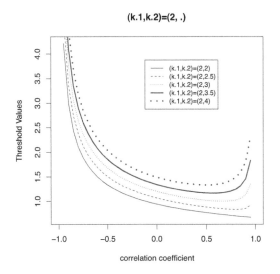

FIGURE 7.1: Threshold values of $C_M(0,0)$ for various values of ρ_{12}, ($k_{.1} = 2.0$ and $k_{.2} = 2.0, 2.5, 3.0, 3.5, 4.0$).

Table 7.1 and Figure 7.1 show that for $k_{.1} = k_{.2}$, $C_M^{(T)}(0,0)$ decreases with ρ_{12}. But for $k_{.1} \neq k_{.2}$, $C_M^{(T)}(0,0)$ decreases for certain values of ρ_{12} and then begins to increase. Also, for a fixed ρ_{12}, the values of $C_M^{(T)}(0,0)$ will remain the same for $(k_{.1}, k_{.2}) = (x, y)$ and $(k_{.1}, k_{.2}) = (y, x)$. Moreover, for $k_{.1} = k_{.2} = k_{.} = 3$, i.e., if the ith quality characteristic has $T_i \pm 3\sigma_i$ specification limits, for $i = 1, 2$, then the specification region becomes symmetric about T and consequently, $C_M^{(T)}(0,0) = C_G^{(T)}(0,0)$, the threshold value of $C_G(0,0)$.

7.4.2 For Multivariate Case

While generalizing the above result for q-variate case, for computational simplicity, we assume that all the process variables have the same correlation coefficient (ρ) with each other and also the values of $k_{.i}, i = 1(1)q$ are all equal. Then, from equation (7.47), the threshold value of $C_M(0,0)$, viz., $C_M^{(T,q)}(0,0)$, is

$$C_M^{(T,q)}(0,0) = \frac{k_{.}}{3}\sqrt{\frac{q}{1+\rho}}, \qquad (7.48)$$

where $k_{.} = min\{k_{.1}, k_{.2}, \cdots, k_{.q}\}$ with $k_{.i} = min(k_{Ui}, k_{Li})$ for $i = 1(1)q$.

Even if in practice, unequal correlation coefficients among the variables is observed, one can define $\rho_{\max} = \max\{\rho_{ij}\}$ and $\rho_{\min} = \min\{\rho_{ij}\}$ for $i \neq j = 1(1)q$, where ρ_{ij} is the correlation coefficient between ith and jth quality characteristics. Then from equation (7.48), $C_M^{(T,q)}(0,0)_{\min} \leq C_M^{(T,q)}(0,0) \leq C_M^{(T,q)}(0,0)_{\max}$, where $C_M^{(T,q)}(0,0)_{\min} = \frac{k}{3}\sqrt{\frac{q}{1+\rho_{\max}}}$ and $C_M^{(T,q)}(0,0)_{\max} = \frac{k}{3}\sqrt{\frac{q}{1+\rho_{\min}}}$.

Finally, the threshold value of $C_M(0,0)$ can be considered as the threshold value of $C_M(u,v)$ for $u \geq 0, v \geq 0$ in general. This is due to the fact that for $\boldsymbol{\mu} = \boldsymbol{M} = \boldsymbol{T}$, all the member MPCI of this superstructure boil down to $C_M(0,0)$ and the index value obtained at this stage is the maximum attainable capability value of a process under the given specification set-up. When $C_M(0,0) \geq C_M^{(T,q)}(0,0)$ but $C_M(u,v) < C_M^{(T,q)}(0,0)$ for $(u,v) \neq (0,0)$, the process is expected to be off-target. On the other hand, if $C_M(u,v) \geq C_M^{(T,q)}(0,0)$ for all u and v, the process, apart from being potentially capable, is also supposed to deliver the good. It is interesting to note that the same approach is followed in practice of univariate PCI, where a process with $C_p(u,v) \geq 1$, for $u \geq 0, v \geq 0$, is considered to be capable while "1" is merely the threshold value of $C_p = C_p(0,0)$. This is true for $C_p''(u,v)$ and $C_G(u,v)$ as well.

7.4.3 Plug-in Estimators of the Member Indices of $C_M(u,v)$ for $u = 0,1$ and $v = 0,1$ and Their Estimation Procedures

Following Chatterjee and Chakraborty [5], plug-in estimator of $C_M(u,v)$ can be defined as

$$\widehat{C}_M(u,v) = \frac{1}{3}\sqrt{\frac{(\mathbf{d}^* - u\widehat{\mathbf{G}}^*)'\widehat{\Sigma}^{-1}(\mathbf{d}^* - u\widehat{\mathbf{G}}^*)}{1 + v\widehat{\mathbf{G}}'\Sigma^{-1}\widehat{\mathbf{G}}}}, \qquad (7.49)$$

where $\widehat{\mathbf{G}} = \widehat{A}\mathbf{d}$ and $\widehat{\mathbf{G}}^* = \widehat{A}\mathbf{d}^*$, where $\widehat{A} = ((\widehat{a}_i))$ and $\widehat{a}_i = [\max\{\frac{\overline{X}_i - T_i}{D_{iU}}, \frac{T_i - \overline{X}}{D_{iL}}\}]$.

$$\widehat{C}_M(0,0) \sim \{C_M(0,0)\} \times \sqrt{n-1} \times \chi_{n-p}^{-1} \qquad (7.50)$$

where χ_{n-p}^{-1} denotes the inverse chi distribution with $n-p$ degrees of freedom. In this context, the inverse chi-square distribution is a continuous probability distribution of a positive valued random variable whose reciprocal (multiplicative inverse) follows chi-square distribution. The values of the density functions and the random number generators of the inverse chi-square distribution are available in *geoR* package of the R software [Ribeiro and Diggle [15]].

Thus, for $b_{n-p} = \frac{2}{n-1} \times \frac{\Gamma(\frac{n-p-1}{2})}{\Gamma(\frac{n-p}{2})}$

$$E[\widehat{C}_M(0,0)]$$
$$= \sqrt{n-1} \times \left\{ \frac{\Gamma(\frac{n-p-1}{2})}{\Gamma(\frac{n-p}{2})} \right\} \times C_M(0,0) \tag{7.51}$$

i.e., $E[\widetilde{C}_M(0,0)] = E[b_{n-p}\widehat{C}_M(0,0)] = C_M(0,0)$

$$\tag{7.52}$$

Therefore, $\widetilde{C}_M(0,0)$ is an unbiased estimator of $C_M(0,0)$.

From equation (7.49), the plug-in estimator of $C_M(1,0)$ is

$$\begin{aligned} \widehat{C}_M(1,0) &= \frac{1}{3} \times \sqrt{(d^* - \widehat{G}^*)'\widehat{\Sigma}^{-1}(d^* - \widehat{G}^*)} \\ &= \frac{\sqrt{n-1}}{3} \times \sqrt{(d^* - \widehat{G}^*)'S^{*-1}(d^* - \widehat{G}^*)} \end{aligned} \tag{7.53}$$

where $\widehat{G}^* = \widehat{A}d^*$ is a $(q \times 1)$ vector whose ith element is given by $\widehat{G}_i^* = \hat{a}_i d_i^* = \max[\overline{X}_i - T_i, (T_i - \overline{X}_i) \times \frac{d_{ui}}{d_{li}}]$, for $i = 1(1)p$ and $S^* = \sqrt{n-1}\widehat{\Sigma}$ is the sum of square-sum of product (SS - SP) matrix corresponding to X.

Let $(d^* - \widehat{G}^*) = H^*$. then for its any particular value, say h^*, we have

$$\begin{aligned} \hat{C}_M(1,0)|_{H^*=h^*} &= \frac{1}{3}\sqrt{h^{*\prime}\widehat{\Sigma}^{-1}h^*} \\ &= \frac{\sqrt{n-1}}{3}\sqrt{h^{*\prime}\Sigma^{-1}h^*} \times \sqrt{\frac{h^{*\prime}S^{*-1}h^*}{h^{*\prime}\Sigma^{-1}h^*}} \end{aligned}$$
$$\tag{7.54}$$

Therefore

$$E\left[\hat{C}_M(1,0)\right] = \frac{\sqrt{n-1}}{3\sqrt{2}} \times \frac{\Gamma\left(\frac{n-q-1}{2}\right)}{\Gamma\left(\frac{n-q}{2}\right)} \times E\left[\sqrt{H^{*\prime}\Sigma^{-1}H^*}\right], \tag{7.55}$$

since $\frac{h^{*\prime}S^{*-1}h^*}{h^{*\prime}\Sigma^{-1}h^*} \sim \chi_{n-p}^{2^{-1}}$, where, $\chi_{n-p}^{2^{-1}}$ stands for inverse chi-square distribution with $(n-q)$ degrees of freedom [Giri [10]] and this is independent of the choice of h^* and hence of $h^{*\prime}\Sigma^{-1}h^*$.

Since derivation of the exact expression of $E\left[\sqrt{H^{*\prime}\Sigma^{-1}H^*}\right]$ is complicated, Chatterjee and Chakraborty [5] have made an extensive simulation study on the bias associated with $E\left[\hat{C}_M(1,0)\right]$, which shows that the bias is in general negative and decreases with the increase in sample size (n). Also, $\hat{C}_M(1,0)$ performs better for highly asymmetric specfication region as compared to moderately asymmetric specification region.

Again, from equation (7.49), the plug-in estimator of $C_M(0,1)$ is

$$\widehat{C}_M(0,1) = \frac{1}{3}\sqrt{\frac{\mathbf{d}^{*\prime}\widehat{\Sigma}^{-1}\mathbf{d}^*}{1+\widehat{\mathbf{G}}^\prime\Sigma^{-1}\widehat{\mathbf{G}}}}$$

(7.56)

where $\widehat{\mathbf{G}} = \widehat{A}\mathbf{d}$ is a $(q \times 1)$ vector whose ith element is given by $\widehat{G}_i = \hat{a}_i d_i = \max[\overline{X}_i - T_i, (T_i - \overline{X}_i)] \times d_i$, for $i = 1(1)p$.

Now, following [see Casella and Berger [2]], since $\overline{X}$ and $\widehat{\Sigma}$ are consistent estimators of μ and Σ, for a continuous function, $h(\overline{X},\widehat{\Sigma}) \to h(\mu,\Sigma)$ almost surely. Thus, from equation (7.56)

$$\hat{C}_M(0,1) \to \frac{1}{3}\sqrt{\frac{\mathbf{d}^{*\prime}\Sigma^{-1}\mathbf{d}^*}{1+\mathbf{G}^\prime\Sigma^{-1}\mathbf{G}}} = C_M(0,1), \text{ almost surely.}$$

(7.57)

Thus, $\hat{C}_M(0,1)$ is a consistent estimator of $C_M(0,1)$.

Chatterjee and Chakraborty [5] have also derived expressions for the expectations of the plug-in estimators of $C_M(u,v)$, for $u = 0,1$ and $v = 0,1$ using multivariate delta method.

7.5 A Real-Life Example

We shall now consider a real life example based on Dataset 1, given in Chapter 1.

The data consists of 25 observations of a process that has two quality characteristics of interest viz., brinell hardness (H) and tensile strength (S). The [USL, LSL] of "H" were [241.3, 112.7] with target set at 177 while the specifications for "S" were [73.30, 32.70] with T = 53. This suggests that, both "H" and "S" were symmetric about their respective targets.

Although the underlying process was initially assumed to be multivariate normal (refer Chen [6]), Chatterjee and Chakraborty [5] have shown that this assumption gets violated. They have transformed the data into multivariate normality using the Box-Cox transformation. The transformed data is given in Table 7.2.

Interestingly, the specification region also gets transformed by virtue of the same transformation. The transformed specification limits and targets for H_{new} and S_{new} are $USL_{H_{new}} = 240.3$, $LSL_{H_{new}} = 111.7$, $T_{H_{new}} = 176$, $USL_{S_{new}} = 2685.945$, $LSL_{S_{new}} = 534.145$, and $T_{S_{new}} = 1404$. Also, the correlation coefficient between H_{new} and S_{new} is 0.846. Thus, after transformation, the transformed specifications for H_{new} remains symmetric, whereas, that of S_{new} becomes asymmetric.

TABLE 7.2: Transformed Data Set Corresponding to Table 1.1

Sample No. Variable	1	2	3	4	5	6	7	8	9	10
H_{new}	143	200	160	181	148	178	162	215	161	141
S_{new}	584.32	1624	1127.625	1425.82	1141.92	1325.625	1052.905	1745.905	1170.78	1118.145

Sample No. Variable	11	12	13	14	15	16	17	18	19	20
H_{new}	175	187	187	186	172	182	177	204	178	196
S_{new}	1641.145	1710.625	1693.12	1624	1219.68	1635.42	1279.68	1517.505	1294.905	1675.705

Sample No. Variable	21	22	23	24	25					
H_{new}	160	183	179	194	181	-	-	-	-	-
S_{new}	1034.625	1452.105	1310.22	1652.625	1545.18	-	-	-	-	-

Boyles [1] also observed that if the original data is transformed, the erstwhile symmetric specification may be transformed into an asymmetric one, by virtue of the same transformation.

Chatterjee and Chakraborty [5] have computed $\widehat{C}_M(0,0) = 1.1672$, $\widehat{C}_M(1,0) = 1.1623$, $\widehat{C}_M(0,1) = 1.1551$, and $\widehat{C}_M(1,1) = 1.1503$ for the transformed data. Also, the threshold value of $\widehat{C}_M(0,0)$ is computed as 1.1672. Thus, the process is potentially just capable as the threshold value coincides with the value of $\widehat{C}_M(0,0)$. All the other MPCIs are found to have values less than the threshold value. This shows that the actual capability level of the process is not satisfactory.

Also, the closer values of $\widehat{C}_M(0,0)$ and $\widehat{C}_M(1,0)$ suggest that the process suffers more due to lack of proximity of the midvalue of the specifications toward the target, than due to the prevailing level of dispersion. This observation is justified by the data itself. The values of S_{new} varies between 584.320 and 1745.905 with the target being 1404; while the range of the values of H_{new} is 141 to 215 and the target is 176. The wide range of S_{new} values strongly suggests that the process suffers from severe off-centeredness corresponding to this quality characteristic.

However, following Chatterjee and Chakraborty [5], one needs to take a look at the prevailing dispersion scenario of the process as well. Because, despite the $\widehat{C}_M(1,0)$ value being close to the $\widehat{C}_M(0,0)$ value, it is still less than the threshold value, indicating high degree of dispersion of the quality characteristics.

Also, for the data in Table 7.2 values of the MPCIs, proposed by Grau are, $\underline{C}_p'' = 0.8864$, $\underline{C}_{pk}'' = 0.8661$, $\underline{C}_{pm}'' = 0.8818$, and $\underline{C}_{pmk}'' = 0.8616$. Observe that here also, the MPCIs have close values to each other. However, due to absence of a threshold value, further comments on these values is difficult.

7.6 Concluding Remark

Asymmetric specification limits, though often observed in practice, is not well covered in the literature. The situations when there are more than one correlated quality characteristics having asymmetric specification limits are even lesser discussed. As of now, only two sets of MPCIs available in the literature are proposed by Grau [11] and Chatterjee and Chakraborty [5]. Both of these sets of MPCIs are actually multivariate analogues of $C_p''(u,v)$, defined by Chen and Pearn [7].

Among these two sets of MPCIs, Grau's [11] MPCIs are apparently difficult to comprehend, though the author has given a very interesting geometrical interpretation for the same.

On the other hand, Chatterjee and Chakraborty's [5] MPCIs are comparatively easier to interpret, though both these sets of MPCIs require more or less similar amount of computational effort.

There are many areas still unexplored in this field. For example, exact relationships between these MPCIs and proportion of nonconformance (PNC), as is done for $C_p^{''}$ and $C_{pk}^{''}$ (refer Chatterjee and Chakraborty [4]). This needs to be explored for multivariate processes as well. Also, the distributional and inferential properties of both these sets of MPCIs, need to be studied in detail, which may lead to further enrichment in the topic and/or proposition of new MPCIs in this field.

Bibliography

[1] Boyles, R. A. (1994). Process Capability with Asymmetric Tolerances. *Communications in Statistics—Simulation and Computation*, Vol. 23, No. 3, pp. 162–175.

[2] Casella, G., Berger, R. L. (2007). *Statistical Inference*, New York: Thompson and Duxbury.

[3] Chatterjee, M., Chakraborty, A. K. (2011). Superstructure Of Multivariate Process Capability Indices for Asymmetric Tolerances. *Proceedings of International Congress on Productivity, Quality, Reliability, Optimization and Modelling*, Vol. 1, pp. 635–647, India: Allied Publishers PVT LTD.

[4] Chatterjee, M., Chakraborty, A. K. (2014). Exact Relationship of $C_{pk}^{''}$ with Proportion of Non-conformance and Some Other Properties of $C_{p}^{''}(u, v)$. *Quality and Reliability Engineering International*, Vol. 30, No. 7, pp. 1023–1034.

[5] Chatterjee, M., Chakraborty, A. K. (2017). Unification of Some Multivariate Process Capability Indices For Asymmetric Specification Region. *Statistica Neerlandica*, Vol. 71, No. 4, pp. 286–306.

[6] Chen, H. (1994), A Multivariate Process Capability Index Over a Rectangular solid Tolerance Zone, *Statistica Sinica*, 4, 749–758.

[7] Chen, K. S., Pearn, W. L. (2001). Capability Indices For Process With Asymmetric Tolerances. *Journal of The Chinese Institute of Engineers*, Vol. 24, No. 5, pp. 559–568.

[8] Fisher, R. A., Yates, F. (1974). *Statistical Tables for Biological, Agricultural and Medical Research*, 6th Edition, Oliver and Boyd, United Kingdom.

[9] Franklin, L. A., Wasserman, G. (1992). Bootstrap Lower Confidence Limits For Capability Indices. *Journal of Quality Technology*, Vol. 24, No. 4, pp. 196–210.

[10] Giri, N. C. (2004). *Multivariate Statistical Analysis*, Marcel & Dekker: New York.

Bibliography

[11] Grau, D. (2007). Multivariate Capability Indices for Processes with Asymmetric Tolerances. *Quality Technology and Quantitative Management*, Vol. 4, No. 4, pp. 471–488.

[12] Jessenberger, J., Weihs, C. (2000). A Note on the Behavior of C_{pmk} with Asymmetric Specification Limits. *Journal of Quality Technology*, Vol. 32, No. 4, pp. 440–443.

[13] Kotz, S., Johnson, N. (2002). Process Capability Indices—a Review, 1992–2000. *Journal of Quality Technology* Vol. 34, No. 1, pp. 2–19.

[14] Kushler, R. H., Hurley, P. (1992). Confidence Bounds for Capability Indices. *Journal of Quality Technology*, Vol. 24, No. 4, pp. 188–195.

[15] Ribeiro Jr, P. J., P. J. Diggle (2001). GeoR: A Package for Geostatistical Analysis, *R News*, 1(2), 15–18.

[16] Rodriguez, R. N. (1992). Recent Developments in Process Capability Analysis. *Journal of Quality Technology*, Vol. 24, No. 4, pp. 176–187.

Chapter 8

Multivariate Process Capability Indices for Unilateral Specification Region

Chapter Summary

Although bilateral specification regions are most commonly encountered in practice, there are ample situations, where only one of the upper or lower specification limits is present for an individual quality characteristic. Such specification regions are called unilateral specification regions. Also, the corresponding quality characteristics are called lower the better (where only upper specification limit (USL) is present) or higher the better (where only lower specification limit (LSL) is present). In Chapter 8, multivariate process capability indices (MPCIs) designed for such quality characteristics are described in detail. A numerical example is given for better understanding.

8.1 Introduction

The multivariate process capability indices (MPCIs) discussed so far, have a number of differences, but still enjoy one commonality – viz., for all these cases, corresponding quality characteristics have bilateral specification region. However, recall from Chapter 3 that, there exist some quality characteristics, which may be of larger the better type or smaller the better type, consequently having either lower specification limits or upper specification limits respectively.

Interestingly, contradicting general convention, Grau [3] has shown that, target plays an important role in the context of unilateral specification in a sense that, deviation from target, toward the opposite side of the existing specification region, incurs loss in quality to some extent, though the loss may not be at per with the deviation toward the existing specification limit.

Chatterjee and Chakraborty [2] have discussed two real life situations in this regard. For making ornaments usually, 10 carat (with purity 41.7%), 14 carat (with purity 58.3%), 18 carat (with purity 75%), or 22 carat (with purity

190

MPCIs for unilateral specification region 191

91.66%–95.83%) gold is used. Although 24 carat gold (with purity 99.9 % and above) is also very much available in the market (in the form of gold bar and gold coin), that is not used for the purpose of making jewelry, precisely due to the fact that, increasing purity of gold beyond 22 carat makes it highly fragile, so much so that it becomes unsuitable for the said purpose.

Surface roughness is another example, where importance of target, in the context of unilateral specification region, can be observed. Theoretically, surface roughness is smaller the better type quality characteristic, i.e., it is desirable to have low surface roughness. However, in the process of reducing surface roughness, beyond one point, it may become so smooth that the surface may become slippery beyond manageability and hence may not be useful in day to day activities.

Although these observations were primarily made for univariate processes, these remain relevant for multivariate processes as well.

PCIs for unilateral specification limits have mostly been defined for univariate processes. A brief discussion on these can be found in Chapter 3. Recall that, two of the most popular PCIs for unilateral specification limits, among both the theoreticians as well as the practitioners, are

$$\left. \begin{array}{l} C_{pu} = \frac{U-\mu}{3\sigma} \\ \text{and} \quad C_{pl} = \frac{\mu-L}{3\sigma} \end{array} \right\} \tag{8.1}$$

(refer Kane [4]). Apart from these, some other PCIs for unilateral specification limits have been proposed by Kane [4], Krishnamoorthy [5], Vannman [9], and Grau [3] among others. A thorough review of these PCIs have been given by Chatterjee and Chakraborty [1].

Although substantial amount of research has been carried out so far for univariate unilateral processes, for multivariate processes, this area of research is somewhat comparatively lesser explored. Only a few MPCIs, for processes with unilateral specification regions, have been defined in recent years. In the present chapter, those will be discussed in detail.

8.2 MPCI for Unilateral Specification Region Based on Proportion of Nonconformance

Wu and Pearn [11] were among the first to define an MPCI for unilateral specification region. For this, they used univariate PCIs viz., C_{pu} and C_{pl} [vide equation (8.1)]. Therefore, their MPCIs are based on multivariate normality assumption of the underlying process distribution.

Observe that

$$C_{pu} = \frac{USL - \mu}{3\sigma}$$

$$= \frac{1}{3}\Phi^{-1}\left\{\Phi\left(\frac{USL - \mu}{\sigma}\right)\right\} \tag{8.2}$$

Generalizing this under multivariate set-up, Wu and Pearn [11] have defined an MPCI for lower the better type of quality characteristics as

$$C_{pu}^T = \frac{1}{3}\Phi^{-1}\left\{\prod_{i=1}^{q}\Phi\left(3C_{pu_i}\right)\right\} \tag{8.3}$$

where $C_{pu_i} = \frac{USL_i - \mu_i}{3\sigma_i}$ is the C_{pu} index for ith quality characteristic, for $i = 1(1)q$.

Similarly, for higher the better type of quality characteristic, one can define

$$C_{pl}^T = \frac{1}{3}\Phi^{-1}\left\{\prod_{i=1}^{q}\Phi\left(3C_{pl_i}\right)\right\} \tag{8.4}$$

where $C_{pl_i} = \frac{\mu_i - LSL_i}{3\sigma_i}$ is the C_{pl} index for ith quality characteristic, for $i = 1(1)q$.

Note that, the product terms in equations (8.3) and (8.4) imply that the quality characteristics are mutually independent. Thus, C_{pu}^T and C_{pl}^T should not be used unless this assumption is satisfied. Consequently, these two MPCIs ignore true essence of being MPCI in a sense that the very idea of using an MPCI instead of a PCI is to capture correlation between the quality characteristics.

It can be seen from equation (8.2), C_{pu}, though primarily ratio based index, can be alternatively expressed as an yield based index. Moreover, since C_{pu}^T is merely a multivariate generalization of this yield based expression of C_{pu}, a one-to-one relationship can be established between C_{pu}^T and the proportion of nonconformance (PNC), viz., p^T.

Now, under univariate set-up and for lower the better type of quality characteristic

$$p = P[X \leq USL]$$

$$= P\left[\frac{X - \mu}{\sigma} \leq \frac{USL - \mu}{\sigma}\right]$$

$$= \Phi\left(3\,C_{pu}\right) \tag{8.5}$$

Hence, if there are "q" independent quality characteristics with the C_{pu} value and PNC for the ith quality characteristic being C_{pu_i} and p_i respectively, then PNC for the overall process will be

$$
\begin{aligned}
p^T &= \prod_{i=1}^{q} p_i \\
&= \prod_{i=1}^{q} \Phi\left(3\,C_{pu_i}\right) \\
&= \Phi\left(3C_{pu}^T\right), \quad \text{from equation (8.3)} \qquad (8.6)
\end{aligned}
$$

Also, since the quality characteristics are mutually independent and consequently, C_{pu}^T is based on individual C_{pu} values, threshold value of the overall process capability can be computed as follows (refer Wu and Pearn [11]) :

Suppose c' denotes minimum required value of C_{pu} for each individual quality characteristic, while c_0 is the minimum required value for C_{pu}^T. Then,

$$
\begin{aligned}
c_0 \le C_{pu}^T &= \frac{1}{3}\Phi^{-1}\left\{\prod_{i=1}^{q} \Phi\left(3C_{pu_i}\right)\right\} \\
&\ge \frac{1}{3}\Phi^{-1}\left\{\prod_{i=1}^{q} \Phi\left(3c'\right)\right\} \qquad (8.7)
\end{aligned}
$$

In equation (8.7), all the individual quality characteristics are assumed to have same threshold value, which is practically not viable. However, if c' is replaced by c'_i for the ith quality characteristic, the formula remains the same, with c' replacing c'_i in the first bracket.

Since C_{pu}^T and C_{pl}^T involve process parameters and hence often are not practically viable, their plug-in estimators should be defined and their properties need to be studied so as to make them ready for practical use. Plug-in estimators of C_{pu}^T and C_{pl}^T can be defined as

$$
\widehat{C}_{pu}^T = \frac{1}{3}\Phi^{-1}\left\{\prod_{i=1}^{q} \Phi\left(\frac{USL_i - \overline{X}_i}{S_i}\right)\right\} \qquad (8.8)
$$

and

$$
\widehat{C}_{pl}^T = \frac{1}{3}\Phi^{-1}\left\{\prod_{i=1}^{q} \Phi\left(\frac{\overline{X}_i - LSL_i}{S_i}\right)\right\} \qquad (8.9)
$$

where $\overline{X}_i$ and S_i are sample mean and sample standard deviation of the ith quality characteristic, for $i = 1(1)q$.

Pearn et al. [7] have derived asymptotic distribution of $\widehat{C}_{pu}^T$ as

$$\widehat{C}_{pu}^T \overset{a}{\sim} N \left(C_{pu}^T, \ \frac{1}{9n \left\{ \phi \left(3 C_{pu}^T \right) \right\}^2} \times \sum_{i=1}^{q} \left(a_i^2 + b_i^2 \right) \right) \qquad (8.10)$$

where

$$a_i = \prod_{i=1; i \neq j}^{q} \left\{ \Phi(3 C_{pui}) \right\} \times \left\{ \phi(3 C_{puj}) \right\} \qquad (8.11)$$

and

$$b_j = \frac{3 C_{puj}}{\sqrt{2}} \times a_j, \ i = 1(1)q \qquad (8.12)$$

From equation (8.10), a $100(1 - \alpha)\%$ lower confidence bound of C_{pu}^T, viz., $C_{pu}^{T(LB)}$, can be obtained as

$$C_{pu}^{T(LB)} \ \approx \ \widehat{C}_{pu}^T - \tau_\alpha \left[\frac{1}{9n \left\{ \phi \left(3 C_{pu}^T \right) \right\}^2} \times \sum_{i=1}^{q} \left(a_i^2 + b_i^2 \right) \right], \qquad (8.13)$$

where τ_α denotes upper α percent point of standard normal distribution.

The authors have also shown that, the maximum value of $C_{pu}^{T(LB)}$ is attained when all the individual C_{pu} values are equal, i.e., $C_{pu_1} = C_{pu_2} = \cdots = C_{pu_q}$. Also, the minimum value of $C_{pu}^{T(LB)}$ is attained when one of these individual C_{pu} values equals C_{pk}^T and the remaining tend to infinity. In that case, the asymptotic distribution of C_{pu}^T can be further simpified as

$$\widehat{C}_{pu}^T \overset{a}{\sim} N \left(C_{pu}^T, \ \frac{1}{9n} + \frac{C_{pu}^{T2}}{2n} \right) \qquad (8.14)$$

and accordingly, the $100(1 - \alpha)\%$ lower confidence bound of C_{pu}^T will be,

$$C_{pu}^{T(LB*)} \ \approx \ \frac{2 \widehat{C}_{pu}^T - \sqrt{\frac{4\tau_\alpha^2}{9n} + \frac{2\tau_\alpha^2}{n} \widehat{C}_{pu}^{T2} - \frac{2\tau_\alpha^4}{9n^2}}}{2 - \frac{\tau_\alpha^2}{n}} \qquad (8.15)$$

For a set of hypothesis

$$\left. \begin{array}{c} H_0 : C_{pu}^T \leq C \\[2mm] \text{against} \quad H_1 : C_{pu}^T > C \end{array} \right\} \qquad (8.16)$$

with "C" being any real number (usually, acting like a threshold value), Pearn et al. [7] have also derived expression for the critical value as

$$c_0 = C + \tau_\alpha \sqrt{\frac{1}{9n} + \frac{C^2}{2n}} \qquad (8.17)$$

Pearn et al. [6] have discussed a step-by-step procedure for product acceptance determination based on C_{pu}^T.

8.3 MPCI for Unilateral Specification Region Based on Principal Component Analysis

The MPCIs discussed in Section 8.2 can be used when there are not too many quality characteristics to consider. However, in practice, an industrial statistician or quality engineer may come across processes having considerably large number of a correlated quality characteristics. Using traditional MPCIs, in such situations, may invite problems like complicated computations and hence one needs to explore alternative way-outs.

Recall from Chapter 5 that, principal component analysis (PCA) plays an important role in dimension reduction of data. Therefore, a number of MPCIs have been defined based on this approach. However, almost all of these MPCIs are designated for bilateral specification region and hence are not suitable for processes having unilateral specification region.

To solve this problem, Perakis and Xekalaki [8] have adopted the approach of Wang and Chen [10] [refer Chapter 5 for more detail] and defined a set of MPCIs analogous to C_{pu} and C_{pl} based on PCA as follows:

$$MCPL = \left(\prod_{i=1}^{v} |C_{pl}^{Y_i}| \right)^{1/v} \qquad (8.18)$$

$$MCPU = \left(\prod_{i=1}^{v} |C_{pu}^{Y_i}| \right)^{1/v} \qquad (8.19)$$

where, $C_{pl}^{Y_i}$ and $C_{pu}^{Y_i}$ are the C_{pu} and C_{pl} values corresponding to the ith principal component, viz., Y_i, for $i = 1(1)v$ and v is the number of significant principal components (PCs).

Observe that, $MCPL$ and $MCPU$ are not applied directly to the original data. Rather concerned significant PCs are used as new variables (as a part of dimension reduction approach). Interestingly, during this transformation it may so happen that, for one or more PCs, the corresponding linear combinations of upper limits may turn into linear combination of lower limits and vice versa, resulting in negative value of some $C_{pl}^{Y_i}$'s or $C_{pu}^{Y_i}$'s, as the case may be. Since MCPL and MCPU are geometric mean type indices, values of $C_{pl}^{Y_i}$ or $C_{pu}^{Y_i}$ should be positive so as to avoid inferential ambiguities.

Moreover, by definition, PCIs assume positive values. To address these issues, Perakis and Xekalaki [8] have used "modulus" operator in equations (8.18) and (8.19),while defining $MCPL$ and $MCPU$, respectively.

However, as has been pointed out by the authors themselves, the MPCIs defined by them, viz., $MCPL$ and $MCPU$ suffer from a major drawback. These MPCIs cannot be used unless all the quality characteristics are either of smaller the better type or larger the better type.

The MPCIs discussed so far in this chapter, make a common assumption. Here equal weihtage is given to all the quality characteristics or PCs (as the case may be), which in turn means that all the quality characteristics or PCs are assumed to have equal importance. However, this is not a very pragmatic assumption in real life. To be more precise, different quality characteristics may have different importance from overall quality perspective of a process. Similarly, it is very unlikely that all the PCs will explain same amount of variance prevailing in the process and hence different PCs are likely to have different importance as well.

To address this issue, instead of considering geometric mean of individual capability index values of significant PCs, Perakis and Xekalaki [8] have advocated use of weighted arithmetic mean type indices where weights are the amount of process variation explained by each significant PC. The authors, thereby, have redefined MCPL and MCPU as follows:

$$MCPL' = \frac{1}{\Lambda} \times \sum_{i=1}^{v} \lambda_i |CPL^{Y_i}| \tag{8.20}$$

$$MCPU' = \frac{1}{\Lambda} \times \sum_{i=1}^{v} \lambda_i |CPU^{Y_i}| \tag{8.21}$$

where λ_i, $i = 1(1)v$ are the eigen values of the significant PCs and $\Lambda = \sum_{i=1}^{v} \lambda_i$. Thus, here the weights are proportional to the amount of variance explained by each principal component, viz., $\frac{\lambda_i}{\Lambda}$, for $i = 1, 2, \cdots, v$, "v" being the number of significant PCs. In this context, note that, one can also retain "all the PCs" instead of "significant PCs" only. In that case "v" will be replaced by "q" in equations (8.18), (8.19), (8.20), and (8.21), keeping all the other things unchanged.

8.4   A Numerical Example

Consider the following data on three most important quality characteristics of thin-film transistor type LCD, viz., response time (rising), response time

MPCIs for unilateral specification region

(falling), and brightness. The data was originally given by Pearn et al. [6]. Observe that, here all the quality characteristics are of smaller the better type, i.e., all are having USLs only. USLs of the three quality characteristics are $USL_1 = 7\ ms$, $USL_2 = 18\ ms$, and $USL_3 = 5\%$, respectively.

Table 1: Data on response time (rising), response time (falling) and brightness of thin-film transistor type LCD

rtr	rtf	brightness
5.975	15.413	12.196
6.416	15.171	12.702
5.719	14.960	12.565
5.772	14.691	13.181
6.008	14.585	13.544
5.594	15.241	12.872
5.453	15.582	12.444
5.535	14.997	12.928
5.824	14.844	13.604
5.917	14.834	12.463
6.381	14.182	12.750
6.234	14.795	12.921
6.056	15.426	12.201
5.341	15.298	13.748
6.099	14.950	12.752
5.849	15.357	12.293
5.870	14.484	12.648
6.067	15.309	12.778
6.298	14.740	13.951
6.053	15.524	12.845
6.031	15.386	12.727
6.119	14.376	12.743
6.368	15.057	13.176
6.154	15.143	13.141
6.455	14.835	13.295
6.164	15.299	13.588
6.426	14.748	12.443
5.816	15.028	12.215
6.220	15.201	12.747
6.024	15.468	12.973
6.006	15.347	12.253
5.936	14.829	13.439
5.679	14.821	13.077
6.454	15.265	13.779
6.384	14.839	12.874

6.129	14.348	12.323
6.030	15.047	13.404
6.028	14.481	12.667
6.035	14.691	12.802
6.488	15.216	12.852
5.626	14.709	13.147
7.314	15.505	13.36
6.387	15.413	12.849
6.297	15.240	12.979
6.619	14.750	13.171
6.403	15.618	13.404
6.468	14.737	14.111
5.930	14.773	13.145
6.032	15.202	12.916
6.132	15.456	12.684
6.320	15.134	13.425
6.226	14.337	12.816
6.172	15.030	12.705
6.159	16.048	13.067
6.062	15.266	12.217
5.677	15.027	13.441
5.755	15.212	13.193
6.107	15.259	12.586
6.162	14.824	13.411
5.973	15.398	13.381
6.396	14.568	12.773
5.451	14.661	12.975
5.566	15.115	12.742
6.722	14.790	13.028
5.867	14.941	13.042
6.442	15.045	12.556
6.360	15.291	12.379
5.964	14.874	12.957
5.241	15.591	12.870
5.305	15.188	13.743
5.678	15.135	13.386
5.542	15.421	13.709
5.939	15.511	12.933
5.884	15.397	13.104
5.524	14.653	12.904
5.889	14.855	13.118
6.142	14.404	13.241
6.191	14.255	12.924
5.883	15.042	12.722

Based on this data, C_{pu} values of Response time (rising), Response time (falling), and brightness are $C_{pu1} = 0.9122$, $C_{pu2} = 2.6839$, and $C_{pu3} = 1.5723$ and hence $C_{pu}^T = 0.9122$.

Also, $MCPU = 1.8391$ and the weighted MCPU, when all the PCs are retained, is $MCPU' = 1.8127$. Interestingly, here $MCPU$ and $MCPU'$ have very close values. If however, the third PC, which explains the lowest amount of process variability, is dropped, then we have $MCPU' = 1.4545$. This is, however, achieved at the cost of losing 26.47% of information.

Also, for none of these MPCIs, mathematical expression for threshold value is computed. As a result, if following conventional approach, "1" is considered as the threshold value in general, then C_{pu}^T concludes the process to be incapable, while $MCPU$ and $MCPU'$ consider it as capable. This ambiguity can only be avoided by defining an appropriate threshold value for each of these MPCIs.

8.5 Concluding Remarks

MPCIs for processes with unilateral specification regions are less explored as compared to those with bilateral specification limits. The few MPCIs, which are available in literature, for unilateral specifications are mostly based on the most primitive univariate PCIs, viz., C_{pu} and C_{pl}. Recall that these two PCIs suffer from a number of drawbacks (refer Section 3.3 of Chapter 3 for more detail) which are inherited by the MPCIs discussed in this chapter. Also, although some simulation studies have been carried out for these MPCIs, extensive study of their statistical properties is yet to be done.

Moreover, MPCIs like C_{pu}^T and C_{pl}^T, do not take into account the inherent correlation structure of the quality characteristics and thereby miss the real essence of a true MPCI.

Thus there remains ample scope of research in this area, starting from defining new MPCIs which are not mere generalization of C_{pu} and C_{pl}, to studying properties of new and existing MPCIs and finding out appropriate threshold values of each of the MPCIs.

Bibliography

[1] Chatterjee, M., Chakraborty, A. K. (2012). Univariate Process Capability Indices for Unilateral Specification Region: A Review & Some Modifications. *International Journal of Reliability, Quality and Safety Engineering*, Vol. 19, No. 4, pp. 1250020 (1–18).

[2] Chatterjee, M., Chakraborty, A. K. (2015). Distributions and Process Capability Control Charts for C_{pu} and C_{pl} Using Subgroup Information. *Communications in Statistics—Theory and Methods*, Vol. 44,No. 20, pp. 4333–4353.

[3] Grau, D. (2009). New Process Capability Indices for One-Sided Tolerances. *Quality Technology and Quantitative Management*, Vol. 6, No. 2, pp. 107–124.

[4] Kane, V. E. (1986). Process Capability Index. *Journal of Quality Technology*, Vol. 18, No. 1, pp. 41–52.

[5] Krishnamoorthy, K. S. (1990). Capability Indices for Processes Subject to Unilateral and Positional Tolerances. *Quality Engineering*, Vol. 2, No. 4, pp. 461–471.

[6] Pearn, W. L.,Wu, C. H., Hung, H. N., Kao, C. M. (2013). An Extension of the Product Acceptance Determination for One-Sided Process with Multiple Characteristics. *Quality and Reliability Engineering International*, vol. 29, pp. 277–284.

[7] Pearn, W. L., Wu, C. H., Tsai, M. C. (2013). A Note on Capability Assessment for Processes with Multiple Characteristics: A Generalization of the Popular Index C_{pk}". *Quality and Reliability Engineering International*, Vol. 29, pp. 159–163.

[8] Perakis, M., Xekalaki, E. (2012). On the Implementation of the Principal Component Analysis—Based Approach in Measuring Process Capability. *Quality and Reliability Engineering International*, Vol. 28, pp. 467–480.

[9] Vannman, K. (1998). Families of Process Capability Indices for Ones-Sided Specification Limits. *Statistics*, Vol. 31, No. 1, pp. 43–66.

[10] Wang, F. K., Chen, J. C. (1998). Capability Index Using Principal Component Analysis. *Quality Engineering*, Vol. 11, No. 1, pp. 21–27.

[11] Wu, C. W., Pearn, W. L. (2005). Measuring Manufacturing Capability for Couplers and Wavelength Division Multiplexers. *The International Journal of Advance Manufacturing Technology*, Vol. 25, pp. 533–541. DOI 10.1007/s00170-003-1793-9.

Chapter 9

Multivariate Process Capability Indices Based on Proportion of Nonconformance

Chapter Summary

Apart from process capability indices (both univariate and multivariate), an alternative way to assess process performance, is to compute proportion of non-conformance (PNC), i.e., proportion of items which fail to meet the specifications. Bridging these two parallel concepts makes the decision regarding the health of the process easier. In Chapter 9, such PNC-based multivariate process capability indices (MPCIs) are discussed in detail.

9.1 Introduction

Capability Index is useful when we try to relate the actual variability of the process with that of the admissible one. This admissible variability is connected to the nonconforming proportion. Hence, study of the relationship of the capability index with nonconforming proportion becomes important. In general, a process is considered to be capable if the probability of getting nonconforming items (outside the specifications) is small. Though we are interested in proportion of nonconforming items, Process Capability Indices (PCIs) are generally unitless quantity which becomes easier to interpret. Typically, a PCI compares the natural variability of a stable process and the allowed variability (Gonzalez and Sanchez, 2009). In other words, a PCI represents the quality of a process that should be able to measure the chance of producing defective articles due to natural variability of the process. In manufacturing industries the usage of PCI is the maximum. In a univariate set-up, quality characteristic is represented by one variable and the engineering requirements are usually represented by two specification limits; the upper and the lower specification limits. Whereas, in the multivariate set up, quality of the product is characterized by several (more than one) parameters each having different specification limits resulting in having the overall specification as a tolerance

202

region rather than an interval. We will however discuss in this chapter the MPCIs based on proportion of nonconformance. Gonzalez and Sanchez [9], however proposed a slightly different way of approaching the problem. Their idea is how much to reduce the variation of the process in order to get a fixed level of nonconformance or below. In the multivariate case, it boils down to how much of the variability of each of the parameters to be reduced to ensure that the process variation remains within the specification region.

9.2 MPCIs Based on Location-Scale Family of Distributions

A univariate quality characteristic X whose cumulative distribution function (cdf) F can be written as $\{F(x; \mu, \sigma) : -\infty < \mu < \infty, \sigma > 0\}$, where

$$F(x) = H\left(\frac{x - \mu}{\sigma}\right) \tag{9.1}$$

and H(y), assumed known, has a symmetric probability density function (pdf) $H'(y) = h(y)$ about the origin is said to belong to a location-scale family of distributions. The parameters μ and σ are, respectively, the location parameter and the scale parameter of X. The random variable Y having cdf H(y) is related to X by $X = \sigma Y + \mu$. Apart from the normal distribution, Laplace distribution, Cauchy distribution, Student's t distribution are some examples of location-scale family of distributions.

Boyles [2] introduced a yield based index S_{pk}, defined in Chapter 3 , where the process yield is given as $2\Phi(3S_{pk}) - 1$, where $\Phi(.)$ is the cumulative distribution function of the standard normal variable.

If P denotes the percentage of products that satisfies the specification, then P= F(USL)—F(LSL). If F (.) comes from the location scale family of distributions defined in equation (9.1) above, then

$$P = H\left(\frac{USL - \mu}{\sigma}\right) - \left\{1 - H\left(\frac{\mu - LSL}{\sigma}\right)\right\} \tag{9.2}$$

$$= H\left(\frac{USL - \mu}{\sigma}\right) + H\left(\frac{\mu - LSL}{\sigma}\right) - 1 \tag{9.3}$$

Using $H^{-1}(x)$ as the inverse function of H, one can define

$$H_{pk} = \frac{1}{3}H^{-1}\left[\frac{1}{2}H\left(\frac{USL - \mu}{\sigma}\right) + \frac{1}{2}H\left(\frac{\mu - LSL}{\sigma}\right)\right] \tag{9.4}$$

Note that when $H(x) = \Phi(x)$, the cdf of the standard normal distribution, H_{pk} directly corresponds to S_{pk}. From equations (9.2) and (9.4), it can be noticed that

$$P = 2H(3H_{pk}) - 1 \tag{9.5}$$

which shows that H_{pk} is related to the process yield directly.

Dharmasena and Zeephongsekul [7] studied the asymptotic properties of $\hat{H}_{pk}$, the estimate of H_{pk} obtained using the estimates of μ and σ from the sample observations. An approximate $(1 - \alpha)$ level confidence interval for P is given by

$$\left(\hat{P} - \frac{6h(3\hat{H}_{pk})\sqrt{\hat{k}}}{\sqrt{n}} \, Z_{\frac{\alpha}{2}} \, , \, \hat{P} + \frac{6h(3\hat{H}_{pk})\sqrt{\hat{k}}}{\sqrt{n}} \, Z_{\frac{\alpha}{2}} \right)$$

where

$$\hat{k} = \frac{1}{36h^2(3\hat{H}_{pk})} \left[\hat{\lambda}^2 S^2 + \frac{\hat{\tau}^2(\hat{\mu}_4 - S^4)}{4S^2} \right]$$

$\hat{\lambda}$ and $\hat{\tau}$ are estimates of λ and τ, respectively, which are functions of the observations (see Dharmasena and Zeephongsekul [7] for exact details).

The same authors then extended the univariate index for location-scale family of distributions to the multivariate set up. Suppose that $X = (X_1, X_2, \cdots, X_\nu)$ represents a ν-dimensional quality characteristic where each X_i comes from different location-scale family,
$\{F_i(x; \mu_i, \sigma_i) : -\infty < \mu_i < \infty, \sigma_i > 0\}$, where

$$F_i(x) = H_i \left(\frac{x - \mu_i}{\sigma_i} \right) \tag{9.6}$$

and $H_i(y)$ is a cdf with a symmetric pdf $h_i(y)$ about the origin. Under such a set up the total yield index generated by the location-scale family of distributions with carrier function $G(.)$, where $G(.)$ is any strictly increasing, continuous, and bounded function having $G(.) = g(.)$ can be written as

$$TH_{pk} = \frac{1}{3} G^{-1} \left\{ \left[\prod_{j=1}^{\nu} (2H_j(3H_{pkj}) - 1) + 1 \right] / 2 \right\} \tag{9.7}$$

where H_{pkj} is the univariate yield index corresponding to X_j discussed in equation (9.4).

For this multivariate yield based index the asymptotic results also are derived in Dharmasena and Zeephongsekul [7] which also gives several examples both for the univariate and multivariate indices.

9.3 Other MPCIs Based on Proportion of Conformance or Nonconformance

Several other authors have developed MPCIs based on either proportion of conformance or proportion of nonconformance. Perakis and Xekalaki [13] developed one such index for the univariate set up (refer Chapter 3). However, other authors like Khadse and Shinde [11] have questioned the utility of such an index particularly when it comes to interpreting the results. They have, however suggested several other indices for the univariate case which have been briefly discussed in Chapter 3. They have also suggested some multivariate counterparts to their univariate PCIs which they claim to be related with proportion of conformance.

Under the assumptions of (i) the process is in statistical control; (ii) target for each quality characteristic being the midpoint of a symmetric specification limit; (iii) the underlying distribution being multivariate normal; they defined the following to propose three MPCIs.

$$p_1 = P(\boldsymbol{X} \in S \mid \boldsymbol{\mu} = T, \Sigma) \tag{9.8}$$

$$p_2 = P(\boldsymbol{X} \in S \mid \boldsymbol{\mu}, \Sigma) \tag{9.9}$$

$$p_3 = P\left(\boldsymbol{X} \in S \mid \boldsymbol{\mu} = T, \Sigma = \Sigma_{\gamma}^{'}\right) \tag{9.10}$$

where S denotes the specification region, $\boldsymbol{T}$ denotes the target vector, and $\Sigma_{\gamma} = E[(\boldsymbol{X} - \boldsymbol{T})(\boldsymbol{X} - \boldsymbol{T})^{'}]$. The three MPCIs proposed are

$$MC_{p(p_1)} = -\frac{1}{3}\Phi^{-1}\left(\frac{1-p_1}{2}\right) \tag{9.11}$$

$$MC_{pk(p_2)} = -\frac{1}{3}\Phi^{-1}\left(\frac{1-p_2}{2}\right) \tag{9.12}$$

$$MC_{pm(p_3)} = -\frac{1}{3}\Phi^{-1}\left(\frac{1-p_3}{2}\right) \tag{9.13}$$

$MC_{p(p_1)}$ and $MC_{pk(p_2)}$ being measures of process capability related to potential proportion of conforming and actual proportion of conforming, respectively, the two measures are related among themselves like C_p and C_{pk} in the univariate case. In fact

$$MC_{pk(p_2)} \leq MC_p(p_1) \tag{9.14}$$

$$MC_{pm(p_3)} \leq MC_p(p_1) \tag{9.15}$$

Equality in (9.15) occurs when the process is on target. It may be noted that that $MC_{p(p_1)}$ is associated with Σ, whereas, $MC_{pm(p_3)}$ is associated with Σ_{γ} and not Σ.

If the second assumption is not met for even one quality characteristics, they suggested a new MPCI as

$$MC_{p(p_1^*)} = -\frac{1}{3}\Phi^{-1}\left(1 - \frac{p_1^*}{2}\right) \tag{9.16}$$

where

$$p_1^* = P\left(\mathbf{X} \in S \mid \boldsymbol{\mu} = \frac{1}{2}(\mathbf{USL} + \mathbf{LSL}), \Sigma\right)$$

Estimates for p_1, p_2, p_3, and p_1^* can be obtained from the sample observations easily in order to get estimates of the respective MCPIs.

Gu et al. [10] used the concept of Six Sigma originally developed in Motorola in the eighties and initially developed an yield based capability index for univariate case, which is later extended to multivariate case as well. If θ denotes the process yield for a univariate normal process, then a quantity Q is defined by them corresponding to θ as

$$\theta = \Phi(1.5 + Q) - \Phi(1.5 - Q) \tag{9.17}$$

Then they defined an equivalent PCI in the form of EC_{pk} which is given as

$$EC_{pk} = \frac{Q}{3} - 0.5$$

It may be noted that EC_{pk} can be applied to processes having unilateral specification.

Extending the concepts to the multivariate case, and assuming that the process follows multivariate normal distributions if θ denotes the true process yield and Q is defined as in equation (9.17), then the MPCI, MEC_{pk} is defined as

$$MEC_{pk} = \frac{Q}{3} - 0.5 \tag{9.18}$$

The MPCI defined in (9.18) appears to be more general in nature and can be applied to the cases where the underlying process distribution is not multivariate normal. The overall process yield θ is affected by not only the magnitude of correlation among the quality characteristics, but also its sign.

Pearn et al. [12] developed a generalized yield index by generalizing S_{pk} introduced by Boyels [2]. In fact, they have modified the MPCI proposed by Chen et al. [5] which assumed that the process quality characteristics are independent normal variables. Chen et al. [5] suggested the following index

$$S_{pk}^T = \frac{1}{3}\Phi^{-1}\left\{\left[\prod_{j=1}^k (2\Phi(3S_{pkj}) - 1) + 1\right]/2\right\} \tag{9.19}$$

where S_{pkj} denotes the *Spk* value of the jth quality characteristics for $j = 1, 2, 3 \cdots k$, k denotes the number of quality characteristics in the process.

To make use of the structure of S_{pk}^T given in (9.19) where independence among the variables are required, Pearn et al. [12] adopted the principal components analysis approach which ensures independence among the principal components. Also principal components being a linear function of the original variables, automatically satisfies that their distributions will remain normal, if the original variables are normally distributed. Peam et al.(2006) then proposed the modified S_{pk}^T as

$$ TS_{pk;PC} = \frac{1}{3} \, \Phi^{-1} \left\{ \left[\prod_{j=1}^{k} \left(2\Phi(3S_{pkj:PC_j}) - 1 \right) + 1 \right] / 2 \right\} \qquad (9.20) $$

where S_{pk_j,PC_j} represents the process yield index of the ith principal component. The overall process yield thus becomes

$$ \text{yield} = 2\Phi(3TS_{pk;PC}) - 1 \qquad (9.21) $$

An approximate $100(1 - \alpha)\%$ confidence interval for $TS_{pk;PC}$ is given as

$$ \frac{1}{3} \, \Phi^{-1} \left\{ \left[\prod_{j=1}^{k} \left(2\Phi(3m_j) - 1 \right) + 1 \right] / 2 \right\} \leq TS_{pk;PC} $$

$$ \leq \frac{1}{3} \, \Phi^{-1} \left\{ \left[\prod_{j=1}^{k} \left(2\Phi(3k_j) - 1 \right) + 1 \right] / 2 \right\} \qquad (9.22) $$

where $m_j = \hat{S}_{pk;PC} - \frac{\sqrt{\hat{a}_{j;PC}^2 + \hat{b}_{j;PC}^2}}{6\sqrt{n}\Phi(3\hat{H}_{S_{pk;PC}})} \, Z_{\alpha/2}$ and $k_j = \hat{S}_{pk;PC} + \frac{\sqrt{\hat{a}_{j;PC}^2 + \hat{b}_{j;PC}^2}}{6\sqrt{n}\Phi(3\hat{H}_{S_{pk;PC}})} \, Z_{\alpha/2}$, with $\hat{a}_{j;PC}$ and $\hat{b}_{j;PC}$ being the respective estimates of a and b given by Pearn et al.(2006) for the jth principal component.

Making use of the eigen values and eigen vectors that come from a principal component analysis, Wang [16] suggested another MPCI as follows:

$$ TS_{pk;PC} = \sum_{i=1}^{k} \frac{\lambda_i}{\sum\limits_{i=1}^{k} \lambda_i} S_{pk;PC_i} \qquad (9.23) $$

where S_{pk,PC_i} represents the yield index for the ith principal component calculated from Boyles's formula, λ_i, $i = 1, 2, \cdots, k$ being the eigen values of S, and S denotes the kxk symmetric covariance matrix obtained from the observations. They have changed the specification limits for the new independent variables obtained from the principal component analysis. Finally, the overall process yield is obtained as

$$P_{PC} = 2\Phi\left(3TS_{pk;PC}\right) - 1 \qquad (9.24)$$

The asymptotic distribution of $\hat{T}S_{pk;PC}$ and the confidence interval for $TS_{pk;PC}$ can then be obtained.

Principal Component Analysis (PCA) based MPCIs are data dependent since the Principal Components are chosen based on the observations. However, if the process is already under the influence of some factors, the PCA based MPCI will be affected, but would not be able to find the reasons for changes in MPCI values. To this end Foster et al. [8] suggested a process oriented basis representation (POBREP) approach for multivariate capability measure of a process. This approach is a generalization of a similar approach for univariate process (refer Barton and Gonzalez—Barreto [1].

For bivariate processes Cheng et al. [6] used the ratio of two estimators of univariate PCIs given by Boyles [3] and found out the probability density of the ratio, assuming asymptotic normality of the PCI $\hat{C}_{pk}^T$. Thus $R = \frac{C_{pk2}^{\hat{T}}}{C_{pk1}^{T}}$, whose pdf can be obtained by using convolution of two normal distributions. They then used the pdf of R to differentiate between different hi-tech manufacturing processes where it is expected that the fraction defective will be very low.

Some authors like Wang [15] tried to deal with multivariate data in a different way. Following Wang and Hubele [18], Wang converted all multivariate data into a single variable by taking geometric distances between the observations. However, it is assumed that the number of observations for all the variables under consideration remains the same. Also, by taking the Euclidean measure as geometric distance, the correlation aspect between the variables was made redundant.

Wang and Chu [17] modified the proposed MPCI by dividing the variables into two broad groups: one set of variables which together follows multivariate normal distribution, and the other set of variables which does not follow multivariate normal distribution. For the first set of variables which jointly follow multivariate normal distribution Wang and Chu [17] suggested to use Mahalanobis distance (MD) as the distance measure between the observations. For the other group they suggested taking the Euclidian distance which Wang [15] referred to as the geometric distance (GD). The process yield for the GD variables can be defined as

$$Yield_{GD} = \int_{0}^{MRD_{GD}} f(x)dx \qquad (9.25)$$

where MRD_{GD} denotes the maximum radial distance from the target to the perimeter of the tolerance region and f(x) denotes the density function of the three-parameter Burr XII distribution.

Similarly, for the MD variables the process yield is obtained by

$$Yield_{MD} = \int_0^{MRD_{MD}} f(x)dx \qquad (9.26)$$

where MRD_D is again the maximum radial distance from the target to the perimeter of the tolerance region for the MD variables, f(s) denotes the pdf of normal distribution. The process yield index, I_{yield}, can be obtained by using the equation

$$yield = 2\Phi(3I_{yield} - 1) \qquad (9.27)$$

Finally, the estimated overall process yield is given by

$$P_{Overall} = \prod_{i=1}^{m} \int_0^{MRD_{GD_i}} f(x_i)dx_i \prod_{i=1}^{r} \int_0^{MRD_{MD_i}} f(s_i)ds_i \qquad (9.28)$$

where m and r represent the number of GD metrics and the number of MD metrics respectively. Using a similar equation as in (9.27) the overall process yield index can be calculated.

Especially for bivariate processes Castagliola and Castellano [4] defined BC_{pk} as follows:

$$BC_{pk}$$
$$= \frac{1}{3} \min \left\{ -\Phi^{-1}(2p_1), -\Phi^{-1}(2p_2), -\Phi^{-1}(2p_3), -\Phi^{-1}(2p_4) \right\} \qquad (9.29)$$

where $p_i = \frac{1}{4} - q_i$, $i = 1, 2, 3, 4$, and $q_i = P(\boldsymbol{X} \in Q_i)$, $Q_i = A_i \cap A$, where A denotes the specification region and A_i, for $i = 1, 2, 3, 4$ denotes the four regions obtained by dividing the plane by the rotation of the original axes to the directions of the two principal components where also the origin was moved to the process mean. It is easy to note that (9.29) can also be written as

$$BC_{pk}$$
$$= -\frac{1}{3} \max \left\{ \Phi^{-1}(2p_1), \Phi^{-1}(2p_2), \Phi^{-1}(2p_3), \Phi^{-1}(2p_4) \right\} \qquad (9.30)$$

Since Φ^{-1} is a strictly increasing function, one can write

$$BC_{pk} = -\frac{1}{3}\Phi^{-1}\{2p_{\max}\} \qquad (9.31)$$

where

$$p_{\max} = \frac{\max}{\max} \{p_1, p_2, p_3, p_4\}.$$

In other words

$$p_{\max} = \frac{1}{2}\Phi\left(-3BC_{pk}\right) \tag{9.32}$$

It may be noted that the percentage nonconformance denoted by % NC, will have both a lower bound and an upper bound given by

$$p_{\max} \le \%NC \le 4p_{\max} \tag{9.33}$$

A reachable lower bound for percentage yield can be obtained from equation (9.33) as

$$2\Phi(3BC_{pk}) - 1 \le \% \text{ yield} \tag{9.34}$$

In a similar way an upper bound for the percentage yield can be obtained from equation (9.33).

A multivariate generalization of BC_{pk} for k characteristics, $k > 2$, can now be defined when we divide the Euclidian space $\mathbb{R}^k$ into 2^k hyperquadrants by using the k principal components as axes of the k-variate distribution as

$$
\begin{aligned}
MC_{pk} \\
&= \frac{1}{3}\min\left\{-\Phi^{-1}(2^{k-1}p_1), -\Phi^{-1}(2^{k-1}p_2), \cdots, -\Phi^{-1}(2^{k-1}p_{2^k})\right\} \\
&= -\frac{1}{3}\max\left\{\Phi^{-1}(2^{k-1}p_1), \Phi^{-1}(2^{k-1}p_2), \cdots, \Phi^{-1}(2^{k-1}p_{2^k})\right\} \\
&= -\frac{1}{3}\Phi^{-1}(2^{k-1}p_{\max}) \tag{9.35}
\end{aligned}
$$

where p_i represents the probability that a randomly selected sample is in the ith hyper quadrant but not is the specification region for $i = 1, 2, \cdots, 2^k$ and $p_{\max} = \max\{p_1, p_2, \cdots, p_{2^k}\}$. From equation (9.35)

$$p_{\max} = \frac{1}{2^{k-1}}\Phi(-3MC_{pk}) \tag{9.36}$$

Using (9.36) and the fact that, $p_{\max} \le \%NC \le 2^k p_{\max}$, we can get a bound for the yield as

$$2\,\Phi(3MC_{pk}) - 1 \le \%\text{Yield} \le 1 - \frac{1}{2^{k-1}}\,\Phi(-3MC_{pk}) \tag{9.37}$$

Shiau et al. [14] proposed an algorithm to get an estimate of MC_{pk} which may be used in the inequalities like (9.37) and an estimate of the lower and the upper bound on yield can be obtained.

BC_p for the bivariate case and MC_p for the multivariate case can be obtained using the steps given Shiau et al. [14].

Bibliography

[1] Barton, R.R. and Gonzalez-Barreto, D.R.(1996). Process-Oriented Basis Representation for Multivariate Process Diagnostics. *Quality Engineering*, Vol. 9, pp. 107–118.

[2] Boyles, R. A. (1991). The Taguchi Capability Index. *Journal of Quality Technology*, Vol. 23, No. 1, pp. 17–26.

[3] Boyles, R. A. (1994). Process Capability with Asymmetric Tolerances. *Communications in Statistics—Simulation and Computation*, Vol. 23, No. 3, pp. 162–175.

[4] Castagliola, P., Castellanos, J. V. G. (2005). Capability Indices Dedicated to the Two Quality Characteristics Case. *Quality Technology and Quantitative Management*, Vol. 2, No. 2, pp. 201–220.

[5] Chen, K. S., Pearn, W. L., Lin, P. C. (2003). Capability Measures for Processes with Multiple Characteristics. *Quality and Reliability Engineering International*, Vol. 19, pp. 101–110.

[6] Cheng, F. T., Wu, M. F., Pearn, W. L. (2011). Hi-tech Manufacturing Process Selection Problem for Very Low Fraction of Defectives with Multiple Characteristics. *International Journal of the Physical Sciences* Vol. 6, pp. 4802–4815

[7] Dharmasena, L. S., Zeephongsekul, P. (2014). Univariate and Multivariate Process Yield Indices Based on Location-Scale Family of Distributions. *International Journal of Production Research*, Vol. 52, pp. 3348–3365.

[8] Foster, E. J., Barton, R. R., Gautam, N., Truss, L. T., Tew, J. D. (2005). The Process-Oriented Multivariate Capability Index. *International Journal of Production Research*, Vol. 43, pp. 2135–2148.

[9] Gonzalez, I., Sanchez, I. (2009). Capability Indices and Nonconforming Proportion in Univariate and Multivariate Processes. *International Journal of Advanced Manufacturing Technology*, Vol. 44, pp. 1036–1050.

[10] Gu, K., Jia, X., Liu, H., You, H. (2015). Yield-Based Capability Index for Evaluating the Performance of Multivariate Manufacturing Process. *Quality and Reliability Engineering International*, Vol. 31, pp. 419–430.

[11] Khadse, K. G., Shinde, R. L. (2009). Probability based Process Capability Indices. *Communications in Statistics—Simulation and Computation*, Vol. 38, pp. 884–904.

[12] Pearn, W. L., Wang, F. K., Yen, C. H. (2006). Measuring Production Yield for Processes with Multiple Quality Characteristics. *International Journal of Production Research*, Vol. 44, pp. 4649–4661.

[13] Perakis, M., Xekalaki, E. (2002). A Process Capability Index that is Based on the Proportion of Conformance. *Journal of Statistical Computation and Simulation*, Vol. 72, pp. 707–718.

[14] Shiau, J. J. H., Yen, C. L., Pearn, W. L., Lee, W. T. (2013). Yield-Related Process Capability Indices for Processes of Multiple Quality Characteristics. *Quality and Reliability Engineering International*, Vol. 29, pp. 487–507.

[15] Wang, F. K. (2006). Quality Evaluation of a Manufactured Product with Multiple Characteristics. *Quality and Reliability Engineering International*, Vol. 22, 225–236.

[16] Wang, F. K. (2010). A General Procedure for Process Yield with Multiple Characteristics. *IEEE Transactions on Semiconductor Manufacturing*, Vol. 23, pp. 503–508.

[17] Wang, F. K., Chu, D. (2013). Process Yield for a Manufactured Product. *Quality Technology and Quantitative Management*, Vol. 10, pp. 483–494.

[18] Wang, F. K., Hubele, N. F., Lawrence, F. P., Miskulin, J. D., Shahriari, H. (2000). Comparison of Three Multivariate Process Capability Indices. *Journal of Quality Technology*. Vol. 32, pp. 263–275.

Chapter 10

Multivariate Process Capability Indices for Quality Characteristics Having Nonnormal Statistical Distributions

Chapter Summary

Most of the multivariate process capability indices (MPCIs) available in literature, are defined under the assumption that, the underlying process distribution is multivariate normal. However, in many practical situations this assumption is found to be unrealistic. In Chapter 10, MPCIs for such processes are discussed in detail. These include MPCIs for nonnormal characteristics based on principal component analysis (PCA), geometric distance approach, skewness reduction approach, nonparametric methods and using multivariate nonnormal distribution (e.g., multivariate g and h distribution). A numerical example is also discussed to supplement the theories discussed in this chapter.

10.1 Introduction

Initially, process capability indices were defined based on two basic assumptions, viz., (i) the process is under statistical control and (ii) underlying process distribution is normal. While the first assumption owes to the fact that unless a process is statistically stable, it is impractical to assess capability of a process; the second assumption is made primarily to have some computational advantage.

However, in practice, often one encounters processes having nonnormal statistical distributions. On the other hand, there is no denial of the fact that, univariate and multivariate PCIs, based on normality assumption, are predominant in quality control literature.

Unfortunately, the common industrial practice is to apply PCIs with normality assumption, viz., C_p, C_{pk}, C_{pm}, and C_{pmk} in particular, without even checking whether the assumption holds good or not. This often leads to mis-

214

MPCIs for Nonnormal Distributions 215

leading and erroneous conclusion regarding process performance. The situation is even worse for multivariate processes (refer Chatterjee [8], Han [14] and the references there-in).

To address this problem, one may either transform the nonnormal (both univariate and multivariate) data to normality by using Box- Cox power transformation (refer Box and Cox [5]) or Johnson's transformation system (refer Johnson [15]) or use PCIs (univariate or multivariate as the case may be) specially defined for processes having nonnormal distributions.

Interestingly, for the normal distribution, the quantity 3σ is the distance of median (which is equal to mean, particularly for normal distribution) from both the upper 99.865 percentile and the lower 0.135 percentile. Therefore, for assessing the capability of a process with nonnormal distribution of the quality characteristic, the idea is to generalize the formulae for standard indices by replacing μ and 3σ with plausible alternatives like appropriate quantiles and so on.

While defining PCIs for nonnormally distributed quality characteristics, Clements [10] suggested replacing 6σ by the length of the interval between the upper and lower 0.135 percentile points of the actual distribution. The author defined PCIs analogous to C_p and C_{pk} for nonnormal distributions as follows:

$$\left.\begin{array}{l} C'_p = \frac{U-L}{\xi_{1-\alpha}-\xi_\alpha} \\ C''_{pk} = \frac{d-|\xi_{0.5}-M|}{(\xi_{1-\alpha}-\xi_\alpha)/2} \end{array}\right\}$$

where $\xi_{1-\alpha}$ and ξ_α are the upper and lower α percentiles of the distribution of the corresponding random variable X and $\xi_{0.5}$ is the corresponding median. Generally, $\alpha = 0.00135$ is considered for computational purposes.

Wright proposed the following PCI which is sensitive to skewness:

$$C_s = \frac{\frac{d}{\sigma} - \frac{|\mu-M|}{\sigma}}{3\sqrt{1 + \left(\frac{\mu-T}{\sigma}\right)^2 + |\sqrt{\beta_1}|}} \tag{10.1}$$

where $\sqrt{\beta_1} = \frac{\mu_3}{\sigma^{3/2}}$ is a widely used measure of skewness and μ_3 is the third order raw moment of the corresponding random variate "X."

Since at present our primary concern is multivariate process capability analysis, we shall confine our discussion to MPCIs for nonnormal distributions for the rest of this chapter.

10.2 MPCIs for Nonnormal Data Using Principal Component Analysis

Wang and Du [34] were among the first to define MPCI for multivariate non-normal process distributions. Recall from Chapter 5 that, Wang and

Chen [33] and Wang and Du [34] have made use of principal component analysis (PCA) as dimension reduction technique for multidimensional process capability analysis. Although Wang and Chen [33] confined their discussion to multivariate normally distributed processes only, Wang and Du [34] incorporated multivariate nonnormal processes as well in their study.

Also recall that, in the context of multivariate normal distributions, to define MPCIs for PCs, Wang and Chen [33] and Wang and Du [34] considered C_p, C_{pk}, C_{pm}, and C_{pmk} values for all the (significant) principal components (PC) and then have taken their geometric mean. For processes following multivariate nonnormal statistical distributions, Wang and Du [34] have adopted a similar approach, the only diffference being here for individual PCs, they have used Luceno's [18] PCI.

Suppose a random variable X characterizes a quality characteristic of a univariate process whose upper and lower specification limits are given by USL and LSL, respectively. Define $M = \frac{USL+LSL}{2}$. Then following Luceno [18], a PCI for univariate nonnormal processes can be defined as

$$C_{pc} = \frac{USL - LSL}{6\sqrt{\pi/2}\ E(|X - M|)} \qquad (10.2)$$

Suppose there are "q" quality characteristics which are considered as "q" variables on which PCA is applied and "v" PCs are found to be statistically significant. Then an MPCI for processes having multivariate nonnormal distribution can be defined as

$$MC_{pc} = \left(\prod_{i=1}^{v} C_{pc;PC_i}\right)^{1/v} \qquad (10.3)$$

where $C_{pc;PC_i}$ stands for C_{pc} value of the ith PC, for $i = 1(1)v$. Note that, similar to the MPCIs discussed in Chapter 5, here also, one can retain all the "q" PCs and consequently, "v" in equation (10.3) will be replaced by "q." While considering significant PCs only may lead to some amount of loss of information, considering all the "q" PCs is not a good alternative either, as although no information is lost in this case, the dimension of the data is not reduced at all (betraying the true spirit of PCA). Situation worsens when one has to deal with a huge number of correlated quality characteristics simultaneously. Therefore, one needs to do a trade off between "v" and "q" according to his/ her necessity.

Now, since MC_{pc} involves process parameter(s) through $E(|X - M|)$, its plug-in estimator can be defined as follows (refer Wang and Du [34]):

$$\widehat{MC}_{pc} = \left(\prod_{i=1}^{v} \widehat{C}_{pc;PC_i}\right)^{1/v} \qquad (10.4)$$

where

$$\widehat{C}_{pc;PC_i} = \frac{USL_{PC_i} - LSL_{PC_i}}{6\sqrt{\pi/2}\ \overline{C}_i}; \qquad (10.5)$$

$$\overline{C}_i = \frac{1}{n}\sum_{j=1}^{n}|PC_{ij} - \frac{USL_{PC_i} + LSL_{PC_i}}{2}| \qquad (10.6)$$

Also, the $(1-\alpha) \times 100\%$ confidence interval for MC_{pc} is given by

$$\left[\left\{\prod_{i=1}^{}\frac{\widehat{C}_{pc,PC_i}}{1 + t_{\alpha/2,n-1}S_{C_i}/(\sqrt{n}\ \overline{C}_i)}\right\}^{1/m},\right.$$

$$\left.\left\{\prod_{i=1}^{}\frac{\widehat{C}_{pc,PC_i}}{1 - t_{\alpha/2,n-1}S_{C_i}/(\sqrt{n}\ \overline{C}_i)}\right\}^{1/m}\right] \qquad (10.7)$$

where

$$S_{C_i} = \frac{1}{n-1}\left[\sum_{i=1}^{n}|PC_{ij} - \frac{USL_{PC_i} + LSL_{PC_i}}{2}|^2 - n\overline{C}_i^2\right] \qquad (10.8)$$

10.3 MPCIs for Multivariate Nonnormal Data Using Distance Approach

Similar to Wang and Du [34], Wang [32] has used Luceno's [18] PCI to define another MPCI, called MC_{pc}^*. In this context, although Wang [32] originally named this MPCI as MC_{pc}, we shall call it as MC_{pc}^* to avoid notational ambiguity with MC_{pc} defined in equation (10.3). Interestingly, unlike the conventional principal component analysis (PCA) approach, Wang [32] has used geometric distance approach, which was originally proposed by Wang and Hubele [35].

Let (X_1, X_2, X_3) is a random vector whose three components represent three correlated quality characteristics of a product. Let (x_1, x_2, x_3) be one particular realization of the product and (T_1, T_2, T_3) be the target vector for this. Then the corresponding geometric distance can be defined as

$$G = \sqrt{(x_1 - T_1)^2 + (x_2 - T_2)^2 + (x_3 - T_3)^2} \qquad (10.9)$$

Therefore, geometric distance is nothing but the Euclidean distance between (x_1, x_2, x_3) and (T_1, T_2, T_3).

Now, among the significant (most important) quality characteristics, of a process, some may be highly correlated, while the rest may be uncorrelated. Suppose based on the underlying correlation structure, "k" groups can be constructed from the total of "q" quality characteristics, such that the members of an individual group are highly correlated, while quality characteristics across the groups are either weakly correlated or are completely uncorrelated. Let G_i be the geometric distance of the ith group and MRD_i is the maximum radial distance of the target from the perimeter of the tolerance region of the ith group, for $i = 1(1)k$. Then using Luceno's [18] PCI, Wang [32] has defined MC_{pc}^* as

$$\widehat{MC}_{pc}^* = \left(\prod_{i=1}^{k} \widehat{C}_{pc(i)} \right)^{1/k} \tag{10.10}$$

where

$$\widehat{C}_{pc(i)} = \frac{MRD_i}{3\sqrt{\frac{\pi}{2}}E[G_i]}, \quad i = 1(1)k \tag{10.11}$$

Note that, here the notation $\widehat{MC}_{pc}^*$ is used instead of MC_{pc}^* as it involves G_i which is defined empirically (as it involves x_1, x_2, x_3 instead of X_1, X_2, X_3).

Also, an approximate $100(1 - \alpha)\%$ confidence interval for MC_{pc}^* will be

$$\left[\left(\frac{\widehat{C}_{pc(i)}}{1 + t_{\alpha/2,n-1}\frac{S_{c_i}}{\overline{c_i}\sqrt{n}}} \right)^{1/k} , \left(\frac{\widehat{C}_{pc(i)}}{1 - t_{\alpha/2,n-1}\frac{S_{c_i}}{\overline{c_i}\sqrt{n}}} \right)^{1/k} \right] \tag{10.12}$$

where $\overline{c_i}$ and S_{c_i} denote, respectively, the arithmetic mean and standard deviation of G_i.

Also, corresponding estimated proportion of nonconformance (PNC) can be given by (refer Wang [32]

$$PNC = 1 - \prod_{i=1}^{k} \int_{0}^{MRD_i} f_i(y)dy \tag{10.13}$$

where $f_i(.)$ denotes p.d.f. of G_i, for $i = 1(1)k$.

However, Ahmad et al. [3] have advocated use of Mahalanobis distance [alternatively known as *covariance distance (CD)*] instead of GD, as the former involves correlation structure of the quality characteristics belonging to that particular group.

Now, what is the difference between GD and CD? Suppose there are "q" quality characteristics represented by the random vector $\boldsymbol{X} = (X_1, X_2, \cdots, X_q)'$ and the corresponding target vector is $\boldsymbol{T} = (T_1, T_2, \cdots, T_q)'$.

Then GD, which is effectively the Euclidean distance between X and T can be defined as

$$
\begin{aligned}
G &= \sqrt{(X - T)'(X - T)} \\
&= \left[(X_1 - T_1)^2 + (X_2 - T_2)^2 + \cdots + (X_q - T_q)^2\right]^{1/2} \quad (10.14)
\end{aligned}
$$

On the contrary, suppose Σ is the dispersion matrix of X. Then CD can be defined as

$$
C = \sqrt{(X - T)'\Sigma^{-1}(X - T)} \quad (10.15)
$$

Then using C, an alternative to MC^*_{PC} can be given as

$$
\widehat{MC}^{**}_{pc} = \left(\prod_{i=1}^{k} \widehat{C}^*_{pc(i)}\right)^{1/k} \quad (10.16)
$$

where

$$
\widehat{C}^*_{pc(i)} = \frac{MRD_i}{3\sqrt{\frac{\pi}{2}}E[C_i]}, \quad i = 1(1)k \quad (10.17)
$$

and C_i is the value of C for the ith group, for $i = 1(1)k$.

In this context, statistical distribution of both G and C have immense impact on MC^*_{PC} and MC^{**}_{PC}, respectively. However, for most of the practical situations, it is hard to get exact statistical distributions of G and C. Wang [32] has used goodness of fit technique to get the approximate statistical distribution of G with the best fit. This can be done using any standard statistical package (the most popular one for the current purpose being "Best-fit" software).

However, instead of handling one particular distribution at a time, Abbasi et al. [1] and Ahmed et al. [3] have advocated for using Burr XII distribution to C.

The Burr system of distributions was given by Burr [4], and Durling [12] has proposed a simplified form of bivariate Burr distribution.

Burr distribution finds ample application in statistical quality control, reliability and survival analysis, and failure time modelling among others. The advantage of using Burr family of distribution, as the name suggests, is that, it incorporates twelve nonnormal distributions (popularly known as Type I − Type XII) which do not require difficult computations as is required by Pearsonian system of distributions. Interested readers may refer to Kotz et al. [17] for more detail discussion on Burr distribution.

Among the twelve types of Burr distributions type XII Burr distribution is particularly important from statistical quality control perspective.

The probability density function (p.d.f.) of Burr XII distribution is given by

$$f(x) = \begin{cases} \frac{cdx^{c-1}}{(1+x^c)^{d+1}}, & x \geq 0, c \geq 1, d \geq 1 \\ \\ 0, & \text{Otherwise} \end{cases} \tag{10.18}$$

and its cumulative distribution function (c. d. f.) is given by

$$F(x) = 1 - \frac{1}{(1+x^c)^{d+1}} \tag{10.19}$$

Here c and d are distributional parameters.

By merely changing the values of c and d, one can have other statistical distributions like normal, log-normal, beta, gamma, Weibull, and extreme value Type $-I$ distributions.

Takahashi [30] has also extended Burr XII distribution to multivariate case.

Now, the log-likelihood function corresponding to Burr XII distribution is given by [refer Wingo [36]]

$$\ln L(c, d, x_1, x_2, ..., x_q) = n \ln c + n \ln k - (1 + k) \sum_{i=1}^{q} \ln(1 + x_i^c)$$

$$+ (c - 1) \sum_{i=1}^{q} \ln x_i \tag{10.20}$$

where $\ln a$ denotes $\log_e a$.

In this context, $L(c, d, x_1, x_2, ..., x_q)$ is the likelihood function of Burr XII distribution, which is nothing but the p. d. f. of $\boldsymbol{X} = (X_1, X_2, \cdots, X_q)'$, the only difference being, here the parameters c and d are considered as variables instead of $\boldsymbol{X}$ (as is done in case of p.d.f.).

Now, to derive expressions for the maximum likelihood estimators (MLE) of c and d, one needs the log-likelihood function in equation (10.20) to be differentiated with respect to c and d and solve the two differential equations thus obtained. Ahmed et al. [3] have derived the expressions for these differential equations as follows:

$$\frac{\delta \ln L}{\delta c} = \frac{q}{c} + \sum_{i=1}^{q} \ln(x_i) - (1+d) \sum_{i=1}^{q} \frac{x_i^c \ln(x_i)}{1 + x_i^c} = 0 \tag{10.21}$$

$$\frac{\delta \ln L}{\delta d} = \frac{q}{d} - \sum_{i=1}^{q} \ln(1 + x_i^c) = 0 \tag{10.22}$$

While solving equations (10.21) and (10.22), there may exist a number of local optimums (maximums in this case) and hence usual approaches will not work efficiently. To address this problem, Ahmed et al. [3] have used the method of simulated annealing while solving equations (10.21) and (10.22).

What is simulated annealing (SA)? SA is a stochastic algorithm to solve optimization problems, particularly when one has to search for global optimum in a dataset having a number of local optimum.

SA method was first proposed by Metropolis et al. [19]. The term annealing originated from the process of physical annealing of metals, which is a thermal process for obtaining low-energy state of a solid in a heat bath. The so-called "Metropolis algorithm" uses Monte Carlo method to give an optimization algorithm which works similar to the physical annealing.

In many real life datasets, the assumption of unimodality is not valid. Consequently, Newton-Raphson method is not applicable. SA can be used in such cases.

SA is easy to compute and interpret and can be applied to both combinatorial as well as continuous optimization problems. New age software, like minitab, python, and R among others, make the computation even easier.

Compared to GD, CD takes into account process dispersion and hence is more relevant to the multivariate process capability problem. However, success of both MC_{PC}^* and MC_{PC}^{**} depend on the fact that the "k" groups thus obtained are mutually independent. Unless this assumption holds good, these MPCIs will fail to perform satisfactorily.

10.4 MPCIs Using Multivariate g and h Distribution

g and h distribution finds ample application in risk modelling (refer Moscoso and Arunachalam [20]). Univariate g and h distribution was first introduced by Tukey [31]. If $Z \sim N(0, 1)$, then the pdf of Y_{gh} is defined as

$$Y_{gh}(Z) = A + B \, \frac{e^{gZ-1}}{g} \, e^{\frac{hZ^2}{2}} \tag{10.23}$$

where A and $B(> 0)$ are the location and scale parameters and g and h are the skewness and kurtosis measures of the corresponding statistical distribution.

Field and Gelton [13] have proposed a multivariate counterpart of g and h distribution. Let the random vector $Z \sim N_q(\mathbf{0}, I_q)$. Define a random vector $\boldsymbol{Y} = \left(\tau_{g_1,h_1}(Z_1), \tau_{g_2,h_2}(Z_2), \cdots, \tau_{g_q,h_q}(Z_q)\right)'$ and

$$\boldsymbol{\tau}_{g,h}(\boldsymbol{Z}) = \frac{e^{g\boldsymbol{Z}} - 1}{g} \, e^{\frac{h\boldsymbol{Z}^2}{2}} \tag{10.24}$$

Then, multivariate g and h distribution can be represented, in terms of $\boldsymbol{Z}$, as

$$\boldsymbol{Y} = \Sigma^{\frac{1}{2}} \, \boldsymbol{\tau}_{g,h}(\boldsymbol{Z}) + \boldsymbol{\mu} \tag{10.25}$$

where $\boldsymbol{\mu}$ and Σ are, respectively, the mean vector and dispersion matrix of the distribution.

Das and Dwivedi [11] have defined an MPCI based on multivariate g and h distribution as follows:

$$C_p = \left[\frac{\left| \prod_{i=1}^{q} (USL_i - LSL_i) \right|}{\left| \prod_{i=1}^{q} (UPL_i - LPL_i) \right|} \right]^{\frac{1}{q}} \tag{10.26}$$

where

$$LPL_i = \sigma_i \frac{e^{-3g} - 1}{g} \, e^{\frac{9h}{2}} + \mu_i \tag{10.27}$$

$$UPL_i = \sigma_i \frac{e^{3g} - 1}{g} \, e^{\frac{9h}{2}} + \mu_i \tag{10.28}$$

$$\tag{10.29}$$

10.5 MPCIs for Multivariate Nonnormal Processes Using Skewness Reduction Approach

Recall from introductory section that, a way to handle nonnormality, while assessing process capability, is to transform the data to multivariate normal using Box-Cox transformation(refer Box and Cox [5]) or similar type of transformations. This makes the PCIs or MPCIs defined for normal distribution (which are ample in number) readily applicable. Alternatively, one can use PCIs or MPCIs (as the case may be) specially designed for nonnormal processes.

Niaki and Abbasi [21] have adopted a mid-way approach between these two, called *"Root Transformation Technique"*. Now onwards it will be abbreviated as RTT. Observe that skewness plays a major role in discriminating a nonnormal distribution from a normal one.

RTT is usually used for right-skewed nonnormal data. Suppose X (for univariate process) or $\boldsymbol{X}$ (for multivariate process) characterize the quality characteristic(s) of the process. At first one has to numerically search for a root r, with $0 < r < 1$, such that X^r has a distribution having almost zero skewness. For $\boldsymbol{X}$, this is done for individual X_i's separately using separate r_i's altogether, for $i = 1(1)q$. The numerical search for r can be done easily using bisection method (refer Scarborough [27] for more detail).

Suppose under multivariate set-up, for $\boldsymbol{X} = (X_1, X_2, \cdots, X_q)'$, after applying root r_i to X_i, it becomes almost symmetric. Let $Y_i = X_i^{r_i}$, i.e., Y_i is the root-transformed version of X_i. Also let Z_i is a standardized variable obtained from Y_i, such that $Z_i = \frac{Y_i - \widehat{\mu}_{Y_i}}{\widehat{\sigma}_{Y_{ii}}}$, where, $\widehat{\mu}_Y = (\widehat{\mu}_{Y_1}, \widehat{\mu}_{Y_2}, \cdots, \widehat{\mu}_{Y_q})'$ is the observed mean vector of $\boldsymbol{Y}$ and $\widehat{\Sigma}_Y = ((\widehat{\sigma}_{Y_{ij}}))$ is the observed dispersion matrix of Y. Thus, $\boldsymbol{Z} \sim N_q(\boldsymbol{0}, \widehat{\Sigma}_Z)$, where $\widehat{\Sigma}_Z$ is the observed dispersion matrix of $\boldsymbol{Z}$.

Note that, the multivariate normality of $\boldsymbol{Z}$, which has thus been established, is an approximate one. This is due to the fact that, root transformation technique reduces skewness of the data, but often cannot eliminate it completely; while normal distribution is symmetric about its mean.

Now, as is observed by Boyles [6], when a data is transformed, its specification limits also get transformed by virtue of the same transformation. Thus, if $\boldsymbol{USL_X} = (USL_{X_1}, USL_{X_2}, \cdots, USL_{X_q})'$ and $\boldsymbol{LSL_X} = (LSL_{X_1}, LSL_{X_2}, \cdots, LSL_{X_q})'$ are the original vector of upper and lower specification limits of $\boldsymbol{X}$, respectively, then for the ith quality characteristics, USL and LSL corresponding to Z_i will, respectively, be

$$USL_{Z_i} \;\; = \;\; \frac{(USL_{X_i})^{r_i} - \widehat{\mu}_{Y_i}}{\widehat{\sigma}_{Y_i}} \tag{10.30}$$

$$LSL_{Z_i} \;\; = \;\; \frac{(LSL_{X_i})^{r_i} - \widehat{\mu}_{Y_i}}{\widehat{\sigma}_{Y_i}} \tag{10.31}$$

Once, $\boldsymbol{Z}$, $\boldsymbol{LSL_Z}$ and $\boldsymbol{USL_Z}$ are obtained, these are then used as representative of the original data $\boldsymbol{X}$ and the corresponding $\boldsymbol{LSL}$ and $\boldsymbol{USL}$, respectively.

Also, in the context of process capability analysis, the general convention is to first compute the PCI or MPCI value and then calculate corresponding PNC value by establishing the relationship between PNC and PCI (or MPCI, as the case may be). However, contradicting this general convention, Abbasi and Niaki [2] have first computed PNC generated by the transformed data $\boldsymbol{Z}$ with respect to $\boldsymbol{USL_Z}$ and $\boldsymbol{LSL_Z}$ and then from that, computed PCI value.

MPCIs for Nonnormal Distributions

For this, a considerably large sample is simulated from $N_q(\boldsymbol{\mu}, \Sigma_{\boldsymbol{Z}})$ distribution (i.e., the approximate distribution of $\boldsymbol{Z}$) and from that, PNC is calculated using following formulae:

$$PNC = \begin{cases} 1 - P\left[\boldsymbol{Z} \leq \boldsymbol{USL_Z}\right], \\ \quad \text{if only upper specification is available} \\ \\ 1 - P\left[\boldsymbol{LSL_Z} \leq \boldsymbol{Z} \leq \boldsymbol{USL_Z}\right], \quad \text{Otherwise} \end{cases}$$

Thus, for bilateral specification (i.e., when both $\boldsymbol{USL_Z}$ and $\boldsymbol{LSL_Z}$ are available), a multivariate analogue of C_p can be computed as

$$C_p^{AN} = \frac{\Phi^{-1}\left[0.5 + 0.5(1 - PNC)\right]}{3} \tag{10.32}$$

Similarly, when only $\boldsymbol{USL_Z}$ is available, a multivariate analogue of C_{pu} can be defined as

$$C_{pu}^{AN} = \frac{\Phi^{-1}\left(1 - PNC\right)}{3} \tag{10.33}$$

Interestingly, no multivariate analogue of C_{pl} is defined, since RTT performs better for right skewed (positively skewed) data.

Note that, success of C_p^{AN} and C_{pu}^{AN} depend largely upon the proximity of distribution of $\boldsymbol{Z}$ toward multivariate normality. As a thumb-rule for finding the root r_i, Abbasi and Niaki [2] suggested having either 20000 iterations or skewness less than 0.05, whichever is attained first. Therefore, there is a possibility (though may be rare) that, one has reached 20000 iterations, though skewness is still not satisfactorily eradicated. Also, in the course of transforming the specification region, the original "unit of measure" gets distorted in an inexplainable way [refer Pan et al. [23]]. Although PCI is a unit-free measure, such distortion may have some impact on the overall interpretation of the index.

Pan et al. [23] defined an MPCI, for nonnormal distributions, using multivariate weighted standard deviation method (MWSD), which is robust to the skewness level of a distribution.

Chang and Bai [7] were first to propose MWSD method. This method approximates an original q-variate nonnormal density to 2^q components each of which is a q-variate normal distribution with common and original mean vector $\boldsymbol{\mu}$ and dispersion matrix.

$$\Sigma^{(W)} \quad = \quad W\Sigma W$$

$$= \quad \begin{pmatrix} \left(\sigma_1^{(W)}\right)^2 & \rho_{12}\sigma_1^{(W)}\sigma_2^{(W)} & \cdots & \rho_{1q}\sigma_1^{(W)}\sigma_q^{(W)} \\ \rho_{12}\sigma_1^{(W)}\sigma_2^{(W)} & \left(\sigma_2^{(W)}\right)^2 & \cdots & \rho_{2q}\sigma_2^{(W)}\sigma_q^{(W)} \\ \vdots & \vdots & \cdots & \vdots \\ \rho_{1q}\sigma_1^{(W)}\sigma_q^{(W)} & \rho_{2q}\sigma_q^{(W)}\sigma_q^{(W)} & \cdots & \left(\sigma_q^{(W)}\right)^2 \end{pmatrix}$$

$$(10.34)$$

where

$$W_i = \begin{cases} 2p_i, & \text{If } X_i > \mu_i \\ 2(1 - p_i), & \text{Otherwise} \end{cases} \tag{10.35}$$

$W = \text{diag } \{W_1, W_2, \cdots, W_q\}$

$\sigma_i^{(W)} = W_i\sigma_i$ and $p_i = P\left(X_i \leq \mu_i\right)$, for $i = 1(1)q$.

Now, recall from Chapter 6 that, Pan and Lee [22] have defined multivariate analogues of C_p and C_{pm}, under the assumption of multivariate normality of the process distribution, as

$$NMC_p \quad = \quad \frac{|A^*|}{|\Sigma|} \tag{10.36}$$

$$NMC_{pm} \quad = \quad NMC_p/D \tag{10.37}$$

where ith element of A^*, viz., a_{ij}^*, is given by

$$a_{ij}^* = \rho_{ij} \left(\frac{USL_i - LSL_i}{2c}\right) \times \left(\frac{USL_j - LSL_j}{2c}\right) \tag{10.38}$$

,

for $i = 1(1)q$, $j = 1(1)q$ with $c = \sqrt{\chi_{1-\alpha,q}^2}$ and

$$D^{-1} = \sqrt{1 + (\boldsymbol{\mu} - \boldsymbol{T})'\Sigma^{-1}(\boldsymbol{\mu} - \boldsymbol{T})} \tag{10.39}$$

To define an MPCI similar to NMC_p, Pan et al. [23] suggested replacing Σ by $\Sigma^{(W)}$ in equation (10.36). However, as has been discussed earlier, MWSD method segregates Σ in 2^q different dispersion matrices, each of order "q". Suppose these matrices are given by $\Sigma_1^{(W)}$, $\Sigma_2^{(W)}, \cdots$, $\Sigma_q^{(W)}$. Since Σ is in the denominator of NMC_p, i.e., the value of NMC_p decreases if Σ increases, hence Pan and Lee [23] have proposed a conservative MPCI similar to NMC_p as

$$RNMC_p = \left(\frac{|A^*|}{|\Sigma_{\max}^{(W)}|} \right)^{1/2} \tag{10.40}$$

where $|\Sigma_{\max}^{(W)}| = \max \left\{ |\Sigma_1^{(W)}|, \ |\Sigma_2^{(W)}|, \cdots, \ |\Sigma_q^{(W)}| \right\}$.

Thus, $RNMC_p$ is basically the minimum value of segment-wise index $\left(\frac{|A^*|}{|\Sigma_i^{(W)}|} \right)^{1/2}$ for $i = 1(1)2^q$.

Also, similar to NMC_{pm} [vide equation (10.37)], Pan et al. [23] have defined $RNMC_{pm}$ as

$$
\begin{aligned}
RNMC_{pm} &= \frac{RNMC_p}{D^{(W)}} \\
&= \frac{RNMC_p}{\sqrt{1 + (\boldsymbol{\mu} - \boldsymbol{T})' \left(\Sigma_{\max}^{(W)} \right)^{-1} (\boldsymbol{\mu} - \boldsymbol{T})}}
\end{aligned}
\tag{10.41}
$$

where $D^{(W)} = \sqrt{1 + (\boldsymbol{\mu} - \boldsymbol{T})' \left(\Sigma_{\max}^{(W)} \right)^{-1} (\boldsymbol{\mu} - \boldsymbol{T})}$ takes care of the deviation of process centering from the stipulated target. Note that, $D^{(W)}$ is a corrected version of D, where Σ has been replaced by $\Sigma_{\max}^{(W)}$.

Since MWSD method segregates the original $(q \times q)$ Σ matrix in 2^q dispersion matrices, it has direct impact on $RNMC_p$ and $RNMC_{pm}$ and hence one may face the following situations in practice:

1. If q is small, say less than 4, and if the dispersion level is quite high, then taking $\Sigma_{\max}^{(W)}$ may be too restrictive. Although $RNMC_p$ measures potential process capability and hence the damage may be less but $RNMC_{pm}$, which is supposed to measure true process capability, may give misleading result due to this.

2. If q is 4 or more, there will be 16 or more $\Sigma_{\max}^{(W)}$ for single Σ. This will be quite difficult to handle and will require substantial amount of programme coding proficiency. Also, as the number of $\Sigma_{\max}^{(W)}$ increases, performance of $\Sigma_{\max}^{(W)}$ becomes lesser efficient.

10.6 Nonparametric MPCIs for Nonnormal Processes

The MPCIs discussed so far make use of some distributional assumption or another of the original variables. However, there are some MPCIs which are completely based on nonparametric set-up and hence do not require any such assumption. Yeh and Chen [38] and Polansky [25], among others, have defined such nonparametric MPCIs.

It is evident, from all the discussions made so far that, a primary hurdle in multivariate process capability assessment is formulating the specification region. Depending upon the nature and complexity of the process, specification regions may be hyper-rectangular, elliptical, or may be of more complicated form, which requires geometric dimensioning and tolerancing for mathematical expression of its form (refer Karl et al. [16]).

Chen [9] have proposed a general form of specification region from multivariate perspective as follows:

$$V = \{\boldsymbol{x} \in \mathbb{R}^q : h(\boldsymbol{x} - \boldsymbol{T}) \le r\} \tag{10.42}$$

where r is a positive constant. In practice often r is so chosen that proportion of non-conformance, viz., $P[\boldsymbol{X} \in V] \le \alpha_0$, where α_0 is a prespecified small value lying between 0 and 1. For example, when the underlying distribution of the process is multivariate normal, the common industrial practice is to assume $\alpha_0 = 0.0027$. In this context, note that this 0.0027 value is actually meant for univariate normal distribution and not for multivariate normal distribution in general.

Observe that, V can accommodate any shape of the specification region by merely using appropriate functional form of $h(.)$. A detailed discussion on Chen's [9] MPCI is given in Chapter 9.

Yeh and Chen [38] have defined a nonparametric MPCI-based V as follows:

$$MC_f = \frac{\alpha_0}{\alpha} \tag{10.43}$$

where α is the actual value of PNC. Interestingly, although Chen [9] originally defined $h(.)$ to be a "positive homogeneous function of degree 1," so that one can have a unique value of the associated MPCI, Yeh and Chen [38] dropped this assumption as this is not required for MC_f.

Observe from equation (10.43) that, a process is deemed to be capable if $MC_f \ge 1$, as then the numerator of the index (viz., α_0), giving acceptable amount of PNC, is more than the denominator (viz., α), i.e., actual PNC, indicating healthy state of the process.

It is evident that computation of α involves computation of tail probability of the concerned distribution. For this, Yeh and Chen [38] have adopted the approach given by Pickands [24] and Smith [29].

Polansky [25] has proposed a probability based MPCI using "kernel estimation method". Let $\boldsymbol{X} = (X_1, X_2, \cdots, X_q)'$ denotes a q-component random vector characterizing correlated quality characteristics of a q-variate process with the corresponding pdf $f(\boldsymbol{x})$ and cdf $F(\boldsymbol{x})$. Then, as has already been discussed, PNC, with respect to the specification region V, can be defined as

$$p = 1 - P[X \in V]$$

$$= 1 - \int_V f(x)dx \tag{10.44}$$

Polansky [25] has adopted nonparametric kernel estimation process to estimate p, without making any distributional assumption.

Let κ be a continuous q-variate kernel function satisfying the conditions:

1. $\int_{\mathbb{R}^q} \kappa(x)dx = 1$;

2. $\int_{\mathbb{R}^q} x\kappa(x)dx = 0$

3. $\int_{\mathbb{R}^q} xx'\kappa(x)dx = diag\,(\mu_2(\kappa))$, where $diag\,(\mu_2(\kappa))$ denotes a diagonal matrix whose all the diagonal elements are the same, viz.,

$$\mu_2(\kappa) = \int_{\mathbb{R}^q} x_i^2 \kappa(x)dx \tag{10.45}$$

has the same value for all $i = 1(1)q$.

Let us now define a $(q \times q)$ symmetric positive definite (p. d.) matrix "H" which is known as the band width matrix of the kernel function κ, such that

$$\kappa_H(x) = |H|^{-1/2}\kappa\left(H^{-1/2}x\right) \tag{10.46}$$

Based on these, a kernel based nonparametric estimate of "p" can be obtained as

$$\widehat{p}(H,V) = 1 - \int_V \widehat{f}(x;H)\,dx$$

$$= 1 - \frac{1}{n}\sum_{i=1}^n \int_V \kappa_H(x - X_i)\,dx \tag{10.47}$$

For computational simplicity, Polansky [25] simplified the expression of H as $H_q = diag\left(h_1^2, h_2^2, \cdots, h_q^2\right)$, i.e., he retained only the diagonal elements of H and assumed off diagonal elements to be zero such that $\kappa(x) = \prod_{i=1}^q k(x_i)$, where $k()$ is the corresponding univariate kernel density function. Accordingly, $\widehat{p}(H,V)$ gets modified into

$$\widehat{p}(H_q,V) = 1 - \frac{1}{n}\sum_{i=1}^n \int_V \left[\prod_{j=1}^q \frac{k\left\{(x_i - X_{ij})/h_j\right\}}{h_j}\right]dx$$

$$\tag{10.48}$$

Finally, Polansky [25], has proposed an estimated multivariate analogue of C_{pm} as

$$\widehat{C}_p^{Polansky} = -\frac{1}{3}\Phi^{-1}\hat{p}(\hat{H}, V)$$

$$(10.49)$$

Simon [28] has proposed another nonparametric MPCI analogous to C_p based on the concept of the so called "half-space depth region". (Refer to Rousseeuw [26] and Zuo and Serfling [39] for more elaborate discussion on the concept of half-space depth.)

Simon [28] have observed that, although proportion of nonconformance is one of the most prominent representation of process capability, it is highly sensitive to the distributional assumption, in a sense that, even the slightest change in the population distribution may change the PNC value to a large extent. Therefore, using nonparametric approach, is an ideal alternative.

Suppose for a process having q correlated quality characteristics, the specification region is given by $\mathcal{S}$, which is a convex and compact set in $\mathbb{R}^q$. This includes the most common shapes of specification region, like elliptical and polyhedral, as special cases. Also, convexity of $\mathcal{S}$ ensures that, if $x \in \mathcal{S}$ is any particular observation, then all the line-segments joining x to S will be included in $\mathcal{S}$.

Now, consider $\nu \in \mathbb{R}$, where, depending upon the situation, ν is the coverage probability p or the probability mass ξ enclosed by supporting hyperplanes. Define $\mathcal{Q}_\nu(.)$ as the "multivariate half-space depth region" indexed by ν. Then $\mathcal{Q}_\nu(X)$ is the intersection of all closed half-spaces.

Then, Simon [28] has defined a multivariate analogue of C_p as

$$MC_p^{(Simon)} = \kappa_\nu \times S_{\max} \qquad (10.50)$$

where κ_ν is a positive normalizing scale factor and $S_{\max}$ is defined as

$$S_{\max} = \sup\{s > 0 : \mathcal{Q}_\nu(sX + c_s) \subset \mathcal{S}, \ c_s \in \mathbb{R}^q\} \qquad (10.51)$$

Observe that, both Polansky [25] and Simon [28] have defined only multivariate analogues of C_p, which measures potential process capability only. One possible reason may be to keep the proposed MPCIs as simple as possible, since incorporating the concepts like process centering viz., μ, target vector T and so on, may complicate the expressions of the MPCIs. Moreover, apart from the symmetric specification region, other types of specification regions, viz., asymmetric, unilateral, and so on, also need to be explored. These would definitely give interesting future scopes of study.

10.7 Numerical Example

Wang [32] has provided a real life dataset on a product named "connector" obtained from a computer industry in Taiwan. The dataset contains 100 observations on each of the seven quality characteristics viz., contact gap, contact loop Tp, LLCR, contact xTp, contact loop diameter, LTGAPY, and RTGAPY. The corresponding random variables are named as X_1, X_2, X_3, X_4, X_5, X_6, and X_7, respectively. Specification limits for these quality characteristics are, 0.10 ± 0.04 mm., $0 + 0.50$ mm., 11 ± 5 $m\Omega$, $0 + 0.2$ mm., 0.55 ± 0.06 mm., 0.07 ± 0.05 mm, and 0.07 ± 0.05 mm, respectively. It is evident from this list of specifications that, for X_2 and X_4, the specification limits are unilateral and for the rest, specification limits are symmetric bilateral.

The dispersion structure of the quality characteristics is as follows:

1. X_1, X_2 and X_3 are mutually correlated;

2. X_6 and X_7 are mutually correlated;

3. X_4 and X_5 are individually independent of all the other variables.

Recall that, Wang [32] advocated grouping of variables having strong correlation among themselves. Hence, from the above discussion, four groups can be formed, viz., $\{X_1, X_2, X_3\}$, $\{X_4\}$, $\{X_5\}$, and $\{X_6, X_7\}$. Euclidean distance variables for each of these four groups will, respectively, be, G_1, G_2, G_3, G_4. These groups, having no strong correlation among themselves, can be now handled individually.

Wang [32] has observed that, G_1 follows gamma distribution, G_2 and G_4 follow Weibull distribution, while G_3 follows normal distribution.

The individual group index values are found to be $\widehat{C}_{pc(1)} = 1.342$, $\widehat{C}_{pc(2)} = 1.849$, $\widehat{C}_{pc(3)} = 0.902$ and $\widehat{C}_{pc(4)} = 0.703$ which can be consolidated as $\widehat{MC}_{pc}^* = 1.120$ with PNC $= 0.0046$.

Apparently, this gives an impression of satisfactory performance of the process. However, a deep insight into the above values shows that $\widehat{C}_{pc(i)}$ values for the four groups differ sigificantly among themselves and $\widehat{MC}_{pc}^*$ tends to smooth out this phenomenon. As a result, though the process is actually not performing satisfactorily (refer Wang [32]), it is not readily noticeable from the computed values above. In fact the seemingly high value of $\widehat{MC}_{pc}^*$ makes the corresponding PNC low, which also misleads the end-user. A mathematically formulated threshold value is required to address this problem. Nonetheless $\widehat{MC}_{pc}^*$ tends to overestimate process capability.

Ahmad et al. [3] used the same groups as Wang [32] but used Mahalanobis distances C_1, C_2, C_3, and C_4. Based on their computation, PNC for the given data is, 0.6372 which strongly suggests that the process is not performing satisfactorily.

MPCIs for Nonnormal Distributions

However, note that, success of such grouping largely depends upon the mechanism of having such groups. To be more precise, in practice, apart from the situation discussed in the context of Wang's [32] data, one may face situations like the following:

1. All the quality characteristics have moderate to high correlation among themselves, so much so that, no further grouping can be made from them;

2. All the quality characteristics are mutually independent (a situation hardly encountered in practice) and hence they can, individually, be considered as group. This phenomenon, however, fails to reduce data dimension as the number of variables, after grouping, remains the same.

Pan et al.'s [23] $RNMC_p$ and $RNMC_{pm}$ have a peculiar problem from the perspective of analyzing the present dataset. Recall that the dataset consists of seven variables, which means, following Pan et al.'s [23] approach, the original distribution will be approximated by $2^7 = 128$ normal distributions with same mean and 128 different dispersion matrices . It is evident that this will involve too much computational complexities. To avoid this, Pan et al. [23] considered only the first three quality characteristics as the most important one and consequently retained X_1, X_2, and X_3 only. Based on this abridged dataset, $\widehat{RNMC_p} = 0.799$ and $\widehat{RNMC_{pm}} = 0.426$ indicating poor performance of the process. However, selection of these three variables or in general reducing dimension of the data should have been done based on some statistical analysis, say, principal component analysis, among others.

10.8   Concluding Remark

There is no denial of the fact that nonnormality (both from univariate and multivariate perspective) is more difficult to handle than normality. In the present chapter some MPCIs, specially designed for nonnormal processes have been discussed. Success of PCA based MPCIs largely depends upon the amount of variability explained by the PCs retained. On the other hand, MPCIs based on some multivariate nonnormal distributions or classes of distributions (viz., type XII Burr distribution) are applicable to some particular distributions only. Nonparametric MPCIs, though, are more robust in that sense, but are the most computation centric. However, the issue of difficulty in computation can be handled by using statistical package based numerical computations.

Although a substantial amount of research work has been carried out on multivariate nonnormal process capability analysis, the area is still among those lesser explored ones, keeping ample scope for further research. To be more precise, different types of specification regions (viz., asymmetric bilateral specification region among others) are yet to be taken into account. The MPCIs defined so far are primarily multivariate analogue of C_p, which actually measures potential process performance and not the actual one. Very few multivariate analogues of C_{pk} or C_{pm} are available. Defining these indices would be an interesting future scope of study. Mathematical formulation of the threshold value is required for almost all the MPCIs discussed in this chapter. For example, computed value of Wang's [32] MPCI, viz., $\widehat{MC}_{pc}^{*}$ is greater than 1 (which conventionally implies satisfactory performance of the process), while Wang [32], himself, observed that the manufactured products fail to comply preassigned specifications. Had there been a mathematically well formulated threshold value, this ambiguity could easily be addressed. Defining some multivariate nonnormal MPCIs based on quartiles or percentiles (similar to Celements [10]) will also be an interesting future scope of study as it will have a direct correspondence to the univariate nonnormal PCIs and hence should be more acceptable among practitioners.

Finally, while defining multivariate nonnormal MPCIs, the basic agenda should be to define MPCIs as simple as possible, because the end users of these MPCIs are mostly the shop floor people, who are often not comfortable with higher mathematics. Use of computer programs or software also often fail to address their apprehensions, as many of these MPCIs become difficult to visualize. As a result, although in recent years, a substantial number of multivariate nonnormal MPCIs have been defined, only a few of them are used in practice.

Bibliography

[1] Abbasi, B., Ahmad, S., Abdollahian, M., Zeephongsekul. (2007). Measuring Capability for Bivariate Non-normal Process Using Bivariate Burr Distribution. *WSEAS Transactions on Business and Economics*, Vol. 4, pp. 71–77.

[2] Abbasi, B., Niaki, S. T. A. (2010). Estimating Process Capability Indices of Multivariate Nonnormal Processes. *International Journal of Advanced Manufacturing Technology*, Vol. 50, pp. 823–830.

[3] Ahmad, S., Abdollahian, M., Zeephongsekul, P, Abbasi, B. (2009). Multivariate Non-normal Process Capability Analysis. *International Journal of Advanced Manufacturing Technology*, Vol. 44, pp. 757–765.

[4] Burr, I. W. (1942). Cumulative Frequency Distribution. *Annals of Mathematical Statistics*, Vol. 13, pp. 215–232.

[5] Box, G. E. P., Cox, D. R. (1964). An Analysis of Transformation. *Journal of Royal Statistical Society, Series B*, Vol. 26, No. 2, pp. 211–252.

[6] Boyles, R. A. (1994). Process Capability with Asymmetric Tolerances. *Communications in Statistics—Simulation and Computation*, Vol. 23, No. 3, pp. 162–175.

[7] Chang, Y. S., Bai, D. S. (2004). A Multivariate T^2 Control Chart for Skewed Populations Using Weighted Standard Deviations. *Quality and Reliability Engineering International*, Vol. 20, pp. 31–46.

[8] Chatterjee, M. (2019). Impact of Multivariate Normality Assumption on Multivariate Process Capability Indices. *Communications in Statistics — Case Studies and Data Analysis*, Vol. 5, pp. 314–345.

[9] Chen, H. (1994). A Multivariate Process Capability Index Over a Rectangular Solid Tolerance Zone. *Statistica Sinica*, vol. 4, pp. 749–758.

[10] Clements, J. A. (1989). Process Capability Calculations for Non-normal Distributions. *Quality Progress*, Vol. 22, No. 9, pp. 95–100.

[11] Das, N., Dwivedi, P. S. (2014). Multivariate Process Capability Index: A Review and Some Results. *Economic Quality Control*, Vol. 28, No. 2, pp. 151–166. DOI: https://doi.org/10.1515/eqc-2013-0022.

Bibliography

[12] Durling, F. C. (1975). The Bivariate Burr Distribution. *Statistical Distributions in Scientific Work*, Vol. 1, pp. 329–335.

[13] Field, C., Genton, M. C. (2006). The Multivariate g-and-h Distribution. *Technometrics*, Vol. 48, pp. 104–111.

[14] Han, C. -P. (2006). Effect of Testing Normality on Estimating Process Capability Indices. *Quality Engineering*. Vol. 18, pp. 391–395.

[15] Johnson, N.L. (1949). System of Frequency Curves Generated by Methods of Translation. *Biometrika*, Vol. 36, pp. 149–176.

[16] Karl. D. P., Morisette, J., Taam, W. (1994). Some Applications of a Multivariate Capability Index in Geometric Dimensioning and Tolerancing. *Quality Engineering*, Vol. 6, pp. 649–665.

[17] Kotz, S., Balakhrishnan, N., Johnson, N. L. (2000) Continuous Multivariate Distributions. Vol. I. John Wiley and Sons, INC. Second Edition.

[18] Luceno, A (1996). A Process Capability Index with Reliable Confidence Intervals. *Communications in Statistics—Simulation and Computation*, Vol 25, pp. 235–245.

[19] Metropolis, N., Rosenbluth, A. W., Teller, A. H. Teller, E. (1958). Equations of State Calculations by Fast Computing Machines.*Journal of Chemical Physics*, Vol. 21, pp.10087–1092.

[20] Moscoso, J.A.J., Arunachalam, V. (2011) Using Tukey's g and h Family of Distributions to Calculate Value-at-risk and Conditional Value-at-risk. *Journal of Risk* , Vol. 13, No. 4, pp. 95–116.

[21] Niaki, S. T. A., Abbasi, B. (2007). Skewness Reduction Approach in Multi-attribute Process Monitoring. *Communicationsnin Statistics – Theory and Methods*, Vol. 36, pp. 2313–2325.

[22] Pan, J. N., Lee, C. Y. (2010). New Capability Indices for Evaluating the Performance of Multivariate Manufacturing Processes. *Quality and Reliability engineering International*, Vol. 26, No. 1, pp. 3–15.

[23] Pan, J. N., Li, C. I., Shih, W. C. (2016). New Multivariate Process Capability Indices for Measuring the Performance of Multivariate Processes Subject to Non-normal Distributions. *International Journal of Quality and Reliability Management*, Vol. 33, pp. 42–61.

[24] Pickands, J. (1975). Statistical Inference Using the Extreme Order Statistics. *Annals of Statistics*, Vol. 3, pp. 119–131.

[25] Polansky, A. (2001). A Smooth Nonparametric Approach to Multivariate Process Capability. *Technometrics*, Vol. 53, No. 2, pp. 199–211.

Bibliography 235

[26] Rousseeuw, P. J., Ruts, I. (1999). The depth function of a population distribution. *Metrika*, Vol. 49, pp. 213–244.

[27] Scarborough. J. B. (2005). *Numerical Mathematical Analysis*. Oxford and IBH Publishing Co.

[28] Simon, M. (2014). Precision index in the multivariate context. *Communications in Statistics—Theory and Methods*, Vol. 43, No. 2, pp. 377–387.

[29] Smith, R. L. (1987). Estimating tails of probability distribution. (1987). *Annals of Statistics*, Vol. 15, pp. 1174–1207.

[30] Takahashi, K. (1965). Note on the multivariate Burr's distribution. *Annals of Institute of Statistical Mathematics*, Vol. 17, pp. 257–260.

[31] Tukey, J. W. (1977). Modern techniques in data analysis, NSF-sponsored regional research conference at Southern Massachusetts University, 1977, North Dartmouth, MA.

[32] Wang, F. K. (2006). Quality evaluation of a manufactured product with multiple characteristics. *Quality and Reliability Engineering International*, Vol. 22, pp. 225–236.

[33] Wang, F. K., Chen, J. C. (1998). Capability Index Using Principal Component Analysis. *Quality Engineering*, Vol. 11, No. 1, pp. 21–27.

[34] Wang, F. K., Du, T. C. T. (2000). Using Principal Component Analysis in Process Performance for Multivariate Data. *Omega*, Vol. 28, No. 2, pp. 185–194.

[35] Wang, F. K., Hubele, N. F. (2002). Quality evaluation of geometric tolerance regions in form and location. *Quality Engineering*, Vol. 14, pp. 203–209.

[36] Wingo, D. R. (1993). Maximum likelihood methods for fitting the Burr type XII distribution multiply (progressively) censored life test data. *Metrika*, Vol. 40, pp. 203–210.

[37] Wright, P. A. (1995). A Process Capability Index Sensitive to Skewness. *Journal of Statistical Computation and Simulation*, Vol. 52, pp. 195–203.

[38] Yeh, A. B., Chen, H. (2001). A nonparametric multivariate process capability index. *International Journal of Modelling and Simulation*, Vol. 21, pp. 218–223.

[39] Zuo, Y., Serfling, R. (2000). General notions of statistical depth functions. *Annals of statistics*, Vo. 28, pp. 461–482.

Chapter 11

Multivariate Process Capability Indices Based on Bayesian Approach

Chapter Summary

The literature of process capability indices (both univariate and multivariate) is dominated by frequentist approach. In Chapter 11, multivariate process capability indices (MPCIs) using another alternative approach, viz., the Bayesian one, are discussed along with some of their important statistical properties. A numerical example, comparing performances of these MPCIs is also described.

11.1 Introduction

The MPCIs discussed so far, despite having a number of differences from various perspectives (viz., types of specification, underlying distribution and so on) share one commonality, i.e., all of those MPCIs are defined using *frequentist approach*. In the present chapter, we shall discuss about MPCIs using *Bayesian approach*.

To begin with, one should know about the origin of the term "Bayesian". Thomas Bayes, a philosopher and statistician had formulated the so called *"Bayes theorem"*, which is discussed below:

Bayes Theorem

Suppose $B_1, B_2, \cdots, B_n$ be mutually exclusive and collectively exhaustive events such that $P(B_i) > 0$ for $i = 1(1)n$. Also, let A be another event, apart from $B_1, B_2, \cdots, B_n$, such that $P(A) > 0$. Then

$$P(B_1 \mid A) = \frac{P(B_i) \ P(A \mid B_i)}{\sum\limits_{i=1}^{n} P(B_i) \ P(A \mid B_i)}, \ \forall i = 1(1)n \qquad (11.1)$$

Proof:

From the definition of conditional probability,

$$P(A \mid B_i) \;=\; \frac{P(A \cap B_i)}{P(B_i)}$$

$$\Rightarrow P(A \cap B_i) \;=\; P(B_i) \times P(A \mid B_i) \tag{11.2}$$

$$P(B_i \mid A) \;=\; \frac{P(A \cap B_i)}{P(A)}$$

$$\Rightarrow P(A \cap B_i) \;=\; P(A) \times P(B_i \mid A) \tag{11.3}$$

Therefore, from equations (11.2) and (11.3),

$$P(A) \times P(B_i \mid A) \;=\; P(B_i) \times P(A \mid B_i)$$
$$\Rightarrow P(B_i \mid A) \;=\; \frac{P(B_i) \times P(A \mid B_i)}{P(A)} \tag{11.4}$$

Now, since $B_1, B_2, \cdots, B_n$ are assumed to be mutually exclusive and A is any other event apart from $B_1, B_2, \cdots, B_n$, hence, $A \cap B_1, A \cap B_2, \cdots, A \cap B_n$ are also mutually exclusive. Thus

$$
\begin{aligned}
P(A) \;&=\; P[\,(A \cap B_1) \cup (A \cap B_2) \cdots (A \cap B_n)\,] \\
&=\; \sum_{i=1}^{n} P(A \cap B_i) \\
&=\; \sum_{i=1}^{n} P(B_i)\, P(A \mid B_i), \text{ since } P(B_i) > 0 \tag{11.5}
\end{aligned}
$$

[The above is popularly known as theorem of total probability.]

Now, substituting the expression for $P(A)$ from equation (11.5) in equation (11.4) we have

$$
\begin{aligned}
P(B_i \mid A) \;&=\; \frac{P(B_i) \times P(A \mid B_i)}{P(A)} \\[2ex]
&=\; \frac{P(B_i) \times P(A \mid B_i)}{\sum\limits_{i=1}^{n} P(B_i)\, P(A \mid B_i)} \tag{11.6}
\end{aligned}
$$

This completes the proof of Bayes theorem.

Contradicting frequentist school of thought, Bayesian approach takes into

Bayesian MPCIs 238

account the prior information available from various sources along with the data in hand. This previous knowledge about the unknown parameter is popularly known as "prior distribution". Based on this and the available data, the actual expression of the distribution of the unknown parameter is constructed and this distribution is known as the posterior distribution.

A thorough discussion on Bayesian statistics is beyond the scope of this book. However, interested readers may refer to Gelman et al. [5], Ghosh et al. [6] and the references therein for a detail discussion on this topic.

It has been observed that like in the other streams of statistics, the literature of statistical quality control and in particular, process capability analysis is primarily dominated by frequentist or classical approach. As a result, PCIs (both univariate and multivariate), defined from Bayesian perspective, are grossly out numbered by classical indices.

Cheng and Spiring [4] were among the first to handle process capability problem from Bayesian perspective. They suggested an alternative way to compute proportion of nonconformance based on C_p and the available data, using Bayesian approach. Shiau et al. [11] have derived a mathematical expression for the posterior probability that a process under consideration is capable. They have also derived expression for the credible interval (Bayesian analogue of the so called confidence interval) for the popular univariate PCI, C_{pm}. Lin et al. [7] have proposed a Bayesian interval estimate of C_{pmk}''', a univariate PCI for asymmetric specifiction region. Interestingly, for both C_{pm} and C_{pmk}'', the underlying statistical distribution is too much complicated to have any simple formulation for their interval estimates confidence interval using frequentist approach. However, both Shiau et al. [11] and Lin et al. [7] have shown that this can be easily handled using Bayesian approach. Interested readers can refer to Pearn and Kotz [10] and the references therein, for a detailed discussion on Bayesian univariate process capability indices.

For multivariate processes, the field of research, viz., Bayesian process capability analysis, is grossly unexplored. The few Bayesian MPCIs, available in literature, will be discussed in detail now.

11.2 $C_b(D)$: A Bayesian MPCI Analogous to C_{pk}

Bernardo and Irony [1] have proposed a Bayesian PCI, which is applicable to both univariate and multivariate processes. In case of most of the existing MPCIs, it is assumed that the data in hand is merely a sample from a multivariate distribution. Also, due to the limitations of the measuring instruments and lack of expertise of the people handling those instruments, often accuracy of the data fluctuates. This apparent discretization of the otherwise continuous data affects its true nature. Unfortunately, these problems are seldom taken into consideration during process capability studies. To address this, Bernardo and Irony [1] have considered the problem of multivariate process capability analysis as a decision theoretic problem with two possible outcomes:

d_1 : Accept i.e., maintain the process at its current state;

d_2 : Reject i.e., look into the process for sorting out the problem.

Suppose in a production process, "N" numbers of items are produced of which a random sample of size "n" is drawn. Also suppose, there are "q" significant quality characteristics corresponding to the manufactured product under consideration. Consider the following notations.

1. x_i' is a q-component vector of unobserved values of the ith item corresponding to its actual measurement x_i, for $i = 1(1)N$. Here the notation " $'$ " segregates unobserved items from the observed ones.

2. $Z_N = \left\{x_1', x_N', \cdots, x_N'\right\}$ be a $(q \times N)$ matrix of unobserved observations for all the items produced;

3. y_i denotes actual measurement corresponding to x_i', $i = 1(1)n$. Note that, since y_i is sample data, it is subject to sampling error of various extent.

4. $D = \{y_1, y_2, \cdots, y_n\}$ is a $(q \times n)$ matrix of observed data.

5. $u(d_i, Z_N)$ is the utility function based on performance of the decision maker regarding acceptability of the two actions d_i, $i = 1, 2$.

6.
$$\overline{u}(d_i \mid D) = \int_{Z_N} u(d_i, Z_N) \, P(Z_N \mid D) \, dZ_N, \quad i = 1, 2 \qquad (11.7)$$

is the expected utility of the ith decision, for $i = 1, 2$.

For the purpose of computational simplicity, Bernardo and Irony [1] have considered linear utility function.

7. A : Acceptance region corresponding to the process.

Based on the above notations, Bernardo and Irony [1] have defined a Bayesian MPCI as,

$$C_b(D) = \frac{1}{3} \, \Phi^{-1} \left[P \, \{x \in A \mid D\}\right] \qquad (11.8)$$

$C_b(D)$ has a unique characteristic viz., it is invariant under any one-one transformation of the concerned quality characteristics. This is due to the fact that, $C_b(D)$ is a monotone function of $P \, \{x \in A \mid D\}$. Moreover, since $C_b(D)$ is a data based index, no estimation related complication is faced in this case.

Again, let $P\left(y_1', y_1', \cdots, y_n' \mid y_1, y_2, \cdots, y_n\right)$ be the joint posterior predictive distribution of an unknown sample $\left(y_1', y_1', \cdots, y_n'\right)$, which is of the same size as that of $(y_1, y_1, \cdots, y_n)$. Then, as required from the practical view-point, the robustness of this MPCI can be measured using the posterior predictive distribution which is given by

$$P(C_b \mid D) = P\left(C_b \mid y_1, y_2, \cdots, y_n\right)$$
$$= \int_{y_1} \int_{y_2} \cdots \int_{y_n} P\left(C_b \mid y_1', y_2', \cdots, y_n'\right)$$
$$\times P\left(y_1', y_1', \cdots, y_n' \mid y_1, y_2, \cdots, y_n\right) dy_1' \, dy_2' \cdots dy_n'$$

$$(11.9)$$

Bernardo and Irony [1] also established $C_b(D)$ as asymptotically equivalent to the popular univariate PCI, C_{pk}, under the following regulatory conditions:

1. Since C_{pk} is primarily defined for univariate normal distribution, the underlying process distribution for $C_b(D)$ is also assumed to be normal, to bring the indices to the same platform.

2. There is no error associated with the data, so that the original observation coincides with the observed one, i.e., $y_i = x_i$ for $i = 1(1)n$.

3. The sample under consideration is sufficiently large.

Observe that, unlike C_{pk}, which considers only one of the two specification limits (viz., the specification limit having smaller distance from μ), $C_b(D)$ takes both the specification limits into account and hence is more accurate than C_{pk}.

However, in practice measurement error is an inevitable part of data, whatever sophisticated the measuring instrument or whatever well trained the data collector may be. To take care of the measurement error occuring due to limitations of the measuring mechanism, Bernardo and Irony [1] have suggested a hierarchical model.

11.3 Vector Valued Multivariate Analogues of C_p and C_{pk} from Bayesian Perspective

By now, readers are acquainted to the fact that PCIs or MPCIs are mostly **single valued** assessment of capability of a process to produce items within a stipulated specification limits. However, this is not completely true. There are a number of vector valued MPCIs available in literature, a detail discussion on which is made in Chapter 13. Although most of these vector valued MPCIs are defined under frequentist approach, Niverthi and Dey [9] have proposed two vector valued MPCIs for multivariate analogues of C_p and C_{pk} and have studied their properties from Bayesian perspective. Since this chapter is dedicated to Bayesian multivariate process capability analysis, we found it logical to discuss these MPCIs in this chapter only.

Recall that, C_p and C_{pk} can be defined as

$$
\begin{aligned}
C_p &= \frac{USL - LSL}{6\sigma} \\
C_{pk} &= \min\left\{\frac{USL - \mu}{3\sigma}, \frac{\mu - LSL}{3\sigma}\right\}
\end{aligned}
\tag{11.10}
$$

Here, it is assumed that a random variable X characterizes the quality characteristic of interest and $X \sim N(\mu, \sigma^2)$. Now, under multivariate set-up, let there be "q" correlated quality characteristics represented by a q-component random vector $\boldsymbol{X}$ such that $\boldsymbol{X} \sim N_q(\boldsymbol{\mu}, \Sigma)$. Then analogous to C_p and C_{pk}, Niverthi and Dey [9] have defined

$$
C_p^{(ND)} = \frac{1}{c} \times \Sigma^{-1/2} (\boldsymbol{USL} - \boldsymbol{LSL})
\tag{11.11}
$$

$$
C_{pk}^{(ND)} = \frac{1}{c} \times \min\left\{\Sigma^{-1/2}(\boldsymbol{U} - \boldsymbol{\mu}), \Sigma^{-1/2}(\boldsymbol{\mu} - \boldsymbol{L})\right\}
\tag{11.12}
$$

where, c is a constant whose value can change based on the concerned MPCI. For example, C_p and C_{pk} have 6 and 3, respectively, as constants in their denominators. Similarly, one can assume $c = 3$ and $c = 6$ for $C_p^{(ND)}$ and $C_{pk}^{(ND)}$, respectively.

Now, since $\boldsymbol{\mu}$ and Σ are practically unobservable, one needs to use their plug-in estimators (natural estimators) as follows:

$$
\widehat{C_p}^{(ND)} = \frac{1}{c} \times \widehat{\Sigma}^{-1/2} (\boldsymbol{USL} - \boldsymbol{LSL})
\tag{11.13}
$$

$$
\widehat{C_{pk}}^{(ND)} = \frac{1}{c} \times \min\left\{\widehat{\Sigma}^{-1/2}(\boldsymbol{U} - \widehat{\boldsymbol{\mu}}), \widehat{\Sigma}^{-1/2}(\widehat{\boldsymbol{\mu}} - \boldsymbol{L})\right\}
\tag{11.14}
$$

where $\widehat{\boldsymbol{\mu}}$ and $\widehat{\Sigma}$ denote sample mean vector and sample dispersion matrix, respectively.

Evidently, the statistical distributions of $\widehat{C_p}^{(ND)}$ and $\widehat{C_{pk}}^{(ND)}$ are mathematically intractable. Niverthi and Dey have advocated use of Bayesian framework as a more pragmative alternative.

Suppose "n" samples are drawn from the process under consideration such that, $X_i \sim N_q(X, \Sigma)$ for $i = 1(1)n$. Now, unlike frequentist approach, where μ and Σ are assumed to be unknown constants, in Bayesian set-up, these are considered as random vectors/ matrices (as the case may be) having specific statistical distributions. Niverthi and Dey [9] have considered the following prior distributions of μ and Σ:

$$\mu \sim N_q(\mu_0, \tau^2 I_q) \tag{11.15}$$

$$\text{and } R = \Sigma^{-1} \sim W_q(\nu, R_0) \tag{11.16}$$

where $E[R] = \nu R_0$; μ_0 and τ are noninformative hyper-parameters, whose values are assumed to be known from the data in hand; I_q is a q- dimensional identity matrix; $W_q(\nu, R_0)$ denotes a q- variate Wishart distribution with degrees of freedom ν and scale matrix R_0. Based on these, conditional distributions of (i) X given μ and $R = \Sigma^{-1}$; (ii) μ given μ_0 and τ^2 and (iii) R given ν and R_0 can be obtained as follows:

$$f(X \mid \mu, R) = \frac{1}{(2\pi)^{nq/2}} \times |R|^{n/2} \times e^{-\frac{1}{2} \sum_{i=1}^{n} (X_i - \mu)' R (X_i - \mu)}$$

$$\tag{11.17}$$

$$f(\mu \mid \mu_0, \tau^2) = \frac{1}{(2\pi)^{q/2} \times |\tau^2 I_q|^{\frac{1}{2}}}$$
$$\times e^{-\frac{1}{2}(\mu - \mu_0)' (\tau^2 I_q)^{-1} (\mu - \mu_0)} \tag{11.18}$$

$$f(R \mid \nu, R_0) \propto |R|^{\frac{\nu - q - 1}{2}} \times e^{-\frac{1}{2 \, tr(RR_0^{-1})}} \tag{11.19}$$

To generate the posterior statistical distributions of μ and R, Gibbs sampling technique has been used. Based on those posterior distributions, the posterior distributions of C_p^{ND} and C_{pk}^{ND} can be obtained.

However, this being a data driven approach, one must make sure that the data quality is satisfactory. Also observe that, both $C_p^{(ND)}$ and $C_{pk}^{(ND)}$ are vector valued MPCIs, ith component of the vector giving capability index value for the ith quality characteristic, for $i = 1(1)q$. The authors themselves have acknowledged that this research do not include the case where one has to decide about the overall process capability level while for some of the quality characteristics the component index values are poor, and for the others, the values are satisfactory. In fact, the quality characteristics being correlated and this being taken care of by Σ, it may not often be logical to consider component level index values. Also, similar to all other vector based MPCIs, it becomes difficult to compare two processes based on their $C_p^{(ND)}$ and $C_{pk}^{(ND)}$ values as one process may have higher values of some component level indices, while for the rest, the other process may show better result. Finally, Mingoti and Oliviera [8] have shown that $C_p^{(ND)}$ and $C_{pk}^{(ND)}$ tend to under estimate process capability particularly, when the process is off-centered.

11.4 A Numerical Example

Niverthi and Dey [9] have discussed a dataset on aircraft manufacturing, originally collected by Pratt and Whitney Company. In the dataset, there are 10 different quality characteristics all belonging to engine of the aircrafts under consideration and for each of these quality characteristics, 50 measurements (in centimeter) have been taken. Thus, here $q = 10$. Also, vectors of upper and lower specification limits for the process are

$$\begin{aligned} \boldsymbol{USL} \quad = \quad & (6.397, 0.060, 8.302, 7.896, 22.051, \\ & 1.856, 7.302, 6.396, 3.052, 23.6810)' \end{aligned}$$

and

$$\begin{aligned} \boldsymbol{LSL} \quad = \quad & (6.393, 0.594, 8.294, 7.892, 22.047, \\ & 1.852, 7.298, 6.390, 3.038, 23.6770)' \end{aligned}$$

respectively.

The detailed data are available in Niverthi and Dey's [9] article.

In order to have the so-called noninformative prior, Niverthi and Dey [9] have considered $\nu = 13$, $R_0 = 10^7 I_{10}$. Note that, here choice of R_0 as a diagonal matrix ensures computational simplicity. Values of the other hyper parameters are

$$\begin{aligned} \boldsymbol{\mu_0} \quad = \quad & (6.395, 0.597, 8.298, 7.894, 22.049, \\ & 1.854, 7.300, 6.393, 3.045, 23.679)', \end{aligned}$$

which is precisely the midpoint between $\boldsymbol{USL}$ and $\boldsymbol{LSL}$, and $\tau^2 = 10^7$. Values of the components of $C_p^{(ND)}$ and $C_{pk}^{(ND)}$ are given in Table 11.1.

From Table 11.1, it is evident that, except MQI445, all the other quality characteristics have indices values more than one. Moreover, although Niverthi and Dey [9], going by the general convention, considered 1 as the threshold value for component level index values of each quality characteristics, no mathematical justification was given for this. In fact, in many of the cases, for processes having multiple correlated quality characteristics, threshold value is found to be a function of the dispersion matrix itself (refer Chatterjee and

TABLE 11.1: Component level $C_p^{(ND)}$ and C_{pk}^{ND} values for the 10 quality characteristics (refer Niverthi and Dey [9])

Name of Quality Characteristic	$C_p^{(ND)}$	$C_{pk}^{(ND)}$
MQI128	3.0903	2.8862
MQI444	1.1872	1.1370
MQI445	0.9604	0.9034
MQI504	1.8472	1.7311
MQI512	1.2465	1.1014
MQI519	2.3974	1.9423
MQI203	1.5014	1.3155
MQI434	1.5099	1.4043
MQI482	1.6676	1.3108
MQI514	2.7970	2.5961

Chakraborty [2, 3]). Also, in a correlated set-up, making a decision about the individual quality characteristics, as is done here, may not always lead to right conclusion. Finally, as has already been discussed, Niverthi and Dey [9], themselves, have pointed out that it is difficult to make a consolidated decision about the process performance-based on the values in Table 11.1, as some of the quality characteristics (in this case MQI445 only) may not show satisfactory result, while the others may be performing well.

Let us now apply Bernardo and Irony's [1] MPCI viz., $C_b(D)$ to the same dataset. The computed values using 1000 bootstrap samples and considering the importance sample estimate of the index, are given in Table 11.2.

TABLE 11.2: Computed values of $C_b(D)$ using 1000 bootstrap samples [9]

	Conformance Probability	$C_b(D)$
Mean	0.9367	0.5091
Standard Deviation	0.00312	0.13795

From table 11.2, it is evident that the process produces considerably high amount of nonconforming items (around 6.33%) and the average $C_b(D)$ value so also low, viz., 0.5091, indicating toward poor capability level of the process.

Thus, here Bernardo and Irony's [1] bayesian MPCI is better conclussive than that of Niverthi and Dey [9]. The problem with the later being the common problem of almost all vector valued MPCIs, i.e. one component of the capability vector may indicate toward satisfactory process performance, while another may show completely opposite result (refer to chapter 13 for more detail discussion on this).

11.5 Concluding Remark

Parallel to the frequentist approach, process capability analysis and in general, statistical quality control from Bayesian perspective is gaining interest of researchers day by day. However, still the researches in this field are largely out-numbered by those carried out using classical approach. To the best of our knowledge, only two research articles, dedicated to bayesian approach, are available in literature. As a result, there remains ample scope of research in this area. Finally, although some Bayesian MPCIs (discussed in this chapter) are available in literature, they are hardly used in practice. Infact, practitioner, who are the end users of these MPCIs, are often apprehensive about using Bayesian techniques due to lack of knowledge about it. A proper training regarding this is an utmost necessity.

Bibliography

[1] Bernardo, J. M. and Irony, T. Z. (1996). A General Multivariate Bayesian Process Capability Index. *The Statistician*, Vol. 45, No. 3, pp. 487–502.

[2] Chatterjee, M., Chakraborty, A. K. (2016). Some Process Capability Indices for Unilateral Specification Limits—Their Properties and the Process Capability Control Charts. *Communications in Statistics—Theory and Methods*. Vol. 45, No. 24, pp. 7130–7160.

[3] Chakraborty, A. K., Chatterjee, M. (2020). Distributional and Inferential Properties of Some New Multivariate Process Capability Indices for Symmetric Specification Region. *Quality and Reliability Engineering International*. DOI:10.1002/qre.2783.

[4] Cheng, S. W., Spiring, F. A. (1989). Assessing Process Capability: A Bayesian Approach. *IIE transactions*, pp. 97–98. DOI: 10.1080/07408178908966212.

[5] Gelman, A., Carlin, J. B., Stern, H. S., Dunson, D. B., Vehtari, A., Rubin, D. B. (2013) . Bayesian Data Analysis. CRC Press, 2nd edn.

[6] Ghosh, J.K., Delampady, M., Samanta, T. (2006). An Introduction to Bayesian Analysis—Theory and Methods. Springer.

[7] Lin, T. Y., Wu, C. -W., Chen, J. C., Chiou, Y. H. (2011) Applying Bayesian Approach to Assess Process Capability for Asymmetric Tolerances Based on $C_{pmk}^{''}$ index. *Applied Mathematical Modelling*, Vol. 35, pp. 4473–4489.

[8] Mingoti, S. A., Oliveira, F. L. P. (2011). On Capability Indices for Multivariate Autocorrelated Processes. *Brazilian Journal of Operations and Production Management*, Vol. 8, pp. 133–152.

[9] Niverthi, M., Dey, D. (2000). Multivariate Process Capability a Bayesian Perspective. *Communications in Statistics—Simulation and Computation*, Vol. 29, No. 2, pp. 667–687.

[10] Pearn, W. L., Kotz, S. (2007). *Encyclopedia and Handbook of Process Capability Indices—Series on Quality, Reliability and Engineering Statistics*. Singapore: World Scientific.

[11] Shiau, J. J. H., Chiang. C. T., Hung, H. N. (1999). A Bayesian Procedure for Process Capability Assessment. *Quality and Reliability Engineering International*, Vol. 15, pp. 369–368.

Chapter 12

Multivariate Process Capability Indices for Autocorrelated Data

Chapter Summary

One of the major problems of handling data, both for one -dimensional and multidimensional processes, is the presence of autocorrelation(s). Unless proper care is taken, this may lead to misinterpretation of the computed values of the multivariate process capability indices (MPCIs). In Chapter 12, methods are described to handle autocorrelation, while computing MPCIs. Using numerical examples, it is shown that, the modified versions of the well known MPCIs (discussed in this chapter) for autocorrelated data are safer even when the practitioner is not sure about the possible existence of autocorrelation.

12.1 Introduction

The multivariate process capability indices (MPCIs) discussed so far inherently make a strong assumption, viz., all the observations are mutually independent. However, if a process is observed closely, then it can be easily noticed that, this assumption is often not valid, i.e., outcome of a process at a particular time point is closely related to its predecessor.

Addressing this problem will be easier, if the sequence of observed values of the quality characteristics under consideration are considered to be originated from a time series model. This naturally raises the question *"What is a time series model?"*

In the simplest of its form, a time series may be defined as a collection of observations X_t, each of which is recorded at a time "t". Alternatively, when a data is collected sequentially over time, it is known as a time series data. Thus, in time series, each observation may be correlated to its neighbour.

Suppose $\{X_t\}$ is a time series data with finite mean $\mu_t = E(X_t)$. Then its auto-covariance function of lag, say, "h" is defined as the simple covariance between the tth observation and $(t + h)^{\text{th}}$ observation, for $h = 0, 1, 2, \cdots$. Notationally,

$$\gamma(h) \quad = \quad Cov\,(X_{t+h}, X_t) \tag{12.1}$$
$$= \quad E\,[(X_{t+h} - \mu_t t + h)\,(X_t - \mu_t)] \tag{12.2}$$

Accordingly, the autocorrelation function (acf) can be defined as

$$\rho(h) \quad = \quad Corr\,(X_{t+h}, X_t)$$
$$= \quad \frac{\gamma(h)}{\gamma(0)} \tag{12.3}$$

Thus, acf measures correlation between the current and the previous observations and hence plays an important role in process capability analysis and statistical quality control in general. Infact, if the observations are positively correlated, then there is a general tendency of the PCIs to overestimate actual process capability (refer Mingoti and Oliveira [3]). Thorough study on the impact of autocorrelation on univariate PCIs, C_p and C_{pk}, have been carried out by Zhang [9]. Later Guevara and Vargas [1] extended this study for C_{pm} and C_{pmk}. Capability analysis of autocorrelated processes is even more complicated, since here one has to deal with more than one correlated quality characteristics and the observations are not mutually independent either.

In the present chapter, some MPCIs defined for autocorrelated data have been discussed.

12.2 MPCIs Analogous to C_p for Autocorrelated Processes

As has already been discussed time and again, C_p is the simplest measure of univariate process capability and is widely accepted among practitioners. As a result, when multiple correlated quality characteristics are required to be simultaneously, C_p has been the motivation for defining many MPCIs. This is true for autocorrelated processes as well.

Recall from our earlier discussions in Chapter 6 that, Taam et al. [8] defined a multivariate analogue of C_p viz, MC_p as

$$MC_p \quad = \quad \frac{(\prod\limits_{i=1}^{q} d_i) \times \pi^{q/2} \times [\Gamma\left(\frac{q}{2}\right) + 1]^{-1}}{|\Sigma|^{1/2} \times (\pi k_q)^{q/2} \times [\Gamma(q/2 + 1)]^{-1}} \tag{12.4}$$

where q is the number of correlated quality characteristics and $d_i = \frac{USL_i - LSL_i}{2}$, for $i = 1(1)q$.

Later Pan and Lee [7] showed that, while defining modified engineering tolerance region, MC_p does not take the prevailing correaltion structure among the variables into account and hence has a general tendency to overestimate process capability. They modified MC_p to define a new MPCI, viz.,

$$
\begin{aligned}
NMC_p &= \frac{|A^*|^{1/2}(\pi\chi^2_{1-\alpha,q})^{q/2}[\Gamma\left(\frac{q}{2}+1\right)]^{-1}}{|\Sigma|^{1/2}(\pi\chi^2_{1-\alpha,q})^{q/2}[\Gamma\left(\frac{q}{2}+1\right)]^{-1}} \\
&= \frac{|A^*|}{|\Sigma|}
\end{aligned} \tag{12.5}
$$

where A^* is a $(q \times q)$ matrix whose $(i,j)^{\text{th}}$ element is given by

$$
\rho_{ij}\left(\frac{USL_i - LSL_i}{2\sqrt{\chi^2_{q,1-\alpha}}}\right) \times \left(\frac{USL_j - LSL_j}{2\sqrt{\chi^2_{q,1-\alpha}}}\right)
$$

It is quite logical that, for a multivariate process, the quality characteristics being correlated, the corresponding MPCIs will be defined as functions of the dispersion matrix Σ. Now, for an autocorrelated process, this Σ matrix will be contaminated by the autocorrelations among the observations. To address this issue, Mingoti and Oliveira [3] and Pan and Huang [6] advocated replacing the Σ matrix by the corresponding auto-covariance matrix, say $\Gamma(0)$, where, $\Gamma(0)$ is defined as

$$
\Gamma(0) = \Phi\Gamma(0)\Phi' + \Theta\Sigma\Theta' - \Phi\Sigma\Theta' - \Theta\Sigma\Phi' + \Sigma \tag{12.6}
$$

where Θ and Φ are the moving average matrices corresponding to the time series data under consideration.

Accordingly, Pan and Huang [6] modified MC_p and NMC_p to define new MPCIs suitable for autocorrelated data as

$$
MAC_p = \frac{\prod\limits_{i=1}^{q} r_i}{\left(\chi^2_{1-\alpha,q}\right)^{q/2} \times |\Gamma(0)|^{1/2}} \tag{12.7}
$$

$$
NMAC_p = \left(\frac{|A^*|}{|\Gamma(0)|}\right)^{1/2} \tag{12.8}
$$

12.3 MPCIs Analogous to C_{pm} for Autocorrelated Processes

Again, recall from Chapter 3 that, in the context of univariate process capability analysis, since C_p remains invariant to the change in process centering, C_{pm} was defined to take into account the squared error loss incurred due to deviation of process mean from the stipulated target. Later, Taam et al. [8] and Pan and Lee [7], among others, have proposed multivariate analogues of C_{pm} as follows:

$$MC_{pm} \quad = \quad \frac{MC_p}{D} \tag{12.9}$$

$$NMC_{pm} \quad = \quad \frac{NMC_p}{D} \tag{12.10}$$

where, $D = \sqrt{1 + (\boldsymbol{\mu} - \boldsymbol{T})'\Sigma^{-1}(\boldsymbol{\mu} - \boldsymbol{T})}$,

and MC_p and NMC_p are as defined in equations (12.4) and (12.5), respectively. A detailed discussion on these MPCIs is available in Chapter 6.

Then, by replacing the process dispersion matrix viz., Σ by the corresponding auto-covariance matrix $\Gamma(0)$, in equations (12.9) and (12.10), Pan and Huang [6] have defined MPCIs for auto-correlated processes as

$$MAC_{pm} \quad = \quad \frac{MC_p}{D_\Gamma} \tag{12.11}$$

$$NMAC_{pm} \quad = \quad \frac{NMC_p}{D_\Gamma} \tag{12.12}$$

where, $D_\Gamma = \sqrt{1 + (\boldsymbol{\mu} - \boldsymbol{T})'\Gamma(0)^{-1}(\boldsymbol{\mu} - \boldsymbol{T})}$

12.4 MPCIs for Autocorrelated Processes Having Unilateral Specification Region

The autocorrelated MPCIs discussed so far, are designed for processes having bilateral specification regions. However, many a times the quality characteristics under consideration may be of smaller the better or larger the better types, requiring only one specification limit. This makes the specification region unilateral. Now, for univariate processes, the most popular PCIs for unilateral specification region are

$$C_{pu} = \frac{USL - \mu}{3\sigma} \tag{12.13}$$

$$C_{pl} = \frac{\mu - LSL}{3\sigma} \tag{12.14}$$

Then, following Niverthy and Dey's [4] approach, multivariate analogues of C_{pu} and C_{pl} can be defined as

$$NMC_{pu} = \frac{1}{3}\Sigma^{-1} \times (\boldsymbol{USL} - \boldsymbol{\mu}) \tag{12.15}$$

$$NMC_{pl} = \frac{1}{3}\Sigma^{-1} \times (\boldsymbol{\mu} - \boldsymbol{LSL}) \tag{12.16}$$

Similar to the previous cases, Pan and Huang [6] have defined MPCI for autocorrelated processes, when the quality characteristics are of smaller the better type as

$$NMAC_{pu} = \frac{1}{3}\,\Gamma(0)^{-1} \times (\boldsymbol{USL} - \boldsymbol{\mu}) \tag{12.17}$$

Similarly, for larger the better type of quality characteristics, one may define

$$NMAC_{pl} = \frac{1}{3}\,\Gamma(0)^{-1} \times (\boldsymbol{\mu} - \boldsymbol{LSL}) \tag{12.18}$$

However, both C_{pu} and C_{pl}, though widely used in practice for their computational simplicity, suffer from a number of drawbacks. These are discussed in detail in Chapter 3. As a result, mere generalization of these indices in mutivariate dimensions, as are done in cases of NMC_{pu}, NMC_{pl}, $NMAC_{pu}$, and $NMAC_{pl}$ inherits all these drawbacks.

12.5   Data Analysis

Pan and Huang [6] have discussed, using a numerical example, the applications of MAC_p and $NMAC_p$ when data sufers from autocorrelation. Unfortunately, in practice, often possible existence of autocorrelation is not checked before applying an MPCI. In order to handle those cases, we shall now consider Pal's [5] data, which does not suffer from autocorrelation. In this context, Pal [5] has discussed about a dataset on a particular type of bobbin having two major quality characteristics viz., its height and weight.

MPCIs for autocorrelated data 253

A detailed discussion on the data is available in Chapter 4. We shall now explore performances of MC_p, MAC_p, NMC_p, and $NMAC_{pm}$ based on Pal's [5] dataset. The computed values are given in Table 12.1.

TABLE 12.1: Data on the coordinates of the centers of 20 drilled holes

MC_p	MAC_p	MC_{pm}	MAC_{pm}	NMC_p	$NMAC_p$	NMC_{pm}	$NMAC_{pm}$
1.1674	1.1846	0.2732	0.2889	1.1548	1.0148	0.2703	0.2474

From Table 12.1 it is evident that, similar to Pal's [5] original conclusion about the process, the small values of MC_{pm}, MAC_{pm}, NMC_{pm}, and $NMAC_{pm}$ indiate toward poor performance of the process. On the contrary, although the computed values of MC_p, MAC_p, NMC_p, and $NMAC_p$ are quite high, unlike Pal's [5] case, it is difficult to conclude whether the process is potentially capable or not, due to unavailability of any threshold value.

Interestingly, here MC_p and MAC_p; NMC_p and $NMAC_p$; MC_{pm} and MAC_{pm}; NMC_{pm} and $NMAC_{pm}$ have very close values, which implies, if the data do not suffer from autocorrelation, the new MPCIs by Pan and Huang [6] perform similar to the original ones given by Taam et al. [8] and pan and Lee [7]. To be more precise, in such cases, the computed values of MAC_p and MAC_{pm} are slightly higher than those of MC_p and MC_{pm}; while the computed values of $NMAC_p$ and $NMAC_{pm}$ are slightly lower than those of NMC_p and NMC_{pm}.

Therefore, if existence of (multivariate) autocorrelation is not checked before-hand, which is usually the case, one should use Pan and Huang's [6] MPCIs to be on the safer side.

12.6 Concluding Remarks

Autocorrelation in a dataset is like a myth, which almost all believe to exist, but very few dare to face. The problem gets more acute with the increase in the dimension of the data. Pan and Huang [6] and Mingoti and Oliveira [3] have made a significant contribution by raising this issue in the context of multivariate process capability analysis. However, similar studies need to be carried out for other types of MPCIs as well. For example, MC_p and MC_{pm} and to some extent, NMC_p and NMC_{pm} tend to overestimate process capability. This drawback is likely to be inherited by MAC_p, MAC_{pm}, $NMAC_p$, and $NMAC_{pm}$ as well. Similarly, C_{pu} and C_{pl} are very primitive PCIs for univariate processes having unilateral specification limits. Hence their direct generalizations, (as is done in cases of NMC_{pu} and consequently, $NMAC_{pu}$) will also have same limitations.

Bibliography

[1] Guevara, R. D., Vargas, J. A. (2007). Revista Colombiana de Estadistica, Vol. 30, pp. 301–316.

[2] Mingoti, S. A., Gloria, F. A. A. (2008). Comparing Mingoti and Glória's and Niverthi and Dey's Multivariate Capability Indices. Produção, Vol. 18, No. 3, pp. 598–608. http://dx.doi.org/10.1590/S0103-65132008000300014.

[3] Mingoti, S. A., Oliveira, F. L. P. (2011). On Capability Indices for Multivariate Autocorrelated Processes. *Brazilian Journal of Production and Management*, Vol. 8, No. 1, pp. 133–152.

[4] Niverthi, M., Dey, D. (2000). Multivariate Process Capability a Bayesian perspective. *Communications in Statistics—Simulation and Computation*, Vol. 29, No. 2, pp. 667–687.

[5] Pal, S. (1999). Performance Evaluation of a Bivariate Normal Process. *Quality Engineering*, Vol. 11, No. 3, pp. 379–386.

[6] Pan, J. N., Huang, W. K. C. (2015). Developing New Multivariate Process Capability Indices for Autocorrelated Data. *Quality and Reliability Engineering International*, Vol. 31, pp. 431–444.

[7] Pan, J. N., Lee, C. Y. (2010). New Capability Indices for Evaluating the Performance of Multivariate Manufacturing Processes. *Quality and Reliability engineering International*, Vol. 26, No. 1, pp. 3–15.

[8] Taam, W., Subbaiah, P., Liddy, W. (1993). A Note on Multivariate Capability Indices. *Journal of Applied Statistics*, Vol. 20, No. 3, pp. 339–351.

[9] Zhang, N.F. (1998). Estimating Process Capability Indexes for Autocorrelated data. *Journal of Applied Statistics*, Vol. 25, pp. 559–574.

Chapter 13

Multivariate Process Capability Vectors

Chapter Summary

Most of the multivariate process capability indices (MPCIs) are, by definition, single valued. However, a parallel school of thought is to consider a vector of indices for multicharacteristic processes. According to them, such a vector of indices will represent capability of that process more accurately, than its single valued counter-part. These type of MPCIs are called multivariate process capability vectors (MPCVs). In Chapter 13, some MPCVs, available in literature, are discussed in detail. These MPCVs include MPCVs for bilateral and unilateral specification regions and MPCVs measuring incapability of a process. A numerical example is also discussed to explore merits and demerits of using MPCVs in practice.

13.1   Introduction

A process capability index for univariate situation, by definition, is a single valued measurement of the overall capability of a process. This definition mostly holds good, even when the process consists of multiple correlated quality characteristics.

However, some researchers advocate vector valued representation of process capability indices, particularly for multivariate processes (refer Hubele et al. [9], Kotz and Johnson [10], Shahriari and Abdollahzadeh [15] and Shahriari et al. [16]). In order to have proper knowledge of the performance of a process, one has to consider process centering, process dispersion, and position of the process region with respect to the specification region. According to this school of thought, combining all these parameters to unify them and have a single valued assessment of process performance, may over-simplify the scenario resulting in erroneous conclusion. Though the concern for, the necessity of having a single value indicating capability of a multivariate process, can not be denied.

256

Multivariate Process Capability Vectors 257

In the present chapter, a thorough discussion has been made about some multivariate process capability vectors (MPCVs) available in literature. These MPCVs cover both bilateral and unilateral specification regions.

13.2 Multivariate Process Capability Vectors for Bilateral Specification Region − A Modification of Traditional MPCIs

The MPCV defined by Hubele et al. [9] was further improvised by Shahriari et al. [16].

Both Hubele et al. [9] and Shahriari et al. [16] considered a three-component MPCV. Suppose a q- component random vector $\boldsymbol{X}$ characterizing the process region is such that, $\boldsymbol{X} \sim N_q(\boldsymbol{\mu}, \Sigma)$. Then the first component of the MPCV is defined as

$$
C_{pM} = \left[\frac{\text{Volume of the engineering tolerance region}}{\text{Volume of the modified process region}} \right]^{\frac{1}{q}}
$$

(13.1)

Note that, in its most general form, the engineering tolerance region is not restricted to the most popular rectangular tolerance region only. Rather, it may be of any feasible shape supported by geometric dimensioning and tolerancing (GD & T), as discussed by Taam et al. [17]. Also, here the term "modified process region" implies "the smallest region similar in shape to the engineering tolerance region, circumscribing a specified probability contour" (refer Wang et al. [18]). Under multivariate normality assumption, this constant contour process region is nothing but the ellipsoid given by

$$
(\boldsymbol{X} - \boldsymbol{\mu})' \Sigma^{-1} (\boldsymbol{X} - \boldsymbol{\mu}) \leq \chi^2_{(\alpha, q)}
$$

(13.2)

Therefore, this ellipsoid is centered at $\boldsymbol{\mu}$.

Now, when the specification region is rectangular, with the upper specification limit (USL) and lower specification limit (LSL) of the ith quality characteristic being given by USL_i and LSL_i, respectively, for $i = 1(1)q$, then equation (13.1) may be modified as

$$
C_{pM} = \left[\frac{\text{Volume of rectangular specification region}}{\text{Volume of the modified process region}} \right]^{\frac{1}{q}}
$$

$$
= \left[\frac{\prod_{i=1}^{q} (USL_i - LSL_i)}{\text{Volume of the modified process region}} \right]^{\frac{1}{q}}
$$

(13.3)

Also, the modified process region being of the same shape as the specification region, it will now be the smallest rectangle circumscribing the elliptical process region. Shahriari et al. [16] have shown that edges of this rectangular modified process region can be obtained by solving the system of equations obtained from the first derivative of the quadratic form

$$(\boldsymbol{X} - \boldsymbol{\mu})'\Sigma^{-1}(\boldsymbol{X} - \boldsymbol{\mu}) = \chi^2_{(\alpha,q)} \tag{13.4}$$

with respect to X_i, for $i = 1(1)q$. Observe that for each X_i, there will be two solutions to the above quadratic form, which will give the upper and lower limits corresponding to the ith quality characteristic. Let these be named as UPL_i and LPL_i, respectively. Then

$$\text{UPL}_i = \mu_i + \sqrt{\frac{\chi^2_{(\alpha,q)}|\Sigma_i^{-1}|}{|\Sigma^{-1}|}} \tag{13.5}$$

$$\text{LPL}_i = \mu_i - \sqrt{\frac{\chi^2_{(\alpha,q)}|\Sigma_i^{-1}|}{|\Sigma^{-1}|}} \tag{13.6}$$

for $i = 1(1)q$, where $\chi^2_{(\alpha,q)}$ is the upper $100\alpha\%$ point of χ^2 distribution with "q" degrees of freedom and Σ_i is a matrix obtained by deleting ith row and ith column from Σ (refer Shahriari et al. [16] and Wang et al. [18]).

Therefore, from equation (13.3), the final expression of the first component of the MPCV, viz., C_{pM} can be obtained as

$$C_{pM} = \left[\frac{\prod_{i=1}^{q}(USL_i - LSL_i)}{\prod_{i=1}^{q}(UPL_i - LPL_i)}\right]^{\frac{1}{q}}$$

$$= \left[\prod_{i=1}^{q}\left\{\frac{(USL_i - LSL_i)}{(UPL_i - LPL_i)}\right\}\right]^{\frac{1}{q}} \tag{13.7}$$

Wang et al. [18] have observed that, since UPL_i and LPL_i are functions of the probability contour (determined by the underlying process distribution), the modified process region is not obtained as a proportional change to the specification region.

It is evident from equation (13.7) that, when C_{pM} assumes a value greater than 1, i.e., when the volume of the so-called "modified process region" is smaller than the volume of the specification region, it indicates satisfactory process performance.

On the contrary, for a value of C_{pM} less than 1, the situation is just the opposite. In such a case, the rectangular "modified process region" is not fully accommodated by the specification region, which means, the process

Multivariate Process Capability Vectors 259

suffers from high level of dispersion and hence their remains ample scope for improvement.

Thus, C_{pM}, though sounds like the univariate PCI, C_{pm}, actually acts like the univariate PCI C_p and takes care of the process dispersion only.

The second component of MPCV is for process centering. Here it is assumed that the specification region is perfectly centered on target, i.e., the specification region is symmetric about the stipulated target.

The second component of MPCV is then defined as

$$PV = P\left(T^2 > \frac{q(n-1)}{n-q} \times F_{q,n-q}\right) \tag{13.8}$$

where $F_{q,n-q}$ denotes F distribution with q and $n-q$ degrees of freedom. Here

$$T^2 = n(\overline{X} - \mu)'\widehat{\Sigma}^{-1}(\overline{X} - \mu) \tag{13.9}$$

is a Hotelling T^2 statistic.

Observe that, unlike C_{pM}, PV is a probability and hence its value ranges between 0 and 1. A value of PV close to 1 implies that the process center is close to the stipulated target; while PV value close to 0 implies that the process is highly off-centered.

The third component of MPCV compares position of the modified process region with respect to the specification region. For a bivariate process, i.e., for $q = 2$, Hubele et al. [9] have defined LI as

$$\begin{aligned}
LI \quad = \quad \max\bigg[&1, \frac{|UPL_1 - LSL_1|}{USL_1 - LSL_1}, \frac{|LPL_1 - USL_1|}{USL_1 - LSL_1}, \\
&\frac{|UPL_2 - LSL_2|}{USL_2 - LSL_2}, \frac{|LPL_2 - USL_2|}{USL_2 - LSL_2}\bigg]
\end{aligned}$$

$$\tag{13.10}$$

which can be easily generalized, for $q > 2$, as

$$LI \quad = \quad \max\left[1, \max_{i=1(1)q} \frac{|UPL_i - LSL_i|}{USL_i - LSL_i}, \frac{|LPL_i - USL_i|}{USL_i - LSL_i}\right]$$

$$\tag{13.11}$$

Shahriari et al. [16] have redefined LI as

$$LI = \begin{cases} 1, & \text{If modified rectangular process region is fully} \\ & \quad \text{accommodated within the tolerance region} \\ 0, & \text{Otherwise} \end{cases} \tag{13.12}$$

Thus, from equations (13.7), (13.8), and (13.12), the final form of the MPCV will be a three component vector given by $[C_{pM}, PV, LI]$.

Wang et al. [18] have observed that, since computation of MPCV involves the tolerance region and the modified process region, which is reshaped similar to the tolerance region, the geometric aspects and the associated computations may become challenging at times, especially when the original tolerance region itself is complicated, say frustum shaped.

It may be noted that, the basic difference between the first component of Shahriari et al.'s [16] MPCV and Taam et al's [17] MC_p is that, in the first case, process region is modified to give it the form of the tolerance region; while in the second case, the tolerance region is modified to the shape of the process region.

We have discussed in detail in Chapter 6 that, the problem of over-estimation while using MC_p and MC_{pm} is due to the fact that, the volume of the tolerance region (numerator of MC_p) is independent of the process dispersion matrix (refer Pan and Lee [14]).

Shahriari and Abdollahzadeh [15] have proposed a modification to the above problem by proposing a new MPCV. Following Shahriari and Abdollahzadeh [15], the modified tolerance region may be defined as

$$(\boldsymbol{X} - \boldsymbol{T})' \Sigma^{-1} (\boldsymbol{X} - \boldsymbol{T}) \leq c'^2, \tag{13.13}$$

where c' may be defined as

$$c' = \begin{cases} \min\left\{ \frac{USL_i - T_i}{\sqrt{\sigma_{ii}}}, \ i = 1(1)q \right\}, & \text{when } T_i = \frac{USL_i + LSL_i}{2} \\[2em] \min\left\{ \min\left\{ \frac{USL_i - T_i}{\sqrt{\sigma_{ii}}}, \frac{T_i - LSL_i}{\sqrt{\sigma_{ii}}} \right\}, \ i = 1(1)q \right\}, \\[1em] \qquad\qquad \text{when } T_i \neq \frac{USL_i + LSL_i}{2} \end{cases}$$

where σ_{ii} is the ith diagonal element of Σ.

Thus, similar to the computations of MC_p [vide Chapter 6], the volume of the modified tolerance region (R_1) will be

$$V(R_1) = \frac{2}{q} \pi^{q/2} \, \Gamma\left(\frac{q}{2}\right) |\Sigma|^{1/2} c'^q \tag{13.14}$$

Shahriari and Abdollahzadeh [15] retained the form of modified 99.73% process region (R_2) as proposed by Taam et al. [17] and thus defined a new MPCI as

$$NMC_p^{(SA)} = \frac{\frac{2}{q}\pi^{q/2}\,\Gamma\left(\frac{q}{2}\right)|\Sigma|^{1/2}c'^q}{\frac{2}{q}\pi^{q/2}\,\Gamma\left(\frac{q}{2}\right)|\Sigma|^{1/2}(\chi_{0.0027,q}^2)^{q/2}}$$

$$= \frac{c'}{\sqrt{\chi_{0.9973,q}^2}} \tag{13.15}$$

It is to be noted that, Shahriari and Abdollahzadeh [15] denoted this index as NMC_{pm}. But the same notation was also used by Pan and Lee [14]. Also, the authors themselves have shown that the index in equation (13.15) performs better than when it is divided by $D = \sqrt{1 + (\boldsymbol{\mu} - \boldsymbol{T})'\Sigma^{-1}(\boldsymbol{\mu} - \boldsymbol{T})}$, i.e., an index similar to MC_{pm}. Thus, the index in equation (13.15) can be thought to be similar to MC_p rather than to MC_{pm}. Therefore, to avoid ambiguity in nomenclature, we have used here the notation $NMC_p^{(SA)}$. Other terms of the MPCV remain the same as those in the MPCV defined in Shahriari et al/'s.[16]

Jalili et al. [11] have pointed out that, $NMC_p^{(SA)}$ is very much dependent on the process dispersion matrix, which in turn, makes the index very much sensitive to the angle between the two axes of the elliptical process region. Consequently, for two bivariate processes having the same values of variance of the quality characteristics, but different correlation coefficients, the $NMC_p^{(SA)}$ values will be different. This observation needs to be considered always while calculating MPCIs, particularly when the multiple characteristics involved are not mutually independent; since correlation between the quality characteristics plays a major role for multivariate process capability study and has commendable influence on an MPCI.

Jalili et al. [11] have also observed that $NMC_p^{(SA)}$ is not applicable if one or more of the quality characteristics have unilateral specification limits. Handling such cases need a careful thinking and sufficient process knowledge. We give below a possible way of dealing with such situations.

For univariate processes with unilateral specification limits, Grau [8] has shown that, quite often when only one specification limit (either USL or LSL) is quoted, actually, deviation from target toward the other limit is not very critical and hence is often ignored. Grau [8] opined that in such cases, loss is still incurred due to deviation from target and hence, if for a process the quality characteristic is of smaller the better type, i.e., only USL is available, one can still have the LSL using the formula $T - LSL = k(USL - T)$. Accordingly, for a quality characteristic with only LSL, the hypothetical USL should be such that $USL - T = k(T - LSL)$. Here, the value of k (> 1) is such that the deviation of μ from T toward the opposite side of the existing specification limit is "k" times less serious than deviation toward the existing specification limit. Chatterjee and Chakraborty [1] have formulated mathematical expression for k based on the concept of loss incurred due to deviation of process centering from target. Generalizing this for multivariate case, suppose that for a q-variate process, only the vector of upper specification limits, viz., $USL = (USL_1, USL_2, \cdots, USL_q)'$ is available. For this, define $T_i - LSL_i = k_i(USL_i - T_i)$, $i = 1(1)q$. Otherwise, suppose only the lower specification limits, viz., $LSL = (LSL_1, LSL_2, \cdots, LSL_q)'$ is available, then define $USL_i - T_i = k_i(T_i - LSL_i)$, $i = 1(1)q$. Then c' can be redefined as,

$$
c' = \begin{cases}
\min\left\{\frac{USL_i - T_i}{\sqrt{\sigma_{ii}}}, \ i = 1(1)q\right\}, \\
\qquad \text{when} \ \ T_i = \frac{USL_i + LSL_i}{2} \\[2em]
\min\left\{\min\left\{\frac{USL_i - T_i}{\sqrt{\sigma_{ii}}}, \frac{T_i - LSL_i}{\sqrt{\sigma_{ii}}}\right\}, \ i = 1(1)q\right\}, \\
\qquad \text{when} \ \ T_i \neq \frac{USL_i + LSL_i}{2} \\[2em]
\min\left\{\min\left\{\frac{USL_i - T_i}{\sqrt{\sigma_{ii}}}, \frac{k_i(USL_i - T_i)}{\sqrt{\sigma_{ii}}}\right\}, \ i = 1(1)q\right\}, \\
\qquad \text{when only} \ \ USL_i \ \text{is available for} \ \ i = 1(1)q \\[2em]
\min\left\{\min\left\{\frac{k_i(T_i - LSL_i)}{\sqrt{\sigma_{ii}}}, \frac{T_i - LSL_i}{\sqrt{\sigma_{ii}}}\right\}, \ i = 1(1)q\right\}, \\
\qquad \text{when only} \ \ LSL_i \ \text{is available for} \ \ i = 1(1)q
\end{cases}
\tag{13.16}
$$

Unlike the three component MPCVs discussed so far, Ganji and Gildeh [7] proposed a two component MPCV viz.,

$$
MPCVG = \left[NMC_p^{(SA)}, PV\right]
\tag{13.17}
$$

where $NMC_p^{(SA)}$ is a ratio-based MPCI defined by Shahriari and Abdollahzadeh [15], [refer equation (13.15)] and PV is defined by Shahriari et al. [16], [refer equation (13.8)].

Thus, Ganji and Gildeh [7] dropped the usual third component of classical MPCV, which are originally used to show the proportion of coverage of the process region by the tolerance region. However, there may be cases where for two different processes, the so called first two components of an MPCV may come out to be equal, though their performances are not equivalent. Without the third component, the index may become inadequate for comparison purposes (refer Ciupke [4]).

Also the drawbacks of $NMC_p^{(SA)}$, discussed by Jalili et al. [11] are valid for the vector $MPCVG$ as well.

Ganji and Gildeh [7] also have established a relationship between $NMC_p^{(SA)}$ and the corresponding proportion of non-conformance. Suppose, individual quality characteristics follow normal distribution, i.e., $X_i \sim N(\mu_i, \sigma_{ii})$, $\forall i = 1(1)q$.

Define

$$pl_i = P[X < LSL_i] = \Phi\left(-\frac{\mu_i - LSL_i}{\sigma_i}\right) \tag{13.18}$$

$$Pu_i = P[X > USL_i] = \Phi\left(-\frac{USL_i - \mu_i}{\sigma_i}\right) \tag{13.19}$$

$$p_{\max} = \max\left\{\max\left(pl_i, pu_i\right), \forall i = 1(1)q\right\} \tag{13.20}$$

where $\Phi(.)$ is the c.d.f. of a standard normal distribution and σ_i is the diagonal element of Σ and $p_{\max}$ is the lower bound of the corresponding proportion of non-conformance. Therefore

$$NMC_p^{(SA)} = -\frac{1}{\sqrt{\chi_{0.9973,q}^2}} \times \Phi^{-1}\left(p_{\max}\right), \tag{13.21}$$

from equation (13.15)

$$\Rightarrow p_{\max} = \Phi\left(-\sqrt{\chi_{0.9973,q}^2}\, NMC_p^{(SA)}\right) \tag{13.22}$$

13.3 Multivariate Process Capability Vector Based on One-Sided Models

Ciupke [4] has proposed an MPCV which can accommodate both normal and non-normal processes under multivariate set-up and also both correlated and uncorrelated data. He has proposed a model called "one-sided" model, for such situations.

According to Ciupke [4], the classical approach of defining MPCIs suffer from a common problem, viz., in almost all the cases, the process region is modified to give it either a ellipsoidal shape (or elliptical, in case of bivariate processes) or to the shape similar to the specificatiion region. As a result,many a times the process region gets modified to a shape which is far from the actual one and hence becomes difficult to explain. One way to handle this problem is to use the "one-sided" models.

One sided model was first introduced by Cholewa and Kicinski [3] to handle the problem of unknown model accuracy in the context of fitting a regression model. Unlike the usual approach of defining a single ellipsoid or hyper-rectangle, as the case may be, in the case of one-sided model, a pair of curves (usually second degree polynomial) are defined, which cover the observed values of the quality characteristics from the top and the bottom simultaneously.

Suppose for a regression model, there are two variables, viz., X_1 and X_2, of which X_1 is an independent variable and X_2 is a dependent variable. Define a pair of functions $\{\widehat{X_2}^-(X_1), \widehat{X_2}^+(X_1)\}$, where $\widehat{X_2}^-(X_1)$ is used to limit the data from the bottom and $\widehat{X_2}^+(X_1)$ is used to limit the data from the above. To retain notational simplicity, now onward, $\{\widehat{X_2}^-(X_1), \widehat{X_2}^+(X_1)\}$ will be replaced by $\{\widehat{X_2}^-, \widehat{X_2}^+\}$. Usually, polynomials of suitable degree are used for these one sided models.

Ciupke [4] has used the method of linear programming to model $\widehat{X_2}^-$ and $\widehat{X_2}^+$. For example, the model for $\widehat{X_2}^-$ will be

$$\text{Maximize} \quad \sum_{i=1}^{n} \widehat{X_{2i}} \tag{13.23}$$

subject to the constraints

$$\widehat{X_{2i}} \leq X_{2i} \quad, \forall i = 1(1)n \tag{13.24}$$

where n denotes the number of observations and $\widehat{X_{2i}}^-$ stands for the fitted value of X_2 for $i = 1(1)n$.

Similarly, the model for $\widehat{X_2}^+$ will be

$$\text{Maximize} \quad \sum_{i=1}^{n} \widehat{X_{2i}} \tag{13.25}$$

subject to the constraints

$$\widehat{X_{2i}} \geq X_{2i} \quad, \forall i = 1(1)n \tag{13.26}$$

where $\widehat{X_{2i}}^+$ stands for the fitted value of X_2 for $i = 1(1)n$.

Ciupke [4] has shown that, a pair of one-sided models defined in this way, cover all the observed data irrespective of the underlying statistical distribution and is not based on any assumption regarding the form of the model. Therefore, one-sided model is robust and is applicable to a wide range of practical problems.

Recall that, the very idea of introducing one-sided model was to redefine the process region. Ciupke [4] modified the MPCV proposed by Shahriari et al. [16] using one-sided model. The first component of Ciupke's MPCV is a ratio-based MPCI C_{pV}, which is defined as

$$C_{pV} = \left(\frac{\text{Volume of tolerance region}}{\text{Volume of process region}}\right)^{1/q} \times 100\%$$

$$= \left(\frac{\prod_{i=1}^{q}(USL_i - LSL_i)}{\text{Volume of process region}}\right)^{1/q} \times 100\% \qquad (13.27)$$

To compute the volume of the process region, Ciupke [4] considered second degree polynomial to define the required one sided models. Thus, suppose, among the q random variables viz., $X_1, X_2, \cdots, X_q$, X_k is independent and the rest of $(q-1)$ variables are considered as dependent to it. Thus, there will be a set of pair of one-sided models

$$\widehat{\boldsymbol{X}} = \bigcup_{i \in I} \left\{\widehat{X_i}^{-}, \widehat{X_i}^{+}\right\} \qquad (13.28)$$

where $\widehat{X_i}$ is the abbriviated expression of $\widehat{X_i}(X_k)$ and I assumes all the values from $1, 2, \cdots, q$ except k.

Now, for each X_i, consider the following second degree polynomial:

$$\widehat{X_i}^{\pm} = a_0 + a_1 X_k + a_2 X_k^2, \quad i \in I \qquad (13.29)$$

where a_0, a_1 and a_2 are model parameters, such that $a_2 \geq 0$ for $\widehat{X_i}^{-}$ and $a_2 \leq 0$ for $\widehat{X_i}^{+}$.

For bivariate process, Ciupke [4] has derived expression for volume of the process region as

$$\text{Vol. [Process region]} = \sum_{i=1}^{n} \prod_{j=1; j \neq k}^{q} \left[\widehat{X_j}^{+}(X_{ki}) - \widehat{X_j}^{-}(X_{ki})\right] \qquad (13.30)$$

where

$$h = \frac{\max(\boldsymbol{X}_k), \min(\boldsymbol{X}_k)}{I}, \text{ for fixed number of sub-intervals I} \qquad (13.31)$$

and

$$X_{ki} = \min(\boldsymbol{X}_k) + (i-1)h, \ \forall i = 1(1) \ \overline{I+1} \qquad (13.32)$$

Thus, C_{pV} takes care of only the process dispersion through the suitably chosen one sided models.

Multivariate Process Capability Vectors 266

Although no threshold value is yet defined for C_{pV}, but a value nearing 100% means volume of the process region is close to the volume of the tolerance region.

Like the MPCV of Shahriari et al. [16], the second component of Ciupke's [4] MPCV takes care of process centering. However, unlike other MPCVs discussed so far, Ciupke [4] considers process median as a measure of process centering instead of process mean so that it can be used for nonnormal processes as well. Consider the vector of medians $\boldsymbol{m_e} = (m_{e1}, m_{e2}, \cdots, m_{eq})$, where, m_{ei} is the median of the ith quality characteristic, $i = 1(1)q$.

Then, following Ciupke [4], the second component of his proposed MPCV can be defined as,

$$PS = \max_{i=1,2,\cdots,q} \left(\frac{|T_i - m_{ei}|}{S_i} \right) \tag{13.33}$$

where

$$S_i = \begin{cases} USL_i - T_i, & \text{if } m_{ei} \geq T_i, \ \forall i = 1(1)q \\ T_i - LSL_i, & \text{Otherwise} \end{cases} \tag{13.34}$$

From equation (13.34), it can be observed that when median of a particular quality characteristic is on its stipulated target, $PS = 0\%$ and as the distance between m_{ei} and T_i increases, the value of PS increases. The highest value of PS will be 100%, which is attained, when m_{ei} lies on either of LSL_i or USL_i. Therefore, unlike C_{pV}, PS is a lower the better type index.

Interestingly, theoretically, PS can assume a value greater than 100%, when $|T_i - m_{ei}| > S_i$. However, in such a case the process will not be under statistical control (refer Montgomery [13]) and hence there is no point in computing the corresponding PS, since we know that a primary assumption for computing a PCI (both univariate and multivariate) is that, the process must be under statistical control (refer Kotz and Johnson [12]).

Finally, Cipuke [4] considered the third element of his proposed MPCV as "the minimal relative distance of the one-sided models from the target" which is mathematically defined as

$$PD = \max_{i=1,2,\cdots,q} \left[\frac{\max(\widehat{\boldsymbol{X}_i}^+) - \boldsymbol{T}}{\boldsymbol{USL} - \boldsymbol{T}}, \frac{\boldsymbol{T} - \max(\widehat{\boldsymbol{X}_i}^-)}{\boldsymbol{T} - \boldsymbol{LSL}} \right] \times 100\% \tag{13.35}$$

It is evident from the above expression that for $PD \leq 100\%$, the process region is fully within the tolerance region while for $PD > 100\%$, numerator of equation (13.35) is greater than its denominator, implying at least some part of the process region is not covered by the tolerance region. Thus, PD is also a lower the better type index.

Note that, the purpose of both LI (refer Shahriari et al. [16] and Shahriari and Abdollahzadeh [15]) and PD are the same. PD gives clearer picture regarding process span as compared to LI, which, being binary, tends to loose some vital information in this respect.

Although Ciupke's [4] MPCV based on the concept of one sided models is free from distributional assumptions and hence may find more practical applications, it suffers from some drawbacks as well, which are enlisted below:

1. For processes of higher order (viz. $q \geq 3$), computational complexity increases and it becomes very difficult to have closed-form expressions in such cases. One then has to consider numerical methods to derive expression for C_{pV}.

2. Selection of the degree of polynomial may at times invite subjectivity. Ciupke [4] has considered second degree polynomial as a logical generalization of ellipse or ellipsoid (as the case may be). However, if one intends to retain the true essence of this MPCV, then higher order polynomials or even more complicated mathematical functions may be employed, which will make the situation even worse.

3. Since formulation of the one-sided model depends on the observed values, it is difficult to get a robust model.

4. Ciupke [4] considered C_{pV} as smaller the better type of characteristic. However, the volume of the process region is in the denominator of C_{pV} and hence smaller the volume of the process region compared to the tolerance region (numerator of the MPCV), better should be the performance of the process. Thus, C_{pV} should be higher the better (as is usually the case).

5. Use of percentage makes the interpretation even more difficult as for a process performing satisfactorily, the value of C_{pV} will be greater than 100%.

6. PS, by its definition suffers from a unique anomaly. To explain this, consider the following diagram:

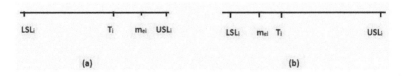

FIGURE 13.1: Relative position of median of a variable with respect to its target, USL and LSL

> In part (a) of Figure 13.1, for a particular quality characteristic i, $m_{ei} > T_i$ and hence S_i only covers the region $[T_i, USL_i]$. On the other hand, in part (b) of the Figure, for the particular quality characteristic i, $m_{ei} < T_i$ and hence S_i only covers the region $[LSL_i, T_i]$. Thus in either of the

Multivariate Process Capability Vectors 268

cases, only a subset of the whole tolerance region is taken into account i.e., one part of the tolerance region remains unattended. As a result, PS tend to under-estimate process capability, since S_i is in the denominator of PS.

13.4 Multivariate Process Incapability Vector

The MPCVs discussed so far in this chapter measure process performance through its capability, while Ganji [5] proposed a vector valued index measuring incapability of a process.

Let us recall from Chapter 3, a super-structure of MPCIs proposed by Chen and Pearn [2] , which is defined as

$$C_p''(u, v) = \frac{d^* - uF^*}{3\sqrt{\sigma^2 + vF^2}} \tag{13.36}$$

where, $d_u = USL - T$, $d_l = T - LSL$, $d^* = min(d_l, d_u)$, $F = \max\left\{\frac{d(\mu - T)}{d_u}, \frac{d(T - \mu)}{d_l}\right\}$ and $F^* = \max\left\{\frac{d^*(\mu - T)}{d_u}, \frac{d^*(T - \mu)}{d_l}\right\}$.

To make this super-structure capture the direction of shift, along with the magnitude, of the process centering from the target, Ganji and Gildeh[6] modified the expression of $C_p''(u, v)$ as follows:

$$C_{pp}'''(u, v) = \frac{d^* - uA^*}{3\sqrt{\sigma^2 + vA^2}} \tag{13.37}$$

Observe that, the indicator functions viz., $I_{\{\mu > T\}}$ and $I_{\{\mu \leq T\}}$ take care of the direction of shift of the process centering from target.

Using $C_{pp}'''(u, v)$, Ganji [5] defined an univariate process incapability index (i.e., a PCI measuring incapability of a process – rather than its capability) as

$$
\begin{aligned}
IC_{pp}'''(u, v) &= \left(\frac{1}{C_{pp}'''(u, v)}\right)^2 \\
&= \frac{9(\sigma^2 + vA^2)}{(d^* - uA^*)^2} \\
&= \left(\frac{6\sigma}{2(d^* - uA^*)^2}\right)^2 + \left(\frac{9vA^2}{(d^* - uA^*)^2}\right) \tag{13.38} \\
&= IC_a'''(u, v) + IC_p'''(u), \text{ say, for, } u, v \geq 0
\end{aligned}
$$

$$\tag{13.39}$$

where $IC_a'''(u, v)$ and $IC_p'''(u, v)$ stand for inaccuracy index and imprecision index, respectively. As the names suggest, inaccuracy index measures degree of deviation from process centering and imprecision index measures degree of dispersion.

Ganji [5] proposed a two-component multivariate process incapability vector (MPICV). The first copmponent, viz., $MIC_{pp}'''(u,v)$ of this MPICV is obtained by generalizing $IC_{pp}'''(u,v)$ to a multivariate set-up as follows:

$$MIC_{pp}'''(u,v) \quad = \quad MIC_a'''(u,v) + MIC_p'''(u), \text{ say, for, } u,v \geq 0$$

$$(13.40)$$

where $MIC_a'''(u,v)$ and $MIC_p'''(u,v)$ stand for inaccuracy index and imprecision index, respectively, under multivariate set-up.

Before going into the mathematical formulation of $MIC_a'''(u,v)$ and $MIC_p'''(u,v)$, consider the notations enlisted below:

1. $d_{ui} = USL_i - T_i$;

2. $d_{li} = T_i - LSL_i$;

3. $d_i^* = \min\{d_{li}, d_{ui}\}$;

4. $d_i = \frac{USL_i - LSL_i}{2}$;

5. $I_{\mu_i > T_i} = \begin{cases} 1, & \text{If } \mu_i > T_i \\ 0, & \text{Otherwise} \end{cases}$;

6. $I_{\mu_i \geq T_i} = \begin{cases} 1, & \text{If } \mu_i \geq T_i \\ 0, & \text{Otherwise} \end{cases}$;

7. $A_i = \frac{d_i(\mu_i - T_i)}{d_{ui}} I_{\mu_i > T_i} + \frac{d_i(T_i - \mu_i)}{d_{li}} I_{\mu_i \leq T_i}$;

8. $A_i^* = \frac{(\mu_i - T_i)^2}{d_{ui}} I_{\mu_i > T_i} + \frac{(T_i - \mu_i)^2}{d_{li}} I_{\mu_i \leq T_i}$;

9. $r_i(u) = |d_i^* - uA_i^*|$, for $i = 1(1)q$;

10. $\boldsymbol{d}^* = \begin{pmatrix} d_1^* \\ d_2^* \\ \vdots \\ d_q^* \end{pmatrix}$;

11. $A = \begin{pmatrix} A_1 \\ A_2 \\ \vdots \\ A_q \end{pmatrix}$;

12. $A^* = \begin{pmatrix} A_1^* \\ A_2^* \\ \vdots \\ A_q^* \end{pmatrix}$;

13. $r(u) = \begin{pmatrix} r_1(u) \\ r_2(u) \\ \vdots \\ r_q(u) \end{pmatrix}$.

Ganji [5] defined the multivariate inaccuracy index $MIC_a'''(u,v)$ as

$$MIC_a'''(u,v) = \frac{9vA'A}{r(u)'r(u)}, \quad u,v \geq 0 \tag{13.41}$$

and the multivariate imprecision index $MIC_p'''(u)$ as

$$MIC_p'''(u) = \left[\frac{\text{Volume of 99.73\% of the process region}}{\text{Volume of the modified tolerance ellipsoid}} \right]^2$$

$$= \left[\frac{|\Sigma|^{1/2} \left(\pi\chi_{1-\alpha,q}^2\right)^{q/2}}{(\Gamma(\frac{q}{2}+1)) \times \pi \times r_1(u)r_2(u)\cdots r_q(u)} \right]^2, \quad u \geq 0 \tag{13.42}$$

As before, the second component of MPICV is defined as

$$LI = \begin{cases} 1, & \text{if the process region is fully accommodated within the tolerance region} \\ 0, & \text{Otherwise} \end{cases} \tag{13.43}$$

Thus, the final form of Ganji's [5] MPICV will be

$$MPICV = \left[MIC_{pp}'''(u,v), \quad LI_{Ganji} \right] \tag{13.44}$$

Ganji [5] has enlisted (without explanation) some recommended values of $MPICV$ as follows:

1. A process will be **incapable**, if $MIC_{pp}'''(u,v) \geq 1$ or $LI = 0$;

2. A process will be **capable**, if $0.56 \leq MIC_{pp}'''(u,v) < 1$ and $LI = 1$;

3. A process will be **satisfactory**, if $0.44 \leq MIC_{pp}'''(u,v) < 0.56$ and $LI = 1$;

Multivariate Process Capability Vectors 271

4. A process will be **excellent**, if $0.25 \leq MIC_{pp}'''(u, v) < 0.44$ and $LI = 1$;

5. A process will be **super**, if $0 \leq MIC_{pp}'''(u, v) < 0.25$ and $LI = 1$;

Ganji[5] has also defined plug-in estimator of $MIC_{pp}'''(u, v)$ by replacing process mean vector μ and dispersion matrix Σ by sample mean vector $\overline{X}$ and S respectively in equation (13.39), as

$$\widehat{MIC_{pp}}'''(u, v) = \widehat{IC_a}'''(u, v) + \widehat{IC_p}'''(u), \text{ say, for, } u, v \geq 0 \tag{13.45}$$

However, statistical properties of $\widehat{MIC_{pp}}'''(u, v)$ are yet to be studied.

Although Ganji [5] introduced the concept of incapability index under the multivariate set-up, there are a few inconsistencies with her proposed *MPICV*. The first component of Ganji's [5] MPICV measures incapability of a process,while the second component is a usual one, measuring capability of the process in some sense. This contradiction may prove to be confusing at times and consequently, the name "incapability **vector**" may not be fully justified.

13.5 An MPCV for Both the Unilateral and Bilateral Specification Regions

Jalili et al. [11] have suggested an MPCV which is applicable for processes having both unilateral (for quality characteristics of higher the better or lower the better type) and bilateral (for quality characteristics of nominal the best type) specification regions.

Let us denote the conformance volume (CV) as the area or volume of the portion of the process region that is covered by the modified specification region; and the nonconformance volume (NCV) denotes area or volume of the residual portion, i.e., the portion which lies beyond the modified specification region. Also let λ is the sensitivity parameter for process capability with $0 \leq \lambda \leq 1$ and β (> 0) is defined to distinguish between two processes which are completely within the specification region, but are having different levels of dispersion.

Based on these concepts, Jalili et al. [11] have defined a two-component MPCV, for processes with bilateral specification region, as

$$MPC_{NCV}$$
$$= \left[\frac{\lambda \times \text{volume of the process region (PR)} + \text{CV} + \beta}{\text{volume of the process region (PR)} + \text{NCV}}, \frac{1}{D} \right]$$

$$(13.46)$$

where as defined before, $D = \sqrt{1 + (\boldsymbol{\mu} - \boldsymbol{T})' \Sigma^{-1} (\boldsymbol{\mu} - \boldsymbol{T})}$ measures the amount of deviation of the center of the process from the stipulated target.

Jalili et al.[11] have made a thorough study on the possible values of λ. Recall that, here λ plays the role of a sensitivity parameter, in a sense that, higher the value of λ, the more sensitive is the first component of MPC_{NCV} toward the CV region. The authors have shown (for detailed proof refer Jalili et al. [11]) that

$$NCV \leq \frac{\lambda}{2} \times PR \qquad (13.47)$$

Thus, $0 \leq \lambda \leq 1$ such that λ is inversely proportional to the correlation between the quality characteristics. Also, for processes with bilateral specification region with the process region being completely within the modified specification region (i.e., when the process is capable) with a very small value of NCV, Jalili et al. [11] have recommended $\lambda = 0.54$. In all the other cases, viz., when the process region coincides with the modified specification region and when the process region is not fully within the modified specification region (though within the original rectangular specification region), the recommended value of $\lambda = 0.27$.

Also, based on a simulation study, Jalili et al. [11] have β value as follows:

$$\beta = \begin{cases} 0.05 \times \text{volume of the tolerance region,} \\ \quad \text{if volume of tolerance region is less than } 1 \\ \\ 0.1, \quad \text{Otherwise} \end{cases} \qquad (13.48)$$

Thus, it may be noted that, when PR is completely within the modified tolerance region or is completely outside of that, the first component of MPC_{NCV} measures process dispersion and the second component measures distance of process centering from the target. On the other hand, when PR lies partly within the modified tolerance region and partly outside of it, the first component measures both process centering and dispersion, while the second component distinguishes between two processes with respect to their proximity toward the stipulated target (refer Jalili et al. [11]).

For processes with one or more unilateral specification limits, Jalili et al. [11] have slightly modified MPC_{NCV} as

$$MPC'_{NCV}$$
$$= \left[\frac{\lambda \times \text{volume of the process region (PR)} + \text{CV} + \beta}{\text{volume of the process region (PR)} + \text{NCV}}, \frac{1}{D'} \right]$$
$$(13.49)$$

To define D', following Jalili et al. [11], consider a bivariate process such that, one of its quality characteristics (characterized by X_1, say) has bilateral specification limits, while the other (characterized by X_2, say) is of smaller the better type and therefore has unilateral specification limit.

Define D_1 as the distance between the line parallel to USL_{X_1} and passing through the reference point viz., $(\frac{USL_{X_1} + LSL_{X_1}}{2}, USL_{X_2})$ and the mean vector and D_2 as the distance between USL_{X_2} and a its parallel line which passes through the mean vector. Note that, since the second quality characteristic is of smaller the better type, D_2 should be as large as possible. Then D' can be defined as,

$$D' = \frac{1 + D_1}{1 + D_2} \qquad (13.50)$$

Thus, the first component remains same for both MPC_{NCV} and MPC'_{NCV}, while the second component varies depending upon availability of the specification limits.

Also, for processes with unilateral specification region, Jalili et al. [11] recommended $\lambda = 0.27/2 = 0.135$.

Moreover, for unilateral tolerance region, if the distance between mean of the process region and the reference point is quite large, then D' needs some modification. In such a case

$$D' = \begin{cases} \frac{1 + D_1}{1 + D_2}, & \text{if } \mu_2 \leq USL_{X_2} \\ \\ \frac{1}{1 + D_1} \times \frac{1}{1 + D_2}, & \text{Otherwise} \end{cases} \qquad (13.51)$$

Finally, Jalili et al. [11] have modified D' to generalize this for higher dimensional cases as,

$$D' = k^a \times \frac{1}{(1 + D_{i2})^b} \qquad (13.52)$$

where
a : Number of quality characteristics having unilateral specification limits;
b : Number of quality characteristics having bilateral specification limits.

$$k = \begin{cases} 1 + D_{i1}, & \text{if } \mu_i \le USL_{X_i} \text{ or, } \mu_i \ge LSL_{X_i} \\ \frac{1}{1+D_{i1}}, & \text{Otherwise} \end{cases} \qquad (13.53)$$

Here, D_{ij} stands for the value of the ith quality characteristic of D_j class, for $i = 1(1)q$ and $j = 1, 2$.

Since by definition, the first component remains the same for both MPC_{NCV} and MPC'_{NCV}, Jalili et al. [11] have derived expression for its $100(1 - \alpha)\%$ confidence interval as

$$\left[\frac{F_Y^{-1}(1 - \frac{\alpha}{2}) + CV}{NCV + \beta}, \frac{F_Y^{-1}(\frac{\alpha}{2}) + CV}{NCV + \beta} \right], \qquad (13.54)$$

where $Y \sim \chi_{n,q}^2$ and $F(.)$ is its cumulative distribution function (c. d. f.). Observe that, MPC_{NCV} and MPC'_{NCV} have the following drawbacks:

1. Since Jalili et al. [11] has adopted Taam et al.'s [17] approach of modified tolerance region, their MPCVs naturally inherits all its drawbacks including over-estimation of process capability (refer Chapter 6 for more detail).

2. D' ignores prevailing correlation structure of the process.

3. Since β value is suggested purely based on simulation study, it keeps room for favorable manipulation.

Nonetheless, Jalili et al.'s [11] MPCI is unique of its kind as it accommodates unilateral tolerances as well.

13.6   A Numerical Example

Recall the data discussed in Chapter 6, pertaining to two quality characteristics coded as "7J" and "6J" from a chemical industry. The complete data is given in Table 6.1 of chapter 6.

Recall that, Hubele et al. [9] and Shahriari et al. [16] suggested modifying the process region to give it the shape similar to that of the specification region, which is rectangular in the present context. Figure 13.2 shows the corresponding plot.

Based on the data in Table 6.1, $\widehat{C_{pM}} = 1.8964$ and $\widehat{PV} \approx 0$. Also, since the entire process region is within the tolerance region, $LI = 1$. Therefore, computed value of Shahriari et al.'s MPCV is $[1.8964, 0, 1]$.

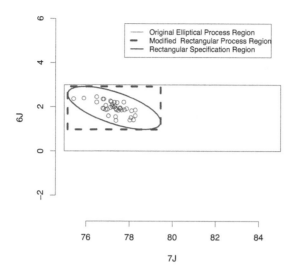

FIGURE 13.2: Relative positions of tolerance region, original elliptical process region and modified rectangular process region

Again, as has already been discussed, Shahriari and Abdollahzadeh [15] advocated modification of the tolerance region – rather than the specification region and as such the corresponding plot for the process and tolerance regions will be as given in Figure 13.3. Accordingly, $\widehat{NMC_p^{(SA)}} = 1.5442$. Therefore, computed value of Shahriari and Abdollahzadeh's [15] MPCI will be [1.5442, 0, 1].

Also, for the present data, computed values of Ganji's [5] multivariate imprecision index and inaccuracy index will, respectively, be $\widehat{MIC}_p'''(1) = 0.1087$ and $\widehat{MIC}_a'''(1,1) = 4.6524$. Thus, $\widehat{MIC}_{pp}'''(1,1) = 4.7611$ and consequently, computed value of Ganji's [5] multivariate process incapability vector will be [4.7611, 1].

Again, for computing Jalili et al.'s [11] MPC_{NCV}, from Figure 13.3 observe that, the process region is not fully covered by the modified tolerance region, which means both CV and NCV do exist. To be more precise, almost half of the process region lies within the modified tolerance region, while the remaining half part outside of it.

Following Taam et al.'s [17] approach, volume of the modified specification region is 23.5691 and that of process region is 5.0162. Also, following Jalili et al.'s [11] recommendation, $\lambda = 0.27$, $\beta = 0.1$, and $D = 4.6949$.

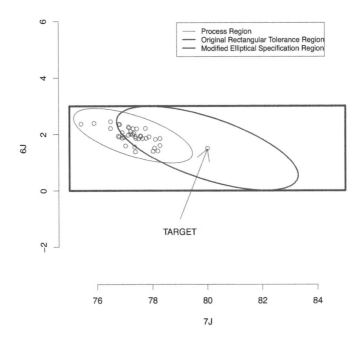

FIGURE 13.3: Relative positions of original rectangular tolerance region, modified elliptical tolerance region and original elliptical process region

Therefore, $MPC_{NCV} = (0.5266, 4.6949)$. Recall that, as observed by Jalili et al. [11], when the process region is not fully covered by the modified tolerance region, the first component represents both process centering and dispersion. This is evident from the computed value as well, since despite having satisfactory dispersion level, the first component of the index is quite low, while the second component is quite high indicating toward remarkable off-centeredness of the process.

From the above discussion, following observations can be made of the data given in Table 6.1.

1. All the MPCVs agree to the fact that the process is highly off centeredness, though its dispersion scenario is satisfactory.

2. C_{pM} over estimates process dispersion, as compared to $NMC_p^{(SA)}$. However, due to unavailability of mathematically formulated threshold value, no further comment can be made in this regard.

3. Although, $LI = 1$, since $\widehat{MIC}_{pp}^{'''}(1,1) > 1$, the process is considered to be "incapable".

4. Interestingly, for the MPCVs defined by Shahriari et al.[16] and Shahriari and Abdollahzadeh [15], computed value of the second component viz., PV is close to zero, while from Figures 13.2 and 13.3, it can be easily observed that, in both the cases the process region is completely within the tolerance region (though highly off centered). Thus, here PV tends to under-estimate process capability. Consequently, second and third components of these MPCVs tend to give contradictory result, to some extent.

5. Since Ganji's [5] consolidated index $MIC_{pp}'''(1,1)$ sums up two seperate indices, viz., $MIC_a'''(1,1)$ and $MIC_p'''(1)$, some crucial aspects of process capability get smoothed out. For example, in the present scenario, $\widehat{MIC_p}'''(1)$ is quite satisfactory, while the situation is just the opposite for $\widehat{MIC_a}'''(1,1)$. However, after getting summed up, this feature is not reflected in $\widehat{MIC_{pp}}'''(1,1)$. A possible solution to this problem may be to retain these individual indices viz., $MIC_a'''(1,1)$ and $MIC_p'''(1)$ seperately in the incapability vector.

6. Jalili et al.'s [11] MPC_{NCV}, captures capability scenario perfectly. However, since its success depends on some external parameters viz., λ and β, it needs to be used carefully. Also, a proper threshold value needs to be developed for taking any decision regarding the process performance.

13.7 Concluding Remark

For multivariate processes, being inherently more complicated than their univariate counter parts, a single-valued assessment of their capability may be easy to understand but may pose some problems when one needs to improve it. Kotz and Johnson [12] have rightly observed that, while assessing capability of a process, it is often better to judge its dispersion and centering seperately.

Although a few MPCVs have been defined so far in literature, statistical properties of their estimators are still not studied extensively. This will definitely make an interesting future scope of study.

Also, one common major drawback of all these MPCVs is that, while comparing two or more processes using these MPCVs, dispersion-wise a process may be in a better position than the other process(es), while another process may depict better centering. In such cases (which may not be very rare in practice), taking decisions based on vector valued MPCVs may pose a challenging problem.

Bibliography

[1] Chatterjee, M., Chakraborty, A. K. (2012). Univariate Process Capability Indices for Unilateral Specification Region A Review & Some Modifications. *International Journal of Reliability, Quality and Safety Engineering*, Vol. 19, No. 4, pp. 1250020 (1–18).

[2] Chen, K. S., Pearn, W. L. (2001). Capability Indices For Process With Asymmetric Tolerances. *Journal of The Chinese Institute of Engineers*, Vol. 24, No. 5, pp. 559–568.

[3] Cholewa, W., Kicinski, J. (1997). Technical diagnostics. Reverse diagnostic models. (In Polish) Gliwice

[4] Ciupke, K. (2015). Multivariate Process Capability Vector Based on Onesided Model. *Quality and Reliability Engineering International*, Vol. 31, No. 2, pp. 313–327.

[5] Ganji, Z. A. (2018). Multivariate Process Incapability Vector. *Quality and Reliability International*, URL: https://doi.org/10.1002/qre.2435.

[6] Ganji, Z. A., Sadeghpour, G. B. (2016). A Class of Process Capability Indices for Asymmetric Tolerances. *Quality Engineering*, Vol. 28, pp. 441–454.

[7] Ganji, Z. A., Sadeghpour, G. B. (2016). A Modified Multivariate Process Capability Vector. *International Journal of Advanced Manufacturing Technology*. Vol. 83, pp. 1221–1229.

[8] Grau, D. (2009). New Process Capability Indices for One-Sided Tolerances. *Quality Technology and Quantitative Management*, Vol. 6, No. 2, pp. 107–124.

[9] Hubele, N. F., Shahriari, H., Cheng,C.S. (1991). A bivariate Process Capability Vector, in Statistics and Design in Process Control. *"Statistical Process Control in Manufacturing"* edited by J. B. Keats and D. C. Montgomery, Marcel Dekker, New York, pp. 299–310.

[10] Kotz, S., Johnson, N. L. (1993). Process Capability Indices. *Chapman & Hall, London.*

[11] Jalili, M., Bashiri, M., Amiri, A. (2012). A New Multivariate Process Capability Index under both Unilateral and Bilateral Quality Characteristics. *Quality and Reliability engineering International*, Vol. 28, pp. 925–941.

[12] Kotz, S., Johnson, N. (2002). Process Capability Indices - a Review, 1992 - 2000. *Journal of Quality Technology*, Vol. 34, No. 1, pp. 2–19.

[13] Montgomery, D. C. (2000). *Introduction to Statistical Quality Control*, 5th ed., John Wiley & Sons, New York.

[14] Pan, J. N., Lee, C. Y. (2010). New Capability Indices for Evaluating the Performance of Multivariate Manufacturing Processes. *Quality and Reliability engineering International*, Vol. 26, No. 1, pp. 3–15.

[15] Shahriari, H., Abdollahzadeh, M. (2009). A New Multivariate Process Capability Vector. *Quality Engineering*, Vol. 21, No. 3, pp. 290–299.

[16] Shahriari, H., Hubele, N. F., Lawrence, F. P. (1995). A Multivariate Process Capability Vector. *Proceedings of the 4th Industrial Engineering Research Conference*, Institute of Industrial Engineers, pp. 304–309.

[17] Taam, W., Subbaiah, P., Liddy, W. (1993). A Note on Multivariate Capability Indices. *Journal of Applied Statistics*, Vol. 20, No. 3, pp. 339–351.

[18] Wang, F. K., Hubele, N. F., Lawrence, F. P., Maskulin, J. D., Shahriari, H. (2000). Comparison of Three Multivariate Process Capability Indices. *Journal of Quality Technology*, Vol. 32, pp. 263–275.

Chapter 14

MPCIs Defined by Other Miscellaneous Approaches

Chapter Summary

Chapter 14 discusses almost all those broad classes of multivariate process capability indices (MPCIs), which are not included in any of the previous chapters. These include priority-based MPCIs, MPCIs defined from linear algebra perspective, multivariate viability index based on the concept of window of opportunity, single valued and vector valued MPCIs using fuzzy logic, MPCIs for linear and nonlinear profiles and so on. These diversified types of MPCIs are of immense importance from practical application point of view.

14.1 Introduction

Apart from the various approaches for finding out process capability of multidimensional processes discussed so far, there are some other interesting ways to assses miltivariate process capability. In the present chapter, we shall discuss some of those MPCIs.

14.2 Priority-Based Multivariate Process Capability Indices (MPCIs)

Throughout this book, it has been discussed that, in most of the practical situations, a process will have more than one correlated quality characteristics and a number of MPCIs are available in literature to measure its performance. However, almost all of these MPCIs (barring a few) grossly overlook a very basic property of a multidimensional process, viz., often all the quality characteristics are not of same importance to a production engineer. Based on its impact on overall performance and functionality of a product, Juran

280

and Gryna [16] have classified all the quality characteristics into three major classses, which are discussed below:

Critical The quality characteristics which have the potential to cause severe damages to human, environment, or may impart irrevocable impact on those, if the corresponding specifications are violated.

Major Out of specification or highly off-target values of these quality characteristics lead to malfunction of the corresponding product, though the amount of damage is not as much as that caused by critical characteristic(s).

Minor Out of specification or highly off- target values of these quality characteristics do not usually cause grave damage, as is done by other two types of quality characteristics, under such circumstances. However, the product's overall usability gets deteriorated,

Based on this classification of quality characteristics, Byun et al. [4] have proposed an MPCI which takes into account "productibility" of multiple correlated quality characteristics of a process. For all practical purposes, for a multidimensional process, all the quality characteristics may never be of equal importance and accordingly, their deviation from stipulated target will not have equal impact on a product. Apart from this, cost of production is another important aspect, because, while targeting for increment of process capability, management cannot afford to increase the manufacturing cost beyond certain level. Unfortunately, most of the MPCIs do not incorporate the aspect of cost in their definitions.

In order to address these two factors, Byun et al. [4] have proposed a so called "producibility measure" of quality characteristics.

According to Carruba and Gordon [5], producibility is a measure of desirability of a product and process design in terms of the consistency of quality and the economy of production.

Suppose, for a particular product, there are n quality characteristics, of which n_1 are critical, n_2 are major, and n_3 are minor type. The corresponding random variables are named as $X_1, X_2, \cdots, X_{n_1}$; $Y_1, Y_2, \cdots, Y_{n_2}$, and $Z_1, Z_2, \cdots, Z_{n_3}$, respectively.

Then, Byun et al. [4] defined producibility vector as

$$PV^{(Byun)}$$
$$= [PCI_{critical}, \quad PCI_{major}, \quad PCI_{minor}, \quad PCI_{overall}, MC] \tag{14.1}$$

where, $PCI_{critical} = \min_{1 \le i \le n_1} \{PCI_{X_i}\}$,
$PCI_{major} = \min_{1 \le i \le n_2} \{PCI_{Y_i}\}$ and

$PCI_{minor} = \min\limits_{1 \le i \le n_3} \{PCI_{Z_i}\}$, with $PCI_.$ denoting the value of the process capability index for the corresponding quality characteristic. Also

$$
\begin{aligned}
PCI_{overall} &= \left[\left(PCI_{X_1} \, PCI_{X_2} \, \cdots PCI_{X_{n_1}}\right)^{1/n_1}\right]^{W_1/\sum\limits_{i=1}^{3} W_i} \\
&\quad \times \left[\left(PCI_{Y_1} \, PCI_{Y_2} \, \cdots PCI_{Y_{n_2}}\right)^{1/n_2}\right]^{W_2/\sum\limits_{i=1}^{3} W_i} \\
&\quad \times \left[\left(PCI_{Z_1} \, PCI_{Z_2} \, \cdots PCI_{Z_{n_3}}\right)^{1/n_3}\right]^{W_3/\sum\limits_{i=1}^{3} W_i} \\
&= \left[\left(\prod_{j=1}^{n_1} PCI_{X_j}\right)^{W_1/n_1} \times \left(\prod_{j=1}^{n_2} PCI_{Y_j}\right)^{W_2/n_2} \right. \\
&\quad \left. \times \left(\prod_{j=1}^{n_3} PCI_{Z_j}\right)^{W_3/n_3}\right]^{\frac{1}{\sum\limits_{i=1}^{3} W_i}}
\end{aligned}
$$

(14.2)

where W_1, W_2, and W_3 denotes relative importance for critical, major, and minor quality characteristics, respectively. Observe that, Byun et al. [4] have used weighted geometric mean (G. M.), instead of weighted arithmetic mean (A. M.), which is the most popular among measures of central tendency, as G. M. is more sensitive to small values of a variable than A. M.

Finally, the fifth component of $PV^{(\mathrm{Byun})}$, viz., MC is the manufacturing cost per unit of production and is estimated from several cost elements derived from a process.

One of the major set-back of $PV^{(\mathrm{Byun})}$ is that, it completely ignores correlation structure of the quality characteristics and hence fails to capture the true essence of an MPCI. Also, the importance ratio viz., $\dfrac{W_j}{\sum\limits_{i=1} W_i}$, for $i = 1, 2, 3$ is completely subjective and hence one can have different $PV^{(\mathrm{Byun})}$ values with different importance ratios for the same process, which is highly misleading. Also, for a particular class (say, critical) of quality characteristics, considering the minimum PCI value may not always be a good representation. For example, suppose for a process, $PCI_{critical}$ is 1.02 and for the remaining critical quality characteristics, corresponding PCI values do not exceed 1.07. Also let there be another process for which $PCI_{critical}$ is 1.005, but all other remaining critical quality characteristics have PCI values of 1.60 or above. Thus in this case, the first process will be considered better than the second one, for critical quality characteristics, though ideally the decision should not be that simple.

Finally, drawbacks of vector-valued MPCIs are naturally inherited by $PV^{(\mathrm{Byun})}$. For example, between two processes, one may have better

MPCIs Defined by Other Miscellaneous Approaches

$PCI_{overall}$ value, while the other process may be more cost-effective. $PV^{(Byun)}$ fails to provide any concrete solution in this regard.

To address these issues, Khadse and Shinde [19] have proposed two sets of MPCIs, under multivariate normality assumption of the correlated quality characteristics, putting emphasis on relative importance of quality characteristics.

For differentiating between critical, major, and minor quality characteristics, Khadse and Shinde [19] have considered Montgoemry's recommended minimum values of C_p, which are given in Table 14.1 below:

TABLE 14.1: Montgoemry's Recommended minimum values of C_p for different types of quality characteristics having two-sided specification limits

Critical/ Noncritical characteristics	Noncritical characteristics Minimum value of C_p
Existing Processes (Noncritical parameter)	1.33
New Processes (Noncritical parameter)	1.50
Existing Processes (Critical parameter)	1.50
New Processes (Critical parameter)	1.67

In order to define the MPCIs, Khadse and Shinde [19] have made the following assumptions:

1. The process is under statistical control.

2. If $\boldsymbol{X}$ is a random vector characterizing the quality characteristics, then $\boldsymbol{X} \sim N_q(\boldsymbol{\mu}, \Sigma)$.

3. α is the maximum PNC that may be allowed.

4. The specification region of the process is hyper-rectangular, whose sides are constituted by the upper and lower specification limits.

5. The specification limits of each of the quality characteristics is symmetric about its target, i.e., $USL_i - T_i = T_i - LSL_i$, for $i = 1(1)q$.

Let k_1, k_2, and k_3 are the minimum required values of C_p for critical, major, and minor quality characteristics, respectively.

Then in order to construct modified specification region, the authors modified $d_i = \frac{USL_i - LSL_i}{2}$, for $i = 1(1)q$, as

$$d_i' = \begin{cases} \frac{2d_i}{k_1} & \text{if } i\text{th characteristic is critical,} \\ \frac{2d_i}{k_2} & \text{if } i\text{th characteristic is major,} \\ \frac{2d_i}{k_3} & \text{if } i\text{th characteristic is minor,} \end{cases}$$

such that $LSL_i' = T_i - \frac{d_i'}{2}$ and $USL_i' = T_i + \frac{d_i'}{2}$. Interestingly, here the target

MPCIs Defined by Other Miscellaneous Approaches   284

vector, viz., $\boldsymbol{T} = (T_1, T_2, \cdots, T_q)'$ is kept unchanged. One possible reason for this may be, for a process, usually, the targets for individual quality characteristics are first set and once this is done, the corresponding USL and LSL are defined based on how much deviation can be allowed on either side of the specification region.

Khadse and Shinde [19] defined MPCIs based on modified specification regions as

$$WMP_1' = P[\boldsymbol{X} \in S' | \boldsymbol{X} \sim N_p(\boldsymbol{T}, \Sigma)], \tag{14.3}$$
$$\text{when the process is centered at } \boldsymbol{T} = (T_1, T_2, \cdots, T_q)'$$

$$WMP_2' = P[\boldsymbol{X} \in S' | \boldsymbol{X} \sim N_p(\boldsymbol{\mu}, \Sigma)], \tag{14.4}$$
$$\text{when the process is centered at } \boldsymbol{\mu} = (\mu_1, \mu_2, \cdots, \mu_q)'$$

where $S = \left\{ \boldsymbol{x} | \bigcap_{i=1}^{q} (LSL_i \leq X_i \leq USL_i) \right\}$ is the original specification region and S' is the revised one, which is defined as, $S' = \left\{ \boldsymbol{x} | \bigcap_{i=1}^{q} (LSL_i' \leq X_i \leq USL_i') \right\}$.

Observe that, WMP_1' considers the process to be perfectly centred at target and hence, similar to C_p, WMP_1' measures potential process capability. Also, since the underlying process distribution is assumed to be multivariate normal, Khadse and Shinde [19] considered the process to be potentially capable, if $WMP_1' \geq 0.9973$.

WMP_2', on the other hand, assumes that the process is not centred on $\boldsymbol{T}$ and hence its mean viz., $\boldsymbol{\mu}$ is assumed to be its center. Therefore, WMP_2' measures the actual capability of a process, similar to C_{pk} and the process is considered to be capable only when $WMP_2' \geq 0.9973$.

Apart from the relative-importance-of-quality-characteristics-based MPCIs viz., WMP_1' and WMP_2', which are defined by making necessary corrections to the corresponding specification regions, Khadse and Shinde [19] have also defined a set of MPCIs based on modified process region.

In order to construct the modified process region, Khadse and Shinde [19] replaced the $(i, j)^{\text{th}}$ components σ_{ij} of the variance- covariance matrix of the quality characteristics by $\sigma_{ij}' = (k_i k_j) \sigma_{ij}$ according to the importance of ith and jth characteristics, for $i, j = 1(1)q$.

Also, let $\mu_i' = T_i - \sigma_{ii} Z_i$, where, $Z_i = \frac{(T_i - \mu_i)}{\sigma_{ii}} \sim N(\mu_i, \sigma_{ii})$ and σ_{ii} is the ith diagonal element of Σ, for $i = 1, 2, \cdots, q$. Moreover, when σ_{ij} is the (ij)th element of Σ; then, Σ', the modified variance-covariance matrix, can be obtained as follows:

$$\sigma_{ij}' = \begin{cases} k_1^2\sigma_{ij}, & \text{if both the } i\text{th and } j\text{th quality} \\ & \quad \text{characteristics are critical,} \\ k_2^2\sigma_{ij}, & \text{if both the } i\text{th and } j\text{th quality} \\ & \quad \text{characteristics are major,} \\ k_3^2\sigma_{ij}, & \text{if both the } i\text{th and } j\text{th quality} \\ & \quad \text{characteristics are minor,} \\ k_1 k_2\sigma_{ij}, & \\ & \quad \text{if out of the } i\text{th and } j\text{th quality characteristics,} \\ & \quad \quad \text{one is critical and the other is major,} \\ k_1 k_3\sigma_{ij}, & \\ & \quad \text{if out of the } i\text{th and } j\text{th quality characteristics,} \\ & \quad \quad \text{one is critical and the other is minor,} \\ k_2 k_3\sigma_{ij}, & \\ & \quad \text{if out of the } i\text{th and } j\text{th quality characteristics,} \\ & \quad \quad \text{one is major and the other is minor,} \end{cases}$$

where σ_{ij}' is the $(i,j)^{\text{th}}$ element of Σ', for $i,j = 1,2,\cdots,q$.

Then Khadse and Shinde's [19] MPCIs based on modified process regions are defined as

$$WMP_1 = P[\boldsymbol{X} \in S | \boldsymbol{X} \sim N_p(\boldsymbol{T}, \Sigma')], \qquad (14.5)$$
$$\text{when the process is centered at } \boldsymbol{T};$$
$$WMP_2 = P[\boldsymbol{X} \in S | \boldsymbol{X} \sim N_p(\boldsymbol{\mu}', \Sigma')], \qquad (14.6)$$
$$\text{when the process is centered at}$$
$$\boldsymbol{\mu}' = (\mu_1', \mu_2', \cdots, \mu_q')'$$

Similar to WMP_1' and WMP_2', WMP_1 and WMP_2 measure potential and actual process capability, respectively.

Although WMP_1', WMP_2', WMP_1, and WMP_2 are defined from a very pragmatic point of view, calculation of the probability may be quite difficult, at some point, particularly when the specification region is of a very complicated shape. Numerical computations may however be used to handle this issue. Also note that, although Khadse and Shinde [19] considered the probability value of 0.9973 as some sort of a threshold to decide whether a process is performing satisfactorily or not, the value 0.9973 is actually the probability of a point lying within $\mu \pm 3\sigma$ limits for a univariate $N(\mu, \sigma^2)$ distribution and may not hold good for a multivariate normal distribution.

Raissi [24] proposed a weighted average method to incorporate relative importance of individual quality characteristics in a consolidated MPCI. Note that, the very idea of using weighted average is to assign different weightage to different items. Infact, in simple average (i.e., the average which does not use any kind of weight), an inherent assumption is made that all the items/ quality

MPCIs Defined by Other Miscellaneous Approaches 286

characteristics are of equal importance – an assumption which is hardly viable in practice. An weighted average-based MPCI is, therefore, more realistic.

Suppose C_{pi}, C_{pki}, C_{pmi}, and C_{pmki} denote, respectively, the C_p, C_{pk}, C_{pm}, and C_{pmk} value corresponding to the ith quality characteristic. Then Raissi [24] has defined the following set of MPCIs:

$$MC_p^{(R)} = \sum_{i=1}^{q} W_i C_{pi} \tag{14.7}$$

$$MC_{pk}^{(R)} = \sum_{i=1}^{q} W_i C_{pki} \tag{14.8}$$

$$MC_{pm}^{(R)} = \sum_{i=1}^{q} W_i C_{pmi} \tag{14.9}$$

$$MC_{pmk}^{(R)} = \sum_{i=1}^{q} W_i C_{pmki} \tag{14.10}$$

where, W_i is the "normalized importance weight", such that $\sum_{i=1}^{q} W_i = 1$. Values of W_i's are to be decided based on customers' preference.

It is evident that, though W_i is incorporated in the definitions of the MPCIs to give proper weightage to the individual quality characteristics, absence of any mathematical or analytical formulation of W_i makes indices subjective to preferable manipulation.

14.3   MPCIs Based on Concepts of Linear Algebra

Kirmani and Polansky [20] have proposed a linear algebra-based MPCI, using the concept of Lowner partial ordering or positive semidenite ordering.

A symmetric matrix A of order $q \times q$ is called a positive semi definite (p.s.d.) matrix, if all of its eigen values are nonnegative. Similarly, a symmetric matrix is called positive definite (p. d.) if all of its eigen values are strictly positive. Two of the most useful characterizations of a p.s.d. matrix are as follows:

$$A \succeq 0 \iff x' A x \geq 0, \ \forall x \in \mathbb{R} \tag{14.11}$$
$$A \succeq 0, \text{if and only if there exists a}$$
$$\text{matrix V such that, } A = VV'$$

$$\tag{14.12}$$

Similar characterizations of a p.d. matrix will be as follows:

$$A \succ 0 \iff x' Ax > 0, \ \forall x \in \mathbb{R} \tag{14.13}$$

$$A \succ 0, \text{if and only if there exists a}$$
$$\text{matrix V such that, } A = VV' \tag{14.14}$$

Partial ordering of p.d. and p.s.d. matrices play important roles in many statistical studies. There are different types of partial orderings, viz., star ordering, minus ordering or rank subtractivity, Lowner ordering and so on. Interested readers may refer to Baksalary et al. [2] and Groß [14] for detail discussion on partial ordering of matrices.

Kirmani and Polansky [20] have used Lowner partial ordering to define a new MPCI.

Lowner ordering or positive semidefinite ordering can be used to partially order symmetric matrices. Let A and B be two $q \times q$ symmetric matrices, such that $A - B \succeq 0$, i.e., $A - B$ is p.s.d. Then one may write $A \succeq B$. Similarly, for $A - B \succ 0$, $A - B$ will be p.d.

Some interesting properties of Lowner ordering (refer Kirmani and Polansky [20] and Baksalary et al. [2]) are as follows:

1. Suppose, A_1 and A_2 are two symmetric matrices of order "q" with λ_{ij} being the jth eigen value for the ith Matrix, for $i = 1, 2$ and $j = 1(1)q$, such that, the eigen values are arranged in descending order, i,e., for a fixed i, $\lambda_{i1} \geq \lambda_{iq} \geq \cdots \geq \lambda_{iq}$. Then, If $A_1 \geq A_2$, $\lambda_{1j} \geq \lambda_{2j}$, for $j = 1(1)q$, i.e. jth eigen value of A_1 will be greater than or equal to the jth eigen value of A_2, provided the eigen values are arranged in descending order.

2. If A_1 and A_2 are two p.s.d. matrices, such that $A_1 \succeq A_2$, then $tr(A_1) \geq tr(A_2)$, $|A_1| \geq |A_2|$ and $rank(A_1) \geq rank(A_2)$.

3. If A_1 and A_2 are two symmetric p.d. matrices, then $A_1 > A_2$ implies and is implied by $A_2^{-1} > A_1^{-1}$.

Kirmani and Polansky [20] have used the concept of Lowner ordering along with the celebrated Anderson's theorem (refer Anderson [1]), to define a probability-based MPCI. Suppose a process having q-correlated quality characteristics is characterized by a q-component random vector $X = (X_1, X_2, \cdots, X_q)'$ such that, $X \sim N_q(\mu, \Sigma)$. Let T be the target vector, which, without loss of generality, is assumed to be 0, i.e., $T = 0$. Suppose $C_0 = \left\{ x \in \mathbb{R}^q : x' \Sigma_0^{-1} x \leq \chi^2_{q,\alpha} \right\}$, where Σ_0 is a specified $q \times q$ p.d. matrix and $\chi^2_{q,\alpha}$ is the upper α point of a χ^2 distribution with q degrees of freedom. Then the proportion of items conforming to the stipulated target will be

$$P(X \in C_0) \geq 1 - \alpha \tag{14.15}$$

MPCIs Defined by Other Miscellaneous Approaches 288

As such, a process will be capable if $\Sigma \leq \Sigma_0$. To ascertain this, Kirmani and Polansky [20] have adopted Roy's [27] Union- intersection test. Based on this test procedure, the authors have argued that, the largest eigen value of $\Sigma\Sigma_0^{-1}$ can be considered as a relevant measure of potential process capability and this is valid for multivariate nonnormal distribution as well.

The major drawback of this approach is that the expression for the specification region C_0 is not a very practical one, as on most of the occassions, specification regions are not defined in this manner.

14.4   Viability Index

Veevers [31] has defined a PCI and an MPCI, measuring potential process capability, which take into account viability of a process region with respect to the stipulated specification region. For this, a new concept has been introduced, viz., "window of opportunity".

Let us first begin with a univariate process. Suppose a random variable X characterizes the process distribution as, $X \sim N(\mu, \sigma^2)$. Suppose, for a univariate process with the underlying distribution as normal, $6\sigma < (USL - LSL)$. Then the entire process region can be allowed to shift within the specification region, until no part of the process region goes beyond either of the specification limits. Then this range of scope of variation can be considered as the window of opportunity. To have a clearer idea, consider Figures 14.1 to 14.6, assuming normality of the process distribution.

In Figures 14.1 and 14.2, tail of the process region coincides with LSL and USL, respectively. Recall that, Veever's viability index measures potential process capability, which means that, only process variability is an issue. Infact, in both the figures, process distribution can be shifted (only by change of location) away from LSL and USL, respectively, without making any part of the process region, out of the specification region.

In Figure 14.3, lower and upper tails of the process distribution coincide with LSL and USL, respectively. Unlike Figures 14.1 and 14.2, here even the slightest shift of origin of the process region will result in increase in nonconforming items, because a part of the process region will move out of the specification region. More the shift of origin, more will be the proportion of nonconformities.

In Figure 14.4, the situation is just the opposite. Here the process region is well into the specification region, i.e., the process span viz., 6σ is much less than the specification span, viz., USL–LSL. Consequently, the process centering may be allowed to shift to either of its two sides, until one of its tails coincides with USL or LSL.

In Figure 14.5, the process region is not fully accommodated by the specification region, i.e., the process span viz., 6σ is more than the specification

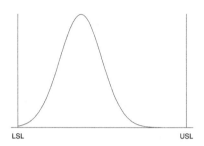

FIGURE 14.1: Lower tail of process distribution coincides with LSL.

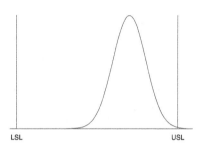

FIGURE 14.2: Upper tail of process distribution coincides USL.

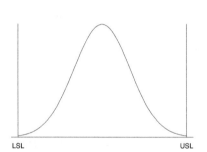

FIGURE 14.3: Process region just meets specification region.

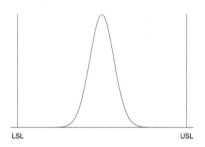

FIGURE 14.4: Process region is smaller than specification region.

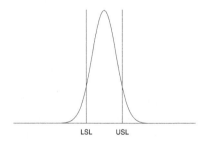

FIGURE 14.5: Process region exceeds both USL & LSL.

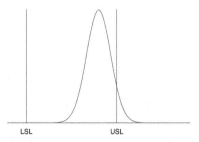

FIGURE 14.6: Process region exceeds only USL.

MPCIs Defined by Other Miscellaneous Approaches 290

span, viz., USL–LSL. Also, unlike Figures 14.1 and 14.2, shift of process centering will not deliver the good, as even then also, the process region will fail to come within the specification region. Controlling process variability is the only way to improve this process.

In Figure 14.6, although a part of the process region lies outside USL, the process is potentially capable. This is due to the fact that, similar to Figures 14.1 and 14.2, here also, mere shift of the process centering will bring the process region within the specification region.

Note that throughout this discussion, we have not mentioned any particular value of USL, LSL, μ, and σ^2, since the above observations hold good for any of their values, till the criteria mentioned above are satisfied.

Thus, summing up all the above situations and under normality assumption of the process distribution, "window of opportunity" can be defined as

$$6\sigma + \omega = USL - LSL \qquad (14.16)$$
$$\Rightarrow \omega = USL - LSL - 6\sigma \qquad (14.17)$$

where ω is the window of opportunity. Observe that, ω can assume positive, negative, and zero value. For example, when the process region just meets the specification span (as in Figure 14.3), i.e., $6\sigma = USL - LSL$, then $\omega = 0$. Likewise, if $6\sigma > (USL - LSL)$, i.e., if the process region exceeds specification span (as in Figure 14.5), then $\omega < 0$. For all the other cases, $\omega > 0$.

The viability index can, then, be defined as

$$V_t = \frac{\omega}{USL - LSL}, \qquad (14.18)$$

Now, since V_t, similar to C_p, measures potential process capability, they should be functionally related. Observe that

$$V_t = \frac{w}{USL - LSL}$$
$$= \frac{USL - LSL - 6\sigma}{USL - LSL} \qquad (14.19)$$
$$= 1 - \frac{1}{C_p} \qquad (14.20)$$
$$\Rightarrow C_p = \frac{1}{1 - V_t} \qquad (14.21)$$

Interestingly, unlike conventional PCIs, for V_t, threshold value is not "1". Infact, for $C_p = 1$, $V_t = 0$ and hence 0 can be considered as threshold of V_t, with its positive values indicating capable processes while negative values indicate that the process region is not even accommodated by the specification region.

The concept of viability index is not restricted to normally distributed prcesses; rather, with slight modification, it can be applied to nonnormal processes as well. Observe that, for any nonnormal process, the span of "6σ" is equivalent to the span of the concerned distribution between 0.00135^{th} quantile, say $q_{0.00135}$ and 99.865^{th} quantile, say $q_{99.865}$. Therefore substituting these values in equation (14.19), expression for the viability index, for non-normal processes, can be obtained as

$$
\begin{aligned}
V_t' &= \frac{USL - LSL - (q_{99.865} - q_{0.00135})}{USL - LSL} \\
&= \frac{USL - LSL - q_{99.865} + q_{0.00135}}{USL - LSL}
\end{aligned}
\tag{14.22}
$$

Veevers [31] has generalized the concept of viability index for multivariate processes as well. For this, the authors have considered rectangular specification region, with USL_i and LSL_i being the upper and lower specification limits of the ith quality characteristic, for $i = 1(1)q$.

Then, for multiresponse prosesses, the definition of viability index may be generalized as

$$
V_t^{(q)} = \frac{\text{Volume of window of opportunity}}{\text{Volume of specification region}}
\tag{14.23}
$$

To begin with, suppose, there are two correlated quality characteristics X_1 and X_2 and their corresponding responses are x_1 and x_2, respectively. Suppose the process region is rectangular with the sides W_1 and W_2. Also let $V_t(x_1)$ and $V_t(x_2)$ are the viability index values for these two quality characteristics, respectively.

When the two quality characteristics are individually viable, viability index for the process as a whole can be defined as

$$
\begin{aligned}
V_t^{(2)} &= \frac{(USL_1 - LSL_1 - W_1) \times (USL_2 - LSL_2 - W_2)}{(USL_1 - LSL_1) \times (USL_2 - LSL_2)} \\
&= \frac{USL_1 - LSL_1 - W_1}{USL_1 - LSL_1} \times \frac{USL_2 - LSL_2 - W_2}{USL_2 - LSL_2} \\
&= V_t(x_1) \times V_t(x_2)
\end{aligned}
\tag{14.24}
$$

Since $V_t(x_1) > 0$ and $V_t(x_2) > 0$, here $V_t^{(2)}$ will also be greater than zero. Accordingly, a multivariate analogue of C_p can be defined as

$$
\begin{aligned}
C_p^{(2)} &= \frac{1}{1 - V_t^{(2)}} \\
&= \frac{C_p(x_1) + C_p(x_2)}{C_p(x_1) + C_p(x_2) - 1},
\end{aligned}
\tag{14.25}
$$

where $C_p(x_i)$ is the value of C_p corresponding to the ith quality characteristic, for $i = 1(1)2$.

Again, when one of the two quality characteristics (say, X_2) is not viable, i.e. $V_t(x_1) > 0$ and $V_t(x_2) < 0$, from equation (14.23),

$$V_t^{(2)} = \frac{(USL_1 - LSL_1) \times (USL_2 - LSL_2 - W_2)}{(USL_1 - LSL_1) \times (USL_2 - LSL_2)}$$

$$= V_t(x_2) \qquad (14.26)$$

Similarly, if X_1 is not viable and X_2 is viable, then

$$V_t^{(2)} = V_t(x_1) \qquad (14.27)$$

Accordingly

$$C_p^{(2)} = \begin{cases} C_p(x_2), & \text{when, } X_2 \text{ is not viable} \\ \\ C_p(x_1), & \text{when, } X_1 \text{ is not viable} \end{cases} \qquad (14.28)$$

Interestingly, when one of the two responses is not viable, the overall viability index is nothing but the individual viability index value of that particular non-viable response variable and hence assumes negative value.

Finally, when both the responses are not viable, that is $V_t(x_1) < 0$ and $V_t(x_2) < 0$ and consequently

$$V_t^{(2)} = V_t(x_1) + V_t(x_2) - V_t(x_1) \times V_t(x_2) \qquad (14.29)$$

and

$$C_p^{(2)} = C_p(x_1) \times C_p(x_2) \qquad (14.30)$$

Veervers [31] has generalized this for processes having "q" correlated quality characteristics as follows:

$$V_t^{(q)} = \begin{cases} \prod_{i=1}^{q} V_t(x_i), & \text{when all the quality characteristics are viable} \\ \\ 1 - \prod_{i=1}^{q} [1 - V_t(x_i)]^{I_i}, & \text{when atleast one} \\ \quad \text{quality characteristic is not viable} \end{cases}$$

$$(14.31)$$

where

$$I_i = \begin{cases} 0, & \text{when, } V_t(x_i) \geq 0 \\ 1, & \text{when } V_t(x_i) < 0 \end{cases} \qquad (14.32)$$

Accordingly

$$
C_p^{(q)} = \begin{cases} \dfrac{\prod\limits_{i=1}^{q} C_p(x_i)}{\prod\limits_{i=1}^{q} C_p(x_i) - \prod\limits_{i=1}^{q} [C_p(x_i) - 1]}, \\[3ex] \quad \text{when all the quality characteristics} \\ \quad \text{are potentially capable} \\[2ex] \prod\limits_{i=1}^{q} C_p(x_i)^{J_i}, \\[3ex] \quad \text{when atleast one of the quality} \\ \quad \text{characteristics is not potentially capable} \end{cases}
\tag{14.33}
$$

with

$$
J_i = \begin{cases} 0, & \text{when, } C_p(x_i) \geq 1 \\ 1, & \text{when } C_p(x_i) < 1 \end{cases}
\tag{14.34}
$$

14.5 MPCIs Defined on Process-Oriented Basis

Most of the MPCIs available in literature perform like an indicator function, in a sense that, they signal whether the concerned process is capable or not. When the process is found to be incapable, one major question arises, which one or more of the quality characteristics are responsible for the poor process performance. This question mostly remains unanswered. Often industrial engineers and process designers have to decide their subsequent line of action based on their domain knowledge. This keeps room for subjectivity. To address this issue, Foster et al. [10] and Ranjan and Maiti [25] have advocated use of the so called "Process Oriented Basis Representation (POBREP)" methodology, originally given by Gonzalez and Aviles [13].

In POBREP methodology, a basis vector is constructed, based on process information (i.e., information obtained from the variables characterising the correlated quality charactristics) and based on that, major factors contributing toward fault in process performance, are identified.

Now to understand, what is a basis (from linear algebra perspective); let V be a vector space. Then a subset A of V is a basis for V, if any vector $\boldsymbol{v} \in V$ is uniquely represented as a linear combination

$$
\boldsymbol{v} = r_1 \boldsymbol{a_1} + r_2 \boldsymbol{a_2} + \cdots + r_s \boldsymbol{a_s}
\tag{14.35}
$$

where, a_1, $a_2, \cdots, a_s$ are distinct vectors of A and r_1, r_2, $\cdots, r_s \in \mathbb{R}$. For an n-dimentional process, the standard basis is of the form

$$E = (e_1, e_2, \cdots, e_n), \tag{14.36}$$

where the ith element of E, viz., e_i is a vector whose ith element is "1" and all the other elements are "0", for $i = 1(1)n$.

In SQC, it is often observed that, a special cause of variation is directly linked to the error pattern in the process, caused by it. The basic difference between principal component analysis (PCA)-based MPCIs and POBREP-based MPCIs is that, in the former case, only first few principal components (PC) are retained. PCA, primarily being a data-oriented approach, gives only the direction of the largest amount of variation in the process. This, in turn, often fails to provide any objective answer to the initial question, viz., which of the quality characteristics play major role in poor process performance (as is reflected by error pattern), making the decision of the concerned authority judgemental, to a large extent. On the contrary, POBREP is defined to be process oriented, in a sense that, here the original vector of quality characteristics is represented in terms of the so called process oriented basis, so that one can identify a small set of "potential causes" for poor process performance objectively (refer Foster et al. [10]).

Suppose there are 'q' quality characteristics represented by the random vector $X = (X_1, X_2, \cdots, X_q)$. Let $a_1, a_2, \cdots, a_s$ be s q-component vectors representing "s" distinct error patterns. Define a matrix $A = (a_1, a_2, \cdots, a_s)$. If the error patterns are mutually independent, i.e. $a_1, a_2, \cdots, a_s$ are mutually independent, which is usually the case, then A constitutes an alternative basis. Also let $Y = (y_1, y_2, \cdots, y_q)$ be a matrix of multivariate measurement errors for q quality characteristics.

Since A and Y are both associated with the error data of the measurements of the quality characteristics, by the very definition of basis, Y can be expressed as a linear combination of vectors of A. Let, $Z = (z_1, z_2, \cdots, z_s)$ be a coefficient matrix, which can be obtained by solving

$$AZ = Y, \quad \text{when A is orthogonal} \tag{14.37}$$

$$Z = (A' A)^{-1} A' Y \text{ when A is non-orthogonal} \tag{14.38}$$

Suppose Σ_Z is the covariance matrix of Z. Here Σ_Z is defined such that it is a diagonal matrix, with its ith diagonal element being σ_{Z_i}, for $i = 1(1)s$. Note that, off-diagonal elements of Σ_Z are set to be "0", as the errors are already assumed to be mutually independent. Also let μ_i stands for the mean of the ith column of Z, for $i = 1(1)s$.

Then under multivariate normality assumption of Z, Foster et al [10] has defined a multivariate analogue of C_{pk} as

$$\hat{M}C_{pk}^{(Foster)} = \frac{1}{3} \Phi^{-1}(\hat{\theta}), \tag{14.39}$$

where $\hat{\theta}$ is the estimated proportion of nonconformance.

MPCIs Defined by Other Miscellaneous Approaches 295

Ranjan and Maiti [25] have discussed another multivariate analogue of C_{pk} based on POBREP approach. Suppose for a given process, Y matrix and the corresponding specification limits are obtained. From that, Z matrix and the corresponding specification limits of individual z_i values, for $i = 1(1)s$ are calculated. Suppose C_{pk_i} denotes the corresponding C_{pk} value for the ith variable. Then a multivariate analogue of C_{pk} value, assessing capability of the multivariate process, can be defined as

$$MC_{pk}^{(RM)} = \sqrt[s]{\prod_{i=1}^{s} C_{pk_i}} \qquad (14.40)$$

Foster et al. [10] has argued that, often quality engineers and other stake holders of a process identify possible areas of correction before-hand. The vector z_i, i.e., the ith column of Z gives the contribution of the ith error pattern on overall process performance. Therefore, a poor value of $\hat{MC}_{pk}^{(Foster)}$ indicates that one or more of the preidentied causes of error need further investigation for necessary correction in the process.

14.6 Multivariate Process Performance Analysis with Special Emphasis on Accuracy and Precision

Almost all the MPCIs, discussed so far, suffer from a unique problem of not being able to get clue of the cause of problem with an incapable process. Suppose after applying a suitable MPCI, a process is found to be incapable. Then accuracy, i.e., amount of deviation from target or precision, i.e., degree of variability in the process or both of these two may be responsible for poor performance of the process. However, since a typical MPCI considers both these factors simultaneously, it is almost impossible to identify the main reasons.

Chang et al. [6] have observed that, for an incapable processs, a single valued capability index (both univariate and multivariate) may often fail to address this issue. They have shown that the celebrated super structure of univariate PCIs, viz. $C_p(u,v)$, proposed by Vannman [30], can be expressed in terms of accuracy index $\delta = \frac{\mu - T}{d}$ and the precision index $\gamma = \frac{\sigma}{d}$, where, $d = \frac{USL - LSL}{2}$, as follows:

$$C_p(u,v) = \frac{d - u|\mu - M|}{3\sqrt{\sigma^2 + v(\mu - T)^2}}, \quad u, v \geq 0. \qquad (14.41)$$

$$= \frac{1 - u|\delta|}{3\sqrt{\gamma^2 + v\delta^2}} \qquad (14.42)$$

MPCIs Defined by Other Miscellaneous Approaches

Note that, the absolute value of δ should ideally be as minimum as possible, with a value of it close to zero signifying process centering close to the stipulated target. Similarly, by definition γ is nonnegative and should have value as small as possible.

Now, depending upon the present state of quality, a process may be at $k\sigma$, quality level, for $k = 3, 4, 5, 6$. Accordingly, let δ_k and γ_k denote accuracy and precision of a process operating at $k\sigma$ quality level.

According to Pearn and Chen [23], for a process performing at 6σ level, should have 1.5 sigma unit deviation from target, i.e., $|\delta| = \frac{1.5\sigma}{6\sigma} = \frac{1}{4}$ and $\gamma = \frac{\sigma}{d} = \frac{\sigma}{6\sigma} = \frac{1}{6}$. Now suppose for a process performing at $k\sigma$ quality level, δ_k and γ_k denote process accuracy and process precision, respectively. Then the quality level measurement constraint can be written as

$$QL_k = \left\{ (\delta_k, \gamma_k) \mid -\frac{1.5}{K} \le \delta_k \le \frac{1.5}{K}, \ \gamma_k = \frac{1}{k} \right\} \qquad (14.43)$$

Based on this, Chang et al. [6] have derived the expression for yield as

$$\% \text{ of yield} \quad = \quad \Phi\left(\frac{1 - \delta_k}{\gamma_k}\right) + \Phi\left(\frac{1 + \delta_k}{\gamma_k}\right) - 1$$
$$(14.44)$$
$$= \quad \Phi(k - 1.5) + \Phi(k + 1.5) - 1 \qquad (14.45)$$

Chang et al. [6] have developed a graphical measure for simultaneous assessment of δ_k and γ_k, called process quality level analysis chart (PQLAC). Suppose for a process, there are more than one quality characteristics of nominal the best type. Then the Table 14.2 gives δ_k, γ_k, and percentage of yield corresponding to 3σ to 6σ quality level for each individual quality characteristic.

TABLE 14.2: Values of δ_k, γ_k, and percentage of yield for various quality levels

Quality level	δ_k	γ_k	% of yield
3σ	[-0.5, 0.5]	0.3333	0.9332
4σ	[-0.375, 0.375]	0.25	0.99938
5σ	[-0.3, 0.3]	0.2	0.9998
6σ	[-0.25, 0.25]	0.1667	0.999997

Based on the information in Table 14.2, Chang et al. [6] have drawn the PQLAC chart given in Figure 14.7, for individual quality characteristic.

For a process running at 3σ quality level, if the concerned authority intend to run it at 6σ quality level, following can be observed as guideline from Figure 14.7:

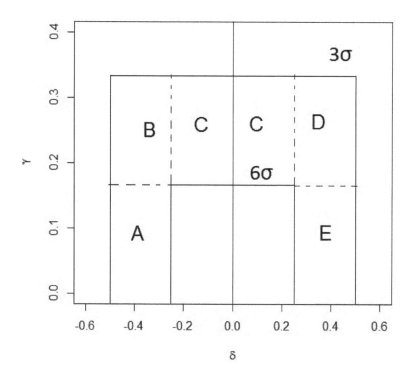

FIGURE 14.7: PQLAC chart for 3σ and 6σ quality level.

1. For any observation lying at zones A and E, although the process precision is less than 0.1667 (refer Table 14.2), process accuracy is beyond the stipulated range viz., [-0.25, 0.25]. Therefore, process centering needs to be re-aligned keeping process dispersion fixed at this level.

2. For any observation lying at zones B and D, both the accuracy and precision index are beyond the stipulated range given in Table 14.2. Therefore, process centering needs to be re-aligned and process dispersion needs to be brought down below 0.1667.

3. In zone C, the process alignment with respect to the target is perfect, but the observations are highly dispersed. Management has to incur huge cost to scale down process dispersion (refer Chang et al. [6]).

Chang et al. [6] have derived expression for the joint $(1 - \alpha_1 - \alpha_2)\%$ confidence interval of δ and γ as

$$P\left[\hat{\delta} - \frac{\hat{\gamma}}{\sqrt{n}}\, t_{\frac{\alpha_1}{2}}(n-1) < \delta < \hat{\delta} + \frac{\hat{\gamma}}{\sqrt{n}}\, t_{\frac{\alpha_1}{2}}(n-1),\right.$$

$$\sqrt{\frac{\hat{\gamma}^2}{\chi^2_{\frac{\alpha_2}{2}}}} < \gamma < \sqrt{\frac{\hat{\gamma}^2}{\chi^2_{1-\frac{\alpha_2}{2}}}}\,\right]$$

$$\geq 1 - P\left[\hat{\delta} + \frac{\hat{\gamma}}{\sqrt{n}}\, t_{\frac{\alpha_1}{2}}(n-1) \leq \delta\right.$$

$$\left. or\ \hat{\delta} - \frac{\hat{\gamma}}{\sqrt{n}}\, t_{\frac{\alpha_1}{2}}(n-1) \geq \delta\right]$$

$$- P\left[\sqrt{\frac{\hat{\gamma}^2}{\chi^2_{1-\frac{\alpha_2}{2}}}} \leq \gamma\ \ or\ \ \sqrt{\frac{\hat{\gamma}^2}{\chi^2_{\frac{\alpha_2}{2}}}} \geq \gamma\right]$$

$$=\ \ 1 - \alpha_1 - \alpha_2 \tag{14.46}$$

PQLAC chart plays an important role in initial decision making regarding process accuracy and precision of individual quality characteristics. However, since under the multivariate set-up, quality characteristics are usually mutually correlated, the aspect which is not considered in the construction of the chart and hence may lead to impractical decisions in quality policy making.

14.7 Multivariate Process Capability Analysis Using Fuzzy Logic

Most of the indices, whether univariate or multivariate, defined in literature and all the allied concepts, are based on the assumption that, the specification set along with the target values are objectively defined. However, in many practical situations, such assumptions may not hold good. In such cases, one can, either use other practical conditions to define specifications and targets distinctly or use the so called fuzzy technique, originally developed by Zadeh [35].

In the simplest way, fuzzy can be defined as something which cannot be "clearly defined". Therefore conceptually, unlike a so called abstract set, a fuzzy set contains elements, which, by definition, may be a partial member of it. This concept of membership plays a key role in constructing a fuzzy set. Laviolette et al. [21] have defined membership function as mapping from a space $\Omega = \{x\}$ of concerned elements to a unit interval $M_A : \Omega \to [0,1]$.

For example, for $s = (s_1, s_2, s_3)' \in \mathbb{R}^3$, a triangular fuzzy membership function may be defined as

$$M_{triag}(x; s_1, s_2, s_3) = \begin{cases} \frac{x - s_1}{s_2 - x}, & \text{if } t \in [s_1, s_2], \ s_1 \neq s_2 \\[2mm] \frac{s_3 - x}{s_3 - s_2}, & \text{if } t \in [s_2, s_3], \ s_2 \neq s_3 \\[2mm] 1, & \text{if } x = s_1 = s_2 = s_3 \\[2mm] 0, & \text{Otherwise} \end{cases} \qquad (14.47)$$

Again, normal fuzzy membership function can be defined as,

$$M_{norm}(x; \mu^*, \lambda) = e^{-\frac{1}{2}\left(\frac{x - \mu^*}{\lambda}\right)^2} \qquad (14.48)$$

Then a fuzzy set A may be defined as follows (refer Kandel and Byatt [17]):

$$A = \{(x, M_A(x))\}, \quad x \in \Omega \qquad (14.49)$$

which is an ordered pair of the elements.

For two "continuous and nonincreasing shape functions", L and R, both of which map $[0, 1] \rightarrow [0, 1]$, Ganji and Gildeh [11, 12] have defined LR fuzzy membership function or LR fuzzy number as

$$M^{(LR)}(t) = \begin{cases} L\left(\frac{a - t}{\alpha}\right), & \text{when, } t \in [a - \alpha, a] \\[2mm] 1, & \text{when } t \in [a, b] \\[2mm] R\left(\frac{t - b}{\beta}\right) & \text{when } t \in [b, b + \beta] \\[2mm] 0, & \text{Otherwise} \end{cases} \qquad (14.50)$$

Now suppose the fuzzy set A contains the elements a, b, c. Then following axioms are satisfied under the operations + and * (refer Kandel and Byatt [17]) :

Idempotent $a + a = a$ and $a * a = a$.

Commutative $a + b = b + a$ and $a * b = b * a$.

associative $(a + b) + c = a + (b + c)$
and $(a * b) * c = a * (b * c)$.

Distributive $a + (b * c) = (a + b) * (a + c)$ and
$a * (b + c) = (a * b) + (a * c)$

Absorption $a + (a * b) = a$ and $a * (a + b) = a$

Complement If $a \in Z$, then there exists a unique complement a^c of a, for which, $a^c \in Z$ and $(a^c)^c = a$, where ^{c} denotes complement of an event.

De-Morgan's Law $(a + b)^c = a^c * b^c$ and $(a * b)^c = a^c + b^c$.

14.7.1 A Fuzzy Logic-Based MPCI

Fayaz et al. [9] have defined a proportion of nonconformance-based MPCI using fuzzy logic.

Recall that, if USL and LSL, respectively, denote upper and lower specification limits of a particular quality characteristic, then, for a single quality characteristic, proportion of nonconformance can be defined as

$$
\begin{aligned}
P_{NC} &= P\,[\text{Value of the quality characteristic} \\
&\quad\; \text{is not within the range [LSL, USL]}] \\
&= 1 - \int_{LSL}^{USL} f(x)dx
\end{aligned}
\tag{14.51}
$$

where, $f(x)$ is the probability density function (p. d. f.) of x.
Accordingly, univariate PCI can be defined as

$$
\begin{aligned}
C_{PNC} &= \int_{LSL}^{USL} f(x)dx \\
&= \int_{-\infty}^{\infty} I(x)f(x)dx
\end{aligned}
\tag{14.52}
$$

where, $I(x)$ is an indiactor function defined as

$$
I(x) = \begin{cases} 1, & \text{when, } x \in [LSL, USL] \\ 0, & \text{when, } x \notin [LSL, USL] \end{cases}
\tag{14.53}
$$

Taking cue from the general expression of a regular univariate PCI, as given in equation (14.52), along with the indicator function $I(x)$, Fayaz et al. [9] have defined a fuzzy PCI, for a single quality characteristic characterized by a continuous random variable (X), as

$$
C_{Fuzzy} = \int_{-\infty}^{\infty} M(x)f(x)dx
\tag{14.54}
$$

where $M(x)$ is the corresponding membership function.

Similarly, suppose a discrete random variable Y assumes values $y_1, y_2, \cdots, y_n$. Then

$$
C'_{Fuzzy} = \sum_{i=1}^{n} M(x)f(x)
\tag{14.55}
$$

MPCIs Defined by Other Miscellaneous Approaches 301

Then using normal or Gaussian fuzzy membership function [vide equation (14.48)], fuzzy PCI, for processes having normal process distribution viz., $X \sim N(\mu, \sigma^2)$, can be defined as

$$C_{Fuzzy}^{norm} = \int_{-\infty}^{\infty} e^{-\frac{1}{2}\left(\frac{x-\mu^*}{\lambda}\right)^2} \frac{1}{\sigma\sqrt{2\pi}} e^{-\frac{1}{2}\left(\frac{x-\mu}{\sigma}\right)^2} dx \tag{14.56}$$

$$= \left[\frac{\lambda}{\sqrt{\sigma^2 + \lambda^2}}\right] \times e^{-\frac{1}{2}\frac{(\mu-\mu^*)^2}{\lambda^2+\sigma^2}} \tag{14.57}$$

Now, extending equation (14.48), for multivariate normal set-up, a fuzzy multivariate PCI (MPCI) may be defined as

$$M_{MVN}(\boldsymbol{x}; \boldsymbol{\mu}^*, \Lambda) = e^{-\frac{1}{2}(\boldsymbol{x}-\boldsymbol{\mu}^*)'\Lambda^{-1}(\boldsymbol{x}-\boldsymbol{\mu}^*)}$$

$$= e^{-\frac{1}{2}\left(\frac{x_1-\mu_1^*}{\lambda_1}\right)^2 + \left(\frac{x_2-\mu_2^*}{\lambda_2}\right)^2 + \cdots + \left(\frac{x_q-\mu_q^*}{\lambda_q}\right)^2} \tag{14.58}$$

$$= \prod_{i=1}^{q} M_{norm}(x_i; \mu_i^*, \lambda_i) \tag{14.59}$$

where $\boldsymbol{\mu}^* = (\mu_1^*, \mu_q^*, \cdots, \mu_q^*)'$ and $\Lambda = diag\left(\lambda_1^2, \lambda_2^2, \cdots, \lambda_q^2\right)$ is a diagonal matrix whose ith diagonal element, i.e., $(i,i)^{\text{th}}$ element is λ_i^2 and all the off diagonal elements are zero.

Then analogous to the univariate case, for a multivariate process having continuous pdf, a general definition of a fuzzy MPCI can be given by (refer Fayaz et al. [9])

$$MC_{Fuzzy} = \int_{-\infty}^{\infty} \int_{-\infty}^{\infty} \cdots \int_{-\infty}^{\infty} M(\boldsymbol{x})f(\boldsymbol{x})d\boldsymbol{x} \tag{14.60}$$

In particular, for a process having multivariate normal process distribution, Fayaz et al. [9] have defined a fuzzy-based Gaussian MPCI as

$$MC_{Fuzzy}^{MVN} = \int_{-\infty}^{\infty} \int_{-\infty}^{\infty} \cdots \int_{-\infty}^{\infty} M_{MVN}(\boldsymbol{x}; \boldsymbol{\mu}^*, \Lambda)f(\boldsymbol{x})d\boldsymbol{x} \tag{14.61}$$

$$= \int_{-\infty}^{\infty} \int_{-\infty}^{\infty} \cdots \int_{-\infty}^{\infty} e^{-\frac{1}{2}(\boldsymbol{x}-\boldsymbol{\mu}^*)'\Lambda^{-1}(\boldsymbol{x}-\boldsymbol{\mu}^*)}$$

$$\times \frac{1}{|\Sigma|(\sqrt{2\pi})^q} e^{-\frac{1}{2}(\boldsymbol{x}-\boldsymbol{\mu})'\Sigma^{-1}(\boldsymbol{x}-\boldsymbol{\mu})} d\boldsymbol{x} \tag{14.62}$$

MPCIs Defined by Other Miscellaneous Approaches 302

Fayaz et al. [9] have also discussed two estimation procedures for MC_{Fuzzy}^{MVN}. In the first approach, process mean vector μ and the process dispersion matrix Σ are replaced by the sample mean vector $\overline{X}$ and the sample dispersion matrix S, respectively, to obtain the so called plug-in estimator of MC_{Fuzzy}^{MVN}.

Alternatively, from equation (14.61)

$$
\begin{aligned}
\hat{MC}_{Fuzzy}^{MVN} &= \int\limits_{-\infty}^{\infty} \int\limits_{-\infty}^{\infty} \cdots \int\limits_{-\infty}^{\infty} M_{MVN}(\boldsymbol{x}; \boldsymbol{\mu}^*, \Lambda) f(\boldsymbol{x}) d\boldsymbol{x} \\
&= E\left[M_{MVN}(\boldsymbol{X}; \boldsymbol{\mu}^*, \Lambda)\right]
\end{aligned}
\tag{14.63}
$$

Therefore, following Fayaz et al. [9], average sample fuzzy membership can be considered as the estimated value of MPCI in fuzzy approach.

14.7.2   Fuzzy Multivariate Process Capability Vector

Ganji and Gildeh [11, 12] have defined a fuzzy multivariate process capability vector (MPCV). To be more precise, they have modified Shahriari and Abdollahzadeh's [28] MPCV from fuzzy perspective.

As has already been discussed, often in practice, upper and lower specification regions and the target may not be distinctly defined. Let $LSL^{(f)} =< l, \beta >$, $USL^{(f)} =< u, \gamma >$ and $T^{(f)} =< t, \delta >$ denote, respectively, the LSL, USL and T from fuzzy perspective, where, $< e, \eta >$ denotes a symmetric triangular fuzzy number with the centre part "e" and the symmetric spread η from either side of "e".

Recall from Chapter 13 that, Shahriari and Abdollahzadeh [28] have defined an MPCV as, $[NMC_p^{(SA)},\ PV, LI]$, where, under multivariate normality assumption of the underlying process distribution, the specification region is given by

$$
(\boldsymbol{X} - \boldsymbol{T})^{'} \Sigma^{-1} (\boldsymbol{X} - \boldsymbol{T}) \le c^{'2},
\tag{14.64}
$$

with

$$
c^{'} = \begin{cases}
\min\left\{ \frac{USL_i - T_i}{\sqrt{\sigma_{ii}}},\ i = 1(1)q \right\}, \quad \text{when } T_i = \frac{USL_i + LSL_i}{2} \\
\\
\min\left\{ \min\left\{ \frac{USL_i - T_i}{\sqrt{\sigma_{ii}}}, \frac{T_i - LSL_i}{\sqrt{\sigma_{ii}}} \right\},\ i = 1(1)q \right\}, \\
\\
\quad \text{when } T_i \neq \frac{USL_i + LSL_i}{2}
\end{cases}
\tag{14.65}
$$

and σ_{ii} is the ith diagonal element of Σ.

$$NMC_p^{(SA)} = \frac{c'}{\sqrt{\chi_{0.9973,q}^2}} \tag{14.66}$$

$$PV = P\left(T^2 > \frac{q(n-1)}{n-q} \times F_{q,n-q}\right), \tag{14.67}$$

where, $T^2 = n(\overline{X} - \mu)'\widehat{\Sigma}^{-1}(\overline{X} - \mu)$
and

$$LI = \begin{cases} 1, & \\ & \text{If modified rectangular process region is} \\ & \quad \text{fully accommodated within the tolerance region} \\ 0, & \text{Otherwise} \end{cases} \tag{14.68}$$

Ganji and Gildeh [11, 12] have redefined this MPCV from fuzzy perspective as follows:

Suppose for a process having q-correlated quality characteristics, the mean vector is $\tilde{\boldsymbol{\mu}} = (\tilde{\mu}_q, \tilde{\mu}_q, \cdots, \tilde{\mu}_q)'$, where, $\tilde{\mu}_i = < \mu_i, \zeta_i >$, for $i = 1(1)q$ and dispersion matrix is $\tilde{\Sigma} = ((\tilde{\sigma}_{ij}))$, with $\tilde{\sigma}_{ij} = < \sigma_{ij}, \xi_{ij} >$.

Ganji and Gildeh [11, 12] have defined a fuzzy version of c' as

$$\tilde{c}' = \min\left\{\min\left\{\frac{U\tilde{S}L_i \ominus \tilde{T}_i}{\sqrt{\tilde{\sigma}_{ii}}}, \frac{\tilde{T}_i \ominus L\tilde{S}L_i}{\sqrt{\tilde{\sigma}_{ii}}}\right\}, \quad i = 1(1)q\right\} \tag{14.69}$$

where $\ominus$ denotes fuzzy substraction. Then, a fuzzy analogue of $NMC_p^{(SA)}$ will be

$$NMC_p^{(fuzzy)} = \frac{\tilde{c}'}{\sqrt{\chi_{0.9973,q}^2}} \tag{14.70}$$

Ganji and Gildeh [11, 12] have fuzzified PV, say $PV^{(fuzzy)}$ using the concept of α cut interval. Let U be a collection of objects, popularly known as universal set in fuzzy nomenclature. For a fuzzy set Z in U and any real number $\alpha \in [0, 1]$, an α- cut set is defined as a set containing all the elements of U having membership function value at least α. Interested readers can refer to Ganji and Gildeh [12] for detail derivation of the expression for PV under fuzzy set-up and its interpretation.

Unlike the previous two members of the fuzzy MPCV, viz., $NMC_p^{(fuzzy)}$ and $PV^{(fuzzy)}$, Ganji and Gildeh [11, 12] have defined an analogue of LI by so called "defuzzifying" all the process parameters, specification limits and targets using ranking function and then using the usual procedure suggested by Shahriari and Abdollahzadeh [28].

14.8 MPCIs for Processes Having Linear and Nonlinear Profiles

Till now while discussing about MPCIs we have assumed processes having two or more interrelated quality characteristics, having no causal relationship among themselves. Interestingly, having strong correlation between two or more variables does not imply existence of causation. However, there are some practical situations, where there exist multiple correlated variables, among which one is a response variable and the rest are the explanatory variables. Often such relationships are modelled by linear or nonlinear regression models depending upon the situation. Interested readers may refer to Mahmoud and Woodall [22], Woodall et al. [33] and Woodall [32] for a detail discussion on simple linear profile monitoring, while for nonlinear profile monitoring, one may refer to Kazemzadeh et al. [18] and the references therein.

In the most general format, a linear or nonlinear profile runs in two phases. In Phase I, historical process data is analysed to estimate in-control process parameter values. In Phase II, the estimated parameter values, as obtained in Phase I, are utilized to detect any shift in the process.

14.8.1 MPCIs for Simple Linear Profile

Suppose from a multivariate process, m random samples of size n are taken. Suppose X_{ij} denotes a particular random observation (out of n) of a random sample (out of m) for the explanatory random variable X, for $i = 1(1)n$, $j = 1(1)m$. Also, for a fixed value of the explanatory variable, there are p- values of the response variable. Thus, for a fixed x_{ij}, values of the response variable may be denoted by $y_{ij1}, y_{ij2}, \cdots, y_{ijp}$.

This can be consolidated in a linear model as

$$Y = XB + E \qquad (14.71)$$

where, Y is a $n \times p$ matrix of response variables, X is a $n \times 2$ matrix of explanatory variables, whose first column consists of 1's (for intercepts of the model) and the second column gives n values of the explanatory variable, B is a $2 \times p$ matrix of model coefficients and E is a $n \times p$ matrix of the corresponding error terms, such that each row of E, which is a p-component random vector of errors follow p-component multivariate normal distribution with mean vector $\mathbf{0}$ and dispersion matrix Σ_E. Ebadi and Amiri [8] have made an additional assumption regarding the model, for computational simplicity as, X values remain unchanged for each sample.

For simple linear profiles, Ebadi and Amiri [8] have proposed three different MPCIs, viz., (i) Proportion of nonconformance (PNC)-based MPCI, (ii)

MPCIs Defined by Other Miscellaneous Approaches 305

Vector valued MPCI or multivariate process capability vector, (iii) Principal component analysis (PCA)-based MPCI.

For the PNC-based MPCI, Ebadi and and Amiri [8] have chosen the index S_{pk}^{T} to generalize for the context of simple linear profiles. Suppose for a process having q correlated quality characteristics, $S_{pk;l}$ stands for a PNC-based PCI for an individual quality characteristic, defined as

$$S_{pk;l} = \Phi^{-1}\left(1 - \frac{P_{NC;l}}{2}\right), \ for \ \ l = 1(1)q \tag{14.72}$$

where $P_{NC;l}$ denotes PNC corresponding to the lth quality characteristic, for $l = 1(1)q$.

Then, Chen et al. [7] have defined a PNC-based MPCI as

$$S_{pk}^{T} = \frac{1}{3} \ \Phi^{-1}\left[\frac{\prod_{l=1}^{q} (2\Phi(3S_{pk;l}) - 1) + 1}{2}\right] \tag{14.73}$$

Now, to adopt S_{pk}^{T} for simple linear profile model perspective, suppose for the kth response variable, $P_{NC;k}^{(L)}$ and $P_{NC;k}^{(U)}$ denote, respectively, PNC incurred due to observations lying below LSL and above USL, respectively, for $k = 1(1)p$. Then Ebadi and Amiri [8] have suggested a consolidated measure for PNC corresponding to the kth response variable as

$$P_{NC;k} = P_{NC;k}^{(L)} + P_{NC;k}^{(U)}, \ \ for \ \ k = 1(1)p \tag{14.74}$$

Then using equation (14.72), S_{pk} value for the kth response variable will be

$$S_{pk;k}^{(SPL)} = \Phi^{-1}\left(1 - \frac{P_{NC;l}}{2}\right), \ for \ \ l = 1(1)q \tag{14.75}$$

and consequently, from equations (14.73), (14.72), and (14.75), Ebadi and Amiri [8] have proposed a PNC-based MPCI for simple linear profile as

$$S_{pk}^{(SPL)} = \frac{1}{3} \ \Phi^{-1}\left[\frac{\prod_{k=1}^{p} \left(2\Phi(3S_{pk;k}^{(RES)}) - 1\right) + 1}{2}\right] \tag{14.76}$$

For vector valued process capability measure, Ebadi and Amiri [8] have used the MPCV defined by Shahriari et al. [29], a detail discussion on which is made in Chapter 13. The first component of the vector, viz., C_{pM} is modified as

$$C_{pM}^{(SPL)} = \left[\frac{\prod\limits_{k=1}^{p} \prod\limits_{i=1}^{n} (USL_{ik} - LSL_{ik})}{(\chi_{\alpha,p}^{2})^{\frac{np}{2}} \, 2^{np} \prod\limits_{k=1}^{p} \sigma_{kk}} \right]^{\frac{1}{pn}} \tag{14.77}$$

where USL_{ik} and LSL_{ik} are, respectively, the lower and upper specification limits of the kth response variable for the ith sample, for $i = 1(1)n$ and $k = 1(1)p$.

As is evident from the discussion so far, process capability analysis for multivariate simple linear profile, response variables are treated as the random variables representing the quality characteristics. Thus, the second component of Shahriari et al.'s [29] MPCV is accordingly modified as

$$PV_i^{(SPL)} = P\left(F_{p,m-p} > \frac{m-p}{p(m-1)} T_i^{(SPL)2}\right) \tag{14.78}$$

where $T_i^{(SPL)2}$ is the Hotelling T^2 statistic for the vector of response variables corresponding to the ith value of the explanatory variable (X). Mathematically

$$T_i^{(SPL)2} = m \left(\overline{Y}_i - T_{Yi}\right)' S^{-1} \left(\overline{Y}_i - T_{Yi}\right), \tag{14.79}$$

where $\overline{Y}_i$ and T_{Yi} are the sample mean vector and the target vector for the response variable corresponding to the ith value of X, for $i = 1(1)n$ and S is the corresponding sample dispersin matrix.

It is evident that, unlike PV, defined by Shahriari et al. [29], $PV_i^{(SPL)}$ is not single values. Rather it is defined for individual values of X.

The third component of the MPCV for simple linear profile, say $LI^{(SPL)}$, is an indicator function assuming value 1 if the modified process regions for all the associated regression models are accommodated by the specification region and 0 otherwise.

Finally, Ebadi and Amiri [8] have defined a PCA-based multivariate analogue of MC_p for simple linear profile as

$$\widehat{MC}_{PC}^{(SPL)} = \left(\prod_{l=1}^{v}\prod_{i=1}^{n} \hat{C}_{p;PC_{il}}\right)^{\frac{1}{vn}}, \tag{14.80}$$

where v is the number to principal components (PC) retained for the analysis

MPCIs Defined by Other Miscellaneous Approaches

$$\hat{C}_{p;PC_{il}} = \frac{\boldsymbol{u}_l' \boldsymbol{USL}_i - \boldsymbol{u}_l' \boldsymbol{LSL}_i}{6 S_{PC;l}} \qquad (14.81)$$

$S_{PC;l} = \boldsymbol{u}_l' \hat{\Sigma}_E$, $\boldsymbol{u}_l$ is the eigen vector corresponding to the lth eigen value λ_l, for $l = 1(1)v$.

However, this being a multivariate analogue of the potential PCI C_p, measures potential process capability only.

14.8.2 MPCIs for Multivariate Nonlinear Profiles

As has been already discussed, the MPCIs defined by Ebadi and Amiri [8] are based on linearity assumption of the multivariate profile under consideration. However, this assumption may often be violated due to various practical reasons. To address this issue, Guevara and Vargas [15] have some new MPCIs for processes having multivariate nonlinear profiles under both the normality and nonnormality assumptions.

Suppose, for a q-dimensional stochastic process, the quality characteristics form a multivariate profile, with the jth component of the random response vector $\boldsymbol{Y} = (Y_1, Y_2, \cdots, Y_q)'$ being a nonlinear regression model given but

$$Y_j(t) = f_j(\boldsymbol{X}_j, \boldsymbol{\beta}_j, t) + \epsilon_j(t), \quad \text{for} \quad j = 1(1)q \qquad (14.82)$$

where i.e., $f_j(\boldsymbol{X}_j, \boldsymbol{\beta}_j, t)$ is a nonlinear function, t is a real number within the range of values of Y_j, say $t \in [a, b]$, $\boldsymbol{X}_j$ is the vector of explanatory variables for Y_j and $\epsilon_j(t)$ is the corresponding error due to regression model, for $j = 1(1)q$. It is further assumed that, for a fixed value of t

$$\boldsymbol{Y}(t) = (Y_1(t), Y_2(t), \cdots, Y_q(t))' \sim N_q \left(\boldsymbol{0}, \Sigma_{\boldsymbol{Y}(t)} \right)$$

where $\Sigma_{\boldsymbol{Y}(t)} = \boldsymbol{Y}(t) \boldsymbol{Y}(t)'$.

using notations similar to Chapter 5, let PC_i denotes ith principal component (PC) corresponding to $\boldsymbol{Y}$ having USL and LSL as $USL_{PC_i} = \boldsymbol{u}_i' \boldsymbol{USL}$ and $LSL_{PC_i} = \boldsymbol{u}_i' \boldsymbol{LSL}$, respectively, for $i = 1(1)q$. Also let $\boldsymbol{u}_i$ and λ_i be, respectively, the eigen vector and eigen value corresponding to PC_i, for $i = 1(1)q$ and ν is the number of PCs explaining 90% or more of the total process variability.

Suppose the random error components follow multivariate normal distribution and accordingly PC_i is also normal. Then, based on these, Guevara and Vargas [15] have defined following PCIs corresponding to the ith PC, for $i = 1(1)\nu$:

$$C_{pu,PC_i}^{(Norm)} = \frac{\int_c^d [USL_{PC_i}(t) - \mu_{PC_i}(t)]\, dt}{3 \int_c^d \sqrt{\lambda_i(t)}\, dt} \qquad (14.83)$$

$$C_{pl,PC_i}^{(Norm)} = \frac{\int_c^d [\mu_{PC_i}(t) - LSL_{PC_i}(t)]\, dt}{3 \int_c^d \sqrt{\lambda_i(t)}\, dt} \qquad (14.84)$$

$$C_{p,PC_i}^{(Norm)} = \frac{\int_c^d [USL_{PC_i}(t) - LSL_{PC_i}(t)]\, dt}{6 \int_c^d \sqrt{\lambda_i(t)}\, dt} \qquad (14.85)$$

$$C_{pk,PC_i}^{(Norm)} = \min\left\{ C_{pu,PC_i}^{(Norm)},\ C_{pl,PC_i}^{(Norm)} \right\} \qquad (14.86)$$

Using these PCIs for individual PCs, Guevara and Vargas [15] have defined MPCIs as

$$MC_{pu,PC}^{(Norm)} = \frac{1}{\nu} \sum_{i=1}^{\nu} C_{pu,PC_i}^{(Norm)} \qquad (14.87)$$

$$MC_{pl,PC}^{(Norm)} = \frac{1}{\nu} \sum_{i=1}^{\nu} C_{pl,PC_i}^{(Norm)} \qquad (14.88)$$

$$MC_{p,PC}^{(Norm)} = \frac{1}{\nu} \sum_{i=1}^{\nu} C_{p,PC_i}^{(Norm)} \qquad (14.89)$$

$$MC_{pk,PC}^{(Norm)} = \frac{1}{\nu} \sum_{i=1}^{\nu} C_{pk,PC_i}^{(Norm)} \qquad (14.90)$$

However, recall from Chapter 5 that, the above MPCIs use no weight for PCs, while even the PCs retained do not explain same amount of process variability and hence are not of same importance. To address this issue, similar to Xekalaki and Perakis [34], Guevara and Vargas [15] have defined weighted MPCIs as

$$MC_{pu,PC}^{(Norm)*} = \frac{1}{\nu} \sum_{i=1}^{\nu} \pi_i C_{pu,PC_i}^{(Norm)} \tag{14.91}$$

$$MC_{pl,PC}^{(Norm)*} = \frac{1}{\nu} \sum_{i=1}^{\nu} \pi_i C_{pl,PC_i}^{(Norm)} \tag{14.92}$$

$$MC_{p,PC}^{(Norm)*} = \frac{1}{\nu} \sum_{i=1}^{\nu} \pi_i C_{p,PC_i}^{(Norm)} \tag{14.93}$$

$$MC_{pk,PC}^{(Norm)*} = \frac{1}{\nu} \sum_{i=1}^{\nu} \pi_i C_{pk,PC_i}^{(Norm)} \tag{14.94}$$

where weight for the ith PC, π_i is the amount of variability explained by the ith PC and is defined as (refer Bernardo et al. [3]),

$$\pi_i = \frac{1}{d-c} \int_c^d \frac{\pi_i(t)}{\sum_{i=1}^{\nu} \pi_i(t)} dt \tag{14.95}$$

Now, suppose the random errors are either nonnormal or unknown in nature. Consequently, PC_i will be either unknown or nonnormal. For this situation, Guevara and Vargas [15] have defined PCI for the ith PC as

$$C_{pu,PC_i}^{(Non-norm)} = \frac{\int_c^d [USL_{PC_i}(t) - PC_{i,0.5}(t)]\, dt}{\int_c^d [PC_{i,0.99865}(t) - PC_{i,0.5}(t)]\, dt} \tag{14.96}$$

$$C_{pl,PC_i}^{(Non-norm)} = \frac{\int_c^d [PC_{i,0.5}(t) - LSL_{PC_i}(t)]\, dt}{\int_c^d [PC_{i,0.5}(t) - PC_{i,0.00135}(t)]\, dt} \tag{14.97}$$

$$C_{p,PC_i}^{(Non-norm)} = \frac{\int_c^d [USL_{PC_i}(t) - LSL_{PC_i}(t)]\, dt}{\int_c^d [PC_{i,0.99865}(t) - PC_{i,0.00135}(t)]\, dt} \tag{14.98}$$

$$C_{pk,PC_i}^{(Non-norm)} = \min\left\{ C_{pu,PC_i}^{(GV)},\ C_{pl,PC_i}^{(GV)} \right\} \tag{14.99}$$

where $PC_{i,0.5}$, $PC_{i,0.99865}$, and $PC_{i,0.00135}$ denote median, 0.99865^{th} quantile and 0.00135^{th} quantile for the ith PC, for $i = 1(1)\nu$.

Similar to the case of normally distributed PCs, for nonnormal PCs also, Guevara and Vargas [15] have defined weighted MPCIs as

$$MC_{pu,PC}^{(Non-norm)*} \quad = \quad \frac{1}{\nu}\sum_{i=1}^{\nu}\pi_i C_{pu,PC_i}^{(Non-norm)} \qquad (14.100)$$

$$MC_{pl,PC}^{(Non-norm)*} \quad = \quad \frac{1}{\nu}\sum_{i=1}^{\nu}\pi_i C_{pl,PC_i}^{(Non-norm)} \qquad (14.101)$$

$$MC_{p,PC}^{(Non-norm)*} \quad = \quad \frac{1}{\nu}\sum_{i=1}^{\nu}\pi_i C_{p,PC_i}^{(Non-norm)} \qquad (14.102)$$

$$MC_{pk,PC}^{(Non-norm)*} \quad = \quad \frac{1}{\nu}\sum_{i=1}^{\nu}\pi_i C_{pk,PC_i}^{(Non-norm)} \qquad (14.103)$$

14.9   Concluding Remark

In this chapter, some miscellaneous MPCIs have been discussed, which do not come under any of the previously discussed chapters. This includes viability indices, fuzzy-based indices, MPCIs based on linear algebraic approach and so on. Apart from these, MPCIs based on machine learning, artificial neural network and loss function-based decision theoretic approach will be interesting future scope of study.

Bibliography

[1] Anderson, T. W. (1955). The Integral of a Symmetric Unimodalfunction Over a Symmetric Convex Set and Some Probability Inequalities. *Proc. American Mathematical Society*, Vol. 6, pp. 170–176.

[2] Baksalary, J. K., Pukelsheim, F., Styan, G. P. H. (1989). Some Properties of Matrix Partial Orderings. *Linear Algebra and its applications*, Vol. 119, pp. 57–85.

[3] Bernerdo, J. R., Justel, A., Svarc, M. (2011). Principal Components for Multivariate Functional Data. *Computational Statistics and Data Analysis*, Vol. 55, pp. 2619–2634.

[4] Byun, J. H., Alsayed, E. A., Chen, A. C. K., Bruins, R. (1997). A Producibility Measure for Quality Characteristics with Design Specifications. *Quality Engineering*, Vol. 10, No. 2, pp. 351–358.

[5] Carruba, E. R., Gordon, R. D. (1988) *Product Assurance Principles: Integrating Design Assurance and Quality Assurance*, McGraw-Hill.

[6] Chang, T. C., Wang, K. J., Chen, K. S. (2014). Capability Performance Analysis for Processes with Multiple Characteristics Using Accuracy and Precision. *Journal of Engineering Manufacture*, Vol. 228, No. 5, pp. 766–776.

[7] Chen, K. S., Pearn, W. L., Lin, P. C. (2003). Capability Measures for Processes with Multiple Characteristics. *Quality and Reliability Engineering International*, Vol. 11, pp. 101–110.

[8] Ebadi, M., Amiri, A. (2012). Evaluation of Process Capability in Multivariate Simple Linear Profiles. *Scientia Iranica E*, Vol. 19, no. 6, pp. 1960–1968.

[9] Fayyaz, S., Ebrahimi, M., Devin, A. G. (2014). Fuzzy Multivariate Process Capability Index for Measuring Process Capability. *Shiraz Journal of System Management*, Vol. 2, No. 4, pp. 41–56.

[10] Foster, E. J., barton, R. R., Gautam, N., Truss, L. T., Tew, J. D. (2005). The Process Oriented Multivariate Capability index. *International Journal of Production Research*, Vol. 43, No. 10, pp. 2135–2148.

[11] Ganji, Z. A., Gildeh, B. S. (2015). On the Fuzzy Multivariate Process Capability Vector. 4th*Iranian Joint Congress on Fuzzy and Intelligent Systems*.

[12] Ganji, Z. A., Gildeh, B. S. (2016). On the Multivariate Process Capability Vector in Fuzzy Environment. *Iranian journal of fuzzy systems*, Vol. 13, No. 5, p. 147–159.

[13] Gonzalez, D., Aviles, E. (1995). Process Diagnostic in Stensil Printing us, No., pp. ing PROBREP. *Proceedings of the 1995 Electronic Packaging Manufacturing Conference*. Hewlett Packard, pp. 203–2011.

[14] Groß, J. (2001). Lowner Partial Ordering and Space Preordering of Hermitian non-negative Definite Matrices. *Linear Algebra and its applications*, Vol. 326, pp. 215–223.

[15] Guevara, R. D., Vargas, J. A. (2016). Evaluation of Process Capability in Multivariate Nonlinear Profiles. *Journal of Statistical Computation and Simulation*, Vol. 86, No. 12, pp. 2411–2428.

[16] Juran, J.M. and Gryna, F.M. (1993). *Quality Planning and Analysis: From Product Development Through Use*, McGraw-Hill international editions.

[17] Kandel, A., Byatt, W. (1978). Fuzzy Sets, Fuzzy Algebraand Fuzzy Statistics. *Proceedings of te IEEE*,Vol. 66, No. 12, pp. 1619–1639.

[18] Kazemzadeh, R. B., Noorssana, R., Amiri, A. (2009). Monitoring Polynomial Profiles in Quality Control Applications. *The International Journal of Advanced Manufacturing Technology*, Vol. 42, pp. 703–712.

[19] Khadse, K. G., Shinde, R. L. (2006). Multivariate Process Capability Using Relative Importance of Quality Characteristics. *IAPQR Transactions*, Vol. 31, No. 2, pp. 85–93.

[20] Kirmani, S. N. U. A., Polansky, A. M. (2009). Multivariate Process Capability via Lowner Ordering. *Linear Algebra and its applications*, Vol. 430, pp. 2681–2689.

[21] Laviolette, M., Seaman, J. W. Jr., Berrett, J. D., W. H. Woodall (1995). A probabilistic and Statistical View of Fuzzy Methods. *Technometrics*, Vol. 37, No. 3, pp. 249–261.

[22] Mahmoud, M. A., Woodall, W. H. (2004). Phase I Analysis of Linear Profiles with Calibration Applications.*Technometrics*, Vol. 46, No. 4, pp. 380–391.

[23] Pearn, W. L., Chen, K. S. (1997). A Practical Implementation of the Process Capability index C_{pk}. *Quality Engineering*, Vol. 9, No. 4, pp. 721–737.

Bibliography

[24] Raissi, S. (2009). Multivariate Process Capability Indices on the Presence of Priority for Quality Characteristics. *Journal of Industrial Engineering International*, Vol. 5, No. 9, pp. 27–36.

[25] Ranjan, C., Maiti, J. (2013). An Approach to Build Process Oriented Basis for Causation Based Multivariate SPC and Process Capability Analysis. *Quality and Reliability Engineering International*, Vol. 29, pp.1221–1234.

[26] Rencher, A. C. (2002). *Methods of Multivariate Analysis*. 2nd edn. Wiley Series in Probability and Statistics.

[27] Roy, S. N. (1953). On a Heuristic Method of Test Construction and its Use in multivariate analysis. *Annals of Mathematical Statistics*, Vol. 24, pp. 220–238.

[28] Shahriari, H., Abdollahzadeh, M. (2009). A New Multivariate Process Capability Vector. *Quality Engineering*, Vol. 21, No. 3, pp. 290–299.

[29] Shahriari, H., Hubele, N. F., Lawrence, F. P. (1995). A Multivariate Process Capability Vector. *Proceedings of the* 4th *Industrial Engineering Research Conference*, Institute of Industrial Engineers, pp. 304–309.

[30] Vannman, K. (1995). A Unified Approach to Capability Indices. *Statistica Sinica*, Vol. 5, No. 2, pp. 805–820.

[31] Veevers, A. (1998). Viability and Capability Indexes for Multiresponse Processes. *Journal of Applied Statistics*, Vol. 25, No. 4, pp. 545–558.

[32] Woodall, W. H. (2007). Current Research on Profile Monitoring. *Rev Producao*, Vol. 17, pp. 420–425.

[33] Woodall, W. H., Spitzner, D. J., Montgomery, D. C., Gupta, S. (2004). Using Control Charts to Monitor Process and Product Quality Profiles. *Journal of Quality Technology*, Vol. 36, pp. 309–320.

[34] Xekalaki, E., Perakis, M. (2002). The Use of Principal Components Analysis in the Assessment of Process Capability Indices. Proceedings of the Joint Statistical Meetings of the American Statistical Association - Section on Physical and Engineering Sciences (SPES), New York, pp. 3819–3823.

[35] Zadeh, L. A. (1965). Fuzzy sets. *Information and Control*, Vol. 8, pp. 338–353.

Chapter 15

Applications of MPCIs

Chapter Summary

The primary objective of defining multivariate process capability indices (MPCIs) is to assess capability of a multidimensional process. Therefore, unless an MPCI finds ample practical application, this objective is not fulfilled. In Chapter 15, some interesting applications of MPCIs are discussed. These include supplier selection for multivariate processes, assessing gauge measurement error and multiresponse optimization among others. These motivate the prospective readers to explore other application areas of MPCIs as well.

15.1   Introduction

In all the previous chapters, almost all the MPCIs available in literature, have been discussed along with some of their important theoretical properties. However, being an application-based topic, any discussion on multivariate process capability analysis is incomplete, unless a vivid discussion is made regarding its applications. In the present chapter, some applications of MPCIs, particularly in manufacturing industries, have been discussed.

15.2   Supplier Selection Based on Multivariate Process Capability Analysis

Not only for assessing capability level of a process, for other quality-related issues also, MPCIs have found ample scopes of application. Supplier selection problem is one such case.

Like other areas of research, for supplier selection also, there are considerable amount of research work in one dimensional case. Interested readers may

Applications of MPCIs   315

refer to Tseng and Wu [29], Chou [9], Pearn et al. [14], Pearn et al. [21], Pearn and Kotz [15], and the references therein, in this regard.

We shall now discuss supplier selection problem from multivariate perspective. In this context, the literature of process capability analysis is mainly concerned with MPCIs measuring potential process capability. This is due to the fact that, if a process, irrespective of its dimension, is not even potentially capable, then there is no point in considering the corresponding supplier for subsequent business.

15.2.1   Supplier Selection Problem for Processes Having Symmetric Bilateral Specification Region

For multivariate processes having symmetric bilateral specification region, Yeh and Pearn [32] have discussed a detailed procedure for supplier selection based on Taam, Subbaiah, and Liddy's [28] MPCI measuring potential process capability, viz., MC_p [Vide equation 15.10]. Recall from Chapter 6 that, the plug-in estimator of MC_p is given by

$$\widehat{MC_p} = \frac{\text{Volume of the modified elliptical tolerance region}}{|S|^{1/2} \times (\pi \chi^2_{q,0.9973})^{q/2} \times [\Gamma(q/2 + 1)]^{-1}},$$

$$(15.1)$$

where S is the sample variance – covariance corresponding to Σ. Yen and Pearn [32] have considered a two suppliers situation. Suppose for the MC_p values for the processes corresponding to these two suppliers are denoted by MC_{p1} and MC_{p2}, respectively. Then, to make a comparison between the performances of these two suppliers, the following hypothesis has been tested:

$$H_0 \quad : \quad MC_{p1} \leq MC_{p2}$$
$$\text{i.e., process/ Supplier I does not}$$
$$\text{perform better than process/ Supplier II}$$

$$\text{Against } H_1 \quad : \quad MC_{p1} > MC_{p2}$$
$$\text{i.e., process/ Supplier I performs better}$$
$$\text{than process/ Supplier II}$$

Now suppose, random samples of sizes n_1 and n_2 were drawn, respectively, from the two processes. Then, at α -level of significance, Yen and Pearn [32] have derived the critical value of the above test as

$$P\left\{\frac{\widehat{MC}_{p1}}{\widehat{MC}_{p2}} > c \mid MC_{p1} = MC_{p2}\right\}$$

$$\text{where } c = F_{2n_2-4,2n_1-4,1-\alpha} \times \frac{(n_1-1)(2N_2-4)}{2n_1-4} \qquad (15.2)$$

If $\frac{\widehat{MC}_{p1}}{\widehat{MC}_{p2}} > c$, H_0 is rejected at α level of significance and otherwise, it is accepted.

15.2.2 Supplier Selection Problem for Processes Having Unilateral Specification Region

Pearn et al. [19, 20] disscussed supplier selection problem for multidimensional processes having quality characteristics with unilateral specification limits. For this, they have considered the MPCI proposed by Wu and Pearn [31], which is given by

$$C_{pu}^T = \frac{1}{3}\Phi^{-1}\left\{\prod_{i=1}^{q}\Phi\left(3C_{pu_i}\right)\right\} \qquad (15.3)$$

where $C_{pu_i} = \frac{USL_i-\mu_i}{3\sigma_i}$ is the C_{pu} index for ith quality characteristic, for $i = 1(1)q$.

Pearn et al. [22] have shown that

$$\widehat{C}_{pu}^T \sim N\left(C_{pu}^T, \frac{1}{9n} + \frac{C_{pu}^{T2}}{2n}\right) \qquad (15.4)$$

Refer to Chapter 8 for detail discussion on C_{pu}^T.

Now, suppose $C_{PU_1}^T$ and $C_{PU_2}^T$ denote C_{PU}^T values for two multidimensional processes corresponding to Supplier I and Supplier II, respectively.

Pearn and Wu [19] have considered two phases for supplier selection problem. In the first phase, objective is to test whether the second process (often, the newer one) performs better than the first process (the existing one).

Thus, similar to Yeh and Pearn [32], Pearn et al. [19] have considered testing the following hypothesis to address the corresponding supplier selection problem:

$$H_0^{(I)} \quad : \quad \frac{C_{pu_1}^T}{C_{pu_2}^T} \leq 1$$

$$\text{Against } H_1^{(I)} \quad : \quad \frac{C_{pu_1}^T}{C_{pu_2}^T} > 1$$

Then the corresponding test statistic will be

$$T_R \quad = \quad \frac{\hat{C}_{pu_1}^T}{\hat{C}_{pu_2}^T} \tag{15.5}$$

which is a ratio of two independent normal distributions, which is related to Cauchy distribution. Pearn and Wu [19] have derived the exact expression of the pdf of T_R as follows:

$$f_{T_R}(r) = \frac{1}{2\pi\sigma_1^* \, \sigma_2^*} \left\{ 2\sigma^{**^2} e^{-\frac{\mu^{**2}}{2\sigma^{**2}}} \right.$$
$$+ \left. \mu^{**}\sigma^{**}\sqrt{2\pi} \left[1 - 2\Phi\left(\frac{\mu^{**}}{\sigma^{**}}\right)\right]\right\} \times e^{-\frac{1}{2}\left(\frac{C_{pu_1}^{T2}}{\sigma_1^{*2}} + \frac{C_{pu_2}^{T2}}{\sigma_2^{*2}} - \frac{\mu^{**2}}{\sigma^{**2}}\right)}$$

$$\tag{15.6}$$

where $\sigma_1^{*2} = \frac{1}{9n_1} + \frac{C_{pu1}^{T2}}{2n_1}$, $\sigma_2^{*2} = \frac{1}{9n_2} + \frac{C_{pu2}^{T2}}{2n_2}$, $\mu^{**} = \frac{r \, C_{pu2}^T \sigma_1^{*2} + C_{pu1}^T \sigma_2^{*2}}{r^2 \, \sigma_1^{*2} \, \sigma_2^{*2}}$.

Equation (15.6) can be used to get the critical value, say c_0 at a pre-determined level of significance α. If the observed value of T_R is more than or equal to c_0, $H_0^{(I)}$ is rejected and Suplier II is considerd to perform better than supplier I; else $H_0^{(I)}$ is accepted.

However, changing an existing supplier brings with it various additional costs and hence often management is not willing to interfere with the existing set-up, unless it shows significant improvement. Therefore, in the second phase of supplier selection procedure, Pearn and Wu [19] have proposed testing of the following hypothesis:

$$H_0^{(II)} \quad : \quad C_{PU_2}^T \leq C_{PU_1}^T + h$$

$$\text{Against } H_1^{(II)} \quad : \quad C_{PU_2}^T > C_{PU_1}^T + h$$

where h is a positive constant to denote the amount of change in process capability, that will be consisidered as significant.

The decision criteria will be same as Phase I, with necessary changes due to inclussion of h.

Note that, process capability analysis, as the name suggests, is a concept of process control; where as, many a times, supplier selection is based on quality assessment of final product and hence product control theories may be applicable here. Pearn et al. [20], thus, have made a fusion of process control and product control to address supplier selection issues.

To be more precise, they have used three major concepts of product control, i.e., operating characteristic (OC) curve, lot tolerance percent defective (LTPD) and average quality level (AQL).

Operating characteristic (OC) is the probability of accepting a lot, whatever be its true proprtion of nonconformance. The so-called OC curve is obtained by plotting OC values against corresponding sample sizes.

Montgomery [11] has defined LTPD as the poorest level of quality which a customer agrees to accept in an individual lot. Thus, LTPD gives a guard against poor quality to a customer. Similarly, Montgomery [11] has defined AQL as the poorest quality level of process that a consumer agrees to consider as the process average.

Thus, for selecting a supplier, Pearn et al. [20] have considered the following two conditions

1. $P\left[\text{Reject the lot} \mid C_{pu}^{T} \geq C_{AQL}\right] \leq \alpha$;

2. $P\left[\text{Accept the lot} \mid C_{pu}^{T} \leq C_{LTPD}\right] \leq \beta$;

where C_{AQL} and C_{LTPD} are critical values corresponding to AQL and LTPD, respectively, as obtained using C_{pu}^{T}.

Pearn et al. [20] have shown that, the above two criteria boil down to the following two nonlinear equations:

$$\alpha \geq \int_{c_0}^{\infty} \frac{\sqrt{n}}{\sqrt{\pi(\frac{2}{n} + C_{AQL^2})}} \, e^{-\frac{n(x - C_{AQL})^2}{(\frac{2}{n} + C_{AQL}^2)}} \, dx \tag{15.7}$$

$$\beta \geq \int_{c_0}^{\infty} \frac{\sqrt{n}}{\sqrt{\pi(\frac{2}{n} + C_{LTPD^2})}} \, e^{-\frac{n(x - C_{LTPD})^2}{(\frac{2}{n} + C_{LTPD}^2)}} \, dx \tag{15.8}$$

where c_0 is the critical acceptance number.

Equations (15.7) and (15.8) are derived directly from the fact that, $\widehat{C}_{pu}^{T} \sim N\left(C_{pu}^{T}, \frac{1}{9n} + \frac{C_{pu}^{T2}}{2n}\right)$.

Solving these two nonlinear quations numerically with fixed values of C_{AQL} and C_{LTPD}, one can have the sample size and acceptance number.

15.2.3 Supplier Selection Problem for Processes Having Asymmetric Specification Region

The supplier selection procedures discussed so far are for processes having specification regions either of symmetric bilateral or unilateral type. However, in practice, many a times the specification region is bilateral but asymmetric with respect to the stipulated target (refer Boyles [4]). Chatterjee [8] has discussed supplier selection problem for such processes, based on the MPCI called $C_M(u, v)$ defined by Chatterjee and Chakraborty [6]. A detailed discussion on $C_M(u, v)$ is made in Chapter 7 of this book.

Suppose there are two processes connected with two suppliers and $C_M^{(1)}(0,0)$ and $C_M^{(2)}(0,0)$ are, respectively, the corresponding values of $C_M(0,0)$ for the two processes. Chatterjee [8] has considered the following hypothesis to test:

$$H_0 \quad : \quad C_M^{(1)}(0,0) \le C_M^{(2)}(0,0)$$

i.e., Supplier I is not better than Supplier II

$$H_1 \quad : \quad C_M^{(1)}(0,0) > C_M^{(2)}(0,0)$$

i.e., Supplier I is better than Supplier II

The critical value corresponding to this test is

$$c^* = \left[\frac{(n_2 - q)(n_1 - 1)}{(n_1 - q)(n_2 - 1)} F_{1-\alpha, n_2-q, n_1-q} \right]^{1/2}, \tag{15.9}$$

where $F_{1-\alpha, n_2-q, n_1-q}$ is the upper α % point of an F distribution with degrees of freedom $n_1 - q$ and $n_2 - q$, respectively.

Suppose, $\hat{C}_M^{(1)}(0,0)$ and $\hat{C}_M^{(2)}(0,0)$ are plug-in estimators of $C_M^{(1)}(0,0)$ and $C_M^{(2)}(0,0)$, respectively. Then, if $\frac{\hat{C}_M^{(1)}(0,0)}{\hat{C}_M^{(2)}(0,0)} < c^*$, then accept H_0 and otherwise reject it.

15.3 Assessing Process Capability of Multivariate Processes Affected by Gauge Measurement Error

Gauge measurement error is an inevitable part of measurement. Since, process capability analysis, irrespective of the dimension of the process, depends upon measurement of the various dimensions of produced items, the decision regarding process capability, gets impacted by the presence of such error to a large extent (refer Montgomery and Runger [10]). Pearn and Liao [17] have made an extensive study on impact of gauge measurement error on univariate

Applications of MPCIs   320

process capability indices particularly, C_p. Pearn and Liao [16] and Baral and Anis [2] have carried out similar analysis for C_{pk} and C_{pm}, respectively.

However, most of these studies assume that the process has only one distinct quality characteristic of interest. Shishebori and Hamadani [24, 25, 26, 27] and Scagliarini [23] have explored this issue of gauge measurement error from multivariate process perspective as well.

15.3.1   Impact of Gauge Measurement Error on MC_p

Recall from Chapter 6 that, MC_p, defined by Taam, Subbaiah, and Liddy [28], is among the earliest MPCIs developed and one of the most famous too. Under the assumption of multivariate normality of the process distribution, i.e., if X is a q- random vector, characterizing the correlated quality characteristics, such that $X \sim N_q(\mu, \Sigma)$, MC_p is defined as

$$MC_p$$

$$= \frac{\text{Volume of the modified elliptical tolerance region}}{\text{Volume of the region which includes 99.73\% of the process spread}}$$

$$= \frac{\text{Volume of the modified elliptical tolerance region}}{|\Sigma|^{1/2} \times (\pi \chi^2_{q,0.9973})^{q/2} \times [\Gamma(q/2+1)]^{-1}}$$

$$(15.10)$$

Now, similar to the univariate study on gauge capability by Montgomery and Runger [10], suppose under the multivariate set-up, considering all the "q" number of correlated quality characteristics together, the random vector of measurement errors is given by M. It is further assumed that, $M \sim N_q(0, \Sigma_{Me})$.

Based on these, Shishebori and Hamadani [24] have proposed a multivariate gauge capability measure as

$$\lambda^M = \frac{|\Sigma|^{1/2} \times (\pi \chi^2_{q,0.9973})^{q/2} \times [\Gamma(q/2+1)]^{-1}}{\text{Volume of the modified elliptical tolerance region}} \quad (15.11)$$

Suppose, for a process, which is affected by measurement error, the random vector of measurement of the quality characteristics is given by $Y = X + M$, such that, $Y \sim N_q(\mu, \Sigma_Y = \Sigma + \Sigma_{Me})$. Then, Shishebori and Hamadani [24, 25, 26, 27] have proposed a modified version of MC_p, for processes affected by measurement error as

$$MC_p^Y = \frac{\text{Volume of the modified elliptical tolerance region}}{|\Sigma_Y|^{1/2} \times (\pi \chi^2_{q,0.9973})^{q/2} \times [\Gamma(q/2+1)]^{-1}}$$

$$(15.12)$$

Plug-in estimator of MC_p^Y is accordingly defined as

$$\widehat{MC}_p^Y = \frac{\text{Volume of the modified elliptical tolerance region}}{|\hat{\Sigma}_Y|^{1/2} \times (\pi \chi_{q,0.9973}^2)^{q/2} \times [\Gamma(q/2+1)]^{-1}}$$

$$= \frac{\widehat{MC}_p}{\sqrt{\left(\hat{\lambda}^M \widehat{MC}_p\right)^2 + \frac{|\hat{\Sigma}_Y| - |\hat{\Sigma}_{Me}|}{|\hat{\Sigma}_Y - \hat{\Sigma}_{Me}|}}} \qquad (15.13)$$

where $\hat{\Sigma}_Y$ denotes the sample variance - covariance matrix.

Again, following Pearn et al. [17], *uniformly minimum variance unbiased estimator* (UMVUE) of MC_p can be obtained as

$$\widetilde{MC}_p = b_q \, \widehat{MC}_p, \qquad (15.14)$$

where $b_q = \left(\frac{2}{n-1}\right)^{q/2} \times \frac{\Gamma\left(\frac{1}{2(n-1)}\right)}{\Gamma\left(\frac{1}{2(n-q)} - \frac{1}{2}\right)}$. Similarly, Shishebori and Hamadani [27] have defined the UMVUE of MC_p as

$$\widetilde{MC}_p^Y = b_q \, \widehat{MC}_p^Y \qquad (15.15)$$

$$= \frac{\widetilde{MC}_p}{\sqrt{\left(\tilde{\lambda}^M \widetilde{MC}_p\right)^2 + \frac{|\hat{\Sigma}_Y| - |\hat{\Sigma}_{Me}|}{|\hat{\Sigma}_Y - \hat{\Sigma}_{Me}|}}} \qquad (15.16)$$

Shishebori and Hamadani [26, 27] have also derived expressions for the *mean square error* (MSE) and confidence interval for $\widehat{MC}_p^Y$. Interestingly, Chatterjee [7] has shown that, MC_p^Y tends to overestimate process capability to a large extent.

15.3.2 MPCIs Based on Principal Component Analysis for Processes Affected by Measurement Error

Apart from Shishebori and Hamadani [24, 25, 26, 27], Scagliarini [23] has also advoccated replacement of the original dispersion matrix Σ by the dispersion matrix Σ_Y in an MPCI, when the concerned multidimensional process is affected by measurement error. For this, Scagliarini [23] has considered MPCIs based on principal component analysis (PCA). A detailed discussion on the PCA based MPCIs is available in Chapter 5 of this book.

Scagliarini [23] has explored various forms of Σ_{Me}, based on different practical considerations. First of all, suppose, same measurement system is used for measuring all the quality characteristics under study. Then it is very likely that the error variances will be homo-scedastic and mutually independent. As such, $\Sigma_{Me} = \sigma^2_{Me} I_q$. Consequently, the eigen vector of Y will be exactly the same as that of the eigen vector of X, though the eigen values will be changed, viz., the eigen value of Y_i will be

$$\lambda_{Y_i} = \lambda_i + \sigma^2_{Me}, \quad for \quad i = 1(1)q, \tag{15.17}$$

where λ_i is the eigen value of X_i.

However, when the concerned quality characteristics have different units of measurements and hence require different measurement systems, the above expression of Σ_{Me} will not be valid.

Also, if the error variable is not homo-scedastic, i.e., if all the diagonal elements of Σ_{Me} are not equal, then it is difficult to obtain any closed form relation between λ_{Y_i} and λ_i, for $i = 1(1)q$.

Scagliarini [23] have assumed the error dispersion matrix to be proportional to the original dispersion matrix, i.e., $\Sigma_{Me} \propto \Sigma$, i.e., $\Sigma_{Me} = k\,\Sigma$, where, $k > 0$ is a constant.

Here also, the eigen vectors will remain unchanged. However, unlike the previous cae, here, the eigen value of Y_i will be

$$\lambda_{Y_i} = (1 + k)\,\lambda_i, \quad for \quad i = 1(1)q, \tag{15.18}$$

In both the cases given in equations (15.17) and (15.18), λ_{Y_i} gets increased as compared to the λ_i, due to the presence of measurement error.

15.4 Multiresponse Optimization Using MPCIs

For a multidimensional process, one of the greatest challenge is to determine optimum levels of process parameters, so that the items produced remain in close vicinity of the target with as minimum variation as possible (refer Bera and Mukherjee [3]). Multivariate process capability indices (MPCIs), being a well accepted quality control tool among the practitioners, find ample scope of application in this sector. Infact, use of MPCI gives insight about maximization of process yield, which, in turn, suggests ways to maximize profit.

Awad and Kovach [1] have used the MPCI $C_{pm}^{(ccs)}$ defined by Chan, Cheng, and Spiring [5]. Recall from Chapter 6 that, $C_{pm}^{(ccs)}$ is defined as

$$C_{pm}^{(ccs)} = \sqrt{\frac{q}{E\left[(X_i - T_i)' A^{-1}(X_i - T_i)\right]}}, \tag{15.19}$$

where A is a $q \times q$ positive definite matrix, such that

$$(\boldsymbol{X}_i - \boldsymbol{T}_i)' A^{-1}(\boldsymbol{X}_i - \boldsymbol{T}_i) \le c^2 \tag{15.20}$$

where A is a $q \times q$ positive definite matrix, such that

$$(\boldsymbol{X}_i - \boldsymbol{T}_i)' A^{-1}(\boldsymbol{X}_i - \boldsymbol{T}_i) \le \chi^2_{\alpha,q} \tag{15.21}$$

is the elliptical specification region.

Interestingly, using the empirical relationship between average and expectation and considering A as the sample dispersion matrix, from equation (15.19), we have

$$\widehat{C_{pm}^{(ccs)}} = \sqrt{\frac{nq}{\sum\limits_{i=1}^{n}(\boldsymbol{X}_i - \boldsymbol{T}_i)' A^{-1}(\boldsymbol{X}_i - \boldsymbol{T}_i)}}, \tag{15.22}$$

In multiresponse optimizaton, it is assumed that, the random vector $\boldsymbol{X}$, characterizing measurements of the quality characteristics, is an output obtained from inputs, say z_1, z_2, $\cdots$, z_n, through a functional relationship viz.,

$$\boldsymbol{X} = f(z_1, z_2, \cdots, z_n) \tag{15.23}$$

Note that, MPCI values are, in general, directly related to the yield, i.e., increase in the value of an MPCI, gets the yield increased. Also, from equation (15.22), for fixed sample size (n) and fixed number of quality characteristics (q), the numerator of $\widehat{C_{pm}^{(ccs)}}$ is fixed. Therefore, minizing denominator of $\widehat{C_{pm}^{(ccs)}}$, viz., $\sum\limits_{i=1}^{n}(\boldsymbol{X}_i - \boldsymbol{T}_i)' A^{-1}(\boldsymbol{X}_i - \boldsymbol{T}_i)$, will automatically increase the yield. Therefore, Awad and Kovach [1] have formulated the optimization problem as

$$\min Y = \sum\limits_{i=1}^{n}(\boldsymbol{X}_i - \boldsymbol{T}_i)' A^{-1}(\boldsymbol{X}_i - \boldsymbol{T}_i)$$

with respect to constraints developed as functions of the mean and variance of each response and using the concept of robust design.

Awad and Kovach [1] have used variablity synthesis method, proposed by Morrison [12], to estimate variability, particularly when there are unreplicated responses. However, unless the value of the standard deviation of each individual quality characteristic is less than 20% of the corresponding mean, Morrison's [12] method can hardly be applied.

Bera and Mukherjee [3] have proposed a multiresponse optimization problem with principal component analysis based MPCI $MC_{pmk}^{(\text{Wang})}$, given by Wang and Chen [30]. Recall from Chapter 5 that, $MC_{pmk}^{(\text{Wang})}$ can be defined by

$$MC_{pmk}^{(\text{Wang})} = \left(\prod_{i=1}^{\nu} C_{pmk;PC_i} \right)^{1/\nu} \tag{15.24}$$

where, ν is the number of principal components retained and $C_{pmk;PC_i}$ is the C_{pmk} index for the ith principal component, for $i = 1(1)\nu$. Under multivariate normality assumption of the process distribution, Bera and Mukherjee [3] have used iterative simplex algorithm given by Nelder and Mead [13] for optimizing $MC_{pmk}^{(\text{Wang})}$.

15.5 Concluding Remark

Although univariate process capability analysis is a long established quality control tool, its multivariate counterpart is a comparatively newer one and more complicated as well. Still it has found ample application in practice. In the present chapter, some of these applications have been discussed.

Apart from manufacturing industries, for which PCIs are primarily defined, exploring its application in other industries including service sector may render mutual benefit to both the theoreticians and practitioners.

Bibliography

[1] Awad, M. I., Kovach, J. V. (2011). Multiresponse Optimization using Multivariate Process Capability Index. *Quality and Reliability Engineering International*, Vol. 27, pp. 465–477.

[2] Baral, A. K., Anis, M. Z. (2015). Assessment of C_{pm} in the Presence of Measurement Errors. *Journal of Statistical Theory and Applications*, Vol. 14, No. 1, pp. 13–27.

[3] Bera, S. Mukherjee, I. (2013). An Integrated Approach Based on Principal Component and Multivariate Process Capability for Simultaneous Optimization of Location and Dispersion for Correlated Multiple Response Problems. *Quality Engineering*, Vol. 25, No. 3, pp. 266–281.

[4] Boyles, R. A. (1994). Process Capability with Asymmetric Tolerances. *Communications in Statistics—Simulation and Computation*, Vol. 23, No. 3, pp. 162–175.

[5] Chan, L. K., Cheng, S. W., Spiring, F. A. (1991). A Multivariate Measure of Process Capability. *International Journal of Modeling and Simulation*, Vol. 11, pp. 1–6.

[6] Chatterjee, M., Chakraborty, A., K. (2017). Unification of Some Multivariate Process Capability Indices for Asymmetric Specification Region. *Statistica Neerlandica*, Vol.71(4), 286- 306.

[7] Chatterjee, M. (2019). Impact of Multivariate Normality Assumption on Multivariate Process Capability Indices. *Communications in Statistics: Case Studies, Data Analysis and Applications*, Vol. 5, pp. 314–345. DOI: https://doi.org/10.1080/23737484.2019.1648193.

[8] Chatterjee, M. (2019). Supplier Selection Problem for Processes Having Asymmetric Specification Region. *Communicated*.

[9] Chou, Y. M. (1994). Selecting a Better Supplier by Testing Process Capability Indices. *Quality Engineering*, Vol. 6, pp. 427–438.

[10] Montgomery, D. C., Runger, G. C. (1993). Gauge Capability and Designed Expeiments, Part I: Basic Methods. *Quality Engineering*, Vol. 6, No. 1, pp. 115–135.

Bibliography

[11] Montgomery, D. C. (2000). *Introduction to Statistical Quality Control*, 5th ed., New York: John Wiley & Sons.

[12] Morroson, S. J. (1957). The Study of Variability in Engineering Design. *Applied Statistics*, Vol. 6, pp. 133–138.

[13] Neler, J. A., Mead, R. (1965). A Simplex Method for Function Minimization. *Computer Journal*, Vol. 7, pp. 308–313.

[14] Pearn, W. L., Hung, H. N., Chuang, Y. S., Su, R. H. (2011). An Effective Powerful Test for One-sided Supplier Selection Problem. *Journal of Statistical Computation and Simulation*, Vol. 81, No. 10, pp. 1313–1331.

[15] Pearn, W. L., Kotz, S. (2007). *Encyclopedia and Handbook of Process Capability Indices—Series on Quality, Reliability and Engineering Statistics*, Singapore: World Scientific

[16] Pearn, W. L., Liao, M. Y. (2005). Measuring Process Capability Based on C_{pk} with Gauge Measurement Errors. *Microelectronics Reliability*, Vol. 45, pp. 739–751.

[17] Pearn, W. L., Liao, M. Y. (2007). Estimating and Testing Process Precision with Presence of Gauge Measurement Errors. *Quality and Quantity*, Vol. 41, No. 5, pp. 757–777.

[18] Pearn, W. L., Wang, F. K., Yen, C. H. (2007). Multivariate Capability Indices: Distributional and Inferential Properties. *Journal of Applied Statistics*, Vol. 34, No. 8, pp. 941–962.

[19] Pearn, W. L., Wu, C. H. (2013). Supplier Selection for Multiple Characteristics Prcesses with One-sided Specifications. *Quality Technology and Quantitative Management*, Vol. 10, No. 1, pp. 133–140.

[20] Pearn, W. L., Wu, C. H., Hung, H. N., Kao, C. M. (2013). An Extension of the Product Acceptance Determination for One-sided Process with Multiple Characteristics. *Quality and Reliability Engineering International*, Vol. 29, pp. 277–284.

[21] Pearn, W. L., Wu, C. W., Lin, H. C. (2004). Procedure for Supplier Selection Based on Cpm Applied to Super Twisted Nematic Liquid Crystal Display Processes. *International Journal of Production Research*, vol. 42, no. 13, pp. 2719–2734.

[22] Pearn, W.L., Wu, C. H., Tsai, M. C. (2013). A Note on Capability Assessment for Processes with Multiple Characteristics: a Generalization of Popular Index C_{pk}. *Quality and Reliability Engineering International*, Vol. 29, No. 2.

[23] Scagliarini, M. (2011). Multivariate Process Capability Using Principal Component Analysis in the Presence of Measurement Errors. *Advances in Statistical Analysis*, Vol. 95, pp. 113–128.

[24] Shishebori, D., Hamadani, A. Z. (2008). Multivariate Capability Index (MC_p) with Presence of Gauge Measurement Errors. 4th International Conference on Wireless Communications, Network and Mobile Computing, pp. 1–4.

[25] Shishebori, D., Hamadani, A. Z. (2010). Gauge Measurement Errors and Multivariate Capability Indices. *International Conferences on Networking and Information Technology*.

[26] Shishebori, D., Hamadani, A. Z. (2010). Properties of Multivariate Process Capability in the Presence of Gauge Measurement Errors and Dependency measure of process variables. *Journal of Manufacturing Systems*, Vol. 29, pp. 10–18.

[27] Shishebori, D., Hamadani, A. Z. (2010). The Effect of Gauge Measurement Capability and Dependency Measure of Process Variables on the MC_p. *Journal of Industrial and Systems Engineering*, Vol. 4, No. 1, pp. 59–76.

[28] Taam, W., Subbaiah, P., Liddy, W. (1993). A Note on Multivariate Capability Indices. *Journal of Applied Statistics*, Vol. 20, No. 3, pp. 339–351.

[29] Tseng, S. T., and Wu, T. Y. (1991). Selecting the Best Manufacturing Process. *Journal of Quality Technology*, Vol. 23, pp. 53–62.

[30] Wang, F. K., Chen, J. C. (1998). Capability Index Using Principal Component Analysis. *Quality Engineering*, Vol. 11, No. 1, pp. 21–27.

[31] Wu, C. W., Pearn, W. L. (2005). Measuring Manufacturing Capability for Couplers and Wavelength Division Multiplexers. *The International Journal of Advance Manufacturing Tecnology*, Vol. 25, pp. 533–541. DOI 10.1007/s00170-003-1793-9.

[32] Yeh, C. H., Pearn, W. L. (2009). Select Better Supplier Based on Manufacturing Precision for Processes with Multivariate Data. *International Journal of Production Research*, Vol. 47, No. 11, pp. 2961–2974.

Conclusion

Process capability indices are unit less measures of capability of processes to produce goods within the specification limits. For the univariate cases, these measures are extensively used in manufacturing processes. However, most of the real-life processes are multivariate in nature and hence it requires multivariate process capability indices to actually measure capability of the process to produce products without much of rejections. MPCIs thus become very important for industrial processes. Unfortunately, though there are quite a few MPCIs developed in the literature, there is no book which deals with such an important development and this book is intended to fill up this void.

To the extent possible, we tried to exhaustively cover the work of several authors whose works are published in the literature till 2019. If we missed some literature, it is an inadvertent error on our part.

In Chapter 1, we introduced the basic concepts of process capability, its uses, including the importance of studying the MPCIs.

Chapter 2 gives some brief details of different statistical distributions that are mostly used in process capability studies, both for univariate and multivariate cases.

To have a complete understanding of the MPCIs, one needs to understand its univariate counterpart very well. Chapter 3 entirely deals with various developments in univariate PCIs. We also discuss various drawbacks of each of the univariate PCIs in this chapter.

Starting with Chapter 4, the remaining part of the book contains discussions on various types of MPCIs starting with bivariate cases which can be considered to be a special case among multivariate processes. We have noted while going through various MPCIs that in many cases the threshold value of an MPCI is not known. This poses a serious problem to the practitioners with respect to the interpretation of the MPCI. It is always better if the expression of the threshold value of an MPCI is developed whenever a new MPCI is proposed. Few authors have understood the importance of developing threshold values for univariate and multivariate PCIs.

In Chapter 5, we discuss the MPCIs, particularly for cases with bilateral specification limits, based on principal component analysis. Principal component analysis helps to reduce the dimensions of the problem and at the same time makes sure that the new principal components, which can be used instead of the original variables, are independent. This ensures that the overall MPCI can be obtained by multiplication of the PCIs calculated for the principal components.

There are several MPCIs, which are defined as a ratio of two quantities. In general, such ratio-based process capability indices are quite common in the literature. Chapter 6 deals with such indices.

Chakraborty and Chatterjee (2016) gave an overview of various kinds of specifications that are used in manufacturing sector. Each of these types of specifications calls for a new type of MPCI. Chapter 7 discusses MPCIs, which are developed for asymmetric specification limits, whereas Chapter 8 covers the developments with respect to unilateral specifications. Many believe that proportion of conformance or nonconformance is the final indicator of the ability of the process to produce goods within specification limits. Hence, there are many MPCIs, which can be directly related to the proportion of conformance or nonconformance of the process. These MPCIs are elaborated in Chapter 9.

Assumption of normality of the distribution of the underlying variables is one of the main strengths as well as the weaknesses of the development of PCIs and MPCIs. There are very few developments in the literature where normality assumption is done away with, whereas many practitioners have to deal with situations where such assumption is not valid. In Chapter 10, we broadly cover the developments in this area as far as MPCIs are concerned.

Chapters 11, 12, and 13 are quite important because each deals with the techniques that statisticians understand the best. Bayesian concepts are the ones that the statisticians and the computer scientists are adopting to do data analysis. Chapter 11 describes a few MPCIs that are built on the Bayesian concepts.

In Chapter 12, we identify the few indices where autocorrelated observations are considered for finding out MPCIs. Some authors chose to use vector valued PCIs where for each quality characteristic, an element of the vector is used as the PCI. Interpretation in such cases becomes quite difficult. However, we describe those MPCIs in Chapter 13.

In Chapter 14, we club all other MPCIs, which cannot be classified properly to be included in any of the other chapters. Chapter 15 gives some applications on real-life data.

Index

acceptance region 239
AQL 318
asymptotic distribution 32, 33
audit 9
autocorrelation 248–250, 252, 253
average quality level *see* AQL

Bayes theorem 33, 236
Bayesian 8, 13, 19, 33, 34, 50, 68, 236, 237, 329
$BC_p^{(CC)}$ 86
$BC_p^{(T)}$ 85
BC_{pk} 84
$BC_{pk}^{(CC)}$ 86
BC_{pm} 83
BC_{pmk} 84
Bessel function 23
beta distribution 80, 220
bivariate folded normal *see* folded normal, bivariate
Box-Cox power transformation 51, 65
Burr XII 208, 219, 220, 231
BVFN *see* folded normal, bivariate

c. d. f. *see* cumulative distribution function
cdf 26, 84, 135, 149, 203, 204, 227; *see also* cumulative distribution function
$C_b(D)$ 238–240
C_{Fuzzy} 300
C'_{Fuzzy} 300
C_{Fuzzy}^{norm} 301
$C_G^{T(2)}$ 159
$C_G^{T(3)}$ 159
$C_G(u, v)$ 158

$C_M(u, v)$ 174
$C_M^{(T)}(0, 0)$ 178
$C_M^{(T,q)}(0, 0)$ 181, 182
C_p 47–50
$C_{p,c}$ 95
$C_{p,c}^T$ 98
$C_{p,c}^{T*}$ 98
$C_{p,c}(u, v)$ 97
$\hat{C}_{p,c}(u, v)$ 98
C_{pk} 47–50
$C_{pk,c}$ 96
$C'_{pk,c}$ 95
C_{pm} 47–50
$C_{pm,c}$ 96
C_{pmk} 47–50
$C_{pmk,c}$ 97
$C_{p,TV}$ 121
$\hat{C}_P$ 93
$\hat{C}_{PK}$ 93
$\hat{C}_p^{Polansky}$ 229
C_p'' 170
$C_p^{(ND)}$ 241
$C_p^{(q)}$ 293
C_{pk}'' 170
$C_{pk}^{(ND)}$ 241
C_{pk}^T 142, 143
$C_{pk}^{T(LB)}$ 146
C_{pM} 257
C_{pm}'' 170
$C_{pm}^{(CCS)}$ 147
$_qC_{pm}$ 148
C_{pmk}'' 170
C_{PNC} 300
C_{pV} 265–267

$C_{pM}^{(SPL)}$ 306
C_{pl} 56, 57, 87, 191, 195, 199
C_{pl}^* 52, 57
C_{pu} 56, 57
C_{pu}^* 52, 57
C_{pl}^T 192
C_{rm} 150, 151
C_{rm}^* 151
circular specification 8, 11, 23, 78, 88–92, 94–98, 105–107
cost 1, 4, 51, 60, 91, 92, 168, 199, 281–283, 297, 317
control chart 2, 19, 25, 30, 31, 33, 34, 68
critical characteristic 281, 283
critical region 82
critical value 135, 194, 315, 318, 319
cumulative distribution function 20, 21, 135, 173, 203, 220, 274
CUSUM 25
defuzzifying 303
delta method: multivariate 40, 184; univariate 19, 39, 40

DFSS 1, 5–7
dimension reduction 12, 13, 38, 39, 112, 125, 195, 216
dynamic programming 34

eigen value 38, 39, 113, 121–123, 149, 196, 207, 286–288, 307, 322
eigen vector *see* eigen value
elliptical integral 24, 103
estimation: interval 134; plug-in 49, 50, 56, 65, 80–82, 87, 98, 99, 102, 104, 107, 114, 118, 120, 122, 133, 139, 143, 146, 148, 152, 156, 159, 182–184, 193, 216, 241, 271, 302, 315, 319, 321; point 49, 134
exponential distribution 19, 28, 29
extreme value Type – I 220

folded normal: bivariate 36, 37; multivariate 19, 36, 37; univariate 24–26, 36

fuzzy 280, 298–303

gamma distribution 65, 220, 230
geometric dimensioning and tolerancing *see* GD&T
geometric mean 7, 79, 117, 195, 196, 216
GD&T 88
Grau, D.: multivariate asymmetric 169, 170, 172, 173, 186; multivariate unilateral 190; univariate 8, 58, 59, 61, 62, 66

hyper-geometric 24
hypothesis testing 49, 68, 122, 134, 135, 146, 315–317, 319

$IC_{q_{//}}'''$ 268
IC_{pp}''' 268
inter-relationship 55, 158, 173, 175
interval estimation *see* estimation, interval
ISO 9

Johnson transformation 65

k_U 60
k_L 60
kernel 66, 227, 228

larger the better 4, 5, 56, 60–62, 150, 190, 196, 251, 252
lean 1, 5–7
log-normal distribution 19, 27, 28, 65, 220
loss function 53, 91, 153, 310
lot tolerance percent defective *see* LTPD
lowner ordering 8, 286, 287
LTPD 318

MAC_p 250
major and minor characteristic 252, 281–283, 285
Markov chain 29

MC_f 227
MC_{Fuzzy} 301
MC_{Fuzzy}^{MVN} 301, 302
MC_p 83
MC_p^{MWSZ} 119
$MC_p^{(R)}$ 286
$MC_p^{(XP)}$ 117
$MC_p^{(Wang)}$ 113, 114, 116
$MC_p^{(Wang*)}$ 124
$MC_{pk}^{(R)}$ 286
$MC_{pk}^{(RM)}$ 295
$MC_{pk}^{(XP)}$ 117
$MC_{pk}^{(Wang)}$ 113, 114
$MC_{pk}^{(Wang*)}$ 124
MC_{pm} 83
MC_{pm}^{MWSZ} 119
$MC_{pm}^{(R)}$ 286
$MC_{pm}^{(XP)}$ 117
$MC_{pmk}^{(R)}$ 286
$MC_{pmk}^{(XP)}$ 117
$MCPL$ 195, 196
$MCPL'$ 196
$MCPU$ 195, 196
$MCPU'$ 196
mfn 90
$MIC_{q_{,,}}'''(u,v)$ 268
$MIC_{pp}''(u,v)$ 268
mgf 36, 37
minimum fraction non-conforming *see* mfn
moment generating function *see* mgf
Monte Carlo 221
Montgomery, D. C. 31, 32, 266, 318–320
MP_1 115
$MP_1^{(emp)}$ 116
MP_2 116
$MP_2^{(emp)}$ 117
MPC_{NCV} 272
MPC_{NCV}' 273
MPCV *see* vector valued index
$MPCVG$ 262

multivariate folded normal *see* folded normal, multivariate
multivariate normal distribution 12, 13, 19, 35, 36; *see also* normal
multivariate threshold: asymmetric specification 175, 177–182, 183, 186; auto-correlated 253; Bayesian 243; non-normal distributions 230, 232; others 290, 328; PCA based 122, 124; symmetric specification 151, 159, 162, 163; unilateral 193, 194, 199; vector based 266, 276, 277
MVC_p^* 140
MVFN *see* folded normal, multivariate

$NMAC_p$ 137, 250
$NMAC_p^{(SA)}$ 261
NMC_p 139, 151, 152
$NMC_p^{(Fuzzy)}$ 303
NMC_{pm} 151, 152, 162, 225
nominal the best 4, 91, 271, 296
non-normal: multivariate 215; univariate 51, 65–67
nonparametric 8, 214, 226–229, 231
normal 2, 19–24, 28, 30–32, 35, 51, 53, 56, 63–65, 67

OC 318
Operating characteristic *see* OC
optimization 221, 313, 314
overestimate 83, 136, 149, 162, 163, 321

p. d. f. *see* probability density function
$\hat{P}_P$ 93
$\hat{P}_{Pk}$ 93
P_T 143
PCA *see* principal component analysis; process capability analysis

PC_P 92
PC_{PK} 92
$PCI_{critical}$ 281, 282
PCI_{major} 281, 282
PCI_{minor} 281, 282
PD 266
$P_{NC;k}$ 305
PNC *see* proportion of
    non-conformance
POBREP 208, 293- 295
point estimation *see* estimation,
    point
point of inflection 22
posterior distribution 238, 242
posterior information 34
PQLAC 296–298
principal component analysis 7, 12,
    13, 19, 35, 38, 112
probability density function 20, 25,
    29, 80, 136, 203, 208, 220
production cost *see* cost
proportion of non-conformance:
    bivariate 83, 84; general
    concept 5, 8, 13;
    multivariate 122, 142, 143,
    173, 187, 191, 192, 202, 218,
    229, 238, 262, 263, 287–289,
    300, 329; univariate 47, 48,
    52, 54, 56, 62, 65,67
prior distribution 238, 242
prior information 34
prioritization 9
PS 266
$PV^{(Byun)}$ 281

R_L 62
R_U 62
radial error 19, 23, 24, 89, 93, 94
rational subgroup 31
rectangular distribution *see* uniform
    distribution
$RNMC_p$ 226
$RNMC_{pm}$ 226
root transformation technique 223

RTT *see* root transformation
    technique

$S_{pk}^{(SPL)}$ 305
$S_{pk;k}^{(SPL)}$ 305
S_{pk}^T 206
simulated annealing 221
six sigma 1, 5–7, 206
skewness 64, 214, 215, 222–224
smaller the better: multivariate 151,
    190, 191, 196, 197;
    univariate 4, 56–58, 60, 62
spectral decomposition 38
static goal 9
stochastic algorithm 221
Sultan, T. L. 10, 11
Super-structure 50, 66, 131, 158

Taylor polynomial 39
Taylor series 39, 143, 145, 153
threshold value: bivariate 84, 85, 87,
    91, 97, 98,106, 107;
    univariate 48, 49, 55, 56, 61;
    see also multivariate
    threshold
$TS_{pk;PC}$ 207

UMVUE 56, 321
under-estimate 268, 277
uniform distribution 19, 26, 27
uniformly most powerful unbiased
    estimator *see* UMVUE

V 115
V' 115
$V*$ 119
V_t 64
$V_t^{(q)}$ 291
Vannman: multivariate 119–122, 124,
    140, 200; univariate 49, 50,
    53, 58, 59, 66, 87, 97, 114,
    158, 191
vector valued index: Bayesian 236,
    237; capability 8, 14,
    251–253, 257, 258; different

specification type 266, 272;
fuzzy 297, 298; incapability
263, 264, 266; priority based
276, 277

viability index 64

Weibull 65, 66, 220, 230
window of opportunity 280, 288, 290,
291
WMP_1 285
WMP_2 285
WMP_1' 285
WMP_2' 285